THE ATHENÆUM PRESS SERIES

G. L. KITTREDGE AND C. T. WINCHESTER
GENERAL EDITORS

Series Announcement

The "Athenæum Press Series" includes the choicest works of English literature in editions carefully prepared for the use of schools, colleges, libraries, and the general reader. Each volume is edited by some scholar who has made a special study of an author and his period. The Introductions are biographical and critical. In particular they set forth the relation of the authors to their times and indicate their importance in the development of literature. A Bibliography and Notes accompany each volume.

Athenæum Press Series

THE MAJOR DRAMAS

OF

RICHARD BRINSLEY SHERIDAN

THE RIVALS
THE SCHOOL FOR SCANDAL
THE CRITIC

EDITED
WITH INTRODUCTIONS AND NOTES

BY

GEORGE HENRY NETTLETON
ASSISTANT PROFESSOR OF ENGLISH IN THE SHEFFIELD SCIENTIFIC SCHOOL
OF YALE UNIVERSITY

GINN & COMPANY
BOSTON · NEW YORK · CHICAGO · LONDON

66.11

The Athenæum Press
GINN & COMPANY · PROPRIETORS · BOSTON · U.S.A.

TO

M. T. N.

PREFACE

No recent student of Sheridan can fail to acknowledge, at the very outset, a heavy debt to the foremost authority upon the subject — Fraser Rae. Before his death, in January, 1905, he had published by far the most important contributions yet made to the knowledge of Sheridan's life and writings. His two exhaustive volumes dealing with Sheridan's life[1] constitute, beyond question, the definitive biography. Even Mr. Augustine Birrell, in the introduction to his edition of *The School for Scandal and The Rivals*, despite good-natured remonstrance with Mr. Rae for seeking to destroy cherished traditions, does not fail to term his biography "a book which very likely will mark a point of departure for subsequent biographers and critics." Mr. Rae's recent publication of the authoritative text of the plays, based on the original manuscripts,[2] has a significance best appreciated by comparison with the text of the two-volume Murray edition on which ultimately rest most reprints of Sheridan's plays. Had he supplemented this work with collation of texts and with critical annotation, there would doubtless have been no occasion for the present volume. That there remained, however, a large and almost unexplored field for investigation in the study of the plays, Mr. Rae himself readily admitted, and from the first gave hearty encouragement to my project of a critical edition based on contemporary documents. To him I owe

[1] *Sheridan, A Biography*, 2 vols., London, Richard Bentley & Son: New York, Henry Holt & Co., 1896. It may be added that Mr. Rae wrote the Sheridan article for the *Dictionary of National Biography*.

[2] *Sheridan's Plays now printed as he wrote them and his mother's unpublished comedy, A Journey to Bath*, London, David Nutt, 1902.

permission to use his authentic text of the plays, and to avail myself freely of the results of his research. Furthermore, his personal answers to vexing questions were always of definite assistance. From the beginning of my correspondence with him some three years ago, it was my hope to submit to him the proofs of this book. His death, before the completion of the manuscript, has denied me both the benefit of his final judgment upon my work, and the opportunity of expressing to him publicly my grateful acknowledgment of his courtesy and generosity. His life-work was a constant incentive to scholarship; his death has brought an increased sense of obligation to complete with zeal and fidelity that portion of the study of Sheridan which he abandoned to other hands.

For the Life of Sheridan in the Introduction to this volume little can be claimed save that it presents, with some additions in the way of "local color," a condensation for the general reader of the eight or nine hundred pages of Fraser Rae's biography. With this exception, however, the present work covers territory diverging widely from his peculiar province. So exhaustive a biography as his cannot fail to furnish incidental aid to any critical study of Sheridan's plays, but to annotation of the text it makes little or no direct contribution. Indeed, notwithstanding the frequency with which the plays have been reprinted, there have been few annotated editions. It is well within bounds to say, that, despite Sheridan's importance in the history of English drama and his continued popularity, no critical edition of his plays has appeared which is either thoroughly accurate or complete. In the *Temple* edition, Mr. G. A. Aitken has brief notes which are usually helpful, though he has been at times betrayed into errors by too implicitly following previous editors. Some of the notes in Brander Matthews's *Sheridan's Comedies* [1] are suggestive.

[1] The first edition, James R. Osgood & Co., 1885, has recently been reprinted, in somewhat revised form, by Thomas Y. Crowell & Co.,

In the *British Theatre*, a collection of English dramas, printed at Leipsic in 1828, are foot-notes to some passages in Sheridan's text which at times have other merit than their delightful quaintness. Save in a few imperative instances, it has seemed sufficient to correct without comment the frequent errors in previous annotations of the plays.

The distinctive aim of this edition has been to give a critical study of Sheridan's major dramas based primarily on contemporary evidence. Directly or indirectly, more than a thousand volumes of eighteenth-century memoirs, diaries, novels, essays, poems, newspapers, and magazines have contributed to the introductions and notes. Contemporary documents, indeed, have often proved the sole possible key to difficulties of the text. If the notes err sometimes on the side of fullness, my plea must be that, with obvious exceptions, the explanatory matter is drawn from original sources, and often deals with questions which have passed unheeded, or at least unanswered.

The introductory sections to the various plays are based, like the notes, chiefly on contemporary evidence. Thus, the picture of Eighteenth-Century Bath is drawn from such sources as Goldsmith's *Life of Richard Nash*, Christopher Anstey's poem, *The New Bath Guide*, Fanny Burney's diary, Horace Walpole's letters, Smollett's novels, and contemporary magazines. The account of The Initial Failure and Final Triumph of *The Rivals* is based on extracts, given in the Appendix, from contemporary newspapers and literary reviews. The Books of Lydia Languish's Circulating Library have been located by means of book-reviews and notices in the monthly magazines and reviews. In the sections discussing the sources of the different plays there is of necessity considerable departure from the general method of dealing only with con-

but most of the errors in the early edition have been allowed to stand uncorrected.

temporary evidence. The aim, here, has been to assemble from all available sources whatever criticisms and suggestions are pertinent to the subject. Even in this field, where ground has been broken more effectually than in most fields of Sheridan investigation, it has been possible to add a considerable amount of new material. In *The Critic*, for example, the elements of Personal Caricature and of Burlesque and Parody of Contemporary Drama have hitherto received infrequent and, at best, casual treatment, while to the study of The Element of Actual History it has been readily possible to contribute original matter from the files of contemporary newspapers.

Since the death of Mr. Rae, the scope of this work has been extended to include a considerable part of that collation of manuscripts and printed editions of Sheridan's plays which he had hoped to undertake. Detailed explanation of this textual work is given in the pages immediately preceding the text of each play.

For the sake of convenience the references to standard works have been taken from readily accessible editions. Thus the *Temple* edition of Shakespeare, the *Mermaid* edition of Restoration dramatists, the two-volume edition of Moore's *Life of Sheridan*, and the recent editions of Walpole, Byron, and Madame d'Arblay, have been adopted. Except, however, in such obvious cases, original documents and editions have been the usual, and often the sole possible, standard of reference.

There remains the pleasant privilege of acknowledging some of the personal debts incurred in the preparation of this volume — to Professor G. L. Kittredge, of Harvard, and to Professor C. T. Winchester, of Wesleyan, the general editors of the Athenæum Series, for the helpful suggestions and annotations which accompanied their acceptance of my manuscript and their inspection of the proofs; to Professors Thomas R.

Lounsbury and Wilbur L. Cross, of Yale, for frequent and valuable criticism of my work in its earlier stages; to Professor Franklin B. Dexter and to Mr. Andrew Keogh, of the Yale Library, for courteous and unfailing help in many times of trouble during the past few years; and to Professor Henry A. Beers, of Yale, to whom, though he has read no part of my present work, I owe my first thorough introduction to the appreciative and critical study of Sheridan and the eighteenth-century drama.

YALE UNIVERSITY,
June 20, 1906.

CONTENTS

CONTENTS

INTRODUCTION

RICHARD BRINSLEY SHERIDAN, 1751–1816

Life

Ancestry. — Richard Brinsley Sheridan inherited in full measure the Anglo-Irish traits of the Sheridan family — wit, ability, geniality, improvidence. His grandfather, the Reverend Dr. Thomas Sheridan, is best remembered as the friend of Swift. The Earl of Orrery unfairly described Dr. Sheridan as "a punster, a quibbler, a fiddler, and a wit,"[1] but paid a somewhat grudging tribute to his merits as a schoolmaster.[2] The most familiar anecdote of Dr. Sheridan's life, however, has perpetuated his failure as a cleric. Through Swift's influence, he had been appointed one of the chaplains to the Lord-Lieutenant of Ireland. When he preached at Cork, on August first, the anniversary of the accession of George I, his text ran, "Sufficient unto the day is the evil thereof." Though the sermon was void of political offense, the text cost him both his place and his hope of preferment. "It is safer for a man's interest," wrote Swift to him in cold comfort, "to blaspheme God, than to be of a party out of power, or even to be thought so."[3] Careless good-nature and thriftlessness in money matters offset Dr. Sheridan's ability as a scholar

[1] *Remarks on the Life and Writings of Dr. Jonathan Swift, . . . in a Series of Letters from John Earl of Orrery to his Son* (1752), p. 86.

[2] *Ibid.*, p. 84.

[3] Thomas Sheridan, *The Life of the Rev. Dr. Jonathan Swift* (1784), p. 382.

and success as a teacher. He was, in his son's phrase, "a perfect child as to the knowledge of the world."[1] In the last year of his life he incurred the enmity of Swift, and the "Character" which the great satirist wrote of him after his death lacks the usual blunt justice which he was wont to mete out to his friend.

Swift was godfather to Dr. Sheridan's third son, Thomas, the father of the dramatist. Thomas Sheridan the younger has been damned with the faint praise of Dr. Johnson, and the hasty judgment of many biographers. It has been somewhat the fashion to exaggerate his defects as a scholar and his vanity as an actor. The truth is that at Westminster school he distinguished himself as a scholar, and later, like his father, took his degree at Trinity College, Dublin. He won marked success, too, both on the Dublin and on the London stage. Even Churchill, the discriminating critic of *The Rosciad*, though rightly pronouncing him inferior to Garrick, concluded his critique of Sheridan as an actor with the couplet,

> Where he falls short, 'tis Nature's fault alone;
> Where he succeeds, the merit's all his own.[2]

Dr. Johnson, comfortable in his own success, disparaged Sheridan's project of a pronouncing dictionary and his attempts to teach oratory. "What influence can Mr. Sheridan have upon the language of this great country, by his narrow exertions? Sir, it is burning a farthing candle at Dover, to shew light at Calais."[3] Yet Dr. Johnson was n[illegible]ove being piqued when the king granted Sheridan a per[illegible]couragement of the dictionary.[4]

A romantic incident introduced Th[illegible]to his

[1] Fraser Rae, *Sheridan*, I, 4–5.
[2] Vv. 1025–1026.
[3] Boswell, *Life of Johnson*, Macmillan ed. (1900), I, 3[illegible]
[4] *Ibid.*, I, 279–280.

future wife. After early successes as an actor, he had become manager of the Theatre Royal in Dublin, where he had conscientiously effected many needed reforms. Resolute defense of one of the actresses of the company from the insults of a drunken spectator named Kelly, who with his friends retaliated by wrecking the theatre and its furnishings, won for Sheridan some anonymous verses of praise. Their author, Frances Chamberlaine, the accomplished daughter of a well-known clergyman, as a pretty sequel to Sheridan's discovery of her identity, became his wife. Some years later the opposition in Dublin culminated in a still more serious riot, and turned the Sheridans toward England. Settling eventually in London, they soon numbered among their friends many of the literary folk, notably Dr. Johnson and Samuel Richardson. Through the friendly interest of Richardson, Dodsley was led to publish Mrs. Sheridan's novel, *Memoirs of Miss Sidney Bidulph* (1761). Critic and general reader hailed it with equal favor. Boswell records Dr. Johnson's unusual compliment: "I know not, Madam, that you have a right, upon moral principles, to make your readers suffer so much."[1] Two years later Garrick produced with marked success a comedy by Mrs. Sheridan, *The Discovery*, in which he himself took a leading part. Other literary efforts were less successful, but Mrs. Sheridan's merits as an author must not be overlooked in tracing the influence of heredity upon her son Richard.

Birth and Schooling. — Richard Brinsley Sheridan was born in Dublin, October 30, 1751. The varying tide of his father's fortunes as manager of the Theatre Royal was then at its height. Presently, however, it ebbed to low-water mark in the disastrous riot at his theatre, in 1754. After two years' absence from Dublin, Thomas Sheridan did indeed resume for a season his old post. But the warmth of his welcome

[1] Boswell, *Life of Johnson*, Macmillan ed. (1900), I, 283.

soon cooled, and in 1758 he took up permanent residence in England. Richard, with his sister Alicia, remained in Dublin eighteen months longer, attending Mr. Whyte's private school. In 1762, the lad was sent to Harrow, where he became a leader with his mates and a laggard with his masters. Boyish letters from Harrow show that he owed his schooling chiefly to his uncle, Richard Chamberlaine, after whom he had been named.

Despite the pension of two hundred pounds a year granted to him in 1762, and his receipts from acting, lecturing, and teaching, Thomas Sheridan was constantly in financial distress. Careless generosity and extravagance were always unheeded enemies in the household of the Sheridans. If circumstances ever grew easier, debts grew heavier. Thomas Sheridan had left behind him in Ireland such debts that his name was generously included in a bill introduced into the Irish House of Commons in 1766 for the relief of insolvent debtors. Two years previous he had sought to economize by settling at Blois, in France. The added hope that the change of climate would benefit Mrs. Sheridan proved ill-founded. She died in 1766, while Richard was still at Harrow.

In 1769, Thomas Sheridan reunited his family, two sons and two daughters, in a London home. The boys had instruction in Latin and mathematics from Mr. Ker, a retired Irish physician, and in fencing and riding from Henry Angelo, a famous teacher, whose friendship with the Sheridan family had been of long standing. Richard Brinsley Sheridan, then, although not a university man, was reasonably schooled to enter the world of society and of letters.

Early writings. — Sheridan's formal introduction into the world of letters was in company with his former schoolmate, Nathaniel Brassey Halhed. At Harrow they had collaborated in some translations from Theocritus. In 1770, letters from Halhed, now an Oxford undergraduate, to Sheridan testify to the abundant literary harvest the two friends planned to reap jointly. A farce, *Ixion*, written by Halhed and revised by Sheridan as *Jupiter*, clearly foreshadows *The Critic*. But hopes of inducing Foote or Garrick to produce it were idle. Another abortive attempt was a periodical miscellany — "Hernan's Miscellany" was Sheridan's suggestion for its title, though Halhed preferred "The Reformer." Halhed, whose vision seems to have been more financial than poetic, had written to Sheridan of *Ixion*, "The thoughts of £200 shared between us are enough to bring tears into one's eyes."[1] Now he looked forward to having, after the payment of the initial expenses of publication, "more money than we shall know how to dispose of."[2] Mr. Ker, Sheridan's former tutor, was more conservative. "As to your intended periodical paper," he wrote to Sheridan, "if it meets with success, there is no doubt of profit accruing, as I have already engaged a publisher of established reputation to undertake it for the account of the authors."[3] A wordy introductory number by Sheridan fortunately remained in manuscript. One production of the two friends, however, appeared in print in August, 1771. This was a translation in verse of *The Love Epistles of Aristænetus*, a deservedly obscure Greek author. Mr. Ker good-naturedly saw the volume through the press after many delays, and somehow it achieved a second edition.

In 1770, Thomas Sheridan had removed his family from London to Bath, hoping to win further patronage in that center of fashion which had already given kindly welcome to his lectures. Before long Richard Sheridan turned his verse from the slow drift of Greek translation into the livelier current of present-day satire. *Clio's Protest; or the Picture Varnished*, in clever rhyme, extols some of the leading beauties

[1] Fraser Rae, *Sheridan*, I, 99.
[2] *Ibid.*, I, 124.
[3] *Ibid.*, I, 125.

of Bath society. One couplet, often quoted — though oftener misquoted[1] — runs thus:

> You write with ease to show your breeding;
> But easy writing's vile hard reading.

Some humorous verses (after the popular style of Christopher Anstey's *The New Bath Guide*) dealing with the opening of the new Assembly Rooms on September 30, 1771, met with such favor that the editor of *The Bath Chronicle*, in which they appeared, had them reprinted for separate circulation. They are cast in the form of an epistle from Timothy Screw, a waiter at Bath, to his brother, a waiter at Almack's in London. These early attempts show a facile pen. Yet, in Sheridan's own case, ease of writing did not produce "vile hard reading."

First Marriage. — While Sheridan was thus striving to gain a literary footing in Bath, prominent among popular artist-folk were the Linleys — in Dr. Burney's words, "a nest of nightingales." The father was a composer, singing-master, and concert-director. The eldest daughter Elizabeth, at sixteen a prima donna in her father's concerts, sang herself into all hearts. In 1764, Mrs. Sheridan had taken singing lessons of Mr. Linley, and the return to Bath of the Sheridans cemented the friendship between the two families. Charles Francis Sheridan fell in love with Miss Linley as readily as his more impulsive brother Richard. Halhed's letters, too, turn from *The Love Epistles of Aristænetus* to passionate love epistles of his own in which he begs Richard to forward his suit with Miss Linley. Halhed was destined to bear disappointment with him to India, whither he sailed in December, 1771, to fill a post in the service of the East India Company.

Miss Linley's parents approved the suit of an elderly gentleman of wealth named Long. When, however, Mr. Long dis-

[1] *E.g.*, by Moore, *Life of Sheridan*, I, 55.

covered that Miss Linley did not favor him, he withdrew his advances and magnanimously settled upon her three thousand pounds. Very different was the constant persecution of Major Matthews, a married rake. So notorious, in fact, were the circumstances of the case, that Samuel Foote made them the theme of a comedy, *The Maid of Bath*, acted in London in June, 1771. Here Miss Linley appears as Miss Linnet, Matthews as Major Rackett, and Long as Flint. The comedy, to be sure, fails to give the literal truth, for it is a far cry from the avarice and unworthiness of Flint to the magnanimity of the real Mr. Long.

Of Miss Linley's first appearance in oratorio at London, Fanny Burney writes in her diary:[1] "The whole town seems distracted about her. Every other diversion is forsaken. Miss Linley alone engrosses all eyes, ears, hearts." Further, she declares that Miss Linley "has had more lovers and admirers than any nymph of these times. She has been addressed by men of all ranks. I dare not pretend to say, *honourably*, which is doubtful; but what is certain is, that whatever were their designs, she has rejected them all. She has long been attached to a Mr. Sheridan, a young man of great talents, and very well spoken of, whom it is expected she will speedily marry." The formal ceremony of marriage did indeed occur that very month. In March, 1772, however — a full year before these jottings in Fanny Burney's diary — Miss Linley had fled to France under the protection of Richard Sheridan to escape in the safe refuge of a French convent the persecutions of Matthews. In France, before temporarily entering the convent at Lille, she consented to a marriage ceremony with Sheridan, perhaps regarded by them rather as a plighting of troth than as the final contract. Mr. Linley, whose arrival at Lille resulted in the prompt return of the runaways

[1] (April) 1773. *The Early Diary of Frances Burney*, edited by Annie Raine Ellis (1889), I, 200–1.

to England, was finally won to consent to the formal marriage which occurred April 13, 1773. Meanwhile Sheridan had fought two duels with Matthews, who had slandered him in *The Bath Chronicle*, the first rather a disgraceful scuffle, the second a more regular meeting in which Sheridan had been wounded. After the marriage the Sheridans retired to love in a cottage at East Burnham, their journeys ended in lovers' meeting.

Dramatic Works. — From the first, Sheridan steadily refused to allow his wife to sing on the public stage — a resolution commended more by Dr. Johnson than by the practical Mr. Linley. Once settled in London in 1774, he turned naturally for a livelihood to the congenial world of the theatre. *The Rivals*, his first play, a temporary failure, but after revision a permanent success, appeared at Covent Garden Theatre, January 17, 1775. An important factor in the final success of *The Rivals* was the actor who replaced the luckless Mr. Lee in the part of Sir Lucius O'Trigger, Mr. Clinch. In gratitude, Sheridan wrote for Clinch's benefit performance on May 2, 1775, the two-act farce, *St. Patrick's Day; or The Scheming Lieutenant.* On November 21 of the same prolific year Sheridan's comic opera — "ballad opera" was Dr. Johnson's term — *The Duenna*, was produced at Covent Garden Theatre. Gay's *Beggar's Opera*, till then an unrivaled favorite, had an initial run of sixty-three nights. On June 1, 1776, *The Duenna* had its seventy-fifth representation. In 1777, Dr. Johnson set the seal of approval on Sheridan by securing his election to the famous Literary Club, among whose members were Fox, Gibbon, Burke, Garrick, and Sir Joshua Reynolds, observing that "he who has written the two best comedies of his age [i.e. *The Rivals* and *The Duenna*] is surely a considerable man."[1]

The tide of affairs now seemed at flood, and Sheridan, determining to take it at its height, thought it would lead on

[1] Boswell, *Life of Johnson*, Macmillan ed. (1900), II, 315.

to fortune. In June, 1776, he succeeded David Garrick as manager of Drury Lane Theatre, raising, perhaps by mortgage, the means to secure his share of the stock.[1] Mr. Linley, his father-in-law, one of the partners in the new management, was equally sanguine of success. But the usual Sheridan incompetence and recklessness in matters financial soon became apparent.

Sheridan opened his first Drury Lane season on September 21, 1776, with a prelude by Colman, called *New Brooms*, whose "main scope," to quote *The London Evening Post*'s review of the performance, "is to convey a handsome compliment to the late Manager and to give some hints of the sentiments and intentions of the new Directors of the Theatre." The popular expectation of a new work from Sheridan's own hand was at length partly realized in his adaptation of Vanbrugh's *The Relapse*, produced under the name of *A Trip to Scarborough*, on February 24, 1777. The difficult feat of expurgating a Restoration comedy Sheridan achieved with some measure of success.

The great triumph came finally in *The School for Scandal*. The opening performance was on May 8, 1777; yet, despite the lateness of production for a new play, it ran twenty nights the first season, and sixty-five the second. In 1779 the treasurer of Drury Lane made this sententious entry in his records: "*School for Scandal* damped the new pieces."[2] It was a

[1] Brander Matthews gives (*Sheridan's Comedies*, ed. 1885, pp. 29–31) an extended conjectural argument on this point, which has Fraser Rae's sanction (*Sheridan*, I, 310–11). It is well, however, to call attention to a very significant passage in Lockhart's *Life of Walter Scott* (Edinburgh, 1837, VI, 189–190), describing under date of January 13, 1826, a visit of Charles Matthews, and alluding to Moore's recently published *Life of Sheridan*: "Mathews says it is very simple in Tom Moore to admire how Sheridan came by the means of paying the price of Drury-Lane Theatre, when all the world knows he never paid it at all; and that Lacy, who sold it, was reduced to want by his breach of faith."

[2] Moore, *Life of Sheridan*, I, 244.

veritable triumph for the Drury Lane actors, as well as for the playwright-manager. Horace Walpole was surprised into declaring in a letter of July 13, 1777, "To my great astonishment there were more parts performed admirably in *The School for Scandal* than I almost ever saw in any play."

But not even this brilliant triumph as dramatist could atone for Sheridan's shortcomings as manager. Thomas Sheridan, appointed stage-manager by his son, was jealous, tactless, and incapable. The supineness of Richard Sheridan contrasted sadly with the business-like activity of his predecessor. On January 20, 1779, Garrick's death accentuated the passing of the old régime. Sheridan's monody in his memory, delivered by Mrs. Yates at Drury Lane on March 2, showed that his verse better fitted the ridiculous than the serious.

On October 30, 1779, was produced the last truly original play of Sheridan, *The Critic*. It was the triumph of sheer wit over the usual transitoriness of burlesque. At twenty-eight, Sheridan stood not merely as monarch of Drury Lane but as the foremost of living dramatists.

Early Political Life. — Even during Sheridan's literary musings, the fire of political ambition burned. In his veins ran the blood of an actor alive to the thrill of personal triumph possible to the orator. Already the power behind the scenes of Drury Lane, Sheridan was eager to hold the center of the stage of politics. Charles James Fox, the brilliant Whig leader in the House of Commons, less than three years older than Sheridan, declared him the wittiest man he had ever met,[1] and welcomed him to his friendship. At the Literary Club Sheridan met Edmund Burke, and at Bath he had known Windham, both Whigs. Wholly natural, then, was his determination to ally himself with the party of his political friends, and to join arms against the waning power of Lord North's ministry. In September, 1780, he was returned member for

[1] Moore, *Life of Sheridan*, I, 289.

Stafford, and within two months was elected a member of Brooks's Club, the center of Whig councils as well as of gambling.

Contrary to usual statements,[1] Sheridan's maiden speech in Parliament was not a failure. He was listened to with marked and uncommon attention. He spoke in answer to charges of bribery and corruption in securing his election, and carried his point triumphantly. His first important speech, on March 5, 1781, attacked the assumption, during the Gordon Riots, by the military of powers belonging constitutionally to the civil authorities. The downfall of Lord North's ministry, in 1782, brought to Sheridan the post of Under-Secretary for Foreign Affairs under Fox. The rapid rise in two years to an office of such distinction in the government parallels the rapidity of his earlier triumphs as manager and dramatist.

Lord Shelburne and Fox, the two Secretaries of State under the new administration of which the Marquis of Rockingham was Prime Minister, were soon at odds over the conduct of peace negotiations between Great Britain and the American Colonies. On the death of Rockingham, on July first, George III, hoping again to enjoy authority as untrammeled as in the days of Lord North's pliant ministry, immediately advanced Shelburne to the post of Prime Minister. On July fourth, Fox resigned office, a step which Sheridan loyally followed. Less honorable was the coalition between Fox and North, his old enemy, against Shelburne. The temporary success of the coalition brought to Sheridan the important post of Secretary to the Treasury. Though the King had been forced to accede to the coalition, he did not scruple to show his enmity toward it, and welcomed an almost immediate chance to turn its members out of office. Fox's India Bill, which, in brief, provided for the control of East Indian matters by commissioners

[1]See for full discussion and references for evidence, Fraser Rae, *Sheridan*, I, 358–360.

appointed by Parliament instead of by the Crown, sounded the knell of the coalition government. William Pitt, realizing the crisis, fanned the opposition to the coalition, and eventually defeated Fox's bill. The administration of Fox and North, begun on April 2, 1783, was concluded on December 18. Within this time Sheridan, as Secretary to the Treasury, had addressed the House of Commons more than a score of times on matters within his department, and had proved himself of great service to his party.

The defeat of the coalition was the triumph of William Pitt. Already, at twenty-three, Chancellor of the Exchequer in Shelburne's brief ministry, he became first Lord of the Treasury and Prime Minister before he was twenty-five. Behind him he soon had a majority of both Houses of Parliament, the King's favor, and the approval of the English people. Before him even the brilliancy of an opposition led by Fox, Burke, and Sheridan was unavailing. Despite the downfall of the coalition, however, Sheridan, in 1784, was again returned for Stafford. To him, as of the minority, fell the task of opposition critic. But before long, fortunately, he emerged from the confines of petty political controversy into broader fields.

Oratorical Triumphs. — Most illustrious in the annals of oratory is the chapter that records the trial of Warren Hastings, ex-Governor-General of India, impeached of high crimes and misdemeanors. On Hastings centered the fire of the opposition orators. High-handed conduct at times, and evident belief in the policy of the end justifying the means, unquestionably had led Hastings into many indefensible acts, but the opposition orators passed over all extenuating circumstances. In June, 1786, the House outvoted Burke and his followers in the charge brought against Hastings on account of his conduct in the Rohilla war, but Fox triumphantly carried the charge concerning extortions from Cheit Singh, an Indian Rajah. Even Pitt approved Fox's charge.

To Sheridan fell the attack upon Hastings's conduct toward the Begums of Oude. This so-called "Begum speech," delivered on Februray 7, 1787, was the supreme triumph of Sheridan's oratory. For five hours and a half he held the crowded House of Commons in breathless attention. Contemporary testimony is unanimous in the most superlative expressions of praise. Sir Gilbert Elliot, member of Parliament, declared that Sheridan's speech surpassed "all I ever imagined possible in eloquence and ability. This is the *universal* sense of all who heard it. You will conceive how admirable it was when I tell you that he surpassed, I think, Pitt, Fox, and even Burke, in his finest and most brilliant orations."[1] Burke, a generous rival, declared that Sheridan's charge was "the most astonishing effort of eloquence, argument, and wit united, of which there was any record or tradition."[2] Fox acknowledged that "all that he had ever heard, all that he had ever read, when compared with it, dwindled into nothing, and vanished like vapour before the sun." Said Pitt, his political adversary, "It surpassed all the eloquence of ancient and modern times." So passionate was the enthusiasm at the conclusion of the speech that, in Elliot's words, "every man was on the floor, and all his friends throwing themselves on his neck in raptures of joy and exultation." The most conclusive proof of Sheridan's triumph was the adjournment of the debate till the next day, on the ground that none could vote dispassionately while "under the wand of the enchanter."[3]

[1] *Life and Letters of Sir Gilbert Elliot* (1874), I, 124.

[2] For Burke's tribute, and those of Fox and Pitt which follow, see *Speeches of the Late Right Honourable Richard Brinsley Sheridan*, edited by a Constitutional Friend (1816), I, 272. They have been given with substantial accord by most of Sheridan's biographers, beginning with Watkins and Moore. Lord John Russell, however, seems a bit suspicious of their authenticity. See *The Life and Times of Charles James Fox* (1859), II, 156.

[3] Pitt's phrase, according to Moore, *Life of Sheridan*, I, 451.

Next day Sheridan's motion was carried, and the impeachment of Hastings was assured.

In the actual trial of Warren Hastings, in June, 1788, Sheridan essayed the dangerous task of rivaling his first almost incredible success. On three separate days he spoke in Westminster Hall. To Thomas Barrett, June 5, 1788, Horace Walpole wrote, "Mr. Sheridan, I hear, did not quite satisfy the passionate expectation that been raised; but it was impossible he could, when people had worked themselves into an enthusiasm of offering fifty — ay, *fifty* guineas for a ticket to hear him." But Sir Nathaniel Wraxall, who voted against Sheridan, frankly declared, "Never perhaps was expectation raised so high as on his appearance; and never, I believe, in the history of modern ages, was it so completely gratified! . . . The most ardent admirers of Burke, of Fox, and of Pitt allowed that they had been outdone, as orators, by Sheridan." [1] Thenceforth the trial of Hastings dragged slowly until his final acquittal in 1795. But in the speeches of 1787 and 1788 Sheridan's star rose to the zenith.

Viewed from the standpoint of permanent literary worth, Sheridan's orations to-day seem somewhat thin and rhetorical in contrast with Burke's. But oratory is, essentially, an appeal not to the eye, but to the ear of the listener. Burke has the verdict of posterity in his favor, but he sometimes spoke to restless benches. Not sounding the depths nor attaining the heights of Burke's logic, Sheridan struck the more popular level. "Theatrical and rather brassy oratory" is the sweeping phrase applied to Sheridan by a modern critic [2] who seemingly forgets that oratory is more than the written word, and ignores not merely the general contemporary verdict, but the

[1] *Posthumous Memoirs of his own Time*, by Sir N. W. Wraxall (1836), III, 102, 104.

[2] George Saintsbury, *A Short History of English Literature* (1898), p. 640.

judgment of consummate masters of oratory — Fox, Pitt, and Burke. Judged as literary essays — especially in the garbled and inaccurate form in which many of them have been preserved — Sheridan's speeches often fail; but Lord Lytton's lines on Sheridan, in the Second Part of *St. Stephens*, strike a true note:

> If eloquence can find its surest test
> In the degree to which it thrill the breast,
> And not the enduring thought, which after-calm
> Retains, then thine the sceptre and the palm:
> For never Fancy shot more gorgeous ray,
> Nor left air duller when it died away.

Manager of Drury Lane. — Sheridan's record of success in politics and in oratory meant inevitable failure in theatrical management. Although his treasure was in Drury Lane, his heart was in Parliament. The wonder is not that he did so ill by Drury Lane, but that he did so well. The strongest factor, perhaps, in averting immediate failure was the brilliancy of a stock company which numbered among its members Mrs. Siddons, Mrs. Jordan, and John Kemble. Mrs. Sheridan, too, brought some order out of her husband's chaos by the method and regularity with which she strove to keep the accounts of the theatre. Furthermore, she read the manuscripts of many new plays submitted to her husband. But the sum of these advantages could not balance the scales against the heavy burdens imposed by Richard Sheridan's own neglect, procrastination, and financial mismanagement.

The inefficiency of his stage-managers had much to do with the confusion at Drury Lane. Thomas Sheridan — "Old Surly Boots," as Mrs. Linley nicknamed him — was as unpopular as King, his successor, was irresponsible. Even Kemble, who became stage-manager late in 1788, was not wholly able to cope with difficulties arising largely from Sheridan's absorption in politics and in the trial of Warren Hastings. Even while holding his post as stage-manager, Thomas Sheridan's jealousy of his son's success is sadly apparent in his letters to his other son, Charles. Richard is dubbed a "wretch," but Charles is "the only treasure I have on earth."[1] Said Dr. Johnson, some years earlier, in reply to Boswell's mention of Thomas Sheridan's complaint of ingratitude on the part of two Scotchmen whom he had helped in early days, "Why, Sir, a man is very apt to complain of the ingratitude of those who have risen far above him."[2] On the death of Thomas Sheridan, in 1788, his will was found to contain no mention of Richard, who had cared for his father's last needs with filial regard.

Deepest grief soon visited Richard Sheridan. The death of his wife, in 1792, seems, in fact, to mark the turning-point in his life. Without a dissenting voice contemporaries extolled the beauty, unaffected grace, and charm of Mrs. Sheridan. Her constant devotion to her husband merited on his part an unquestionable fidelity which he sometimes failed to return. But the sincerity of his love for her, and the poignancy of his grief at her loss, are beyond cavil. To intensify his anguish followed, soon afterward, the loss of the infant daughter Mary, who had been born three months before her mother's death.

The hour was passed, now, when Sheridan could fleet the time carelessly as he had done in the golden world of early success. In 1791, Drury Lane Theatre had been condemned as unsafe. Expenditures for repairs and enlargement vastly exceeded even the enormous original estimate. In addition, temporary quarters had to be secured for the Drury Lane company at the Haymarket Theatre. At last, on April 21, 1794, was given, with an unrivaled cast, the first theatrical production in the new playhouse, *Macbeth.*

[1] Fraser Rae, *Sheridan*, II, 2.

[2] Boswell, *Life of Johnson*, Macmillan ed. (1900), II, 220.

Two years later Sheridan became the victim of a famous literary imposition. William Ireland professed that he had in manuscript an unpublished play by Shakespeare, *Vortigern and Rowena*. Sheridan and Harris, manager of Covent Garden Theatre, vied with each other to secure the right of first production. Malone and other critics did not hesitate to brand the play a forgery, but more learned men than Sheridan were hoaxed. The verdict of the first-night audience, however, was unmistakable. Curiosity gave way to disgust. The catastrophe came in the fifth act, when Kemble, whose disbelief in the genuineness of the play increased his discontent with the part of Vortigern, pronounced the words,

And when this solemn mockery is o'er.

With the words faded hopes of financial success that had led Sheridan to promise Ireland's father not merely a considerable immediate sum, but large future profits.

Two adaptations by Sheridan somewhat retrieved his fortunes. *The Stranger* (1798) and *Pizarro* (1799), though considerably revised from the German of Kotzebue, cannot be regarded as original works of Sheridan.[1] Financially, however, they were admirable successes. The acting of Mrs. Siddons and Kemble, the spectacular effects, and the patriotic appeal of some passages, gave *Pizarro* a popularity attested practically by receipts of fifteen thousand pounds. Rolla's speech to the Peruvians in the second act, long a favorite school

[1] I have in my possession a play published in Dublin, in 1798, whose title runs: "*The Stranger:* a Comedy. Freely translated from Kotzebue's German comedy of Misanthropy and Repentance." The author claims that "it was offered, about a year and a half since, to the Managers of *Drury-Lane Theatre*," and adds that when he saw *The Stranger* "acted, with scarcely any alteration from his own Manuscript, except in the names of the Characters, and with the addition of a Song and some dancing, entirely unconnected with the subject, he could not help feeling that he had been ungenerously treated."

declamation, contained, as Pitt detected, reminiscences of Sheridan's own "Begum speech." But chance roses in his path could not make Sheridan forget "how full of briers is this working-day world."

The final catastrophe of Sheridan's ill-starred career as manager occurred on February 24, 1809, when fire destroyed Drury Lane Theatre. The news was brought to him while the House of Commons was in session, but he refused the courtesy of proposed adjournment on the ground that individual misfortune should not interrupt proceedings of national importance.

Second Marriage. — Long before the public wreck of Sheridan's financial prospects in the Drury Lane disaster, the tide of misfortune had borne down inexorably upon his private life. In April, 1795, less than three years after the death of his first wife, he married Miss Ogle, daughter of the Dean of Winchester. More than two score years of age had begun to render him too crabbed to live with youth of twenty. He had become morbidly anxious about the health of his son Tom. At Brooks's Club, after the death of his first wife, he had entered into bets as reckless as many of his Drury Lane contracts. The second Mrs. Sheridan added her own extravagances to his. A brief fancy for gentleman farming on an estate in Surrey recalls somewhat Sir Walter Scott and his estate at Abbotsford. As Sheridan's fortunes declined, his wife's reproaches and complaints increased. Writing to his wife, in 1810, in all detail of self-defense, Sheridan accounted for his ill-success with pathetic truth: "No one can be in smaller affairs of the world of a more negligent, forgetful and procrastinating habit of mind than I am, united at the same time with a most unfortunately sanguine temper, and a rash confidence that I am capable of exertions equal to any difficulty whenever extremity may call for them." [1]

[1] Fraser Rae, *Sheridan*, II, 217.

Friendship with the Prince of Wales. — Perhaps the crowning misfortune of Sheridan's life was his friendship with the Prince of Wales. "I have been always fond of popularity too indiscriminately," Sheridan once wrote[1] with unerring self-analysis. Prizing so dearly the right to stand forth in that light which beats upon a throne, he forgot that its fierceness blackened every blot in the Prince of Wales and his scapegrace company. The duplicity, scandal, and intrigue of Carlton House needed cloaking, and in return for favor Sheridan was often given the task of defending the Prince. Once he wrote a defense of the Prince in the case of a Newmarket jockey scandal. At another time he rescued him from entering into a disgraceful loan. Again he was put forward to soothe the distress of Mrs. Fitzherbert when the Prince, who had married her, authorized Fox to deny it in order that the House of Commons might be more favorably inclined to vote him the allowances demanded by his extravagances. Sheridan's own integrity helped to blind him to the fact that he was but a tool in unscrupulous hands. After years of acquaintance with the Prince, he wrote to his second wife, "Pray, pray, never suspect or decry the Prince. He is acting as honourably as man can do, and gives me his entire and unqualified confidence."[2] Even during the lifetime of his first wife, Sheridan was engaged in the unhappy intrigue of Carlton House, precipitated by the illness and temporary mental derangement of George III in 1788. The prospect was that, if the Prince became Regent, his friendship with the Whigs would restore them to power. But though he had such supporters as Fox, Sheridan, Burke, and Lord North, the opposition of Pitt was indomitable in the House of Commons. A few time-servers deserted Pitt's party for the rising faction of the Prince, only to find speedily that the opposition was to suffer utter rout in the restoration of the King to health.

[1] Fraser Rae, *Sheridan*, II, 227. [2] *Ibid.*, II, 249.

Later Political Life. — The bitterness of the defeat of Whig hopes of power brought in its wake dissension among the leaders of the party. The advent of the French Revolution fomented differences of opinion. Fox and Sheridan took the reasonable ground that, if the French preferred a republican form of government, they were exercising their rightful prerogative of choice. Burke, mindful of the crimes committed in the name of liberty, maintained a more conservative attitude toward the revolt against monarchy. The general verdict of the English people was against the more radical position of Fox and Sheridan. As years went on, Sheridan, receding somewhat from the position he had assumed at the outset of the war, adopted a more conciliatory attitude toward the ministry than did Fox. With such dissensions among the Whig leaders, it was not surprising that many of the rank-and-file deserted to the united and triumphant ministerial party.

Through the mazes of petty politics it is unprofitable to trace in detail Sheridan's part. Once, in 1797, the mutiny in the fleet at the Nore gave him a chance to appear in a less partisan and more broadly patriotic attitude, his initiative of prompt action unquestionably acting to prevent panic. But Sheridan's political position became more and more isolated. The gulf which separated him from Burke in attitude toward the French Revolution had been widened, no doubt, by natural jealousy of Burke's prominence. Sheridan's differences with Fox were accentuated when he supported the short-lived ministry of Addington. He had to pay the penalty of vacillation, for after the death of Pitt, in the ministry of Fox and Grenville, he failed to obtain a coveted position in the Cabinet, and had to content himself with the less significant post of Treasurer of the Navy.

Declining Fortunes. — The destruction of Drury Lane Theatre in 1809 wrecked Sheridan's finances irrevocably. No doubt he might have turned his political prominence to the profit of his pocket. But, whatever his shortcomings, there seems to be no reason to doubt that he spoke well within the truth when he said to Addington, "My visits to you may possibly be misconstrued by my friends; but I hope you know, Mr. Addington, that I have an unpurchaseable mind."[1] Almost all his political life a member of the Opposition, he would not sell his soul to gain a world of political advantage. When the rebuilding of Drury Lane Theatre was entrusted to a committee headed by Whitbread, it was not surprising that they stipulated that Sheridan should have no further part in its management. Though he was allowed £28,000 for his share in the theatre, most of that sum was absorbed by outstanding claims against him. So low, too, had his fortunes ebbed that, at the general election in 1812, he could not raise the funds essential to return him again as member for Stafford. That defeat sounded the death-knell of a continuous political career in the House of Commons of more than thirty years.

Banished alike from the world of politics and of the theatre, Sheridan was a broken man. When, in 1810, owing to the mental incapacity of George III, the Prince of Wales was appointed Regent, it was too late for the realization of the fond hopes entertained by the Whigs more than a score of years previous. The Tories remained undisturbed in power, and the Whigs vented their disappointment upon Sheridan. Now, if ever, had come the time when his son Tom's words should be fulfilled: "What a situation would yours be could you now stand between the Prince and the people, possessing the confidence of both."[2] Possessing the full confidence of neither, Sheridan stood helplessly between the contending factions. At the end of years of faithful devotion his eyes opened to the fact that he had put trust in a Prince whose word was as worthless as his bond. Thomas Sheridan the elder had

[1] Fraser Rae, *Sheridan*, II, 244.

[2] *Ibid.*, II, 273.

experienced the ingratitude of Swift; Thomas Sheridan the younger had felt the alienation of Dr. Johnson; Richard Sheridan knew both the alienation and the ingratitude of the Prince whom he had served with life-long loyalty.

As creditors pressed upon Sheridan, and the hard-headed Whitbread gave him little relief from the funds due him from Drury Lane, he was forced to the wall. In August, 1813, he was arrested for debt, and confined for a time in a sponging-house. Financial distress was, however, not the darkest cloud which overhung his declining years. Both his wife and elder son were struggling against incurable diseases. His own health was broken, partly, it must be confessed, by excesses into which he had fallen. In justice, however, the usual unpitying verdict against his later years should be tempered by the remembrance that he lived in an age when even Pitt drank to excess.

Death. — Ceaseless struggle against debt and disease brought Sheridan to his death-bed in 1816. An abscess in his throat confined him to the house. But even here a sheriff's writ for debt was served upon him. Death released him mercifully, on July 7, 1816.

Pitiful as is the real record of Sheridan's last days, the truth is far less pitiful than the fictions that have too frequently passed current. That a bailiff stopped the funeral procession and arrested the corpse for debt is a falsehood too flagrant to deceive many. Equally false though less extravagant accounts given by the Prince of Wales to his facile tool Croker,[1] in the effort to excuse his rank ingratitude toward Sheridan, have, however, been accepted by most biographers at face value. They should have recalled the Prince's admission to Lady Spencer, "You know I don't speak the truth"[2] — a confession, indeed, superfluous even in his own day, save to blind loyalty

[1] *The Croker Papers*, edited by Louis J. Jennings, I, 288–312.

[2] Fraser Rae, *Sheridan*, II, 283, foot-note 3.

such as Sheridan's. Modern taste is fortunately too squeamish to relish the picture of filth and stench in Sheridan's death-room, painted by a Prince who — to apply the phrase often attributed to Sheridan — "relied on his imagination for his facts." It is true that in the columns of *The Morning Post* an appeal for help was made by one of Sheridan's friends, but Charles Sheridan, in a letter to his half-brother Tom, wrote: "You will be soothed by learning that our father's death was unaccompanied by suffering, that he almost slumbered into death, and that the reports which you may have seen in the newspapers of the privations and the want of comforts which he endured are unfounded; that he had every attention and comfort which could make a death-bed easy." [1]

The truth is that, however hampered by debts during life, Sheridan at his death had liabilities but slightly exceeding five thousand pounds — a sum insignificant in comparison with the forty thousand pounds which William Pitt left as a debt to be paid by the nation.

A truly royal assemblage attended Sheridan's interment in Westminster Abbey. He was buried, not near Fox, as he would have preferred, but in the Poets' Corner. Especially appropriate this seems to-day, when Sheridan is remembered as a dramatist rather than as a statesman. Yet it is well to recall that on the morning after his death an article in *The London Times* spoke of him as one "whom it has been the fashion for many years to quote as a bold reprover of the selfish spirit of party; and throughout a period fruitful of able men and trying circumstances, as the most popular specimen in the British Senate of political consistency, intrepidity, and honour."

[1] *Ibid.*, II, 286.

SHERIDAN'S RELATION TO THE ENGLISH DRAMA

1. Sheridan and the Elizabethans

In examining the manuscript of *Vortigern and Rowena*, before that supposedly Shakespearean treasure-trove was proved to be Ireland's forgery, Sheridan encountered a line which he pronounced "not strictly poetic." Thereupon he turned to Ireland's father with the words, "This is rather strange; for though you are acquainted with my opinion as to Shakspeare, yet, be it as it may, he certainly always wrote poetry."[1] The remark shows that Sheridan was not in full sympathy with even the greatest of the Elizabethan dramatists. He held the mirror up to art, rather than to nature. Unable to penetrate with Shakespeare the depths of the Human Comedy, Sheridan followed the comic dramatists of the Restoration in the simpler path of the Comedy of Manners. His failure to appreciate Shakespeare was not due to ignorance. The text of *The Critic* quotes phrases in *Hamlet* and *Othello* as readily as it recalls Falstaff's Page or Juliet or Richard. Familiarity with Shakespeare was, indeed, essential for the manager of Drury Lane, but it was a familiarity which led rather to the manager's appreciation of the successful playwright than to the critic's appreciation of supreme genius. Idle, then, must be the attempt to find in Sheridan evidence of more than casual indebtedness to Shakespeare. Even the cherished assertions that Mrs. Malaprop is but Dogberry with a change of sex, and that Bob Acres is a second Sir Andrew Aguecheek, seem as unfair to Shakespeare as to Sheridan. Sheridan was a wit; Shakespeare, a humorist. Sheridan passed lightly over the surface of life, while Shakespeare probed its depths. Sheridan's prospect was bounded by the actual horizon. Beyond his ken lay Prospero's isle and the seacoast of Bohemia.

[1] *Confessions of William-Henry Ireland* (1805), p. 138.

If literary kinship must be proved between Sheridan and the Elizabethans, it is less with Shakespeare than with Ben Jonson. Jonson's Comedy of Manners painted the affectations and vices of London life, largely delineating such individual peculiarities — or "humors" — of character as are implied in the names, Fastidius Brisk, Sir Amorous La-Foole, and Sir Epicure Mammon. Equally suggestive in Sheridan are such names as Absolute, Malaprop, Languish, Careless, Snake, Candour, Backbite, and Sneerwell. Furthermore, Sheridan has two highly developed instances of artificial humors in "the *oath referential*" of Bob Acres, and Mrs. Malaprop's "nice derangement of epitaphs," while, in a broader sense, Faulkland's humor is unreasonable jealousy, as Sir Lucius O'Trigger's humor is love of fighting. Without asserting conscious and direct imitation of Jonson's comedies by Sheridan, the fact is yet apparent that *The Rivals* and *The School for Scandal* incline less toward the Shakespearean Comedy of Character than toward the Jonsonian Comedy of Manners.

Despite frequent exaggeration of certain casual resemblances between Shakespeare and Sheridan, there has been singular disregard of perhaps their most noteworthy similarity in dramatic art. In distinguishing Shakespeare's plays from those of other dramatic poets, Coleridge made a primary point of the use of "expectation in preference to surprise," as a dramatic motive. Shakespeare takes his audience into the secret of Viola's disguise, of Hero's supposed death, of Iago's villainy. With him no "Disinherited Knight" becomes an Ivanhoe; no "Black Knight" eventually unmasks the features of a King of England. In utter contrast to the Shakespearean use of "expectation," two conspicuous Elizabethan dramas sufficiently illustrate the frequent substitution of "surprise" as the dramatic motive. Jonson's *Epicœne; or, The Silent Woman,* hinges on the revelation in the last act that the supposed "Silent Woman" is in reality a boy: Beaumont and Fletcher's *Philaster* concludes with the astounding discovery that the Page, Bellario, is in reality a woman. Sheridan did not sacrifice on the temporary altar to "surprise" the deeper and more lasting effectiveness of "expectation." At the outset, Fag informs the audience that "Captain Absolute and Ensign Beverley are one and the same person"; without delay Lady Sneerwell unmasks the hypocrisy of Joseph Surface. Even in the climax of the "screen scene," the fall of the screen does not startle the audience with an unexpected apparition. The emotion aroused is not curiosity as to the identity of the person concealed behind the screen, but interest in the feelings of the erring wife, the almost dishonored husband, and the unmasked hypocrite. In taking the audience into his confidence, Sheridan followed the Shakespearean method of dethroning mere curiosity and exalting in its place insight into the motives and emotions of his characters.

Whatever Sheridan's indirect debt to Shakespearean methods of dramatic art or to Jonsonian portrayal of manners, his real masters were not the Elizabethans. By far his closest models were the Comic Dramatists of the Restoration.

2. Sheridan and the Restoration Dramatists

Sheridan inherited the genius, but not the immorality, of the Comic Dramatists of the Restoration. Portraying the manners of society rather than the springs of human character, he followed the Restoration Comedy of Manners. In the exaltation of wit over humor and of sparkling dialogue over depth of expression, he harks back to Congreve. In ceaseless brilliancy of wit Congreve was as pre-eminent in Restoration comedy as Sheridan in eighteenth-century comedy. Both sacrificed naturalness on the altar of wit. Puff might have been Congreve's advocate as well as Sheridan's in declaring, "I am not for making slavish distinctions, and giving all the fine language to the upper sort of people"; Congreve's own defense, however unsound, is at least equally applicable to Sheridan: "The saying of humourous things does not distinguish Characters; for every Person in a Comedy may be allow'd to speak them."[1] Without the brutality of Wycherley, and with less grossness than Farquhar or Vanbrugh, Congreve blended wit with grace and fluency of style. The dialogue of *The School for Scandal* recalls that of *The Way of the World;* Lady Teazle breathes the same atmosphere, only purified, as Millamant. In dramatic construction, to be sure, Sheridan and Congreve part company. Congreve's plots are hard to follow, and harder still to recollect; Sheridan was a master of vigorous plot and effective scenes. Broadly viewed, however, Congreve is Sheridan's closest prototype.

Sheridan had much in sympathy, too, with other Restoration dramatists. Etheredge, an earlier and more Gallicized Congreve, was the real founder of that school of society comedy whose most finished product is *The School for Scandal.* In *A Trip to Scarborough* Sheridan strove to "draw some slender covering o'er That graceless wit which was too bare before," in Vanbrugh's comedy, *The Relapse; or, Virtue in Danger.* Lord Foppington, that most exquisite fop of society comedy, must have been a strong magnet to the author of *The School for Scandal.* Though Sheridan followed the spirit of Etheredge and Congreve and adapted the very text of Vanbrugh, he had something in common with Farquhar. The best of Farquhar's comedies, *The Beaux' Stratagem,* has the ingenuity and vigor of plot which Etheredge and Congreve usually lacked, and a spirit of humor sometimes reminiscent of *The Rivals.* Mrs. Dangle's reference to Dorinda in the same breath with Ophelia and Juliet shows the familiarity of Sheridan's age with Farquhar's comedy. Though

[1] Congreve's letter to Dennis, *Concerning Humour in Comedy, Select Works of John Dennis,* 1718, II, 515.

Farquhar's touches of life at inn and country-house, and his blending of farce with comedy, foreshadow Goldsmith rather than Sheridan, *The Beaux' Stratagem* has a certain kinship of spirit, not so much with *The School for Scandal* as with its less witty but more humorous predecessor, *The Rivals*.

Difficult of belief is Sheridan's statement that he never read Wycherley.[1] Moore's assertion[2] that *The Duenna* was "mainly founded upon an incident borrowed from *The Country Wife* of Wycherley" may have been phrased too positively, yet Sheridan could hardly have been ignorant of Garrick's popular adaptation of the play under the title of *The Country Girl*, less than a decade before. Wycherley's *The Plain Dealer* may well have furnished some hints to Sheridan's scandal-scenes,[3] and Lady Teazle is essentially the Restoration "country wife" redeemed from destruction. Lady Teazle is all but singed by the flame of the fire that consumes Mrs. Pinchwife. With cynical brutality Wycherley turned the laugh against the dishonored husband: Sheridan drew Lady Teazle back from the precipice by the path of repentance. As Mrs. Pinchwife seems Molière's *ingénue*, Agnes, in *L'École des Femmes*, befouled by Wycherley's revolting cynicism, Lady Teazle seems, in a sense, Sheridan's redemption of Mrs. Pinchwife out of the hot-house atmosphere of the Restoration into purer air.[4]

With the genius, then, of the Comic Dramatists of the

[1] "They used to annoy him about his plagiarisms from Wycherley, till he at last swore he had never read a line of Wycherley." *Diary of Thomas Moore*, April, 1819, Russell's ed. Moore's *Memoirs*, etc., II, 297–8. [2] *Life of Sheridan*, I, 169.

[3] For more specific reference, see Introduction, *The Sources of The School for Scandal*.

[4] The ingénue was a stock character in Restoration comedy, *e.g.* Miss Prue in Congreve's *Love for Love*, and Miss Hoyden in Vanbrugh's *The Relapse*. Mrs. Pinchwife is here used rather as a general type than as necessarily Sheridan's direct and specific model.

Restoration Sheridan was in hearty accord. Blending with Congreve's dominant spirit of wit occasional touches of other dramatists of Congreve's age, Sheridan freed the Restoration Comedy of Manners from the incubus of immorality.

3. Sheridan and the Eighteenth-Century Sentimentalists

On the crest of the wave of moral reaction which, early in the eighteenth century, engulfed the last real survivals of Restoration Drama, came in Sentimental Comedy. Without the *vis comica* of the Restoration, and with avowed moral intent, Richard Steele sought to reinforce humor with sentiment. As sentiment speedily declined into sentimentality, genuine comedy sank to low-water mark. The birth of the French *comédie larmoyante* and of the English sentimental novel stimulated the tendency of English comedy to substitute tears for laughter. Thus fostered, Sentimental Comedy in England rose to its zenith in such plays as Hugh Kelly's *False Delicacy* (1768) and Richard Cumberland's *The West Indian* (1771). At this juncture Goldsmith put the pertinent query,[1] "Which deserves the preference, — the weeping sentimental comedy so much in fashion at present, or the laughing, and even low comedy, which seems to have been last exhibited by Vanbrugh and Cibber?"

Reaction was inevitable. Fielding had already struck passing blows at Sentimental Comedy, as in the description in *Tom Jones*[2] of the puppet-show of *The Provoked Husband*, that "very grave and solemn entertainment, without any low wit, or humour, or jests," in which there was not "anything which could provoke a laugh." In February, 1773, Samuel

[1] *An Essay on The Theatre; or, A Comparison between Laughing and Sentimental Comedy;* contributed by Goldsmith to *The Westminster Magazine*, December, 1772.

[2] Book xii, chap. 5.

Foote produced on the actual stage of the Haymarket Theatre a "Primitive Puppet-show" entitled *The Handsome House-maid; or, Piety in Pattens*, a burlesque sentimental comedy in which "a maiden of low degree, by the mere effects of morality and virtue, raised herself to riches and honours."[1] A month later, at Covent Garden, a stronger hand than Foote's struck a lasting blow at Sentimental Comedy in *She Stoops to Conquer*. The whirligig of time brought in his revenges to Goldsmith, from whose earlier comedy, *The Good Natur'd Man*, the bailiffs' scene had been excised, in deference to the refined sensibilities of a "genteel" audience.

The attack on Sentimental Comedy, ably led by Foote and Goldsmith, was renewed by Sheridan. In *The Rivals*, he struck at sentimentality both in comedy and in the novel.[2] The apparent concession to the sentimentalists in the Julia-Faulkland under-plot was far more than offset by the prominence of Lydia Languish, who sighs over the sentimental novels of the circulating library and weeps over the prospect of a humdrum wedding in lieu of "one of the most sentimental elopements." Emboldened by the final triumph of *The Rivals*, Sheridan showed plainly, in the "Prologue spoken on the tenth night," his desire to dethrone "the goddess of the woful countenance — the sentimental Muse."

In *The School for Scandal* Sheridan turned even farther away from contemporary sentimentality. In seeking "this Hydra, Scandal, in his den,"[3] he reverted to that spirit of comedy which makes merry with the faults and foibles of society. Purged of immorality, the Restoration Comedy of Manners triumphed over "the weeping sentimental comedy." In the mouth of the hypocrite, Joseph Surface, sentimental

[1] Genest, V, 374–6. See also Oulton, *History of the Theatres of London* (1796), I, 14–23.

[2] See Introduction, *The Books of Lydia Languish's Circulating Library.*

[3] Garrick's Prologue to *The School for Scandal.*

moralizing lost its charm. In *The Critic* Sheridan rained parting blows upon the well-nigh extinct body of Sentimental Comedy. "That's a genteel comedy," says Sneer of the lachrymose play which Dangle mistakes for a tragedy. "It is written in a style which they have lately tried to run down; the true sentimental, and nothing ridiculous in it from the beginning to the end." How effectually Sheridan himself had run down "true sentimental" comedy is easily read between the lines of mock lament given to Sneer: "The theatre, in proper hands, might certainly be made the school of morality: but now, I am sorry to say it, people seem to go there principally for their entertainment!" Sheridan had banished the tears of "the goddess of the woful countenance — the sentimental Muse."

4. Sheridan and Goldsmith

Wit and Humor. — Born on Irish soil, dramatists of the same decade, rebels alike against sentimentalism, authors of the sole English comedies since Shakespeare which to-day hold the stage after more than a century of popularity, Goldsmith and Sheridan challenge comparison. If wit be defined in the subtle phrase of Professor Beers as "the laughter of the head," and humor as "the laughter of the heart," Sheridan was primarily a wit and Goldsmith a humorist. Yet the creator of Bob Acres was not without humor, and the author of *She Stoops to Conquer* was not without wit. Sheridan, like Congreve, has incurred the frequent charge that all his characters are witty; Goldsmith, by avoiding incessant sacrifice to wit, gains naturalness. Contrast Sheridan's Fag and David, who rival their masters in repartee, with Goldsmith's "honest Diggory," who, so far from being witty in himself, is not even the cause of wit in his master Hardcastle. Diggory's utter inability to comprehend how social laws can overrule the law of nature which prescribes hunger "whenever Diggory sees yeating going forward," and of instinct which compels a laugh at "the story of Ould Grouse in the gun-room," contrasts vividly in natural humor with the artificial wit of Fag's reply to Captain Absolute, "Sir, whenever I draw on my invention for a good current lie, I always forge endorsements as well as the bill." The constant sparkle of dialogue, more justifiable in the artificial world of scandal, is hardly to be expected in *The Rivals* from clownish servant and from country bumpkin. Sum up the case against Sheridan however strongly, there yet remains supreme brilliancy of wit to offset disregard of naturalness. Sheridan wrote for the stage, with a deliberate heightening of dialogue for stage effect. If far-fetched Elizabethan conceits and even Shakespearean puns in moments of tragic stress be viewed to-day with kindly toleration, some leniency is due even to artificialities in a dialogue which has never failed to compel laughter. Though the wit is at times polished thin, there remain few verbal crudities. Much of Sheridan's art lies in seemingly artless building up of dialogue toward effective climax. A random illustration is the succession of Sir Peter's and Lady Teazle's speeches, culminating in Lady Teazle's, "For my part, I should think you would like to have your wife thought a woman of taste," and Sir Peter's reply, "Ay — there again — taste! Zounds! madam, you had no taste when you married me!" *The Rivals* and *The School for Scandal* overrun with wit; *The Critic* remains as the most notable triumph in English drama of sheer wit over the usual transitoriness of burlesque.

Character-Drawing. — The character-drawing of Goldsmith and Sheridan cannot fairly be dismissed with the curt summary that Goldsmith's characters are natural, Sheridan's artificial. Goldsmith's greater naturalness is partially accounted for by his choice of a less artificial background than that of Bath and London society. Of necessity, Mr. Hardcastle stands closer to Squire Western than can Sir Anthony Absolute or

Sir Peter Teazle. If Diggory breathes the country atmosphere of the Hardcastle home, Trip absorbs somewhat of Charles Surface's lavishness of wit and of money. "The mimicry of Falstaff's page," to borrow an illustration from Sneer, is somewhat of a precedent for Sheridan's dramatization of the proverb, "Like master, like man." Furthermore, in the deliberate change from Solomon Teazle to Sir Peter Teazle, Sheridan intentionally removed his characters from *bourgeois* to "society" comedy. That *The Rivals* is less artificial in atmosphere than *The School for Scandal* partially enforces the argument. Frank should be the concession that Goldsmith's characters are more natural than Sheridan's, yet the case should not rest here.

If it be granted freely that Sheridan's lavishness of wit sacrifices truth to brilliancy, it is but just to indicate Goldsmith's limitations in character-drawing. Very unconvincing is the conception of young Marlow as a lion among maids and a sheep among ladies. To another anomaly in character Mr. Austin Dobson directs attention:[1] "Tony Lumpkin, who in Act IV is so illiterate as not to be able to read more than his own name in script, is clever enough, in Act I, to have composed the excellent song of *The Three Pigeons.*" Again, Miss Hardcastle and Miss Neville are not strongly differentiated. If it be urged that *The Rivals* is marred by the introduction of "humor characters," the same objection applies to Croaker and young Honeywood in *The Good Natur'd Man*, and to young Marlow himself. In Goldsmith, love-making is as conventional as in Sheridan. If Charles Surface is least at home in the presence of Maria, it may be urged that quite as much interest centers in the recovery of Miss Neville's jewels as in the gaining of her hand. In Goldsmith and Sheridan alike, Jack mates with Jill in accordance with the

[1] *The Good Natur'd Man and She Stoops to Conquer* (Belles-Lettres Series) Introduction, xxviii.

law of comedy rather than of nature. Miss Hardcastle and Miss Neville are as far removed from Rosalind and Viola as are Lydia Languish and Maria. Indeed, it may be questioned whether Goldsmith's comedies offer anything comparable to Sheridan's touch of real sentiment when Lady Teazle, behind the screen, overhears Sir Peter's generous plans for her welfare, and is reclaimed from folly. Dispassionate review of the limitations of Goldsmith's characters will show that injustice is done to a greater dramatist than Sheridan in ascribing to Goldsmith "Shakespearean naturalness."

Weighed in the Shakespearean balance Goldsmith's and Sheridan's characters are alike wanting, yet criticism must not be wholly destructive. Tony Lumpkin, Bob Acres, and Mrs. Malaprop, at least, rank among distinct dramatic creations, maintaining, despite obvious exaggerations of character, undiminished vitality. Charges that Mrs. Malaprop's "derangement of epitaphs" is altogether too "nice" should not ignore Shakespeare's bestowal upon Mrs. Quickly of half a dozen word-blunders in as many lines, and "derangements" as artificial as "honey-suckle" for "homicidal." If the "oath referential" of Bob Acres is an exaggerated "humor," the dramatist's provocation is certainly greater than that of the novelist who insists upon Uriah Heep's "'umble" and Clara Peggotty's constant bursting off of buttons. Sheridan, like Shakespeare, wrote for the stage, and criticism that ignores the vitality of Mrs. Malaprop and Bob Acres is itself as distorted as the peculiarities which it attacks.

Barring Tony Lumpkin — perhaps even including him — the best drawn character in *She Stoops to Conquer* is Mr. Hardcastle. The country squire with long-spun anecdotes of the Duke of Marlborough and stories like that of "Ould Grouse in the gun-room" at which his household has laughed "these twenty years," exhales the country air of *The Vicar of Wakefield.* Mrs. Hardcastle, though farcical, is effective, and

Diggory's brief scene with his master abounds in natural humor. Miss Hardcastle's nimbleness of wit helps to redeem a somewhat unconvincing heroine. Young Marlow falls far below either Captain Absolute or Charles Surface. Sir Charles Marlow is shadowy in comparison with Sir Anthony Absolute. Hastings, though mechanical, is doubtless better than the over-jealous Faulkland, yet even Faulkland has a certain justification as a foil to Bob Acres. Miss Neville, as a heroine of under-plot, is preferable to the sentimental Julia. In Sheridan, there are, apart from Bob Acres and Mrs. Malaprop, Sir Anthony Absolute, especially admirable in the quarrel-scene with his son; Captain Absolute, a far more vital "first lover" than young Marlow; Sir Lucius O'Trigger, who blends Irish wit with love of fighting, and who refuses to spoil "a very pretty quarrel as it stands . . . by trying to explain it"; Lady Teazle, upon whose "woman's wit" Sir Peter in vain endeavors to "make the doors"; Sir Peter, whose generosity, with a touch of real sentiment, reclaims the erring wife; Sir Oliver Surface, an effective stage character; the scandal-group, a many-headed Hydra, to be sure, but with a body of very distinct individuality; Joseph Surface, in whom Charles Lamb over-ingeniously found the real hero, and Charles Surface, the warm-hearted prodigal. Such brief survey of some of Goldsmith's and Sheridan's characters can be neither exhaustive nor conclusive. It should, however, suffice to show that estimates based merely on admitted merits of Goldsmith's character-drawing and admitted faults of Sheridan's, unjustly ignore Goldsmith's shortcomings and Sheridan's positive merits. Justice — to return to the original contention — demands a fairer judgment than that implied in the statement that Goldsmith's characters are natural, Sheridan's artificial.

Dramatic Art. — In dramatic art, Sheridan clearly excels Goldsmith, and indeed is not unworthy of comparison with Shakespeare. True, the Julia-Faulkland under-plot is so poorly linked with the main plot that it is sometimes well-nigh excised from acting versions of *The Rivals*,[1] while the "scandal-scenes" serve rather for "setting" than for advancement of the plot. In general, however, Sheridan's practical knowledge of stage effect is consummate. The "duel scene," the "auction scene," and especially the "screen scene" are among the most successful scenes in English comedy. Yet perhaps Sheridan's most notable triumph is that his scenes, however effective individually, develop naturally from the necessities of the plot. The brilliancy of the "auction scene" would be its own justification, but it serves the essential object of introducing Sir Oliver's test of the character of his scapegrace nephew. Not merely the general conception, but the execution of individual details in scene-construction, reveals Sheridan's dramatic art. Highly ingenious, and highly natural as well, is the device which provides for the fall of the screen not by blunder or accident, but by Sir Peter's curiosity as to the "little French milliner." Hazlitt surely had in mind Sheridan's dramatic art when he pronounced *The School for Scandal*, "if not the most original, perhaps the most finished and faultless comedy which we have."[2]

Contrast with Goldsmith shows Sheridan's triumph in naturalness of incident. So strong are the improbabilities upon which rests the plot of *She Stoops to Conquer* that, to quote Dr. Johnson, it "borders upon farce."[3] The prolongation of Marlow's mistake in thinking Hardcastle's house an inn is hardly justified by the plea that the plot is founded on an actual mistake of Goldsmith. The scene on "Crackskull Common" passes from comedy to farce, when Mrs. Hardcastle fails to recognize either her own garden or her own husband. Equally improbable is Marlow's failure to recognize

[1] See Appendix, *Mr. Joseph Jefferson's Acting Version of The Rivals.*

[2] Lecture viii, in *Lectures on the English Comic Writers* (1819), p. 335.

[3] Boswell, *Life of Johnson*, Macmillan ed. (1900), I, 530.

the mistress in the maid. In Sheridan there is no such wrenching of the probabilities. Mrs. Malaprop has no reason to suspect that "Captain Absolute and Ensign Beverley are one and the same person," nor has Bob Acres reason to suspect that his dreaded adversary will prove to be one of his "particular friends." However effective as a stage-play, *She Stoops to Conquer* cannot compare in naturalness of incident or of plot-development with *The School for Scandal*. As a dramatic artist Goldsmith must yield the honors to Sheridan.

Comparison between Goldsmith and Sheridan has been intentionally confined to the trio of famous comedies. To insist upon comparison of *The Good Natur'd Man* with *The Rivals* and *The School for Scandal* is to hang a millstone around Goldsmith's neck. Croaker and Lofty, doubtless the best characters in Goldsmith's earlier play, can with difficulty rival Sir Fretful Plagiary and Mr. Puff, despite the fact that *The Critic* is merely a burlesque. For scenes, perhaps only the bailiffs' scene and Croaker's reading of the letter may be termed effective. If the rather negative merits of *The Good Natur'd Man* and the positive merits of *The Critic* be urged, Goldsmith's contribution to English drama is obviously inferior in extent and variety to that of Sheridan.

Tested merely by continuance of stage popularity, Sheridan stands in English drama second only to Shakespeare. Judged by purely literary standards, though he cannot be ranked in the school of Shakespeare's Comedy of Nature, he stands as the most finished product of the Comedy of Manners. No more effective and yet rational modern summary of the case for Sheridan can perhaps be found than that given to Fraser Rae by Sir Henry Irving: "Sheridan brought the comedy of manners to the highest perfection, and *The School for Scandal* remains to this day the most popular comedy in the English language. Some of the characters both in this play and in *The Rivals* have become so closely associated with our current speech that we may fairly regard them as imperishable. No farce of our time has so excellent a chance of immortality as *The Critic*."[1]

THE RIVALS

1. The Sources of The Rivals

General Sources Suggested. — The ingenuity of many explorers of the original sources of *The Rivals* is comparable only to the imaginative genius of many of Sheridan's biographers. Were all the charges of borrowing and theft preferred against Sheridan proved, he would at least stand credited with a literary knowledge perhaps as striking in a man of three-and-twenty as the possession of some original dramatic ability. An idea of these supposed borrowings, great and small, in plot and character, may be gained by grouping together a few of the authors from whom, it is alleged, Sheridan drew — Smollett, Garrick, Shakespeare, Molière, Fielding, Colman, Prior, Steele, Mrs. Sheridan, Theodore Hook.[2] So far, moreover, do doctors disagree, that while one suggests Smollett's *Peregrine Pickle*, several insist on *Humphry Clinker;* while one suggests Mrs. Sheridan's novel *The Memoirs of Miss Sidney Bidulph*, others insist on her play, *A Journey to Bath.* Most ingenious is the theory of indebtedness to Theodore Hook, who was born thirteen years after the first performance of *The Rivals.* Not all the other suggestions can be swept aside so conclusively, but the assertion may be made safely that Sheridan's borrowings from any or all of these supposed originals are comparatively slight.

Mrs. Malaprop. — Investigation has centered chiefly on the original of Mrs. Malaprop. The hyper-ingenious Watkins,

[1] Fraser Rae, *Sheridan*, II, 322.

[2] Brander Matthews, *Sheridan's Comedies* (Crowell ed. 1904), *Introduction to the Rivals*, lxviii ff., takes up the cudgels effectively in Sheridan's defense.

Sheridan's first biographer, finds Mrs. Malaprop "a palpable copy from an original in the novel of Joseph Andrews," and thereupon institutes a comparison between Mrs. Slipslop and Mrs. Malaprop in which he maintains that what "gives inimitable humour to the story of Fielding becomes extravagantly absurd in the comedy of Sheridan."[1] Among other suggested originals are Tabitha Bramble in *Humphry Clinker*, Mrs. Heidelberg in Colman and Garrick's *The Clandestine Marriage*, and Dogberry in *Much Ado about Nothing*. The word-blunders of these characters, however, bear but a superficial resemblance to Mrs. Malaprop's "nice derangement of epitaphs." In Tabitha Bramble's letters, for instance, most of the rough comic effect is due to extraordinarily illiterate spelling. Thus, in her first letter, she writes of her "rose-collard neglejay, with green robins," and of the "litel box with my jowls." In the speeches assigned to Mrs. Heidelberg, the spelling shows that her blunders of speech lie chiefly in mispronunciation. In her first scene, for example, occur "pertest," "dishabille," "kivers" (for "covers"), "qualaty," "nataral," and "perdigious." In decided contrast should be remembered Julia's explanation of Mrs. Malaprop's "select words so ingeniously *misapplied*, without being *mispronounced*." Dogberry, indeed, may claim closer kinship to Mrs. Malaprop than can Tabitha Bramble or Mrs. Heidelberg. Yet it must not be forgotten that the word-blunders of the illiterate have long been a stock source of comedy, and that in Shakespeare alone are, besides Dogberry, Elbow the "simple constable," Mistress Quickly, and Launcelot Gobbo.

Whatever the kinship between Mrs. Malaprop and such literary — or rather, illiterate — ancestors, a far nearer relative is to be found in Mrs. Sheridan's unfinished comedy, *A Journey to Bath*. In the fifth scene of the first act Mrs. Tryfort is described as "the yainest poor creature, and the fondest of

[1] *Memoirs of Richard Brinsley Sheridan*, I, 198.

hard words, which, without *miscalling*, she always takes care to *misapply*" — a close parallel to Julia's already quoted description of Mrs. Malaprop. Both Mrs. Tryfort and Mrs. Malaprop use "progeny" for "prodigy," and "contagious" for "contiguous," and there are a few parallels less exact than these. Though the borrowings are not numerous, the conclusion seems inevitable that the immediate suggestion for Mrs. Malaprop came from Mrs. Sheridan's play.

Lydia Languish. — Since the ultra-romantic heroine is a stock comedy character, it is not surprising that critics have found originals for Lydia Languish almost as readily as for Mrs. Malaprop. Among the most frequently suggested prototypes of Lydia Languish are Smollett's Lydia Melford[1] in *Humphry Clinker*, Colman's Polly Honeycombe in the comedy of the same name, and Steele's Biddy Tipkin in *The Tender Husband.* Apart from the similarity in name, Lydia Melford's resemblance to Lydia Languish is best summarized in her uncle Matthew Bramble's phrase, "Truly, she has got a languishing eye, and reads romances." His earlier description of her, however — "a poor, good-natured simpleton; as soft as butter, and as easily melted" — hardly fits Sheridan's character. Lydia Melford faints on discovering that a supposed spectacle-vendor is her disguised lover, Wilson. Lydia Languish speedily overcomes astonishment at the sudden discovery of Beverley (iii, 3), and turns the unexpected opportunity to profit. Smollett's heroine rejoices with all her relatives when finally "the slighted Wilson is metamorphosed into George Dennison, only son and heir of a gentleman whose character is second to none in England";[2] Sheridan's heroine renounces Beverley when she discovers that he is Sir Anthony's

[1] Sanders, *Life of Sheridan*, p. 34, and G. A. Aitken, *The Rivals, Introduction*, vii, speak of Lydia "Bramble" instead of Melford.

[2] Lydia Melford's words in her letter to Mrs. Jermyn, toward the close of *Humphry Clinker.*

son, and laments the destruction of her project for "one of the most sentimental elopements."

The opening scene of Colman's *Polly Honeycombe* certainly bears some resemblance to Lydia Languish's first appearance. Polly bids her Nurse "call at the Circulating Library, as you go along, for the rest of this Novel — The History of Sir George Truman and Emilia — and tell the bookseller to be sure to send me the British Amazon, and Tom Faddle, and the rest of the new Novels this winter, as soon as ever they come out." Like Lydia Languish, Polly thinks of "ladders of ropes" and other accessories of sentimental elopements. The exclamation of Polly's father, "A man might as well turn his daughter loose in Covent-Garden, as trust the cultivation of her mind to A CIRCULATING LIBRARY," recalls in substance, if not in finish of expression, Sir Anthony's "A circulating library in a town is as an evergreen tree of diabolical knowledge!" Colman's Prologue, too, ridicules the sentimental novel in a way that Sheridan might have applauded:

> And then so sentimental is the Stile,
> So chaste, yet so bewitching all the while!
> Plot, and elopement, passion, rape, and rapture,
> The total sum of ev'ry dear — dear — Chapter.

Dibdin implies that Sheridan's debt to Colman is self-evident, by saying,[1] "Polly Honeycomb was better in its former place." Though Dibdin is far too positive in his implication, certain resemblances between the "circulating library scenes" render at least plausible the theory of some slight indebtedness on Sheridan's part. Certainly the idea does not merit the hasty contempt with which it has sometimes been swept aside.

In general conception Lydia Languish resembles Steele's Biddy Tipkin, rather than Smollett's or Colman's heroines.

[1] *A Complete History of the Stage*, V, 296.

As in Colman and in Sheridan, the heroine in Steele's *The Tender Husband* is introduced as a passionate lover of romances — "These idle romances," remarks her aunt, "have quite turned your head." Closer, however, than this general resemblance is the scene in *The Tender Husband* (iv, 2) where Biddy's lover, in disguise, courts her before her unsuspecting aunt. When Biddy remarks *aside*, "But I can't think of abridging our amours, and cutting off all farther decoration of disguise, serenade, and adventure," and a moment later turns to her lover with "But it looks so ordinary, to go out at a door to be married. Indeed, I ought to be taken out of a window, and run away with" — she is at least a sister in spirit to Lydia Languish. Sheridan may well have found here the germ of Lydia's speeches to Julia (v, 1). If, however, Sheridan owes a debt to Steele, it is rather in the general conception of the character than in details of drawing.

When all is said, one returns readily from the uncertain ground of conjecture to the solid basis of the first assertion that the ultra-romantic heroine is a stock comedy character, and that the sum total of Sheridan's possible borrowings is small.

Julia-Faulkland. — The supposed sources of the Julia-Faulkland under-plot may be disposed of briefly. With the positiveness that seems almost a mania with many who investigate literary antecedents, Boaden asserts,[1] with his own italics, "There is *absolute* proof that he [Sheridan] found *some* aid in the genius of his own family. In the *Rivals* Falkland rushes into Julia's dressing-room, tells her that he has killed his adversary, that his life is forfeited, that he wishes first to call her *his*, and then that, without preparation, she would fly the country with him. — Rivals, Act V. Sc. 1. In the Memoirs of Sidney Biddulph, written by his excellent mother, — the hero,

[1] *Memoirs of the Life of John Philip Kemble* (1825), I, Introduction, xiv.

a *Falkland*, too, observe, — enters to the heroine in the same perturbed state, — tells the same distracted story, and urges the same sacrifice from the lady. In the romance the story is true, in the play it is merely feigned to try the constancy of Julia." The radical difference in situation which Boaden himself shows in this last sentence rather mars the alleged absoluteness of the proof. Moore ascribed the origin of this same incident to Prior and Smollett, by maintaining [1] that the imposture which Faulkland practices upon Julia is "perhaps weakened in its effect, by our recollection of the same device in the Nut-Brown Maid and Peregrine Pickle." Dibdin, with self-satisfied assurance, says,[2] "The Nut-brown Maid is only fit for the poem she adorns." Since critics, with equal positiveness, trace the source of Sheridan's under-plot to such different fountain-heads as Prior, Smollett, and Mrs. Sheridan, the fair presumption is, again, that Sheridan's borrowings, if any, were trivial.

Other Characters. —The same general truth may be asserted in reviewing the suggested originals of the remaining characters in *The Rivals.* E. P. Whipple asserts,[3] "Sir Anthony Absolute is the best character of the piece, and is made up of the elder Sheridan and Smollet's [*sic*] Matthew Bramble." To derive Sir Anthony Absolute from Matthew Bramble certainly requires a deal of reading between Smollett's lines. When "the shaping spirit of Imagination" soars thus, it is unfortunate that it overlooked Matthew Bramble's sentence in one of his Bath letters describing his sister Tabitha's flirtation — "This amiable maiden has actually commenced a flirting correspondence with an Irish baronet of sixty-five." Could not one readily find in this single sentence already fully developed Mrs. Malaprop and Sir Lucius O'Trigger! True,

[1] *Life of Sheridan*, I, 142.
[2] *A Complete History of the Stage*, V, 296.
[3] *The North American Review*, January, 1848.

Sir Ulic Mackilligut is speedily dismissed from favor for an inadvertent "kick in the jaws" administered to Tabitha's "dog Chowder, a filthy cur from Newfoundland," but neither this nor other slight discrepancies should be allowed to mar the beauty of a parallel so deadly to Sheridan.

A Picture of Sheridan's Own Life. — It remains only to take decided issue with the ever-recurring theory that *The Rivals* is merely a stage version of Sheridan's own life. Though the original idea is at least as old as Sheridan's first biographer, Watkins,[1] a recent version of the old tradition recurs in Mrs. Oliphant's biography of Sheridan:[2] "The reader who has accompanied Sheridan through the previous chapters of his history will be inclined . . . to feel that the young dramatist has but selected a few incidents from the still more curious comedy of life in which he himself had so recently been one of the actors, and in which elopements, duels, secret correspondences, and all the rest of the simple-artificial round, were the order of the day." More specifically, Lydia Languish is sometimes declared to be Eliza Linley, Bob Acres's duel to be founded on Sheridan's duels with Matthews, and Faulkland, to quote again from Whipple, to be "a satire on a state of mind which Sheridan himself experienced during his courtship of Miss Linley." A more rational judgment would be that the autobiographic element in *The Rivals* consists not in a literal transcript of Sheridan's own experiences, but in the general background of Bath society. It is hardly credible that the man who refused to allow his wife to appear on the public concert stage after their marriage would intentionally trail personal history into the glare of footlights.

Of Bath Society. — Though even the extended treatment here given to the supposed sources of *The Rivals* by no means exhausts the conjectures of the ingenious, attention must now

[1] See his *Memoirs of Richard Brinsley Sheridan*, I, 198.

[2] *Sheridan* (English Men of Letters Series), p. 50.

be diverted from Sheridan's literary antecedents to a consideration of the ample material for comedy which lay ready to his hand. Whatever dramatic prototypes Sheridan may have had perhaps indistinctly in mind, he had distinctly before his eye the familiar types of Bath society — the sentimental maiden, the dashing young subaltern, the Irish fortune-hunter, the pretentious social climber, the dandified country booby. For setting he needed only the lodgings and Parades of Bath. For a faithful portrayal of Bath society Sheridan doubtless cared little or nothing. Dramatic instinct taught him to heighten color for stage effect; but, even if he seems sometimes to turn character into caricature, the faces of his models are still discernible. Fully to understand the real sources of *The Rivals*, and the extent to which Sheridan's drama suggests a basis of real life, one must turn to accounts of Eighteenth-Century Bath.

2. Eighteenth-Century Bath

Wee thre Bath Deities bee:
Humbug; Follee, & Vanitee. — *Old Song.*[1]

The eighteenth century transformed Bath from a health to a pleasure resort. Queen Anne's visit stamped it with the seal of royal favor; Beau Nash raised it to social rank second only to that of London. Thither flocked, on the heels of good society, adventurers of every sort. Fortune-hunters in quest of dowries, spinsters in quest of titles, gamblers in quest of careless purses, joined the company of invalids in quest of health. Manners made the man more readily than in the exclusive circles of St. James, and many counterfeits passed current as to the manner born. Goldsmith, Anstey, Fanny Burney, Horace Walpole, and Smollett are but a few of many who, in biography,

[1] On the title-page of *Rebellion in Bath : or, The Battle of the Upper Rooms. An Heroico-Odico-Tragico-Comico Poem* (1808).

verse, diary, and novel, picture the Bath of Sheridan's day not merely in black-and-white, but in all vividness of local color.

Most readable of accounts of the rise of Bath into social predominance is Goldsmith's *Life of Richard Nash.* A clever fellow was Beau Nash, who set such store by others' rank that they forgot his own lack of it. By inaugurating a band under his own control he became Master of Ceremonies at concerts and assemblies. By common consent he became "King of Bath," and his enormous cream-colored beaver hat acquired almost the dignity of a recognized crown of office. Without fear or favor he enforced not merely the unwritten laws of society, but his own Rules of Behavior posted in the Pump Room. His reforms were not confined to banishing high-boots and riding-dress and white aprons from the assemblies. He successfully attacked extortionate lodging-house keepers and insolent chairmen, arrested duelists, and secured extensive repairs to the public roads. Nash lived on revenue from gaming-houses in which he was a silent partner. The stringent laws against public gaming, culminating in those of 1745, sounded his death-knell. Thereafter his fortunes waned, and with younger generations the Beau's jokes were as much out of fashion as the block of his beaver. Finally the corporation of Bath shelved him with a pension of ten guineas a month, and though Nash lived till he was well-nigh ninety, the "King" had long since been dead.

The daily routine of fashionable life began with the bath, between the hours of six and nine, followed by a general assembly at the Pump House to drink the waters and retail gossip. Public breakfasts, private concerts, lectures, walks on the Parades, visits to the circulating libraries, occupied the day until dinner. In the afternoon came a second visit to the Pump House, with tea at the assembly-houses. The day concluded with cards, the assembly, concert, or theatre. Balls began at six and ended inexorably at eleven — "not a fiddle nor a card after eleven," complains Fag, in the opening scene of *The Rivals*.

Horace Walpole, whose three weeks' visit in October, 1766, disgusted him so thoroughly with Bath that he wrote, "It does one ten times more good to leave Bath than to go to it," has left a vivid account of Captain and Lady Miller's assemblies at Bath Easton. Writes Walpole, in a letter of January 15, 1775, "Alas! Mrs. Miller is returned [from abroad] a beauty, a genius, a Sappho, a tenth muse, as romantic as Mademoiselle Scudéri, and as sophisticated as Mrs. Vesey. The Captain's fingers are loaded with cameos, his tongue runs over with *virtù*, and that both may contribute to the improvement of their own country, they have introduced *bouts-rimés* [verses composed to match given rhymes] as a new discovery. They hold a Parnassus fair every Thursday, give out rhymes and themes, and all the flux of quality at Bath contend for the prizes. A Roman vase dressed with pink ribbons and myrtles receives the poetry, which is drawn out every festival; six judges of these Olympic games retire and select the brightest compositions, which the respective successful acknowledge, kneel to Mrs. Calliope Miller, kiss her fair hand, and are crowned by it with myrtle, with — I don't know what. . . . There are *bouts-rimés* on a buttered muffin, made by her Grace the Duchess of Northumberland; receipts to make them by Corydon the venerable, *alias* George Pitt, others very pretty, by Lord Palmerston; some by Lord Carlisle: many by Mrs. Miller herself, that have no fault but wanting metre."

Five years later, in 1780, Frances Burney thus recorded her impressions:[1] "Lady Miller is a round, plump, coarse-looking dame of about forty, and while all her aim is to appear an elegant woman of fashion, all her success is to seem an ordinary woman in very common life, with fine clothes on.

[1] *Diary and Letters of Madame d'Arblay*, edited by Austin Dobson (1904——), I, 382.

Her manners are bustling, her air is mock-important, and her manners very inelegant." Despite this general verification of Walpole's description, Miss Burney confesses [1] that "notwithstanding Bath Easton is so much laughed at in London, nothing here is more tonish than to visit Lady Miller," and admits [2] that Lady Miller "seems extremely good-natured" and "is I am sure extremely civil."

Interesting as a record of fashionable dress at Bath in the year in which *The Rivals* pictured Bath society on the stage is this extract from *The Gentleman and Lady's Weekly Magazine*, for Wednesday, February 22, 1775: "The Fashionable Dress for February, as established at St. James's and Bath. — FULL DRESS. — The Ladies in general still wear their Hair dressed high, broad at top, with large Flys; — Negligees of rich plain coloured Silks or Sattins, very much trimmed with Chenille, and Gauze Fancy trimmings, ornamented with Tassels of different colours and no Flounce to the Petticoat; — large Hoops and Drop Ear-Rings; — coloured Shoes, and small Rose Buckles."

Side by side with the facts recorded by Goldsmith, Walpole, Fanny Burney, and the contemporary mazagines, should be put some vivid passages from the fiction of Tobias Smollett. The sixty-ninth chapter of *Peregrine Pickle* (1751) gives a striking account of the way in which the hero, aided by a friend who is an expert billiard player, ruins some of the low sharpers of Bath so successfully that, in the next chapter, he is hailed with plaudits in the "long-room." Much more extended, however, are the letters from Bath that form so considerable a part of the earlier pages of *Humphry Clinker* (1771). The hand, to be sure, is the hand of Matthew Bramble, but the voice is the voice of the real Dr. Smollett, out of sorts with Bath on account of his ill-success as a physician. Yet, as in Walpole's case, with due allowance for the personal

[1] *Ibid.*, I, 381. [2] *Ibid.*, I, 382.

equation, no more vivid descriptions than Smollett's can be found of the town and people of Bath. "The Square, though irregular, is, on the whole, pretty well laid out, spacious, open, and airy; and, in my opinion, is by far the most wholesome and agreeable situation in Bath, especially the upper side of it; but the avenues to it are mean, dirty, dangerous, and indirect. . . . The Circus is a pretty bauble, contrived for show, and looks like Vespasian's amphitheatre turned outside in. . . . The chairs stand soaking in the open street, from morning to night, till they become so many boxes of wet leather, for the benefit of the gouty and rheumatic, who are transported in them from place to place." The varied parasites on Bath society are thus depicted: "Every upstart of fortune, harnessed in the trappings of the mode, presents himself at Bath, as in the very focus of observation. Clerks and factors from the East Indies, loaded with the spoil of plundered provinces; planters, negro-drivers, and hucksters, from our American plantations, enriched they know not how; agents, commissaries, and contractors, who have fattened, in two successive wars, on the blood of the nation; usurers, brokers, and jobbers of every kind; men of low birth, and no breeding, have found themselves suddenly translated into a state of affluence, unknown to former ages; and no wonder that their brains should be intoxicated with pride, vanity, and presumption. Knowing no other criterion of greatness but the ostentation of wealth, they discharge their affluence, without taste or conduct, through every channel of the most absurd extravagance; and all of them hurry to Bath, because here, without any further qualification, they can mingle with the princes and nobles of the land. Even the wives and daughters of low tradesmen, who, like shovel-nosed sharks, prey upon the blubber of those uncouth whales of fortune, are infected with the same rage of displaying their importance, and the slightest indisposition serves them for a pretext to insist upon being conveyed to

Bath, where they may hobble country-dances and cotillons among lordlings, squires, counselors, and clergy."

Despite the vividness of these descriptions there yet remains an even more vivid contemporary picture of eighteenth-century Bath — Christopher Anstey's *The New Bath Guide* (1766). In verse of varying meter, Anstey depicts in a series of letters the intimate life of Bath society, with a wealth of detail that almost defies brief quotation.[1] The arrival at Bath — the consultation of physicians — the bathing — the visits to the assembly-rooms — the balls — the dress — the "polite conversation" — the "Bill of Expenses" — the farewell to Bath — such is but a crude summary of the contents of this thoroughly humorous satirical sketch of Bath society."[2]

Such was Bath when Sheridan eloped with Eliza Linley and fought a duel with Captain Matthews; such was Bath when Miss Lydia Languish "projected one of the most sentimental elopements," and Bob Acres felt his valor oozing out as it were at the palms of his hands at King's-Mead-Fields.

3. The Initial Failure and Final Triumph of The Rivals

A most familiar fact in the history of English drama is that the first performance of *The Rivals* was a failure. No complete summary, however, of the real reasons for the failure has ever been given. No biographer save Fraser Rae has presented all the evidence in the case, while, unfortunately for the general reader, his admirably complete material,[3] is accompanied by no selection or summary of the facts therein discoverable.

[1] The Notes to *The Rivals* include various quotations from *The New Bath Guide*, which are often the best commentary on Sheridan's text.

[2] Though this section of the Introduction is intentionally based solely on contemporary evidence, the reader's attention may be called to a very recent book on Bath: *Une ville d'eaux anglaise au xviiie siècle*, par A. Barbeau, Paris, 1904.

[3] *Sheridan's Plays*, Prefatory Notes, pp. xvi–xxxiii.

Thorough analysis, then, of the contemporary evidence will be of decided value both to the general reader and to the specialist who cares to institute minute comparison between the full facts and the usual statements of the case. The familiar, though by no means the best,[1] statement of the matter, may be put in the words of Henry Morley:[2] "*The Rivals* missed success on the first night through bad acting in the part of Sir Lucius O'Trigger. The part was transferred to another actor, and success was complete. In gratitude to Clinch, the actor who thus saved his play, Sheridan wrote his farce of *St. Patrick's Day.*" Beyond question, the implication is that the failure was due wholly to Lee's wretched acting, and that the transfer of his part to Clinch was all that was necessary for complete success.

First of all, even a casual reading of Sheridan's own *Preface* to the play reveals several additional reasons for its non-success. One was its undue length; another the possibility of malicious opposition in the first-night audience, still another the certainty of opposition from some who thought Sir Lucius O'Trigger a reflection on the Irish gentleman. The extracts given in the Appendix,[3] which may be multiplied readily,[4] from

[1] Among the usual omissions in even the best statements of the case are, for example, the wretched acting and utter ignorance of their parts of Shuter and others besides Lee at the first performance, their great subsequent improvement both in acting and in knowledge of the text, and Sheridan's revision of the part of *Sir Lucius* to remove all suggestion that *Sir Lucius* was intended as a national reflection upon the Irish gentleman. [2] *The Plays of Richard Brinsley Sheridan*, Introduction.

[3] Pp. 313–316.

[4] Mention may be made, for example, of the communication to *The Morning Post* of January 20, 1775, a remonstrance against attempts "to create a prejudice against the performance, by every mode that malevolence could suggest," and the statement in *The London Chronicle*, for January 21–24, 1775: "Several people in the galleries, who were evidently planted to disturb the performance, were turned out before the third act."

contemporary newspapers, prove that Sheridan spoke not merely truly, but well within the truth.

But the matter does not stop here. Contemporary evidence gives other weighty reasons for the failure of the play. Shuter, who played Sir Anthony Absolute, is criticised almost as harshly as Lee himself, while the other actors, with but few exceptions, are roundly scored by critics of the first performance. Attention has been called by some of Sheridan's biographers to the fact that in so far as *The Rivals* was a revolt against "sentimental comedy" it ran counter to the dramatic fashion of the day — a fact to which Sheridan's second prologue to the play bears witness. But since Faulkland and Julia pleased the sentimentalists, and since the revised production of the play was instantly successful, despite the retention of much that attacked sentimentalism, this in itself cannot fairly be held accountable for the failure of the first performance.

Before turning from the consideration of the initial failure of *The Rivals*, it will be well to disprove the common assertion [1] that the play was performed a second time before it was withdrawn for alteration. Probably the best explanation of

[1] Brander Matthews, *Sheridan's Comedies*, p. 23; and again, p. 65, 1885 ed. (these mistakes are repeated in the 1904 ed., xxii, lx); Lloyd C. Sanders: *Life of Richard Brinsley Sheridan*, p. 26; G. A. Aitken, *Temple* edition of *The Rivals*, Intro. v. Less readily explainable is the statement of G. G. S. [igmond] in his *Life of Sheridan*, prefixed to the Bohn Library edition of *The Dramatic Works of Richard Brinsley Sheridan*, 1848 ed., p. 39, who, after comment on Lee's wretched acting at the first performance adds: "Fortunately, on the *following night* [the italics are mine] Mr. Clinch was his substitute." Since the discovery of this mistake I have found that Mr. Rae, with his usual accuracy, has in a passing clause (*Sheridan's Plays:* Prefatory Notes, xiii) mentioned "the second [performance] on the 28th." Since, however, this clause can in itself hardly attract the attention it deserves, in view of far more prominent incorrect statements, the massing of the proofs in the case for the first time still seems justifiable.

the mistake[1] is furnished by the following extract, which has seemingly never attracted attention, from *The Town and Country Magazine*, January, 1775. In the course of a critique upon *The Rivals* occurs this sentence: "After a pretty warm contest towards the end of the last act, it was suffered to be given out for the ensuing night." To this, however, is appended the following significant foot-note: "Mr. Sheridan withdrew it after the first night's representation to make some alterations, as we suppose, similar to those here pointed out." Full corroboration of the latter statement is to be found in contemporary newspapers. *The Gazetteer*, January 24, gives notice that *The Rivals* will be performed "for the second time," on Saturday next (the 28th), and on January 30 the same paper says, "The new Comedy of The Rivals, which was performed for the second time on Saturday night, was received with very great applause."[2] The fact is, therefore, that *The Rivals* was withdrawn after the *first* performance. The *second* performance was the successful revision produced January 28.

Quite as obvious as the reasons for the initial failure of *The Rivals* are the reasons for the success of the revised production. The transfer of Lee's part to Clinch was but one of many factors in the final triumph. Shuter and other actors inadequate at first redeemed themselves, while Sheridan himself subjected the play to thorough condensation and revision. His changes included pruning of dialogue, alteration in the action of the plot, and especial revision of the part of Sir Lucius. The oft-put query[3] "How could Sir Lucius possibly have been

[1] The mistake of later commentators seems due to following Genest (V, 459), who is here incorrect.

[2] For additional proofs see the three newspaper extracts *On the Revised Performance*, pp. 316–318, and the extract from *The Critical Review*, p. 318.

[3] *E.g.* "Why any one should object to *Sir Lucius* it is now difficult to discover." Brander Matthews: *Sheridan's Comedies*, 1885 ed., p. 320

misconstrued into an intended reflection upon the Irish gentleman?" is conclusively answered by the statement that Sheridan, in the revision of the no longer extant text of the original performance, "very judiciously removed everything that could give offence in the character of Sir Lucius O'Trigger."

The extracts from contemporary newspapers, which are given in the Appendix,[1] amply prove the contentions already made — the comments on the First Performance giving the reasons for the initial failure of *The Rivals*, the comments on the Revised Performance giving the reasons for its final success.

4. The Books of Lydia Languish's Circulating Library[2]

The Morning Post of February 3, 1775, contains the following communication: "Mr. Editor, I desire you will inform the Author of the *Rivals* that his attack upon *Circulating Libraries* in his first act is unjust, and very impertinent: Besides his sentiments are so inconsistent — He pretends to make such fine speeches in his play about *love*, and to pay such a compliment in the Epilogue to the Ladies, yet would decry novels, which form the very food and sustenance of love. I should be glad to know what are most of the modern comedies but *dialogue novels?* Are the two Play-houses better than circulating libraries? Only that at Mr. *Noble's* we may chuse our entertainment, and there the managers chuse it for us; — So, as our club consequently honour *your* paper with a place at our breakfast-table, I desire you will give this notice a place in it instantly, that the Author may expunge the malicious scene, or we will let him know that Ladies can *hiss* as well as smile. Yours &c. Sukey Saunter."

(1904 ed., p. 253). "Why the audience took offence at the former [*i.e.* Sir Lucius] must pass the wit of man to decide." Lloyd C. Sanders: *Life of Richard Brinsley Sheridan*, p. 40.

[1] Pp. 313–318.

[2] In *The Journal of English and Germanic Philology*, October, 1905, I have already published a considerable part of the results of the investigation of this subject.

The scene to which Sukey Saunter refers is the second scene of the first act. Somewhat covertly in the dialogue between Lydia and Lucy, more openly in Sir Anthony's denunciation of the circulating library as "an evergreen tree of diabolical knowledge," Sheridan strikes effectively at the sentimental novel of the day. This attitude toward the sentimental novel reinforces powerfully his attitude toward the sentimental drama.[1] Popular, however, as were these sentimental novels and dramas, Sheridan did not wage the attack single-handed. Beside his picture of the books of Lydia Languish's circulating library may be put this earlier comment of *The London Magazine*, April, 1770: "'Fatal Friendship' is not a bad title for the novel of a circulating library. — It strikes young, and particularly female minds, with a kind of melancholy curiosity." Equally ironical or plainly contemptuous comments appear in some of the magazine reviews of the novels alluded to in Sheridan's scene. Appreciation, not merely of the text of this scene, but of Sheridan's general attitude to the spirit of sentimentality run riot, is helped by an account of The Books of Lydia Languish's Circulating Library.

The following analysis is based solely upon contemporary evidence. The sometimes differing views of the magazine reviewers throw instructive side-lights on the conflict between sentimentality and sentiment. Worthy of comment, too, is the fact that the mild rain of Sheridan's satire falls on the just and the unjust — if men are to be judged by the company they keep — for Smollett and Sterne appear side by side with Mrs. Fogerty, Mr. and Mrs. Griffith, and others who have passed into the limbo of novelists of a day.

Twenty books are mentioned by Sheridan: *The Reward of Constancy; The Fatal Connexion; The Mistakes of the Heart; The Delicate Distress; The Memoirs of Lady Woodford; The Gordian Knot; Peregrine Pickle; The Tears of Sensibility;*

[1] See Introduction, pp. xliii-xlv.

Humphry Clinker; The Memoirs of a Lady of Quality written by herself; The Sentimental Journey; The Whole Duty of Man; Roderick Random; The Innocent Adultery; Lord Aimworth; Ovid; The Man of Feeling; Mrs. Chapone; Fordyce's Sermons; and *Lord Chesterfield's Letters*.[1]

The Reward of Constancy. — Of the twenty books mentioned by Sheridan this is the only one that I have been unable to identify definitely. My conjecture is that Sheridan had in mind the sub-title of *The Happy Pair; or Virtue and Constancy rewarded. A Novel. By Mr. Shebbeare* — noticed in the *Supplement to The Universal Magazine* (January–June, 1771).[2]

The Fatal Connexion (1773), by Mrs. Fogerty.

Surely Mrs. Fogerty was begotten, born, nursed, and educated in a circulating library, and sucked in the spirit of romance with her mother's milk. — *The Monthly Review*, August, 1773.

Romantic nonsense, as usual. — *The London Magazine*, September, 1773.

Whether Mrs. Fogerty is a real or a fictitious personage, is of no

[1] Notes on some of these books have been given by previous editors. Brander Matthews, in his notes to *Sheridan's Comedies*, pp. 320–1, mentions thirteen of the books, with some mistakes in identification and dates. The 1904 edition repeats the same errors of omission and of commission, pp. 254–5. G. A. Aitken, in notes to the *Temple* edition of *The Rivals*, p. 168, evidently repeats this list, with the omission of *Lord Chesterfield's Letters*, and this addition: "Dr James Fordyce [wrote] *Sermons to Young Women*, 1765, and *The Character and Conduct of the Female Sex*, 1776." [N.B. *The Rivals* appeared January 17, 1775.] To the well-known books, such as *Humphry Clinker* and *Roderick Random*, little space has been given, in order that unfamiliar books, especially those that have never previously been identified, may be described more fully.

[2] In support of this theory it may be pardonable to quote from a personal letter from Mr. Fraser Rae: "I have applied to many friends, of great bibliographical learning, to help me to reply to you. The general opinion is that your guess is correct and that the work in question was *The Happy Pair; or, Virtue and Constancy Rewarded*."

sort of consequence to the public; of less consequence is the production under her name, which has very little to recommend it to their attention. — *The Critical Review*, November, 1773.

The Mistakes of the Heart; *or*, *Memoirs of Lady Caroline Pelham and Lady Victoria Nevil.* By Treyssac de Vergy, Counsellor in the Parliaments of Paris and Bourdeaux, 3 vols. (1769).

This writer imitates Rousseau and Richardson. His performance is not without merit, and we might recommend it to the ladies if there were not some scenes too luxuriant for the eye of delicacy. — *The Town and Country Magazine*, April, 1769.

These memoirs are related in a collection of letters, in the manner of Richardson, to whom this writer is very inferior in point of language, manners, and sentiment. — *The Gentleman's Magazine*, May, 1769.

If Monsieur de Vergy had ever been really acquainted with persons of distinction in this country, or had seen any of their letters, he could not have so egregiously mistaken their style and manner. . . The *mistakes of the pen*, however, may be pardoned in a foreigner, although we are quite wearied with their perpetual repetition, — and the frequent instances of broken English into the bargain. — *The Monthly Review*, February, 1772 (on vol. 4).

The Delicate Distress (1769) and *The Gordian Knot* (1769).

Two Novels, in Letters. By the Authors of *Henry and Frances.* In Four Volumes. The first and second, entitled, *The Delicate Distress*, by Frances; the third and fourth, entitled, *The Gordian Knot*, or *Dignus Vindice Nodus*, by Henry.

In *The Delicate Distress*, Mrs. Griffith, whose productions we have occasionally recommended to the public, has told us an interesting tale, embellished with an agreeable variety of characters.

In *The Gordian Knot*, Mr. G., under the assumed name of Henry, gives us, as his title-page may seem to import, a more complicated and more elaborate, but less sprightly and less pleasing history. — *The Monthly Review*, September, 1769.

The Memoirs of Lady Woodford, written by herself, and addressed to a Friend.

Tenderness and simplicity are the principal characteristics of this innocent novel. — *The Monthly Review*, June, 1771.

The Adventures of Peregrine Pickle: In which are included Memoirs of a Lady of Quality [supposed to be Lady Vane], 4 vols. 1751, and *The Expedition of Humphry Clinker*, 2 vols. 1771, are well-known novels of Tobias Smollett. Cf. Introduction, *Eighteenth-Century Bath*, pp. lxii-lxiv. The fifth edition of *Peregrine Pickle* appeared in 1773.

The Tears of Sensibility, Novels. Namely, 1. The cruel Father. 2. Rosetta. 3. The rival Friends. 4. Sidney and Silli. Translated from the French of M. D'Arnaud, by John Murdoch, 2 vols.

These novels are highly interesting, and written with sentiment and delicacy. The translator has done them ample justice: His version is elegant, and discovers a rare propriety of expression and language. — *The Universal Magazine*, January, 1773.

In this work, as is usual to the French novelists, nature is painted very warmly, but chastely. The translation has preserved the spirit of the original. — *The London Magazine*, January, 1773.

Amongst the various translations which we have read of this kind from the works of our ingenious neighbours, we recollect scarcely any which can come in competition with these productions of M. D'Arnaud. . . . We should be better pleased were not some of the incidents beyond the reach of probability. — *The Critical Review*, March, 1773.

The Author aims, for the most part, to keep his Readers on the rack. He deals only in those virtues and vices which astonish and exercise our sensibility in the extreme. He therefore defeats his own purpose. A tale made up wholly of wonders, never excites admiration; and a novel, which in every page is to harrow up the soul, leaves it in great quietness. — *The Monthly Review*, April, 1773.

A Sentimental Journey through France and Italy, 2 vols., 1768, by Laurence Sterne, best known as the author of *Tristram Shandy.*

The Whole Duty of Man.

The Whole Duty of Man, necessary for all families, with private devotions for severall occasions. [By Lady Pakington? or R. Sterne, Archbishop of York? With a prefatory letter by H. Hammond.] 2 pt. *London*, [December? 1658?–] 1660. [According to the catalogue of the British Museum.]

This famous religious work had about a score of editions during the century after its first publication. It has been ascribed conjecturally to a great variety of authors. It is highly probable that Sheridan's allusion to it may have been prompted by the publication of a new and revised edition advertised very prominently. In *The Universal Magazine*, February, 1773, for example, after a full prospectus of the work, appears this explanatory note:

> It being now upwards of 100 years since the publication of the Old Whole Duty of Man, it need not be a matter of surprise if the generality of readers begin to be little affected by that work.
>
> I have endeavoured to supply all these deficiencies of the Old Whole Duty of Man, by furnishing the age we live in with a Duty of Man much better adapted to the Christian religion, and the occasions of the present time.

The Adventures of Roderick Random, 2 vols., 1748 — Smollett's famous novel. The eighth edition appeared in 1770.

The Innocent Adultery, a thoroughly indecent romance, was a translation of Paul Scarron's *L'Adultère Innocente.* The British Museum has an edition of 1722. The Yale University Library contains an edition of 1729: "*The Innocent Adultery.* Translated from the *French* Original of Monsieur Scarron. London: MDCCXXIX." (Included in vol. 4 of

A Select Collection of Novels and Histories. London, 1729.) The British Museum has several early eighteenth-century editions of *The Whole Comical Works of Monsr. Scarron* (including "All his novels and histories"). There is abundant proof that Scarron's work was well known in English translations.[1]

The History of Lord Aimsworth, and the Honourable Charles Hanford, Esq., in a series of letters.

[1] Brander Matthews, *Sheridan's Comedies*, p. 321, asserts: "The 'Innocent Adultery' was the second title of Southerne's tragedy, the 'Fatal Marriage,' revived as 'Isabella; or, the Fatal Marriage,' for Mrs. Siddons, after Sheridan became manager of Drury Lane theatre." G. A. Aitken, *Temple* edition of *The Rivals*, p. 168, repeats the first statement. In the first place, the context of the play itself is a strong presumption against this theory, for many other novels, including several translations from the French, are mentioned, but no other plays. Definite proof, however, may be had. *The Fatal Marriage; or The Innocent Adultery* was produced at the Theatre Royal in 1694 (Genest, II, 56). It was revived at Drury Lane in 1757.

"Dec. 2. — On this evening will be revived a Tragedy called the Fatal Marriage, altered from Southerne. . . . Garrick omitted the comic underplot." (Genest, IV, 511.)

The printed version of the play reads "Isabella; or The Fatal Marriage. A play. Alter'd from Southern (by David Garrick). London, 1757."

March 31, 1770 — Covent Garden. "Mrs. Bellamy's bt. [*i.e.* benefit] Never acted there, (that is as altered by Garrick) Isabella. (Genest, V, 286.)

November 25, 1774 — Drury Lane. "Acted but once these 14 years, Isabella." (Genest, V, 443.)

Other references in Genest and elsewhere are needless as additional proof that the version known in Sheridan's day, both on the stage and in the library, was Garrick's, and that the play was regularly called *Isabella.* I have been unable to discover any reference whatsoever in Sheridan's day to Southerne's play by its original sub-title, *The Innocent Adultery.* Garrick's revision (1757) dropped the old sub-title entirely. It is doubtful if Sheridan knew any version save Garrick's: it is sure that theatre-goers in 1775 could not have understood a recondite allusion to a sub-title. Sheridan's reference to Scarron's *The Innocent Adultery* is clear.

"A novel in three volumes by the author of Dorinda Catesby and Ermina, or the fair recluse." — *The Gentleman's Magazine*, May, 1773.

In the foot-note quoted at the end of this section of the Introduction (p. lxxvii) from the *British Theatre* (Leipsic, 1828, p. 654), occurs this clause: "Lord Aimworth (see Maid of the Mill) has debased himself by a *mésalliance*." *The Maid of the Mill*, a comic opera, by Isaac Bickerstaffe, was acted at Covent Garden Theatre in 1765. First in the list of Dramatis Personæ is Lord Aimworth. The only possible point in favor of this explanation is the spelling "Aimworth," while the novel is spelled "Aim*s*worth." The context, the date of the novel, its title, and the improbability that the opera would be mentioned by the name of one of the characters instead of by its real title, are some of many reasons for belief that Sheridan refers to the novel. It is hardly necessary to add that Sheridan's text contains many misspellings. Finally, in the *General Index to Fifty-six Volumes of the Gentleman's Magazine* (London, 1818) the above-quoted book-notice is catalogued (II, 237) with the spelling *Aimworth*, presumably a correction of the error.

Ovid. — For numerous eighteenth-century editions of Ovid in English translation see the British Museum catalogue. Apparently the most popular eighteenth-century English translation of Ovid's *Metamorphoses* was that published by Tonson (1717). Its fifth edition was in 1751. It is thus catalogued in the British Museum: "Ovid's Metamorphoses in fifteen books. Translated [into English verse] by the most eminent hands [viz., J. Dryden, J. Addison, L. Eusden, A. Mainwaring, S. Croxall, N. Tate, J. Gay, W. Congreve, and the editor Sir S. Garth, *etc.* Adorn'd with sculptures, pp. 548. *J. Tonson*: *London*, 1717. fol.] Note Sheridan's pun on the word "Metamorphoses" in the first version of *The Rivals*, on which two contemporary comments are given, p. 313.

The Man of Feeling (1771), by Henry Mackenzie.

This performance is written after the manner of Sterne; but it follows at a prodigious distance the steps of that ingenious and sentimental writer. It is not however totally destitute of merit; and the Reader, who weeps not over some of the scenes it describes, has no sensibility of mind. — *The Monthly Review*, May, 1771.

Mrs. Chapone. — Letters on the Improvement of the Mind. Addressed to a young Lady. 2 vols., 1773 [by Mrs. Chapone].

These letters are ten in number, 1. On the first principles of religion. 2 and 3. On the study of the Holy Scriptures. 4 and 5. On the regulation of the heart and affections: these are contained in the first volume — Letter 6. On the government of the temper. 7. On œconomy. 8. On politeness and accomplishments. 9. On geography and chronology. 10. On the manner, and course of reading history, with the conclusion, make up the second. They are addressed from an aunt to her niece, (a young lady in the 15th year of her age) for whose happiness she expresses the most tender concern, and for whose use the letters seem originally to have been written. The language is the language of the heart; and the instructions are conveyed in so kind and engaging a manner, that they cannot fail of being extensively useful. — *The Gentleman's Magazine*, May, 1773.

Fordyce's Sermons. — Sermons to Young Women. 2 vols., 1765. By James Fordyce [Fordyce was a popular Presbyterian divine (1720–1796), whose popularity was waning, however, at the time of *The Rivals*.]

A series of free but affectionate addresses. — *The Gentleman's Magazine*, June, 1766.

There are indeed, to the best of our recollection, no compositions of this kind in the English language, in which are to be found greater delicacy of sentiment, correctness of imagination, elegance of taste, or that contain such genuine pictures of life and manners. — *The Monthly Review*, June, 1766.

Lord Chesterfield's Letters. — Letters written by the Earl of Chesterfield to his son, Philip Stanhope, published by Mrs. Eugenia Stanhope, 2 vols. London, 1774.

The famous Letters of Philip Dormer Stanhope, fourth Earl of Chesterfield (1694–1773), were sold by his son's widow to the publisher, Dodsley, for fifteen hundred pounds. Their immediate popularity is attested by the fact that the fifth edition (in 4 vols.) appeared within a year.

In final review of the books of Lydia Languish's circulating library may be quoted this quaint foot-note from the *British Theatre* (Leipsic, 1828, p. 654):

> These books are introduced in such a manner, that they produce either a very whimsical contrast, or an aptness of allusion; for instance, Peregrine Pickle, as a lady's man, can have no better place than the toilet; Roderick Random's peregrinations are confined to the closet; the innocent Adultery is *not* the most proper thing in the whole duty of man; Lord Aimworth, (see Maid of the Mill) has debased himself by a *mésalliance;* Ovid is to attend the dreams of the love-sick maid; and the Man of Feeling is to direct our charities. Mrs. Chapone has written advice to young women upon marriage, etc.

Comparison of these explanations with the accompanying phrases in Sheridan's text will disclose that the "etc." of the commentator brings to an untimely end a discussion worthy of high rank among the curiosities of criticism.

THE SCHOOL FOR SCANDAL

1. The Sources of The School for Scandal

The same ingenuity of commentators which would deprive *The Rivals* of almost all claim to originality has assailed the originality of *The School for Scandal*, with almost equal fervor, and perhaps fully equal success. Watkins, the earliest biographer of Sheridan, insinuates [1] that *The School for Scandal* was written either by Mrs. Sheridan or by "a young lady, the daughter of a merchant in Thames Street," who put her manuscript into the hands of Sheridan as manager of Drury Lane — "soon after which the fair writer, who was then in a stage of decline, went to Bristol Hot-Wells, where she died."

On the other hand, to claim for *The School for Scandal* strict originality in every detail would be absurd. One of the commonest suggestions — that the Surface brothers resemble the Blifil and Tom Jones of Fielding's novel, *Tom Jones* (1749) — dates back to the first performance of the play, since *The London Chronicle*, May 8–10, 1777, asserts that "Joseph and Charles Surface are the Blifil and Tom Jones of the piece." So obvious, indeed, is the similarity that, though Sheridan may quite possibly have had Fielding immediately in mind, it is well to remember that the hypocrite and his foil are stock characters, common alike to novel and drama. This latter truth is reinforced by the remembrance that different critics have found the original of Joseph Surface in hypocrites so little akin as Fielding's Blifil, Molière's Tartuffe, and Arthur Murphy's Malvil, in *Know Your Own Mind*.[2]

Investigation, further, has been concerned largely with the origin of the scandal-scenes. Again, numerous originals have been suggested. Among them are Molière's scene (ii, 5) in

[1] *Memoirs of Sheridan*, I, 218.

[2] Lloyd C. Sanders well says in this connection (*Life of Sheridan*, p. 79): "Tartuffe and Joseph Surface are both hypocrites, but there the resemblance ends. As to the Malvil theory, which has the authority of Hazlitt, it is more tenable. But all that can safely be asserted is that Sheridan may have seen the play — it was produced at Covent Garden on February 22, 1777 — while he was writing 'The School for Scandal.' From a solitary sentence uttered by Malvil, 'To a person of sentiment like you, madam, a visit is paid with pleasure,' Sheridan may have conceived the idea of making Joseph Surface a sententious hypocrite, but otherwise the two characters have nothing in common beyond being hypocrites."

Le Misanthrope, where Célimène dissects her friends, Wycherley's brief scene (ii, 1) in *The Plain Dealer*, where Olivia and Novel discuss Novel's companions at dinner, and Congreve's scene (iii, 3) in *The Double-Dealer*, where Lady Froth and Brisk are the scandalmongers. A parallel in Congreve's *The Way of the World* has attracted less attention.[1] In the first two scenes of Act I are several suggestive references to "cabal nights," explained by Fainall in these words: "They have 'em three times a-week, and meet by turns at one another's apartments, where they come together like the coroner's inquest, to sit upon the murdered reputations of the week" (Scene 1). While minute comparison of these scenes with Sheridan's scandal-scenes reveals general parallels and suggests, especially in the case of Congreve, more specific borrowings, it is well to remember that, though Sheridan may have directly imitated some touches of other dramatic artists, the general background of scandal-scenes has a common color.

Again, critics who believe in the influence of heredity have found in Mrs. Sheridan's novel, *The Memoirs of Miss Sidney Bidulph*, the episode of the arrival of the Indian uncle and his assumed disguise. Far more certain is the suggestion that Sheridan borrowed the name Surface from her unfinished comedy, *A Journey to Bath*.[2]

In the zealous efforts to discover all the original sources of

[1] Edmund Gosse, *Life of Congreve* (Great Writers Series) p. 138, however, makes a sweeping claim for Congreve: "His Cabal-Night at Lady Wishfort's is the direct original of Sheridan's *School for Scandal*." Possibly these "cabal nights" have escaped general notice since the scandal-scenes are not enacted on the stage, but described. One passage which suggests a specific borrowing by Sheridan from this scene is given in the Notes, p. 290.

[2] In this connection it may be remarked that various critics have suggested that the name Careless may be borrowed from Congreve's *The Double-Dealer*, and that Mr. Premium recalls "little Transfer, the broker," in Foote's *The Minor*.

The School for Scandal, Sir Peter and Lady Teazle have hardly had fair attention. Mr. Sanders has, indeed, suggested a certain similarity between Joseph Surface's relations with Lady Teazle and Maria and Maskwell's relations with Lady Touchwood and Cynthia in Congreve's *The Double-Dealer*. Since, however, Maskwell has already wronged Lady Touchwood's honor prior to the commencement of the play,[1] since Maskwell has already "lost all appetite to her,"[2] and since Lady Touchwood herself arranges a further assignation which the reluctant Maskwell takes care to have interrupted by her nephew, Sheridan's immediate debt in this instance can scarcely be deemed excessive. If Restoration Comedy must be made to furnish the original for the Lady Teazle–Sir Peter plot, the suggestion may be ventured that the same situation, in Wycherley's indescribably brutal hands, may be found in the Mr. and Mrs. Pinchwife of *The Country Wife*. Both Lady Teazle and Mrs. Pinchwife are launched into the same sea of fashionable intrigue, and Lady Teazle is rescued at the verge of the maelstrom which almost inevitably engulfs the Restoration heroine.

Whatever specific borrowings or imitations may be alleged against *The School for Scandal,* its indebtedness to originals has frequently been grossly exaggerated. There is no reason to doubt the answer made by Miss Lefanu, Sheridan's niece, to Dr. Watkins's charges:[3] "The whole story of the supposed manner in which the play of The School for Scandal came into Mr. Sheridan's hands is perfectly groundless, the writer of these lines having frequently heard him speak on the subject long before the play appeared; many of the characters and incidents related to persons known to them both, and were laughingly talked over with his family." To the same effect Sheridan's father has been quoted as

[1] See Congreve's *The Double-Dealer*, i, 3. [2] See *Ibid.*, iii, 1.

[3] Alicia Lefanu, *Memoirs of Mrs. Frances Sheridan* (1824), p. 409.

saying, by no means graciously, "Talk of the merit of Dick's comedy, there's nothing in it. He had but to dip the pencil in his own heart, and he'd find there the characters both of Joseph and Charles."[1]

Final proof that, in a broad sense, *The School for Scandal* is essentially original, is furnished by study of the circumstances of its composition.

2. The Composition of The School for Scandal

Sheridan's first crude sketch, headed The Slanderers. — *A Pump Room Scene*, renders most probable the contention that, like *The Rivals*, *The School for Scandal* grew out of Sheridan's own knowledge of fashionable Bath. The final transfer of the scene of action from the *Pump-Room* to the fashionable drawing-rooms of London was merely a change from the miniature world of fashion to the broader setting of its London original.

From the first rough hints, jotted down under the title *The Slanderers*, to the finished comedy, *The School for Scandal*, is a study in literary evolution traced by Moore in more than a score of pages.[2] Briefly summarized, it is the story of the gradual welding together of two plots — one centering in a group of scandalmongers, the other in an old husband and a young country wife, already plunged in a matrimonial slough of despond. In the former appear Lady Sneerwell, Mrs. Candour, Sir Benjamin Backbite, Maria, and Clerimont (the rough-hewn model of Charles Surface); in the latter, Old Teazle, Mrs. Teazle, Plausible and Captain Harry Plausible (the Surface brothers), and Maria. Side by side with the hammering of the rude ore of dialogue into finely tempered points of sparkling wit went corresponding refinement in the molding of the *dramatis personae*. Solomon Teazle and his

[1] Sanders, *Life of Sheridan*, pp. 79–80.

[2] *Life of Sheridan*, I, 210–234.

wife were advanced from the world of London tradesmen to the dignity of rank and title. Less significant, perhaps, but even more indicative of painstaking, were the successive changes by which Clerimont, Florival, Captain Harry Plausible, Harry Pliant or Pliable, young Harrier, and Frank, became ultimately Charles Surface, while through Plausible, Pliable, Young Pliant, and Tom was evolved Joseph Surface. Revision of names and dialogue extended also to minor characters — Spunge became Trip, Spatter became eventually Snake.

Even brief summary of Moore's details, then, shows that, contrary to popular impression, Sheridan was by no means a genius who never blotted a line. Moore has made much,[1] and others have made still more, of evidences of haste in the composition of the last five scenes of the play. Fraser Rae, with the heavy hand of fact, has crushed certain airy fabrications, by quoting [2] from one of Sheridan's speeches proof that the play was refused a license on the night before its first production — evidence that, in some form, it must have been completed for submission to the examiner of plays. The license, withheld at first on the charge that Moses was intended as a satire on Hopkins, the "Court candidate" for the office of City Chamberlain, was finally readily granted to Sheridan by the Lord Chamberlain.

The circumstances, therefore, of the composition of *The School for Scandal*, though disproving the theory that Sheridan struck off his masterpiece at a blow, furnish perhaps equally effective proof of the essential originality of Sheridan's work. Whatever reminiscences of previous authors may have helped him at times in molding plot or refining dialogue, the fact is indisputable that, whether in crude ore or in finished product, *The School for Scandal* bears always the hallmark of Sheridan.

[1] *Life of Sheridan*, I, 241–2.
[2] *Sheridan*, I, 320.

THE CRITIC

1. Sheridan's Jupiter, a Forerunner of The Critic

Thorough investigation of the sources of *The Critic* demands, as a preliminary, some knowledge of Sheridan's earlier burlesque, *Jupiter*. The general framework of both plays Sheridan derived from *The Rehearsal* (1671), still a favorite farce in Sheridan's early days, with Garrick in the part of Bayes. The real history of Sheridan's indebtedness begins, then, not with *The Critic* itself, but with *Jupiter*.

In 1770, Nathaniel Halhed, a Harrow school-friend of Sheridan, submitted to him for criticism and alteration for the stage a farce called *Ixion*. Sheridan renamed it *Jupiter*, and recast it largely in the form of a mock rehearsal modeled after *The Rehearsal*. A sentence from one of Halhed's letters to Sheridan is significant: "I hope you will keep your plan of a rehearsal — it is a very good one, but I can give you no hints."[1] Moore, who saw the manuscript of *Jupiter* as altered by Sheridan, gives[2] extracts enough to prove his assertion that "in the character of Simile the reader will at once discover a sort of dim and shadowy pre-existence of Puff." He might have added that Simile's companions, who question his dramatic methods before the rehearsal and later interrupt the progress of the play with queries, foreshadow Dangle and Sneer. *Jupiter* failed to secure a hearing, but it evidently fixed in Sheridan's mind the dramatic possibilities of its general framework.

Since Halhed's *Ixion* was a farce dealing with Ixion's attempted intrigue with Juno in the heavens, while Jupiter, disguised as Amphitryon, makes love to the latter's wife on earth, it bears no relation to Puff's tragedy in *The Critic*. Brief

[1] Fraser Rae, *Sheridan*, I, 100.
[2] *Life of Sheridan*, I, 18–22.

quotation, however, from Sheridan's setting of *Ixion* in the form of a stage-rehearsal shows strikingly how *Jupiter* anticipates *The Critic* in general framework:

SIMILE. Sir, you are very ignorant on the subject, — it is the method most in vogue.

O'CUL. What! to make the music first, and then make the sense to it afterwards!

SIM. Just so.

MONOP. What Mr. Simile says is very true, gentlemen; and there is nothing surprising in it, if we consider now the general method of writing *plays* to *scenes*.

O'CUL. Writing *plays* to *scenes!* — Oh, you are joking.

MONOP. Not I, upon my word. Mr. Simile knows that I have frequently a complete set of scenes from Italy, and then I have nothing to do but to get some ingenious hand to write a play to them.

SIM. I am your witness, sir. Gentlemen, you perceive you know nothing about these matters.

. . . .

SIM. Now for it. Draw up the curtain, and (*looking at his book*) enter Sir Richard Ixion, — but stay, — zounds, Sir Richard ought to over-hear Jupiter and his wife quarrelling, — but, never mind — these accidents have spoiled the division of my piece. — So enter, Sir Richard, and look as cunning as if you had overheard them. Now for it, gentlemen, — you can't be too attentive.

. . . .

Sir Richard Ixion then enters, and after a speech of half a dozen couplets retires.

MACD. But pray, Mr. Simile, how did Ixion get into heaven?

SIM. Why, sir, what's that to anybody? — perhaps by Salmoneus's Brazen Bridge, or the Giant's Mountain, or the Tower of Babel, or on Theobald's bull-dogs, or — who the devil cares how? — he is there, and that's enough.

. . . .

SIM. Now for a Phœnix of a song.

Song by JUPITER

You dogs, I'm Jupiter Imperial,
King, Emperor, and Pope ætherial,
Master of th' Ordnance of the sky. —

SIM. Z—ds, where's the ordnance? Have you forgot the pistol? (*to the Orchestra.*)

ORCHESTRA. (*to some one behind the scenes.*) Tom, are not you prepared?

TOM. (*from behind the scenes.*) Yes, sir, but I flash'd in the pan a little out of time, and had I staid to prime, I should have shot a bar too late.

SIM. Oh then, Jupiter, begin the song again. — We must not lose our ordnance.

You dogs, I'm Jupiter Imperial,
King, Emperor, and Pope ætherial,
Master of th' Ordnance of the sky; &c. &c.

[*Here a pistol or cracker is fired from behind the scenes.*

SIM. This hint I took from Handel. — Well, how do you think we go on?

O'CUL. With vast spirit, — the plot begins to thicken.

SIM. Thicken! aye, — 'twill be as thick as the calf of your leg presently. Well, now for the real, original patentee Amphitryon What, ho, Amphitryon! Amphitryon! — 'tis Simile calls. — Why, where the devil is he?

Enter SERVANT

MONOP. Tom, where is Amphitryon?

SIM. Zounds, he's not arrested too, is he?

SERV. No, sir, but there was but *one black eye* in the house, and he is waiting to get it from Jupiter.

SIM. To get a black eye from Jupiter, — oh, this will never do. Why, when they meet, they ought to match like two beef-eaters.

Even the foregoing extracts are sufficient to show that *Jupiter* contains more than the mere framework of *The Critic.*

Though in the earlier play the ore is yet crude, Sheridan's shaft has already struck the rich vein whose polished metal flashes ceaselessly in *The Critic.*

2. The Sources of The Critic

The Rehearsal (1671). — Fitzpatrick's *Prologue* to *The Critic* speaks significantly of the days "when Villiers criticised what Dryden writ." George Villiers, second Duke of Buckingham, was the most conspicuous of the authors who collaborated in the writing of *The Rehearsal* (1671). In the form of a burlesque rehearsal, this farce ridicules the heroic tragedies of the day, notably those of Dryden, parodying not merely their general spirit, but many specific passages. The idea of a burlesque performance given in the presence of some of the *dramatis personae* who interrupt the action with comment was not, indeed, original with the authors of *The Rehearsal.* In Beaumont and Fletcher's *The Knight of the Burning Pestle* (first printed in 1613), a grocer and his wife comment on the performance of their apprentice, Ralph, in a play which burlesques the ultra-romantic drama. Sometimes, too, the burlesque is specific, as in Ralph's last speech — a travesty of a passage in Kyd's *The Spanish Tragedy.* Since, however, Sheridan's debt is not to the Elizabethan but to the later Stuart drama, the discussion of the sources of *The Critic* need be carried no further than Buckingham's play.

(*a*) *General Framework.* In *The Rehearsal*, Bayes, who has admitted Johnson and Smith to the rehearsal of his new play, constantly interrupts its progress with criticism of the players and with answers to his friends' queries as to plot and dramatic methods. To Bayes, his play is as sublime as his dramatic dicta are authoritative; to Smith and Johnson, both play and explanation speedily become ridiculous. To Buckingham's real audience beyond the footlights, *The Rehearsal* burlesqued the mouthing tragedies of the day in general, and Bayes, in particular, caricatured Dryden. Here, then, is Sheridan's essential framework. Bayes and his companions are the prototypes of Simile and his companions in *Jupiter,* and of Puff, Sneer, and Dangle in *The Critic.* Again, Sheridan ridiculed the absurdities in contemporary drama in general, and Sir Fretful Plagiary, in particular, caricatured Richard Cumberland.

(*b*) *Specific Passages.* Besides the general framework and method of *The Rehearsal,* Sheridan doubtless borrowed from it hints for a very few specific passages in *The Critic.* An instance of this, to which attention has been drawn frequently, is the following:

PHYSICIAN. Sir, to conclude.
SMITH. What, before he begins?
BAYES. No, Sir; you must know they had been talking of this a pretty while without.
SMITH. Where? In the Tyring-room?
BAYES. Why ay, Sir.

This passage from *The Rehearsal* (ii, 1) is compared with the following from *The Critic* (ii, 2).

SIR CHRISTOPHER. True, gallant Raleigh!
DANGLE. What, they had been talking before?
PUFF. O, yes; all the way as they came along.

Even if one puts aside, as perhaps too subtle, Fraser Rae's explanation [1] that, in this passage, "a parody on one of the ridiculous situations in *The Rehearsal* had been penned by Sheridan," the borrowing is not serious. Another parallel sometimes cited is that between the speech of Bayes (v, 1) introducing his spectacular scene — "the greatest scene that England saw: I mean not for words, for those I do not value; but for state, show, and magnificence," and the speech of Puff

[1] *Sheridan,* I, 337.

at the end of the play, before his grand *finale* — "Now then for my magnificence! — my battle! — and my procession!" Possibly, too, Sheridan took a hint from this passage in *The Rehearsal* (v, 1):

SMITH. Well; but, methinks, the sense of the song is not very plain.

BAYES. Plain? why, did you ever hear any people in clouds speak plain? They must be all for flight of fancy, at its full range, without the least check, or control upon it. When once you tie up spirits and people in clouds to speak plain, you spoil all.

In *The Critic* (ii, 2) Sheridan gives these lines to *Puff*:

And now, I think, you shall hear some better language. I was obliged to be plain and intelligible in the first scene, because there was so much matter of fact in it; but now, faith! you have trope, figure, and metaphor, as plenty as noun substantives.

Sir Fretful Plagiary's "Commonplace book — where stray jokes and pilfered witticisms are kept" (i, 1), may have been suggested by the one which Bayes calls (i, 1), "My book of *Drama Common-places*, the Mother of many other plays." Trivial as these parallels seem, the critic who compares Sheridan's lines with Buckingham's has difficulty in finding even such as these. Minute study of the two texts reveals wide differences, rather than close parallels. As a sufficient example, however, of the absurdities of some charges of plagiarism preferred against Sheridan may be cited this from Percy Fitzgerald's *The Lives of the Sheridans* (I, 207): "A couple of specimens of Sheridan's borrowings or adaptations from the Duke of Buckingham will serve to show how wholesale was his system." The second exhibit offered by Fitzgerald to illustrate Sheridan's wholesale system of borrowing from the Duke of Buckingham is a passage from Fielding's farce, *The Historical Register for the Year* 1736 (iii, 1).

Fielding's The Historical Register. — Though it is important to assert emphatically the essential originality of the text of *The Critic*, impartial criticism must recognize a few trifling debts to Fielding's farces. Lord Burleigh's scene in *The Critic* (iii, 1) is limited to the two stage-directions:

> "Enter Lord Burleigh, goes slowly to a chair and sits," and "Lord Burleigh comes forward, shakes his head, and exit."

In Fielding's *The Historical Register for the Year* 1736 (first acted in 1737) is this passage:

> Enter four PATRIOTS from different doors, who meet in the centre and shake hands.
>
> SOURWIT. These patriots seem to equal your greatest politicians in their silence.
>
> MEDLEY. Sir, what they think now cannot well be spoke, but you may conjecture a great deal from their shaking their heads.

Puff's elaborate explanation of the reason and meaning of Lord Burleigh's shake of the head offers an interesting parallel. Furthermore, Sourwit and Lord Dapper criticise the rehearsal of Medley's play, much in the same fashion as Sneer and Dangle criticise Puff's tragedy. In the first scene of the rehearsal, Medley explains the silence of one of his characters by saying, "My first and greatest politician never speaks at all, he is a very deep man" — a passage which again recalls Puff's explanation of Lord Burleigh's silence. It is possible that Sheridan borrowed the name Dangle from one of minor characters introduced into Medley's play, though Fielding's Dangle has but three short speeches.

Fielding's The Author's Farce. — Moore implies a borrowing in *The Critic* from Fielding's *The Author's Farce* (1730), by saying,[1] "The manager, Marplay, in 'The Author's Farce,' like him of Drury Lane in 'The Critic,' 'does the town the honour of writing himself.'" Evidently, Moore's quotation is from

[1] *Life of Sheridan*, I, 275.

Witmore's speech to Marplay, Junior (i, 6): "Besides, as I take it, you have done the town the honour of writing yourself." Seemingly, Moore's reference to *The Critic* is the scene (i, 1) where Sneer suggests that Sir Fretful Plagiary's play "might have been cast better at Drury Lane." When Sir Fretful replies, "O Lud! no — never send a play there while I live — hark'ee!" and whispers to Sneer, Sneer rejoins, "Writes himself! — I know he does." Comparison of the contexts in the two plays makes the resemblance very shadowy.

Fielding's Pasquin. — Closest of Fielding's farces in general similarity to *The Critic* is *Pasquin: A Dramatic Satire on the Times: Being the Rehearsal of Two Plays: viz. A Comedy called The Election; and a Tragedy, called The Life and Death of Common Sense* (1736). Here, instead of one author and two critics, as in Sheridan's play, Fielding has two authors, Trapwit and Fustian, and one critic, Sneerwell. The part of second critic is, however, filled by Fustian, during his rival's comedy, though Trapwit, excusing himself from the rehearsal of Fustian's tragedy, fails to return the compliment. Besides general similarity in structure, a few passages in *Pasquin* may have suggested specific hints for *The Critic.* Fustian's speech (i, 1) in which he is delivering a tirade against the work of his rival, is turned instantly, on the appearance of Trapwit himself, to false flattery: "Dear Mr. Trapwit! your most humble servant, Sir; I read your comedy over last night, and a most excellent one it is." A general parallel is suggested in Dangle's abuse of Sir Fretful Plagiary, which, at the entrance of the latter, is readily diverted into insincere compliment: "Ah, my dear friend! — Egad, we were just speaking of your tragedy. — Admirable, Sir Fretful, admirable!" Another possible parallel is between Puff's vehement objections to the "cuts" made in his tragedy, and the following speeches in *Pasquin* (iii, 1):

SNEERWELL. Yes, faith, I think I would cut out a turn or two.

TRAPWIT. Sir, I 'll sooner cut off an ear or two; Sir, that 's the very best thing in the whole play.

It may be added that Fustian objects, likewise (i, 1), to the proposal to "cut the ghost out," by exclaiming "Cut him out, Sir! He is one of the most considerable persons in the play." Moore, who remarks[1] "In Trapwit . . . there are the rudiments of Sir Fretful as well as of Puff," fails to illustrate his point clearly. One of his two illustrations, in which he misquotes Sneerwell's speech already given above, seems to refer to Puff, rather than to Sir Fretful. The other illustration, a speech by Fustian (v, 1) which Moore ascribes unhappily to Trapwit, can with difficulty be made to resemble closely either Puff or Sir Fretful. Close comparative study, then, of the texts of *The Critic* and of *Pasquin* proves, again, that Sheridan's possible borrowings are very few.

Foote's The Minor. — Beside borrowing or theft from *The Rehearsal* and from Fielding's farces, Sheridan has sometimes been charged with very considerable obligation to Samuel Foote's three-act farce, *The Minor* (1760). Watkins declares[2] that the character of Puff "in the leading feature is a palpable imitation, rendered worse, however, by copying, of Shift in Foote's comedy of 'The Minor.'" He rests his case on this broad statement: "Both of these dramatic personages are equally vain of their versatile talents, and eager to gain credit for their ingenuity in deceiving mankind." Fitzgerald has made a more specific charge by asserting[3] that "The passage where Puff gives an account of his various modes of advertising is beyond question suggested by Shift's account of himself in 'The Minor.'" But Puff's "most extraordinary life," in the years when necessity was the mother of the

[1] *Life of Sheridan*, I, 274. [2] *Memoirs of Sheridan*, I, 239.

[3] *The Lives of the Sheridans*, I, 207.

ingenious advertisements by which he subsisted, resembles Shift's progress from link-boy at Drury Lane to professional mimic only in that both characters alike lived by their wits. It is conceivable that, from the second act, where Shift is disguised as an auctioneer, Sheridan may have taken a hint for Puff's long speech (i, 2) in which he explains how he taught the auctioneers to enrich their style — "to crowd their advertisements with panegyrical superlatives, each epithet rising above the other like the bidders in their own auction rooms!" It is also conceivable that Sheridan, who turned Charles Surface into an inimitable auctioneer for the nonce, may not have realized the enormity of his "palpable imitation" of Foote so readily as the biographer who found Puff a poor copy of so illustrious an original as Shift.

Churchill's Rosciad. — After arduous pursuit of elusive parallels in *The Critic* to little known and less read originals, it is a relief to find one instance close enough to satisfy the most exacting critic. Moore has drawn attention [1] to Sir Fretful Plagiary's speech (i, 1), "Steal! — to be sure they may; and, egad, serve your best thoughts as gypsies do stolen children, disfigure them to make 'em pass for their own," in connection with Churchill's lines:

> Still pilfers wretched plans, and makes them worse,
> Like gipsies, lest the stolen brat be known,
> Defacing first, then claiming for his own.[2]

So deadly, indeed, is this parallel, and so different from the intangible borrowings usually ascribed to Sheridan, that one might be tempted to run the gauntlet of critics with the perhaps over subtle suggestion that Sheridan may have put

[1] *Life of Sheridan*, I, 275–6.

[2] Moore has "*their* own." The passage is to be found in *The Apology, Addressed to the Critical Reviewers* (ll. 233–235), which supplemented *The Rosciad.*

these words, possibly familiar to Churchill's own contemporaries, into Sir Fretful's mouth with malice aforethought, the better to show that Sir Fretful's own practice did not coincide with his preaching. Since, however, Moore adds that "this simile was again made use of by him in a speech upon Mr. Pitt's India Bill," it is well to convict Sheridan, on this count, of high plagiarism. If, in other instances, Sheridan has borrowed the "best thoughts" of others, he has at least so disfigured them as to make them pass for his own.

Conclusion. — A fitting climax to the discussion of the sources of *The Critic* is the assertion of Watkins[1] that Sheridan, in taking *The Rehearsal* "as a model for an attack upon his adversaries . . . was assisted by his brother-in-law,[2] Tickell, who had a caustic severity of style in composition, and whose share in this piece may be very easily traced by any one that will take the trouble to compare 'The Critic' with that gentleman's celebrated pamphlet entitled 'Anticipation.'" Investigation of Tickell's "celebrated pamphlet" shows that it was an attempt to satirize the proceedings at the opening of parliament largely by anticipating the speeches to be delivered by prominent members. No modern reader of Tickell's satire will be prompted to apply to it Sir Andrew Aguecheek's "Excellent! why, this is the best fooling, when all is done." It is the irony of Sheridan's fate that part of the excellence of *The Critic* was sometimes attributed to Tickell, while all of the mediocrity of Tickell's "musical entertainment," *The Camp*, was so persistently ascribed to Sheridan that it was more than once printed as Sheridan's work.

In final review of the sweeping charges against the originality of *The Critic*, the dispassionate verdict of whoever will investigate critically all the documents in the case must be this —

[1] *Memoirs of Sheridan*, I, 239.

[2] Tickell did not become Sheridan's "brother-in-law" until after the production of *The Critic*.

for the general framework and method of treatment, as well as for a few more specific hints, Sheridan was indebted to *The Rehearsal;* to Fielding, Foote, and others he owed perhaps an occasional touch; but the text of *The Critic* is essentially original. Resolute, indeed, must needs be the defense of *The Critic* when Leigh Hunt is betrayed into the evil company of Watkins by declaring[1] that *The Critic*, in some of its best passages, "is little better than an exquisite cento of the wit of the satirists before him." In dismissing finally the extravagant charges against Sheridan it is fitting to recall that "trifles light as air are to the jealous confirmations strong as proofs of holy writ." Well in advance of the army of criticasters, Horace Walpole wrote in a letter of December 11, 1779:[2] "I have read Sheridan's *Critic*, but not having seen it, for they say it is admirably acted, it appeared wondrously flat and old, and a poor imitation." The first sentence of his letter shows, however, that he was aggravated by an attack of gout. For those who, without Walpole's provocation, press groundless charges of grand larceny against the text of *The Critic*, one is tempted to recast Walpole's phrase to read — "To those who have read *The Critic*, not having clearly seen its supposed originals, it appears wondrously flat and old, and a poor imitation."

3. Personal Caricature in the Critic

Sir Fretful Plagiary. — Conspicuous among the varied forms of satire with which Sheridan ridiculed the absurdities of the stage is personal caricature of a few of his contemporaries. Bayes in *The Rehearsal* caricatured Dryden, then poet-laureate; Sir Fretful Plagiary in *The Critic* caricatured Richard Cumberland, one of Sheridan's contemporary dramatists.

[1] *The Dramatic Works of Richard Brinsley Sheridan*, with a biographical and critical sketch by Leigh Hunt (1865 ed. p. xi.)

[2] Toynbee ed. (1903–5), XI, 77.

Bayes, however, so far reproduces the petty peculiarities of Dryden as to be essentially the caricature of one individual; Sir Fretful, though reproducing unmistakably the general faults and foibles of Cumberland, is conceived so broadly that he rises above individual caricature to the dignity of generic satire. Had Sir Fretful been merely a figure of temporary burlesque he would have died with Cumberland; but Sheridan, in thrusting at super-sensitiveness and inordinate jealousy, bore his lance at targets that ever invite the shafts of satire.

So admirable was Sheridan's portrayal of Cumberland that even Watkins in the same paragraph[1] in which he maintains that *The Critic* is destitute of "any claim to originality" save in the first act, is constrained to add, "The character of Sir Fretful Plagiary must be admitted to have exhibited a striking sketch, in many respects, of a dramatic writer, whose nervous sensibility often made him ridiculous. The late Mr. Cumberland was so tenderly alive to every thing that affected his literary reputation, as to court the opinions and praises of those who he knew had little regard for him or his works. He stooped sometimes to paltry artifices for the sake of eliciting a compliment; and when any of his pieces failed to give public satisfaction, he was querulous as a child at the loss of a plaything, and vented his lamentations in bitter complaints of the malignity and envy of his rivals." To be sure Watkins at once devotes several pages to "the moral excellence of the dramas of Cumberland," defending them from Sheridan's ridicule with sentiments that would do credit to Joseph Surface: "Merriment is wretchedly procured at the expense of humanity," and "No excuse can be offered for the writer who wantonly perverts his wit in order to render a fellow-creature miserable." Cumberland's life, however, as reflected in his memoirs and letters, shows that Sheridan founded Sir Fretful on a strong basis of fact. A few phrases from a letter by

[1] *Memoirs of Sheridan*, I, 237.

Cumberland, September, 1776, to the elder Colman[1] illustrate the salient characteristics which Sheridan reproduced so adroitly. Cumberland appeals from the adverse verdict of the proprietors of Covent Garden Theatre against his tragedy, *The Battle of Hastings.* Though disclaiming "presumption enough in my own behalf to say that they are not warranted in what they have done," he hastens to add, "At the same time I would in no period of my life desert what may prove to be for the interests of literature in general, what ridicule soever may fall upon me in the upshot. In this light I ask you, as a scholar and an author of genius, if you have any objection to read and judge my piece. . . . . My tragedy cost me great pains and much attention; hath been many years in hand; is entirely original in plan, popular in its subject, and free of all imitation. The opinions of men exceedingly high in the republic of letters have been unanimous, and more than warmly, in its favour." Highly diplomatic was Colman's declination of the honor of reading Cumberland's tragedy on the ground of a previous dispute with the Covent Garden management. Highly diplomatic, too, was the sop he threw to the sensitive dramatist in the suggestion that the merits of the tragedy "may be rested so much more confidently on the testimony of those respectable opinions which you have already collected."

Cumberland's jealousy of his brother dramatists and his accusations of plagiarism are admirably illustrated in his *Prologue* to his comedy, *The Brothers* (1769). Here, after stinging reproaches of those who pilfer from magazines and from French writers, he modestly presents his own work in refreshing contrast:

From no man's jest he draws felonious praise,
Nor from his neighbor's garden crops his bays:
From his own breast the filial story flows,
And the free scene no foreign master knows:

[1] Peake, *Memoirs of the Colman Family*, I, 417–8.

Nor only tenders he his work as new;
He hopes 'tis good, or wou'd not give it you.

Something of an anticlimax is afforded by Cumberland's own statement [1] in discussing this very comedy, *The Brothers:* "I recollect that I borrowed the hint of Sir Benjamin's assumed valour upon being forced into a rencounter from one of the old comedies." Whoever tires of Cumberland's inordinate self-conceit may turn gratefully to Thomas Davies's chapter on him.[2] Here, after attacking with specific charges Cumberland's proud boast to unique originality, Davies epitomizes the author in these words: "Mr. Cumberland is unquestionably a man of very considerable abilities; 'tis his misfortune to rate them greatly above their real value, and to suppose that he has no equal."

Ample proof that Sheridan's portrait of Cumberland is little, if at all, heightened in color, may be drawn from the *Memoirs of Richard Cumberland written by Himself.* Viewed in the light of the events there recorded and of the sentiments therein expressed, one can read Sir Fretful between the lines even in perhaps the most striking *apologia pro sua vita* which Cumberland ever penned [3]: "I solemnly protest that I have never written, or caused to be written, a single line to puff and praise myself, or to decry a brother dramatist, since I had life; of all such anonymous and mean manœuvres I am clearly innocent and proudly disdainful; I have stood firm for the corps, into which I enrolled myself, and never disgraced my colours by abandoning the cause of the *legitimate comedy,* to whose service I am sworn, and in whose defence I have kept the field for nearly half a century, till at last I have survived all true national taste, and lived to see buffoonery, spectacle, and puerility so effectually triumph, that now to be repulsed

[1] *Memoirs of Richard Cumberland written by Himself,* 1807, I, 265.
[2] *Memoirs of the Life of David Garrick* (1780), II, chap. xlviii.
[3] *Memoirs of Richard Cumberland written by Himself,* 1807, I, 270.

from the stage is to be recommended to the closet, and to be applauded by the theatre is little else than a passport to the puppet-show." It was Cumberland who wrote thus: it was Sir Fretful who said, "I say nothing — I take away from no man's merit — am hurt at no man's good fortune — I say nothing. — But this I will say — through all my knowledge of life, I have observed — that there is not a passion so strongly rooted in the human heart as envy."

Discussion of the element of personal caricature in the part of Sir Fretful leads to the remark that, in one passage, Sheridan seems to strike, over the broad back of Sir Fretful, at those who abetted the foolish insinuation that he had stolen *The School for Scandal* from a manuscript left in his hands by "a young lady, the daughter of a merchant in Thames Street." [1]

SIR FRETFUL. Besides — I can tell you it is not always so safe to leave a play in the hands of those who write themselves.

SNEER. What, they may steal from them, hey, my dear Plagiary?

SIR FRET. Steal! — to be sure they may; and, egad, serve your best thoughts as gypsies do stolen children, disfigure them to make 'em pass for their own.

Dangle. — Far less striking as a personal caricature than that of Cumberland as Sir Fretful is the part of Dangle, generally regarded as intended to represent another of Sheridan's contemporaries, Thomas Vaughan. The scant records of Vaughan's life show that his chief passion was the theatre. Some of his own farces obtained a brief hearing on the London stage, one of them, *The Hotel, or the Double Valet*, appearing in 1776. Four years earlier he had contributed to *The London Post* a series of essays on The Richmond Theatre. As early as 1761, Churchill epitomized him in these lines in *The Rosciad* (ll. 611–612):

[1] See Introduction, lxxviii.

Whilst Vaughan or Dapper, call him which you will,
Shall blow the trumpet, and give out the bill.

A decade later George Colman ridiculed him again under the name of Dapper, in the periodical papers entitled *The Genius*. Such facts throw light on the conversation between Dangle and his wife which opens *The Critic*, and in particular these speeches:

MRS. DANGLE. And what have you to do with the theatre, Mr. Dangle? Why should you affect the character of a critic? I have no patience with you! — haven't you made yourself the jest of all your acquaintance by your interference in matters where you have no business? Are you not called a theatrical Quidnunc, and a mock Mæcenas to second-hand authors?

DANGLE. True; my power with the managers is pretty notorious.

Since Vaughan was in his own day far less conspicuous a personage than Cumberland, whatever personal caricature Sheridan may have intended in Dangle was of far less importance than that in Sir Fretful. Again, as with Sir Fretful, particular caricature in Dangle has been subordinated to enduring general satire — satire of the class of theatrical Quidnuncs of which Vaughan was but a type.

Even less attention need be paid to the suggestion that Sheridan intended to ridicule Woodfall, the theatrical critic of *The Morning Chronicle*. The rather considerate and temperate review of the first production of *The Rivals* in *The Morning Chronicle*, probably penned by Woodfall, when Sheridan's fate as a dramatist hung in the balance, renders it unlikely that Sheridan would have returned evil for good.

Personal caricature in *The Critic* is confined chiefly to the opening scene of the first act. Sir Fretful Plagiary, by far the most conspicuous caricature in the play, appears here only. Here, too, occur the most important passages in which Dangle is supposed to represent Vaughan. This point, indeed, needs emphasis in view of assertions that Sheridan intended *The Critic* as a vehicle of personal revenge upon his enemies. One illustration of such charges will suffice. After speaking of the complaints of Cumberland, Watkins adds:[1] "and as other literary persons had similar complaints against the conduct of the manager, a common concern was made of the injury, and the newspapers daily exhibited some severe criticisms upon theatrical subjects and the direction of Drury Lane. To counteract these attempts upon his official character, Sheridan took 'The Rehearsal,' as a model for an attack upon his adversaries." That Sheridan was ready to meet his critics with good-humored banter is obvious, but it is idle to maintain that *The Critic* was designed primarily as a defense of "his official character" or as "an attack upon his adversaries." Circumstantial evidence of the falsity of such accusations is to be found in the expansion in *The Critic* of Sheridan's early burlesque, *Jupiter;* direct evidence is furnished in *The Critic* itself in the subordination of personal caricature to general burlesque. Had Sheridan's primary object been to pillory Cumberland he would not have dismissed Sir Fretful from the boards in the opening scene, but would have assigned to him the chief role filled by Puff in the remaining acts. In *The Rehearsal* Dryden is kept ever in the foreground in the part of Bayes.

Conspicuous, then, as is the element of personal caricature in the opening scene of *The Critic*, it is by no means the primary object of the play. In turning the laugh against the absurdities of the stage, Sheridan was ready to expose good-humoredly the foibles of some of his contemporaries, but his wit was sharpened by neither envy nor malice.

[1] *Memoirs of Sheridan*, I, 239.

4. Burlesque and Parody of Contemporary Drama in The Critic

In *The Rivals* and *The School for Scandal* Sheridan ran counter to the sentimental comedy of the day; in *The Critic* he turned the laugh against bombastic tragedy. So broad and universal, however, is Sheridan's satire that it strikes not so much at individual plays, or even at the extravagances of tragedy alone, as at the general absurdities of the entire drama. Though Puff's play is *A Tragedy Rehearsed*, Sheridan did not fail to administer some final blows to the sentimental comedy whose fate had been so largely sealed by Lydia Languish, the sentimental heroine, and Joseph Surface, the "man of sentiment." An excellent example of ridicule of sentimental comedy is in the opening scene of *The Critic*:

> Dangle. (*reading*) *Bursts into tears and exit.* — What is this a tragedy?
>
> Sneer. No, that's a genteel comedy, not a translation — only taken from the French: it is written in a style which they have lately tried to run down; the true sentimental, and nothing ridiculous in it from the beginning to the end.

By thus ridiculing the spirit, rather than the letter, of absurdities prevalent both in tragedy and comedy, *The Critic* has maintained its vitality. Personal caricature rarely outlives the person caricatured; dramatic travesty rarely outlives the drama travestied. Yet Sir Fretful lives, even if the caricature of Cumberland is unheeded, and *The Critic* lives, though the particular dramas it burlesqued are familiar to few.

A decided contrast may be drawn between the general burlesque of *The Critic* and the individual parodies of *The Rehearsal*. In fairness, it must be conceded that many parts of *The Rehearsal* burlesque general absurdities of the drama of all times. Otherwise it is improbable that even the interpolation into its text of local hits, or the genius of Garrick as Bayes, could have contrived to maintain *The Rehearsal* on the stage until its final eclipse by *The Critic.* Discussion of the prevalence of individual parodies of particular plays in *The Rehearsal* is best furthered by study of the different *Keys* included in Arber's reprint of the play.[1] Here the "Illustrations from Previous Plays" given on the even-numbered pages come somewhat near to balancing the text of *The Rehearsal* given on the odd-numbered pages. Among the plays from which, according to the table of contents, the illustrations are "principally taken," are seven plays of Dryden, three of D'Avenant, two of Killigrew, and single plays of Mrs. Behn, Fanshaw, J. Howard, Col. H. Howard, Porter, Quarles, and Stapylton. Though comparison of some of these extracts with the text of *The Rehearsal* shows but slight suggestion of parody, there remain enough unquestionable parallels to prove that specific parody was a vital part in the authors' conception of *The Rehearsal.*

One fact may help to account in large measure for the prevalence of direct parody in *The Rehearsal*, and its comparative absence in *The Critic.* *The Rehearsal* grew into final form not merely from the collaboration of various authors, but from years of evolution. Though said to have been commenced in 1663,[2] it was not produced until December 7, 1671. The hero seems to have been intended, at first, to burlesque D'Avenant, then Howard, and finally Dryden, who had meantime been appointed poet-laureate. The gradual progress of the burlesque invited constant additions to the exact parodies of contemporary dramas. On the other hand, *The Critic* may fairly be said to have been composed with a rapidity which practically precluded a con-

[1] English Reprints, London, November 2, 1858.

[2] Ward, *A History of English Dramatic Literature*, revised ed. 1899, III, 363.

stant succession of such elaborate specific parodies as are found in *The Rehearsal*.

In the *Memoirs of John Bannister, Comedian*,[1] John Adolphus writes: "I have heard Mr. Holcroft say, that he could make a key to 'The Critic' similar to that which is published with 'The Rehearsal,' by selecting from the works of contemporary tragic writers, passages and lines exactly similar to those in the burlesque drama." This remark, more or less distinctly referred to by some of Sheridan's biographers, has seemingly been allowed to pass, with little comment, as proof that *The Critic* abounds in direct parody of specific passages in contemporary tragedy. In this vein writes Sigmond:[2] "It would not be difficult for any one in the habit of reading the plays of the period to show the different passages that are burlesqued. Holcroft had at one time an idea of publishing a key to the Critic; such has been done for the Rehearsal." Whoever attempts the task pronounced so easy will conclude that Sigmond himself never made the test. Nor should too much stress be laid on a chance remark whose truth Holcroft himself never demonstrated. The next sentence of Adolphus after that already quoted implies some doubt at least of Holcroft's assertion, for it begins, "If that were so." Prolonged though necessarily incomplete, investigation of the tragedies that preceded *The Critic* on the London stage suggests the general subjects of Sheridan's burlesque rather than "passages and lines exactly similar to those in the burlesque drama." The only definite suggestion of Sigmond himself is this:[3] "The family recognition of the Justice, and the wife of the highwayman, is admirable. It is a supposed hit at the tumid language of Home, the author of 'Douglas,' in the 'Fatal Discovery,' a tragedy of bombast and nonsense." Significant is

[1] I, 49–50.

[2] *Life of Sheridan*, Bohn's Standard Library (1848), p. 86.

[3] *Ibid.*, p. 87.

the fact that, instead of positive assertion, the "hit" is said only to be "supposed," and that Sigmond fails to show any particular bit of "tumid language" in Home's play which Sheridan may have parodied. If, by "the wife of the highwayman," Sigmond refers to the Justice's Lady who in the "family recognition" scene proves to be the *mother* of the criminal who is brought before the Justice, the passage occurs in the first part of the third act of *The Critic*. Though one will readily grant that Sheridan hits at such "tumid language" as that of Home's tragedy, careful reading of *The Fatal Discovery* seems to afford no specific passage that is closely parodied. The suggestion is offered, with a diffidence born of long and usually fruitless search in contemporary tragedies for individual passages burlesqued in *The Critic*, that Sheridan may have intended to parody not merely somewhat of the situation, but somewhat of the language in Home's *Douglas* (ii, 1). There Lady Randolph, welcoming the "young stranger" who has saved her husband's life, is instinctively reminded of the lost son of her first husband, Douglas. To her confidante, Anna, she laments:

> I thought, that had the son of DOUGLAS liv'd,
> He might have been like this young gallant stranger,
> And pair'd with him in features and in shape.

So the Justice's Lady, on seeing the youthful prisoner, says:

> Strange bodings seized
> My flutt'ring heart — and to myself I said,
> An' if our Jack had lived he'd surely been
> This stripling's height.

In both cases the unknown turns out to be the long-lost son to whom "some powerful sympathy" has directed the mother's heart. If the similarities be regarded and the dissimilarities be neglected, there is certainly some ground for suggestion of specific parody.

Again, the response of the prisoner in Puff's tragedy to the Justice, "My name's John Wilkins — *Alias* have I none" — may be specific parody of young Norval's most famous speech, long a favorite declamation, "My name is Norval."[1]

It may be hazarded, too, that Tilburina's "confidant" is a burlesque sister to Anna, Lady Randolph's confidante. Yet it should be remembered also that the confidante was a familiar convenience of tragedy. Finally, it may be added that *Douglas* had attained a popularity on the stage which renders it probable that the audience of *The Critic* might have caught the necessarily somewhat subtle allusion of specific parody of individual lines.

Despite such direct parodies as have here been tentatively suggested, the contention that, as compared with *The Rehearsal*, *The Critic* is strikingly free from specific parody of individual passages in contemporary drama, is not only possible, but probable. It is improbable that the manager of Drury Lane would have gone far out of his way to ridicule in unmistakable fashion a multitude of direct passages from playwrights who supplied much of the drama for his own stage. It may be noted, too, that the *Tragedy Rehearsed* in *The Critic* is far shorter than the play of Bayes in *The Rehearsal*. Puff's tragedy appears only in the last two acts of *The Critic*: the tragedy of Bayes appears in all the five acts of *The Rehearsal*. Furthermore, even this comparatively limited extent of text is still further restricted, in its possibilities for definite parody, by the numerous passages which cannot possibly be interpreted save as general hits at the absurdities of the stage. A definite illustration of this is the very opening of Puff's tragedy with the striking of a clock, "to beget an awful attention in the audience — it also marks the time, which is four o'clock in the morning, and saves a description of the rising sun, and a great deal about gilding the eastern hemis-

[1] See note, p. 312.

phere." It is at once apparent that Sheridan burlesques the tediousness of opening scenes and the ornateness and verbosity of descriptive passages. So numerous are the contemporary plays which would meet the requirements of the burlesque that a dozen different keys to the passage could be readily supplied. This is general burlesque, not specific parody of a particular play. It would be profitless to continue the discussion with the great number of similar instances in Puff's tragedy. Futile must be the effort to give to these passages a local habitation and the name of a particular dramatist. Even if Holcroft could have supplied some key to *The Critic*, a modern key would inevitably encounter the pitfalls which proved disastrous to the key to *The Rehearsal* attempted by Bishop Percy some hundred years after the first production of *The Rehearsal*. Arber's words[1] may be most pertinently applied to *The Critic:* "A real Key should confine itself to the identical plays and dramatists satirized, nothing more nor less. Bp. Percy searching through all the antecedent dramatic literature, may find, did find, many parallel passages, but he could adduce nothing to prove these were in the minds of the authors in writing *The Rehearsal*. Indeed it is improbable that they had in view the 40 or 60 plays to which he refers. His references but illustrate the extent of the mock heroic drama."

The extended discussion here given has been necessitated in large measure by the unanimity with which Sheridan's commentators have allowed Holcroft's chance remark to pass unchallenged as proof that *The Critic* is full of direct parody readily recognizable in the contemporary drama. Dogmatic assertion is dangerous, but the contention seems amply supported that *The Critic* cannot be regarded as abounding in passages of specific parody similar to those in *The Rehearsal*. A passage from the critique in *The Public Advertiser* of Lon-

[1] Reprint of *The Rehearsal*, p. 48.

don, November 2, 1779, on the first performance of *The Critic*, may show fittingly how fully, even in its own day, it was held to be not so much a series of individual parodies, as a general burlesque of stage absurdities: "The tedious and unartificial Commencements of modern Tragedies, the inflated Diction, the figurative Tautology, the *Feu de Theatre* of Embraces and Groans, Vows and Prayers, florid Pathos, whining Heroism, and, above all, the Trick of Stage Situation, are ridiculed with a Burlesque which may be thought rather too refined for the Multitude, but certainly is perfect in its Stile."

5. The Element of Actual History in The Critic

So zealously has attention been focused upon some of the more obvious burlesque features of *The Critic* that scant heed has been paid to the marked basis of real history which furnishes to *The Critic* much of its setting. Sheridan's text alludes frequently to events of current history which have, for the most part, been allowed to pass, if not unnoticed, at least unexplained. Accordingly, the detailed explanation of these individual allusions given in the *Notes* to the text should here be prefaced with a brief connected account of the general political situation in England in 1779.

For many months before the production of *The Critic* public attention had been directed with increasing disfavor to the administration of English naval affairs. Contemporary newspapers, periodicals, the *Journals of the House of Commons* — all bear abundant testimony to widespread discontent. John Montagu, fourth Earl of Sandwich, the First Lord of the Admiralty, was a scandalously corrupt partisan. Though the governmental party gave him the doubtful sanction of support, the minority votes in the House of Commons against the conduct of the Admiralty voiced public indignation. One motion, lost by a vote of 118 to 224, on April 19, 1779, reads: "That an humble Address be presented to

His Majesty, that He will be graciously pleased to remove from His Presence and Councils *John* Earl of *Sandwich*, on Account of the general ill State of the Navy under his Administration at the most critical Seasons."[1] When Keppel, who had commanded the English Fleet in an indecisive engagement in the Channel with the French, was acquitted by the court martial, a mob had attacked Sandwich's official residence at the Admiralty. In a word, Sandwich was the constant target of righteous wrath, a man who debauched public honor as fully as he did private morality.

The immediate political situation which confronted the First Lord of the Admiralty in 1779 was hostility between England and the allied forces of France and Spain. On the retirement of Keppel, the command of the Channel Fleet had been eventually assumed by Sir Charles Hardy, long retired from active service. By the middle of the year the French and Spanish fleets threatened an invasion of England. In mid-August the London newspapers announced the appearance of the fleet off Plymouth. Hardy, with a fleet smaller than that of the allies, did not hazard an attack. Before the appearance of *The Critic*, however, public apprehension had been largely allayed by the withdrawal of the hostile fleet. *Lloyd's Evening Post*, October 27–29, gives an "Extract of a Letter from a Lady at Plymouth, dated Oct. 21, 1779. After the terrors of an invasion from the combined fleets, we begin once more to resume our usual gaiete de coeur. Our assemblies and suppers are as gay and lively as the Officers of ten thousand brave troops, now in our environs, can possibly promote." Ten days before *The Critic* appeared at Drury Lane, was produced at Covent Garden "a new musical farce entitled Plymouth in an Uproar." Commenting on this, *The London Chronicle* (October 19–21) says: "This entertainment is founded on the well-known circumstances of the combined

[1] *The Journal of the House of Commons*, vol. 37, p. 334.

fleets appearing off Plymouth last summer, and the consternation occasioned in that part of the world in consequence thereof." *Lloyd's Evening Post* (October 20–22) discusses the same farce as follows: "The business of the French and Spanish fleets appearing off Plymouth was a matter of too serious and alarming a nature to be the subject of wit or humour. The formidable strength of our enemies naturally excites resolutions of opposing them with determined courage, but a truly brave people feel the impropriety of treating them with contempt and ridicule."

Such was the general political situation when Dangle picked up his newspaper in the opening scene of *The Critic* and read in its head-lines "nothing but about the fleet and the nation." Only study of the historical setting of *The Critic* reveals the significance of naming Puff's tragedy *The Spanish Armada*, or the appeal to patriotic pride of Puff's final "magnificence, battle, and procession" when the stage-direction[1] details the destruction of the Spanish Armada by the English Fleet.

Flourish of drums — trumpets — cannon, &c., &c. Scene changes to the sea — the musick plays 'Britons strike home.' — Spanish fleet destroyed by fire-ships, &c. — English fleet advances — musick plays 'Rule Britannia.'

[1] As given in the first printed edition of *The Critic*, 1781, p. 98.

CHIEF FACTS OF SHERIDAN'S LITERARY LIFE

1771. (August) — Publication of *The Love Epistles of Aristænetus*, translated from the Greek into English meter. (Halhed, a Harrow school friend, collaborated with Sheridan.)

1775. (January 17) — First production of *The Rivals* (Comedy), at Covent Garden Theatre.

(January 28) — Revised production of *The Rivals*.

(May 2) — *St. Patrick's Day; or, The Scheming Lieutenant* (Farce), produced at Covent Garden Theatre.

(November 21) — *The Duenna* (Comic Opera), produced at Covent Garden Theatre.

1777. (February 24) — A *Trip to Scarborough* (Comedy altered from Vanbrugh's *The Relapse; or, Virtue in Danger*), produced at Drury Lane Theatre.

(May 8) — *The School for Scandal* (Comedy), produced at Drury Lane Theatre.

1779. (March 2) — *Verses to the memory of Garrick*, spoken as a Monody by Mrs. Yates at Drury Lane Theatre (David Garrick died January 20, 1779).

(October 30) — *The Critic: or A Tragedy Rehearsed* (Burlesque Farce), produced at Drury Lane Theatre.

1799. (May 24) — *Pizarro* (Melodramatic Tragedy adapted from the German drama, *Spaniards in Peru*, by Kotzebue), produced at Drury Lane Theatre.

A BIBLIOGRAPHICAL NOTE

The pages preceding the text of each play in this volume discuss with some detail a few of the early editions of Sheridan's major dramas. Such discussion is supplemented in the following bibliography by (1) a list of collected editions of Sheridan's dramas, and (2) lists of individual editions of the three major dramas prior to 1821. In that year appeared the two-volume edition of Sheridan's works published by Murray, the supervision of which is commonly credited to Thomas Moore.[1] In 1816 Sheridan died, and no edition after Moore's can claim even the doubtful authority of that work, save Fraser Rae's edition of 1902, based on the original Sheridan manuscripts. The extension of the lists of editions of the separate plays after 1821 would accordingly have little significance save as proof of the steady popularity of Sheridan. Most of the collected editions have, however, more or less extended biographies, and some include also critical or explanatory material. So numerous have been the reprints of Sheridan's dramas, and so various the collections in which individual plays have appeared, that even the admirable bibliography by John P. Anderson appended to the *Life of Sheridan* by Lloyd C. Sanders, in the *Great Writers Series*, is suggestive rather than exhaustive. Within the narrower limits of the present pages, it has been possible to expand Mr. Anderson's work, based on the British Museum collection, by the inclusion of many American and English editions not there listed, and by the addition of a considerable number of editions published since his work. In the following lists the only edition which I have not examined personally is the first Dublin edition of *The Critic*, which I have included on the authority of the catalogue of the library of Trinity College, Dublin.

The definitive biography of Sheridan is that by W. Fraser Rae—

[1] But see Fraser Rae, *Sheridan's Plays*, Prefatory Notes, xiv.

Sheridan, A Biography, 2 vols. London, Richard Bentley & Son; New York, Henry Holt & Co., 1896. The best of the briefer biographies is by Lloyd C. Sanders in the *Great Writers Series.* Moore's *Life of Sheridan* handles carelessly and often inaccurately its wealth of material. The work of Watkins, Sheridan's first biographer, is practically worthless. Even the best of the biographies in the collected editions of Sheridan's works should be carefully checked for errors. For works relating to Sheridan, Mr. Anderson's bibliography may be consulted to advantage.

BRITISH MUSEUM,
July 27, 1906.

I. COLLECTED EDITIONS OF SHERIDAN'S DRAMAS

1795? The Dramatic Works of R. B. Sheridan, Esq. Containing, The School for Scandal, The Rivals, The Duenna, The Critic. London [1795?].

1821. The Works of the late Right Honourable Richard Brinsley Sheridan. 2 vols. [Edited by Thomas Moore.] London, 1821.

1828. The Dramatic Works of Richard Brinsley Sheridan. With some observations upon his personal and literary character. Greenock, 1828.

1833. The Works of the late Right Honourable Richard Brinsley Sheridan. Collected by Thomas Moore, Esq. A new edition complete in one volume. With a biographical sketch. Leipsic, 1833.

1840. The Dramatic Works of Richard Brinsley Sheridan. With a biographical and critical sketch. By Leigh Hunt. London, 1840.

———Another edition. London, 1846.

———Another edition. London, 1865.

1848. The Dramatic Works of the Right Honourable Richard Brinsley Sheridan. With a memoir of his life by G. G. S[igmond]. London, 1848. (In *Bohn's Standard Library.* Various editions with different dates.)

1851. Select Comedies by R. B. Sheridan: with explanatory

Italian notes, by John Millhouse. [Includes *The School for Scandal* and *The Rivals.*] Second Milan edition. Milan, 1851.

1854. The Dramatic Works of Richard Brinsley Sheridan, with a biographical and critical sketch, edited by Ludwig Gantter. Stuttgart, 1854. (No. 3 in *The Standard Poets of Great-Britain.*)

1869. The Dramatic Works of the Right Honourable Richard Brinsley Sheridan. [Tauchnitz edition.] Leipzig, 1869.

1873. The Works of the Right Honourable Richard Brinsley Sheridan, with a memoir by James P. Browne, M.D. Containing extracts from the life by Thomas Moore. [Includes *The Camp*, not written by Sheridan.] 2 vols. London, 1873.

——— Same work, in one volume, without *The Camp.* London, 1873.

——— Another edition, in two volumes, with Memoir by Browne. London, 1884.

——— Another edition, two volumes in one. London, New York, and Melbourne, 1891. (In the *Macaulay Library of Great Writers.*)

1874. The Works of Richard Brinsley Sheridan. Dramas, poems, translations, speeches, and unfinished sketches. With a memoir of the author, a collection of ana, and ten chalk drawings. Edited by F. Stainforth. London, 1874. (Also a New York edition, George Routledge & Sons, n. d.)

1879. The Rivals and School for Scandal. Comedies. New York, 1879. (In *Harper's Half-hour Series.*)

1883. The Plays of Richard Brinsley Sheridan, with an introduction by Henry Morley. London, 1883. (In *Morley's Universal Library.* Various editions with different dates. Included also in *Sir John Lubbock's Hundred Books,* 1892.)

1883. The Dramatic Works of Richard Brinsley Sheridan. With an introduction by Richard Grant White. 3 vols. [Includes *The Camp* in vol. 1.] New York, 1883.

1884. Dramatic Works of Sheridan and Goldsmith. With Goldsmith's Poems. 2 vols. London, 1884.

——— Another edition. London [1886]. (In *Cassell's Miniature Library of the Poets.*)

1885. Sheridan's Comedies. The Rivals and The School for Scandal. Edited with an introduction and notes to each play and a biographical sketch of Sheridan, by Brander Matthews. Boston, 1885. (Also a London edition, 1885.)

1886. The Rivals and the School for Scandal. London, 1886. (In *Cassell's National Library.* Various editions with different dates.)

1887. The Dramatic Works of Richard Brinsley Sheridan. London [1887]. (In *Cassell's Red Library.*)

1889. Plays of Sheridan. Containing The Rivals, The School for Scandal, The Critic. London, 1889. (In *Bohn's Select Library.*)

1890. The Rivals, The School for Scandal, and other plays of Richard Brinsley Sheridan. London, 1890.

1891. The Plays of Richard Brinsley Sheridan. Edited, with an introduction, by Rudolf Dircks. London and New York [1891]. (In the *Camelot Series.*)

1896. The School for Scandal and The Rivals, by Richard Brinsley Sheridan, with introduction by Augustine Birrell. London and New York, 1896.

1900. The Plays of Richard Brinsley Sheridan. London and New York, 1900. [Edited by A. W. Pollard.] (In Macmillan's *Library of English Classics.* Various editions with different dates.)

1902. The Dramatic Works of Richard Brinsley Sheridan, with a short account of his life by G. G. S[igmond]. New York and London, 1902.

1902. Sheridan's Plays now printed as he wrote them, and his mother's unpublished comedy A Journey to Bath. Edited by W. Fraser Rae. With an introduction by Sheridan's great-grandson, the Marquess of Dufferin and Ava. London, 1902.

1903. Richard Brinsley Sheridan. Plays. ("A few notes on each of the plays will be found at the end of the volume.") London and New York, 1903. (No. 28 in *The Unit Library.*)

1904. Sheridan's Comedies. The Rivals and The School for Scandal, *etc.* Edited by Brander Matthews. New York, 1904. (A slightly revised edition of the original work published in 1885.)

1905. The Plays of Sheridan. [With introductions by Edmund Gosse.] 3 vols. The Rivals, The School for Scandal, The Critic [in separate vols.]. London, 1905. (In William Heinemann's *Favourite Classics.*)

II. EDITIONS OF SEPARATE PLAYS

(a) *Editions of The Rivals previous to* 1821

1775. The Rivals, a Comedy. As it is acted at the Theatre-Royal, in Covent-Garden. London, 1775.
Second edition. London, 1775.
Another edition. Dublin, 1775.

1776. Third edition. London, 1776.

1778. Another edition. (*A Collection of New Plays by Several Hands*, IV, 143–282.) Altenburgh, 1778.

1791. Fifth edition. London, 1791.

1793. Another edition. Dublin, 1793.
Another edition. (W. Jones's *British Theatre*, V, 191–317.) Dublin, 1793. [Whole vol. dated 1795.]

1798. Sixth edition. London, 1798.

1804. Another edition. (*The British Drama comprehending the best plays in the English Language.* Comedies. Pt. 2, 999–1029.) London, 1804.

1807. Another edition. New York, 1807.

1808. Another edition. (*The British Theatre*, by Mrs. Inchbald, XIX.) London, 1808.

1810. Another edition. (*English Comedy*, II, 1–83.) London, 1810.

1811. Another edition. (*The Modern British Drama*, IV, 619–648.) London, 1811.

1815. Another edition. (*The London Theatre*, by Thomas [John] Dibdin, I.) London, 1815.

1818. Another edition. (*The New English Drama*, by W. Oxberry, I.) London, 1818.

1820. Oxberry's edition. London, 1820.

(*b*) *Editions of The School for Scandal previous to* 1821.

1777? The School for Scandal. A Comedy. Dublin [1777?].

1781. Another edition. Dublin, 1781.

1782. Fourth edition. Dublin, 1782.

1783. Another edition. The real and genuine School for Scandal, a comedy . . . . Written by Brinsley Sheridan, Esquire. London, 1783.

1785. Another edition. (*A volume of plays, as performed at the Theatre* [Royal], *Smoke-Alley, Dublin.*) Dublin, 1785.

1787. Another edition. Dublin, 1787.

1788. Fifth edition. London, 1788.

1792. Another edition. (W. Jones's *British Theatre*, V, 1–116.) Dublin, 1792.

1793. Another edition. (As it is acted at the Theatre [Royal], Smoke-Alley, Dublin.) [Dublin?] 1793.

1798. Another edition. London, 1798.

1807. Another edition. (*Collection of English Plays*, with explanatory notes in the Danish language. By Fredk. Schneider, I, 91–228.) Copenhagen, 1807.

(*c*) *Editions of The Critic previous to* 1821.

1781. The Critic, or a Tragedy Rehearsed. A dramatic piece in three acts as it is performed at the Theatre Royal in Drury Lane. London, 1781.

Second edition. London, 1781.

Another [third?] edition. London, 1781.

Fourth edition. London, 1781.

Another edition. Dublin, 1781.

1785. Another edition. Dublin, 1785.

1793. Another edition. (W. Jones's *British Theatre*, V, 117–190.) Dublin, 1793.

1807. Another edition. (Cawthorn's *Minor British Theatre*, VI.) London, 1807.

Another edition. New York, 1807.

1811. A new edition. London, 1811.

Another edition. (*The Modern British Drama*, V, 642–659.) London, 1811.

1814. Another edition. (*The London Theatre*, by Thomas [John] Dibdin, VIII.) London, 1814.

1815. Another edition. (Mrs. Inchbald's *A Collection of Farces*, III, 201–255.) London, 1815.

1820. Another edition. (*The New English Drama*, by W. Oxberry, IX.) London, 1820.

THE RIVALS

THE TEXT OF THE RIVALS

THE text of *The Rivals* in this edition is taken, by Mr. Fraser Rae's generous permission, from his *Sheridan's Plays now printed as he wrote them* (London, 1902). Of this book he once wrote me: "I copied Sheridan's text in order that a reader might have it before him, just as he would do if he had the original manuscript." This text — "Sheridan's version, printed with absolute fidelity," as his Prefatory Notes describe it — I have tried to reproduce with like fidelity. With this I have collated the first three editions from the copies in the Yale University Library. In the footnotes I have adopted the following method of reference: R 1 — *The Rivals*, first edition, 1775; R 2 — second edition, 1775; R 3 — third edition, 1776; RR — agreement of the first three editions. On the title-page of the third edition are the words, "The Third Edition Corrected." Apart from the verbal changes indicated in the footnotes, the most striking 'corrections' are the omission of certain passages which I have enclosed within guillemets (« »). In his Prefatory Notes (xiv, xv), Mr. Rae seems to imply that the specific omissions which he cites were first made in "the truncated version which Mr. Wilkie prepared for Mr. Murray" — that is, the two-volume Murray edition of Sheridan's plays, in 1821. My collation shows that these changes had been already made in R 3. With his general conclusion, however, that modern editions of *The Rivals* present but a "truncated version," there can, I think, be no dispute. Even disregarding the question of authenticity, Sheridan's version seems to me decidedly the best text. In some places, where the spelling or punctuation may be misleading, I have inserted suggestions in brackets. Even in spelling, however, Mr. Rae's text is usually preferable to R 1, a fact sufficiently illustrated by the use in R 1 of "knawing," "shew," "cloke," and "sopha," for the usual forms found in Sheridan's version. I have disregarded unimportant variants in punctuation, spelling, and stage-directions. Various minor errors may be dismissed by restoring that delightful "oath referential" stolen from Bob Acres by the ruthless corrector — that oath which was an "echo to the sense" when his memory played him false as to a snatch of song — "Odds slips!"

THE RIVALS

A COMEDY

PREFACE

A PREFACE to a play seems generally to be considered as a kind of Closet-prologue, in which — if his Piece has been successful — the Author solicits that indulgence from the Reader which he had before experienced from the Audience: But as the scope and immediate object of a Play is to please a mixed assembly in *Representation* (whose judgment in the Theatre at least is decisive), its degree of reputation is usually as determined by the public,[1] before it can be prepared for the cooler tribunal of the Study. Thus any farther solicitude on the part of the Writer becomes unnecessary at least, if not an intrusion; and if the Piece has been condemned in the Performance, I fear an Address to the Closet, like an Appeal to posterity, is constantly regarded as the procrastination of a suit, from a consciousness of the weakness of the cause. From these considerations, the following Comedy would certainly have been submitted to the Reader, without any further introduction than what it had in the Representation, but that its success has probably been founded on a circumstance which the Author is informed has not before attended a theatrical trial, and which consequently ought not to pass unnoticed.

I need scarcely add, that the circumstance alluded to was the withdrawing of the Piece, to remove those imperfections in the first Representation which were too obvious to escape reprehension, and too numerous to admit of a hasty correction. There are few writers, I believe, who, even in the fullest consciousness of error,

[1] R 1, 2: as determined as public.

do not wish to palliate the faults which they acknowledge; and, however trifling the performance, to second their confession of its deficiencies, by whatever plea seems least disgraceful to their ability. In the present instance, it cannot be said to amount either to candour or modesty in me, to acknowledge an extreme inexperience and want of judgment on matters, in which, without guidance from practice, or spur from success, a young man should scarcely boast of being an adept. If it be said that under such disadvantages no one should attempt to write a play — I must beg leave to dissent from the position, while the first point of experience that I have gained on the subject is, a knowledge of the candour and judgment with which an impartial Public distinguishes between the errors of inexperience and incapacity, and the indulgence which it shews even to a disposition to remedy the defects of either.

It were unnecessary to enter into any farther extenuation of what was thought exceptionable in this Play, but that it has been said, that the Managers should have prevented some of the defects before its appearance to the public — and in particular the uncommon length of the piece as represented the first night. — It were an ill return for the most liberal and gentlemanly conduct on their side, to suffer any censure to rest where none was deserved. Hurry in writing has long been exploded as an excuse for an author; — however, in the dramatic line, it may happen, that both an Author and a Manager may wish to fill a chasm in the entertainment of the Public with a hastiness not altogether culpable. The season was advanced when I first put the play into Mr. Harris's hands: — it was at that time at least double the length of any acting comedy. — I profited by his judgment and experience in the curtailing of it — 'till, I believe, his feeling for the vanity of a young Author got the better of his desire for correctness, and he left many excrescences remaining, because he had assisted in pruning so many more. Hence, though I was not uninformed that the Acts were still too long, I flattered myself that, after the first trial, I might with safer judgment proceed to remove what should appear to have been most dissatisfactory. Many other errors there were, which might in part have arisen from my being by no means conversant with plays in general, either in reading or at the theatre. — Yet I own that, in one respect, I did not regret my ignorance: for as my first wish in attempting a Play was to avoid every appearance of plagiary, I thought I should stand a better chance of effecting this from being in a walk which I had not frequented, and where consequently the progress of invention was less likely to be interrupted by starts of recollection: for on subjects on which the mind has been much informed, invention is slow of exerting itself. — Faded ideas float in the fancy like half-forgotten dreams; and the imagination in its fullest enjoyments becomes suspicious of its offspring, and doubts whether it has created or adopted.

With regard to some particular passages which on the First Night's Representation seemed generally disliked, I confess, that if I felt any emotion of surprise at the disapprobation, it was not that they were disapproved of, but that I had not before perceived that they deserved it. As some part of the attack on the Piece was begun too early to pass for the sentence of *Judgment*, which is ever tardy in condemning, it has been suggested to me, that much of the disapprobation must have arisen from virulence of Malice, rather than severity of Criticism: but as I was more apprehensive of there being just grounds to excite the latter, than conscious of having deserved the former, I continue not to believe that probable, which I am sure must have been unprovoked. However, if it was so, and I could even mark the quarter from whence it came, it would be ungenerous to retort; for no passion suffers more than malice from disappointment. For my own part, I see no reason why the Author of a Play should not regard a First Night's Audience as a candid and judicious friend attending, in behalf of the Public, at his last Rehearsal. If he can dispense with flattery, he is sure at least of sincerity, and even though the annotation be rude, he may rely upon the justness of the comment. Considered in this light, that Audience, whose *fiat* is essential to the Poet's claim, whether his object be Fame or Profit, has surely a right to expect some deference to its opinion, from principles of Politeness at least, if not from Gratitude.

As for the little puny Critics, who scatter their peevish strictures in private circles, and scribble at every Author who has the eminence of being unconnected with them, as they are usually spleen-swoln from a vain idea of increasing their consequence, there will always be found a petulance and illiberality in their remarks, which should place them as far beneath the notice of a Gentleman as their original dulness had sunk them from the level of the most unsuccessful Author.

It is not without pleasure that I catch at an opportunity of justifying myself from the charge of intending any national reflection in the character of Sir *Lucius O'Trigger*. If any Gentlemen opposed the Piece from that idea, I thank them sincerely for their opposition; and if the condemnation of this Comedy (however misconceived the provocation) could have added one spark to the decaying flame of national attachment to the country supposed to be reflected on, I should have been happy in its fate; and might with truth have boasted, that it had done more real service in its failure, than the successful morality of a thousand stage-novels will ever effect.

It is usual, I believe, to thank the Performers in a new Play, for the exertion of their several abilities. But where (as in this instance) their merit has been so striking and uncontroverted, as to call for the warmest and truest applause from a number of judicious Audiences, the Poet's after-praise comes like the feeble acclamation of a child to close the shouts of a multitude. The conduct, however, of the Principals in a theatre cannot be so apparent to the Public. — I think it therefore but justice to declare, that from this Theatre (the only one I can speak of from experience) those Writers who wish to try the Dramatic Line will meet with that candour and liberal attention, which are generally allowed to be better calculated to lead genius into excellence, than either the precepts of judgment, or the guidance of experience.

THE AUTHOR

DRAMATIS PERSONÆ

AS ORIGINALLY ACTED AT COVENT GARDEN THEATRE IN 1775

SIR ANTHONY ABSOLUTE	*Mr. Shuter*
CAPTAIN ABSOLUTE	*Mr. Woodward*
FAULKLAND	*Mr. Lewis*
ACRES	*Mr. Quick*
SIR LUCIUS O'TRIGGER	*Mr. Lee*[1]
FAG	*Mr. Lee Lewes*
DAVID	*Mr. Dunstal*
THOMAS[2]	*Mr. Fearon*
MRS. MALAPROP	*Mrs. Green*
LYDIA LANGUISH	*Miss Barsanti*
JULIA	*Mrs. Bulkley*
LUCY	*Mrs. Lessingham*

Maid, Boy, Servants, &c.

SCENE. — *Bath*

Time of Action — Five Hours[3]

PROLOGUE

By the Author

SPOKEN BY MR. WOODWARD AND MR. QUICK

Enter SERJEANT-AT-LAW, *and* ATTORNEY *following, and giving a paper.*

SERJ. What's here! — a vile cramp hand! I cannot see
Without my spectacles.

ATT. He means his fee.
Nay, Mr. Serjeant, good sir, try again. [*Gives money.*

SERJ. The scrawl improves! [*more*] O come, 'tis pretty plain.
Hey![4] how's this? The Poet's Brief *again.* O ho![5]

[1] RR: Mr. Clinch.
[2] RR: Coachman.
[3] R 3: within one day.
[4] R 1, 2, omit "Hey."
[5] R 3: Hey! how's this?—*Dibble!*—sure it cannot be!

A poet's brief! a poet and a fee! [1]
ATT. Yes,[2] sir! though you without reward, I know,
Would gladly plead the Muse's cause.
SERJ. So! — so!
ATT. And if the fee offends your wrath should fall
On me.
SERJ. Dear Dibble, no offence at all.
ATT. Some sons of Phœbus in the courts we meet,
SERJ. And fifty sons of Phœbus in the Fleet!
ATT. Nor pleads he worse, who with a decent sprig
Of bays adorns his legal waste of wig.
SERJ. Full-bottomed heroes thus, on signs, unfurl
A leaf of laurel in a grove of curl!
Yet tell your client, that, in adverse days,
This wig is warmer than a bush of bays.
ATT. Do you, then, sir, my client's place supply,
Profuse of robe, and prodigal of tie ——
Do you, with all those blushing powers of face,
And wonted bashful hesitating grace,
Rise in the court and flourish on the case. [*Exit.*
SERJ. For practice then suppose — this brief will show it, —
Me, Serjeant *Woodward*, — Council for the Poet.
Us'd to the ground — I know 'tis hard to deal
With this dread *Court*, from whence there's *no appeal;*
No *Tricking* here, to blunt the edge of *Law*,

[1] R 1, 2, substitute for ll. 6–10, as follows:

Cast, I suppose? *Att.* O pardon me — No — No —
We found the Court, o'erlooking stricter laws,
Indulgent to the *merits* of the Cause;
By *Judges* mild, unus'd to harsh denial,
A Rule was granted for *another trial.*
Serj. Then heark'ee, *Dibble*, did you *mend* your *Pleadings*,
Errors, no few, we've *found* in our *Proceedings*.
Att. Come, courage, Sir, we did *amend* our *Plea*,
Hence your new *Brief*, and this *refreshing Fee.*

[2] R 3: Yea.

Or, damn'd in *Equity*, escape by *Flaw:*
But *Judgment* given — *your Sentence* must remain;
No *Writ of Error* lies — to *Drury Lane!*
Yet when so kind you seem — 'tis past dispute
We gain some favour, if not *Costs of Suit.*
No spleen is here! I see no hoarded fury; —
I think I never faced a milder Jury!
Sad else our plight! where frowns are transportation,
A hiss the gallows, and a groan, damnation!
But such the public candour, without fear
My Client waives all *right of challenge* here.
No Newsman from *our* Session is dismiss'd,
Nor Wit nor Critic *we* scratch off the list;
His faults can never hurt another's ease,
His crime at worst — a *bad attempt* to please:
Thus, all respecting, he appeals to all,
And by the general voice will *stand* or *fall.*

PROLOGUE

By the Author

SPOKEN ON THE TENTH NIGHT, BY MRS. BULKLEY[1]

GRANTED our cause, our suit and trial o'er,
The worthy serjeant need appear no more:
In pleasing I a different client choose,
He served the Poet — I would serve the Muse.
Like him, I'll try to merit your applause,
A female counsel in a female's cause.
Look on this form,[2] — where humour, quaint and sly,
Dimples the cheek, and points the beaming eye;
Where gay invention seems to boast its wiles

[1] This Prologue is included in R 3, but not in R 1, 2.
[2] Pointing to the figure of Comedy.

In amourous hint, and half-triumphant smiles;
While her light mask or covers satire's strokes,[1]
Or hides the conscious blush her wit provokes.
Look on her well — does she seem'd form'd to teach?
Should you expect to hear this lady preach?
Is grey experience suited to her youth?
Do solemn sentiments become that mouth?
Bid her be grave, those lips should rebel prove
To every theme that slanders mirth or love.
  Yet, thus adorn'd with every graceful art
To charm the fancy and yet reach the heart ——
Must we displace her, and instead advance
The goddess of the woful countenance —
The sentimental Muse? — Her emblems view,
The Pilgrim's Progress, and a sprig of rue!
View her — too chaste to look like flesh and blood —
Primly portray'd on emblematic wood!
There, fix'd in usurpation, should she stand,
She'll snatch the dagger from her sister's hand:
And having made her votaries weep a flood,
Good heaven! she'll end her comedies in blood —
Bid Harry Woodward break poor Dunstal's crown!
Imprison Quick, and knock Ned Shuter down;
While sad Barsanti, weeping o'er the scene,
Shall stab herself — or poison Mrs. Green.
  Such dire encroachments to prevent in time,
Demands the critic's voice — the poet's rhyme.
Can our light scenes add strength to holy laws
Such puny patronage but hurts the cause:
Fair virtue scorns our feeble aid to ask;
And moral truth disdains the trickster's mask

[1] R 3:

While her light masks or covers satire's strokes,
All hides . . .

For here their favourite stands,[1] whose brow severe
And sad, claims youth's respect, and pity's tear;
Who, when oppress'd by foes her worth creates,
Can point a poniard at the guilt she hates.

ACT I

SCENE I. — *A Street in Bath*

COACHMAN *crosses the Stage; enter* FAG, *looking after him*

FAG. What! Thomas! sure 'tis he? — What! Thomas! Thomas!

COACH. Hay! — Odd's life! Mr. Fag! — give us your hand, my old fellow-servant.

FAG. Excuse my glove, Thomas: — I'm devilish glad to see you, my lad. Why, my prince of charioteers, you look as hearty! — but who the deuce thought of seeing you in Bath?

COACH. Sure, master, Madam Julia, Harry, Mrs. Kate, and the postilion be all come.

FAG. Indeed!

COACH. Aye, master thought another fit of the gout was coming to make him a visit; so he'd a mind to gi't the slip, and whip! we were all off at an hour's warning.

FAG. Aye, aye, hasty in everything, or it would not be Sir Anthony Absolute!

COACH. But tell us, Mr. Fag, how does young Master? Odd! Sir Anthony will stare to see the Captain here!

FAG. I do not serve Captain Absolute now.

COACH. Why sure!

FAG. At present I am employ'd by Ensign Beverley.

COACH. I doubt, Mr. Fag, you ha'n't changed for the better.

FAG. I have not changed, Thomas.

COACH. No! Why didn't you say you had left young Master?

FAG. No. — Well, honest Thomas, I must puzzle you no

[1] Pointing to Tragedy.

farther: — briefly then — Captain Absolute and Ensign Beverley are one and the same person.

COACH. The devil they are!

FAG. So it is indeed, Thomas; and the *Ensign* half of my master being on guard at present — the *Captain* has nothing to do with me.

COACH. So, so! — What, this is some freak, I warrant! — Do, tell us, Mr. Fag, the meaning o't — you know I ha' trusted you.

FAG. You'll be secret, Thomas?

COACH. As a coach-horse.

FAG. Why then the cause of all this is — Love, — Love, Thomas, who (as you may get read to you) has been a masquerader ever since the days of Jupiter.

COACH. Aye, aye; — I guessed there was a lady in the case: — but pray, why does your Master pass only for *Ensign?* — Now if he had shamm'd *General* indeed ——

FAG. Ah! Thomas, there lies the mystery o' the matter. Hark'ee, Thomas, my Master is in love with a lady of a very singular taste: a lady who likes him better as a *half-pay Ensign* than if she knew he was son and heir to Sir Anthony Absolute, a baronet with[1] three thousand a year.

COACH. That is an odd taste indeed! — But has she got the stuff, Mr. Fag? Is she rich, hey?

FAG. Rich! — Why, I believe she owns half the stocks! Z—ds! Thomas, she could pay the national debt as easily[2] as I could my washerwoman! She has a lapdog that eats out of gold, — she feeds her parrot with small pearls, — and all her thread-papers are made of bank-notes!

COACH. Bravo! faith! — Odd! I warrant she has a set of thousands at least: — but does she draw kindly with the Captain?

FAG. As fond as pigeons.

[1] R 3: of. [2] R 1, 2: easy.

COACH. May one hear her name?

FAG. Miss Lydia Languish. — But there is an old tough aunt in the way; though, by-the-by, she has never seen my Master — for we[1] got acquainted with Miss while on a visit in Gloucestershire.

COACH. Well — I wish they were once harnessed together in matrimony. — But pray, Mr. Fag, what kind of a place is this Bath? — I ha' heard a deal of it — here's a mort o' merry-making, hey?

FAG. Pretty well, Thomas, pretty well — 'tis a good lounge. «Though at present we are, like other great assemblies, divided into parties — High-roomians and Low-roomians; however for my part, I have resolved to stand neuter, and so I told Bob Brush at our last committee.

«COACH. But what do the folks do here?

«FAG. Oh! there are little amusements enough»; in the morning we go to the pump-room (though neither my Master nor I drink the waters); after breakfast we saunter on the parades or play a game at billiards; at night we dance; but d—n the place, I'm tired of it: their regular hours stupefy me — not a fiddle nor a card after eleven! — However Mr. Faulkland's gentleman and I keep it up a little in private parties; — I'll introduce you there, Thomas — you'll like him much.

COACH. Sure I know Mr. Du-Peigne — you know his Master is to marry Madam Julia.

FAG. I had forgot. — But, Thomas, you must polish a little — indeed you must. — Here now — this wig! What the devil do you do with a *wig*, Thomas? — None of the London whips of any degree of Ton wear *wigs* now.

COACH. More's the pity! more's the pity! I say. — Odd's life! when I heard how the lawyers and doctors had took to their own hair, I thought how 'twould go next: — odd rabbit it! when the fashion had got foot on the Bar, I guessed 'twould

[1] RR: he.

mount to the Box! — but 'tis all out of character, believe me, Mr. Fag: and look'ee, I'll never gi' up mine — the lawyers and doctors may do as they will.

FAG. Well, Thomas, we'll not quarrel about that.

COACH. Why, bless you, the gentlemen of they professions ben't all of a mind — for in our village now thoff *Jack Gauge*, the *exciseman*, has ta'en to his carrots, there's little Dick the farrier swears he'll never forsake his *bob*, tho' all the college should appear with their own heads!

FAG. Indeed! well said, Dick! — but hold — mark! mark! Thomas.

COACH. Zooks! 'tis the captain. — Is that the lady with him?

FAG. No! no! that is Madam Lucy, my Master's mistress's maid. They lodge at that house — but I must after him to tell him the news.

COACH. Odd! he's giving her money! — Well, Mr. Fag ——

FAG. Good-bye, Thomas. I have an appointment in Gydes' Porch this evening at eight; meet me there, and we'll make a little party. [*Exeunt severally.*

SCENE II. — *A Dressing-room in* MRS. MALAPROP'S *Lodgings*

LYDIA *sitting on a sofa, with a book in her hand.* LUCY, *as just returned from a message*

LUCY. Indeed, Ma'am, I transferr'd[1] half the town in search of it! I don't believe there's a circulating library in Bath I han't been at.

LYD. And could not you get *The Reward of Constancy?*

LUCY. No, indeed, Ma'am.

LYD. Nor *The Fatal Connection?*

LUCY. No, indeed, Ma'am.

LYD. Nor *The Mistakes of the Heart?*

[1] R 3: travers'd.

LUCY. Ma'am, as ill luck would have it, Mr. Bull said Miss Sukey Saunter had just fetched it away.

LYD. Heigh-ho! Did you inquire for *The Delicate Distress?*

LUCY. Or, *The Memoirs of Lady Woodford?* Yes, indeed, Ma'am. I asked everywhere for it; and I might have brought it from Mr. Frederick's, but Lady Slattern Lounger, who had just sent it home, had so soiled and dog's-eared it, it wa'n't fit for a christian to read.

LYD. Heigh-ho! Yes, I always know when Lady Slattern has been before me. She has a most observing thumb; and I believe cherishes her nails for the convenience of making marginal notes. — Well, child, what *have* you brought me?

LUCY. Oh! here, ma'am. — [*Taking books from under her cloke, and from her pockets.*] This is *The Gordian Knot,* — and this *Peregrine Pickle.* Here are *The Tears of Sensibility,* and *Humphry Clinker.* This is *The Memoirs of a Lady of Quality, written by herself,* and here the second volume of *The Sentimental Journey.*

LYD. Heigh-ho! — What are those books by the glass?

LUCY. The great one is only *The Whole Duty of Man,* where I press a few blonds, Ma'am.

LYD. Very well — give me the *sal volatile.*

LUCY. Is it in a blue cover, Ma'am?

LYD. My smelling-bottle, you simpleton!

LUCY. Oh, the drops! — here, Ma'am.

«LYD. No note, Lucy?

«LUCY. No, indeed, Ma'am — but I have seen a certain person —

«LYD. What, my Beverley! Well Lucy?

«LUCY. O Ma'am he looks so desponding and melancholic!»

LYD. Hold! Lucy [1] — here's some one coming — quick! see who it is. (*Exit* LUCY.) — Surely I heard my cousin Julia's voice.

[1] R 3 omits "Lucy."

Re-enter LUCY

LUCY. Lud! Ma'am, here is Miss Melville.

LYD. Is it possible! —

Enter JULIA

LYD. My dearest Julia, how delighted am I! — [*Embrace.*] How unexpected was this happiness!

JUL. True, Lydia — and our pleasure is the greater. — But what has been the matter? — you were denied to me at first!

LYD. Ah, Julia, I have a thousand things to tell you! — But first inform me what has conjur'd you to Bath? — Is Sir Anthony here?

JUL. He is — we are arrived within this hour — and I suppose he will be here to wait on Mrs. Malaprop as soon as he is dress'd.

LYD. Then before we are interrupted, let me impart to you some of my distress! I know your gentle nature will sympathize with me, tho' your prudence may condemn me! My letters have informed you of my whole connexion with Beverley; but I have lost him, Julia! My aunt has discovered our intercourse by a note she intercepted, and has confin'd me ever since! Yet, would you believe it? she has absolutely fallen[1] in love with a tall Irish baronet she met one night since she has[2] been here, at Lady Macshuffle's rout.

JUL. You jest, Lydia!

[illegible] upon my word. — She really[3] carries on a kind of [illegible]e with him, under a feigned name though, till she [illegible] known to him; — but it is a *Delia* or a *Celia*, [illegible]

JUL. Then, surely, she is now more indulgent to her niece.

LYD. Quite the contrary. Since she has discovered her own frailty, she is become more suspicious of mine. [illegible] must inform you of another plague! — That odi[illegible] to be

[1] RR: fallen absolutely. [2] RR: we have. [3] [illegible]ely.

in Bath to-day; so that I protest I shall be teased out of all spirits!

JUL. Come, come, Lydia, hope the best — Sir Anthony shall use his interest with Mrs. Malaprop.

LYD. But you have not heard the worst. Unfortunately I had quarrelled with my poor Beverley, just before my aunt made the discovery, and I have not seen him since, to make it up.

JUL. What was his offence?

LYD. Nothing at all! — But, I don't know how it was, as often as we had been together, we had never had a quarrel! And, somehow I was afraid he would never give me an opportunity. — So, last Thursday, I wrote a letter to myself, to inform myself that Beverley was at that time paying his addresses to another woman. — I sign'd it *your Friend unknown*, showed it to Beverley, charg'd him with his falsehood, put myself in a violent passion, and vow'd I'd never see him more.

JUL. And you let him depart so, and have not seen him since?

LYD. 'Twas the next day my aunt found the matter out. I intended only to have teased him three days and a half, and now I've lost him for ever.

JUL. If he is as deserving and sincere as you have represented him to me, he will never give you up so. Yet, consider, Lydia, you tell me he is but an ensign, and you have thirty thousand pounds!

LYD. But you know I lose most of my fortune, if I marry without my aunt's consent, till of age; and that is what I have determin'd to do, ever since I knew the penalty. Nor could I love the man, who would wish to wait a day for the alternative.

JUL. Nay, this is caprice!

LYD. What, does Julia tax me with caprice? — I thought her lover Faulkland had enured her to it.

I do not love even *his* faults.

LYD. But a-propos — you have sent to him, I suppose?

JUL. Not yet, upon my word — nor has he the least idea of my being in Bath. — Sir Anthony's resolution was so sudden, I could not inform him of it.

LYD. Well, Julia, you are your own mistress (though under the protection of Sir Anthony) yet have you, for this long year, been the [1] slave to the caprice, the whim, the jealousy of this ungrateful Faulkland, who will ever delay assuming the right of a husband, while you suffer him to be equally imperious as a lover.

JUL. Nay, you are wrong entirely. We were contracted before my father's death. — *That*, and some consequent embarrassments, have delay'd what I know to be my Faulkland's most ardent wish. — He is too generous to trifle on such a point — and for his character, you wrong him there, too. — Lydia, he is too proud, too noble to be jealous; if he is captious, 'tis without dissembling; if fretful, without rudeness. — Unus'd to the foppery [2] of love, he is negligent of the little duties expected from a lover — but being unhackney'd in the passion, his love [3] is ardent and sincere; and as it engrosses his whole soul, he expects every thought and emotion of his mistress to move in unison with his. — Yet, though his pride calls for this full return — his humility makes him undervalue those qualities in him, which should [4] entitle him to it; and not feeling why he should be lov'd to the degree he wishes, he still suspects that he is not lov'd enough. — This temper, I must own, has cost me many unhappy hours; but I have learned to think myself his debtor, for those imperfections which arise from the ardour of his love.[5]

LYD. Well, I cannot blame you for defending him. — But tell me candidly, Julia, had he never sav'd your life, do you

[1] R 3: a. [2] R 3: fopperies. [3] R 3: affection.
[4] R 3: would. [5] R 3: attachment.

think you should have been attach'd to him as you are? — Believe me, the rude blast that overset your boat was a prosperous gale of love to him.

JUL. Gratitude may have strengthened my attachment to Mr. Faulkland, but I loved him before he had preserv'd me, yet surely that alone were an obligation sufficient.

LYD. Obligation! — why a water spaniel would have done as much! — Well, I should never think of giving my heart to a man because he could swim!

JUL. Come, Lydia, you are too inconsiderate.

LYD. Nay, I do but jest — What's here?

Enter LUCY *in a hurry*

LUCY. O Ma'am, here is Sir Anthony Absolute just come home with your aunt.

LYD. They'll not come here. — Lucy do you watch.

[*Exit* LUCY.

JUL. Yet I must go. — Sir Anthony does not know I am here, and if we meet, he'll detain me, to show me the town. I'll take another opportunity of paying my respects to Mrs. Malaprop, when she shall treat me, as long as she chooses, with her select words so ingeniously *misapplied*, without being *mispronounced.*

Re-enter LUCY

LUCY. O Lud! Ma'am, they are both coming upstairs.

LYD. Well, I'll not detain you, Coz. — Adieu, my dear Julia, I'm sure you are in haste to send to Faulkland.— There — through my room you'll find another staircase.

JUL. Adieu! [*Embrace.*] [*Exit* JULIA.

LYD. Here, my dear Lucy, hide these books. Quick, quick! — Fling *Peregrine Pickle* under the toilet — throw *Roderick Random* into the closet — put *The Innocent Adultery* into *The Whole Duty of Man* — thrust *Lord Aimworth* under the sofa — cram *Ovid* behind the bolster — there — put *The Man of*

Feeling into your pocket [illegible] — now lay *Mrs. Chapone* in sight, and leave *Fordyce's Ser[illegible]s* open on the table.

LUCY. O burn it, Ma'am! the hair-dresser has torn away as far as *Proper Pri[illegible]*

[illegible] open at *Sobriety*. — Fling me *Lord* [illegible] — Now for 'em. [*Exit* LUCY.

[illegible] PROP, *and* SIR ANTHONY ABSOLUTE

MRS. MAL. There, Sir Anthony, there sits the deliberate Simpleton who wants to disgrace her family, and lavish herself on a fellow not worth a shilling.

LYD. Madam, I thought you once ——

MRS. MAL. You thought, Miss! — I don't know any business you have to think at all — thought does not become a young woman; the point we would request of you is, that you will promise to forget this fellow — to illiterate him, I say, quite from your memory.

[illegible] memories are independent of our [illegible] forget.

[illegible] Miss; there is nothing on earth [illegible] person chooses to set about it. — I'm sure I have as much forgot your poor dear uncle as if he had never existed — and I thought it my duty so to do; and let me tell you, Lydia, these violent memories don't become a young woman.

SIR ANTH. Why sure she won't pretend to remember what she's ordered not! — aye, this comes of her reading!

LYD. What crime, Madam, have I committed, to be treated thus?

MRS. MAL. Now don't attempt to extirpate yourself from the matter; you know I have proof controvertible of it. — But tell me, will you promise to do as you're bid? — Will you tal[illegible] a husband of your friends choosing?

LYD. Madam, I must tell you plainly, tha[illegible]efe

ence for any one else, the choice you have made would be my aversion.

MRS. MAL. What business have you, Miss, with *preference* and *aversion?* They don't become a young woman; and you ought to know, that as both always wear off, 'tis safest in matrimony to begin with a little *aversion.* I am sure I hated your poor dear uncle before marriage as if he'd been a black-a-moor — and yet, Miss, you are sensible what a wife I made! — and when it pleas'd Heaven to release me from him, 'tis unknown what tears I shed! — But suppose we were going to give you another choice, will you promise us to give up this Beverley?

LYD. Could I belie my thoughts so far, as to give that promise, my actions would certainly as far belie my words.

MRS. MAL. Take yourself to your room. — You are fit company for nothing but your own ill-humours.

LYD. Willingly, Ma'am — I cannot change for the worse.

[*Exit* LYDIA.

MRS. MAL. There's a little intricate hussy for you!

SIR ANTH. It is not to be wondered at, Ma'am, — all this is the natural consequence of teaching girls to read. Had I a thousand daughters, by Heavens![1] I'd as soon have them taught the black art as their alphabet!

MRS. MAL. Nay, nay, Sir Anthony, you are an absolute misanthropy.

SIR ANTH. In my way hither, Mrs. Malaprop, I observed your niece's maid coming forth from a circulating library! — She had a book in each hand — they were half-bound volumes, with marbled covers! — From that moment I guess'd how full of duty I should see her mistress!

MRS. MAL. Those are vile places, indeed!

SIR ANTH. Madam, a circulating library in a town is, as an evergreen tree, of diabolical knowledge! — It blossoms through

[1] R 3: heaven.

the year! — And depend on it, Mrs. Malaprop, that they who are so fond of handling the leaves, will long for the fruit at last.

«MRS. MAL. Well, but Sir Anthony, your wife, Lady Absolute, was fond of books.

«SIR ANTH. Aye — and injury sufficient they were to her, Madam — but were I to chuse another helpmate, the extent of her erudition should consist in[1] knowing her simple letters, without their mischievous combinations; — and the summit of her science be — her ability to count as far as twenty. — The first, Mrs. Malaprop, would enable her to work *A. A.* upon my linen; — and the latter would be quite sufficient to prevent her giving me a Shirt, No. 1, and a Stock No. 2.»

MRS. MAL. Fie, fie, Sir Anthony! you surely speak laconically!

SIR ANTH. Why, Mrs. Malaprop, in moderation now, what would you have a woman know?

MRS. MAL. Observe me, Sir Anthony. I would by no means wish a daughter of mine to be a progeny of learning; I don't think so much learning becomes a young woman; for instance, I would never let her meddle with Greek, or Hebrew, Algebra, or Simony, or Fluxions, or Paradoxes, or such lammatory branches of learning — neither would it be neces-ry for her to handle any of your mathematical, astronomical, bolical instruments. — But, Sir Anthony, I would send her, at nine years old, to a boarding-school, in order to learn a little ingenuity and artifice. Then, Sir, she should have a supercilious knowledge in accounts; — and as she grew up, I would have her instructed in geometry, that she might know something of the contagious countries; — but above all, Sir Anthony, she should be mistress of orthodoxy, that she might not mis-spell, and mis-pronounce words so shamefully as girls usually do; and likewise that she might reprehend the true meaning of what she is saying. — This, Sir Anthony, is what

[1] RR: in her.

I would have a woman know; — and I don't think there is a superstitious article in it.

SIR ANTH. Well, well, Mrs. Malaprop, I will dispute the point no further with you; though I must confess, that you are a truly moderate and polite arguer, for almost every third word you say is on my side of the question. — But, Mrs Malaprop, to the more important point in debate — you say, you have no objection to my proposal?

MRS. MAL. None, I assure you. — I am under no positive engagement with Mr. Acres, and as Lydia is so obstinate against him, perhaps your son may have better success.

SIR ANTH. Well, Madam, I will write for the boy directly. — He knows not a syllable of this yet, though I have for some time had the proposal in my head. He is at present with his regiment.

MRS. MAL. We have never seen your son, Sir Anthony; but I hope no objection on his side.

SIR ANTH. Objection! — let him object if he dare! — No, no, Mrs. Malaprop, Jack knows that the least demur puts me in a frenzy directly. — My process was always very simple — in their younger days, 'twas "Jack do this"; — if he demurred, I knocked him down — and if he grumbled at that, I always sent him out of the room.

MRS. MAL. Aye, and the properest way, o' my conscience! — nothing is so conciliating to young people as severity. — Well, Sir Anthony, I shall give Mr. Acres his discharge, and prepare Lydia to receive your son's invocations; — and I hope you will represent *her* to the Captain as an object not altogether illegible.

SIR ANTH. Madam, I will handle the subject prudently. — Well, I must leave you; and let me beg you, Mrs. Malaprop, to enforce this matter roundly to the girl. — Take my advice — keep a tight hand; if she rejects this proposal, clap her under lock and key; and if you were just to let the servants forget to bring her dinner for three or four days, you can't conceive how she'd come about. [*Exit* SIR ANTH.

MRS. MAL. Well, at any rate, I shall be glad to get her from under my intuition. — She has somehow discovered my partiality for Sir Lucius O'Trigger — sure, Lucy can't have betray'd me! — No, the girl is such a simpleton, I should have made her confess it. — Lucy! — Lucy! — [*Calls.*] Had she been one of your artificial ones, I should never have trusted her.

Enter LUCY

LUCY. Did you call, Ma'am?

MRS. MAL. Yes, girl. — Did you see Sir Lucius while you was out?

LUCY. No, indeed, Ma'am, not a glimpse of him.

MRS. MAL. You are sure, Lucy, that you never mention'd ——

LUCY. O Gemini! I'd sooner cut my tongue out.

MRS. MAL. Well, don't let your simplicity be imposed on.

LUCY. No, Ma'am.

MRS. MAL. So, come to me presently, and I'll give you another letter to Sir Lucius; — but mind, Lucy — if ever you betray what you are entrusted with — (unless it be other people's secrets to me) you forfeit my malevolence for ever: — and your being a simpleton shall be no excuse for your locality. [*Exit* MRS. MALAPROP.

LUCY. Ha! ha! ha! — So, my dear *simplicity*, let me give you a little respite. — [*Altering her manner.*] Let girls in my station be as fond as they please of appearing expert, and knowing in their trusts; — commend me to a mask of *silliness*, and a pair of sharp eyes for my own interest under it! — Let me see to what account have I[1] turn'd my *simplicity* lately. — [*Looks at a paper.*] For *abetting Miss Lydia Languish in a design of running away with an Ensign! — in money sundry*

[1] R 1, 2: I have.

times, twelve pound twelve; gowns, five; hats, ruffles, caps, &c., &c., numberless! — *From the said Ensign, within this last month, six guineas and a half.* — About a quarter's pay! — Item, *from Mrs. Malaprop, for betraying the young people to her* — when I found matters were likely to be discovered — *two guineas, and a black paduasoy.* — Item, *from Mr. Acres, for carrying divers letters* — which I never deliver'd — *two guineas, and a pair of buckles.* — Item, *from Sir Lucius O'Trigger, three crowns, two gold pocket-pieces, and a silver snuff-box!* — Well done, *simplicity!* — Yet I was forced to make my Hibernian believe that he was corresponding, not with the *Aunt*, but with the *Niece:* for though not over rich, I found he had too much pride and delicacy to sacrifice the feelings of a gentleman to the necessities of his fortune. [*Exit.*

END OF THE FIRST ACT

ACT II

Scene I. — Captain Absolute's *Lodgings*

Captain Absolute *and* Fag

Fag. Sir, while I was there, Sir Anthony came in: I told him you had sent me to inquire after his health, and to know if he was at leisure to see you.

Abs. And what did he say, on hearing I was at Bath?

Fag. Sir, in my life I never saw an elderly gentleman more astonished! He started back two or three paces, rapt out a dozen interjectoral oaths, and asked what the devil had brought you here!

Abs. Well, sir, and what did you say?

Fag. Oh, I lied, Sir — I forgot[1] the precise lie; but you may depend on't, he got no truth from me. Yet, with submission, for fear of blunders in future, I should be glad to fix what *has*

[1] R 3: forget.

brought us to Bath: in order that we may lie a little consistently. Sir Anthony's servants were curious, Sir, very curious indeed.

ABS. You have said nothing to them ——?

FAG. Oh, not a word, Sir, — not a word! Mr. Thomas, indeed, the coachman (whom I take to be the discreetest of whips) ——

ABS. 'Sdeath! — you rascal! you have not trusted him!

FAG. Oh, *no*, sir — no — no — not a syllable, upon my veracity! — He was, indeed, a little inquisitive; but I was sly, sir — devilish sly! My Master (said I), honest Thomas (you know, Sir, one says *honest* to one's inferiors), is come to Bath to *recruit*. — Yes, sir, I said to *recruit* — and whether for men, money, or constitution, you know, Sir, is nothing to him, nor any one else.

ABS. Well, *recruit* will do — let it be so.

FAG. Oh, Sir, recruit will do surprisingly — indeed, to give the thing an air, I told Thomas that your honour had already inlisted five disbanded chairmen, seven minority waiters, and thirteen billiard-markers.

ABS. You blockhead, never say more than is necessary.

FAG. I beg pardon, Sir — I beg pardon — But, with submission, a lie is nothing unless one supports it. Sir, whenever I draw on my invention for a good current lie, I always forge *indorsements* as well as the bill.

ABS. Well, take care you don't hurt your credit by offering too much security. — Is Mr. Faulkland returned?

FAG. He is above, Sir, changing his dress.

ABS. Can you tell whether he has been informed of Sir Anthony's and Miss Melville's arrival?

FAG. I fancy not, Sir; he has seen no one since he came in, but his gentleman, who was with him at Bristol. — I think, Sir, I hear Mr. Faulkland coming down ——

ABS. Go, tell him, I am here.

FAG. Yes, Sir. — [*Going.*] I beg pardon, Sir, but should Sir Anthony call, you will do me the favour to remember that we are *recruiting*, if you please.

ABS. Well, well.

FAG. And, in tenderness to my character, if your Honour could bring in the chairmen and waiters, I should[1] esteem it as an obligation; for though I never scruple a lie to serve my Master, yet it *hurts* one's conscience to be found out. [*Exit.*

ABS. Now for my whimsical friend — if he does not know that his mistress is here, I'll tease him a little before I tell him ——

Enter FAULKLAND

Faulkland, you're welcome to Bath again; you are punctual in your return.

FAULK. Yes; I had nothing to detain me when I had finished the business I went on. Well, what news since I left you? how stand matters between you and Lydia?

ABS. Faith, much as they were; I have not seen her since our quarrel; however, I expect to be recalled every hour.

FAULK. Why don't you persuade her to go off with you at once?

ABS. What, and lose two-thirds of her fortune? You forget that, my friend. — No, no, I could have brought her to that long ago.

FAULK. Nay, then, you trifle too long — if you are sure of *her*, propose to the aunt *in your own character*, and write to Sir Anthony for his consent.

ABS. Softly, softly; for though I am convinced my little Lydia would elope with me as Ensign Beverley, yet am I by no means certain that she would take me with the impediment of our friends' consent, a regular humdrum wedding, and a reversion of a good fortune on my side; no, no; I must prepare her gradually for the discovery, and make myself necessary to

[1] RR: shall.

her, before I risk it. — Well, but Faulkland, you'll dine with us to-day at the Hotel?

Faulk. Indeed, I cannot; I am not in spirits to be of such a party.

Abs. By Heavens! I shall forswear your company. You are the most teasing, captious, incorrigible lover! — Do, love like a man.

Faulk. I own I am unfit for company.

Abs. Am *I* not[1] a lover; ay, and a romantic one too? Yet do I carry everywhere with me such a confounded farrago of doubts, fears, hopes, wishes, and all the flimsy furniture of a country Miss's brain!

Faulk. Ah! Jack, your heart and soul are not, like mine, fixed immutably on one only object. — You throw for a large stake, but losing — you could stake, and throw again: — but I have set my sum of happiness on this cast, and not to succeed, were to be stript of all.

Abs. But, for Heaven's sake! what grounds for apprehension can your whimsical brain conjure up at present? «Has Julia missed writing this last post? or was her last too tender, or too cool; or too grave, or too gay; or —

«Faulk. Nay, nay, Jack.

«Abs. Why, her love — her honour — her prudence, you cannot doubt.

«Faulk. O! upon my soul, I never have; — but» what grounds for apprehension, did you say? Heavens! are there not a thousand! I fear for her spirits — her health — her life. — My absence may fret her; her anxiety for my return, her fears for me, may oppress her gentle temper. And for her health — does not every hour bring me cause to be alarmed? If it rains, some shower may even then have chilled her delicate frame! — If the wind be keen, some rude blast may have affected her! The heat of noon, the dews of the evening, may endanger

[1] RR: Am not *I*.

the life of her, for whom only I value mine. O! Jack! when delicate and feeling souls are separated, there is not a feature in the sky, not a movement of the elements; not an aspiration of the breeze, but hints some cause for a lover's apprehension!

ABS. Aye, but we may choose whether we will take the hint or no.[1] — Well then, Faulkland, if you were convinced that Julia was well and in spirits, you would be entirely content.

FAULK. I should be happy beyond measure — I am anxious only for that.

ABS. Then to cure your anxiety at once — Miss Melville is in perfect health, and is at this moment in Bath.

FAULK. Nay, Jack — don't trifle with me.

ABS. She is arrived here with my father within this hour.

FAULK. Can you be serious?

ABS. I thought you knew Sir Anthony better than to be surprised at a sudden whim of this kind.—Seriously, then, it is as I tell you — upon my honour.

FAULK. My dear friend! — Hollo, Du-Peigne! my hat — my dear Jack — *now nothing on earth can give me a moment's uneasiness.*

Enter FAG

FAG. Sir, Mr. Acres just arrived is below.

ABS. Stay, Faulkland, this Acres lives within a mile of Sir Anthony, and he shall tell you how your mistress has been ever since you left her. — Fag, show the gentleman up.

[*Exit* FAG.

FAULK. What, is he much acquainted in the family?

ABS. Oh, very intimate: I insist on your not going: besides, his character will divert you.

FAULK. Well, I should like to ask him a few questions.

ABS. He is likewise a rival of mine — that is of my *other self's*, for he does not think his friend Captain Absolute ever saw the lady in question; — and it is ridiculous enough to hear

[1] R 3: not.

him complain to me of *one Beverley*, a concealed skulking rival, who ——

FAULK. Hush! — He's here.

Enter ACRES

ACRES. Hah! my dear friend, noble captain, and honest Jack, how do'st thou? just arrived faith, as you see. — Sir, your humble servant. Warm work on the roads, Jack! — Odds, whips and wheels, I've travelled like a Comet, with a tail of dust all the way as long as the Mall.

ABS. Ah! Bob, you are indeed an excentric planet, but we know your attraction hither — give me leave to introduce Mr. Faulkland to you; Mr. Faulkland, Mr. Acres.

ACRES. Sir, I am most heartily glad to see you: Sir, I solicit your connections. — Hey, Jack — what, this is Mr. Faulkland, who ——

ABS. Aye, Bob, Miss Melville's Mr. Faulkland.

ACRES. Od'so! she and your father can be but just arrived before me — I suppose you have seen them. — Ah! Mr. Faulkland, you are indeed a happy man.

FAULK. I have not seen Miss Melville yet, Sir; — I hope she enjoyed full health and spirits in Devonshire?

ACRES. Never knew her better in my life, Sir, — never better. Odds Blushes and Blooms! she has been as healthy as the German Spa.

FAULK. Indeed! — I did hear that she had been a little indisposed.

ACRES. False, false, Sir — only said to vex you: quite the reverse, I assure you.

FAULK. There, Jack, you see she has the advantage of me; I had almost fretted myself ill.

ABS. Now are you angry with your mistress for not having been sick.

FAULK. No, no, you misunderstand me: — yet surely a

little trifling indisposition is not an unnatural consequence of absence from those we love. — Now confess — isn't there something unkind in this violent, robust, unfeeling health?

ABS. Oh, it was very unkind of her to be well in your absence to be sure!

ACRES. Good apartments, Jack.

FAULK. Well, Sir, but you were saying that Miss Melville has been so *exceedingly* well — what then she has been merry and gay I suppose? — Always in spirits — hey?

ACRES. Merry, Odds Crickets! she has been the belle and spirit of the company wherever she has been — so lively and entertaining! so full of wit and humour!

FAULK. There, Jack, there. — O, by my soul! there is an innate levity in woman, that nothing can overcome. — What! happy and I away!

ABS. Have done: How foolish this is! just now you were only apprehensive for your mistress' *spirits*.

FAULK. Why, Jack, have I been the joy and spirit of the company?

ABS. No, indeed, you have not.

FAULK. Have I been lively and entertaining?

ABS. O, upon my word, I acquit you.

FAULK. Have I been full of wit and humour?

ABS. No, faith, to do you justice, you have been confoundedly [1] stupid indeed.

ACRES. What's the matter with the gentleman?

ABS. He is only expressing his great satisfaction at hearing that Julia has been so well and happy — that's all — hey, Faulkland?

FAULK. Oh! I am rejoiced to hear it — yes, yes, she has a *happy* disposition!

ACRES. That she has indeed — then she is so accomplished

[1] R 1, 2: confounded.

— so sweet a voice — so expert at her Harpsichord — such a mistress of flat and sharp, squallante, rumblante, and quiverante! — There was this time month — Odds Minims[1] and Crotchets! how she did chirrup at Mrs. Piano's Concert!

FAULK. There again, what say you to this? you see she has been all mirth and song — not a thought of me!

ABS. Pho! man, is not music the food of love?

FAULK. Well, well, it may be so. — Pray, Mr. ——, what's his d—d name? — Do you remember what Songs Miss Melville sung?

ACRES. Not I indeed.

ABS. Stay, now, they were some pretty melancholy, purling-stream airs, I warrant; perhaps you may recollect; — did she sing, *When absent from my soul's delight?*

ACRES. No, that wa'n't it.

ABS. Or — *Go, gentle Gales! "Go, gentle Gales!"* [*Sings.*

ACRES. O no! nothing like it. Odds slips?[2] now I recollect one of them — "*My heart's my own, my will is free.*" [*Sings.*

FAULK. Fool! fool that I am! to fix all my happiness upon such a trifler! 'Sdeath! to make herself the pipe and ballad-monger of a circle! to sooth her light heart with catches and glees! — What can you say to this, Sir?

ABS. Why, that I should be glad to hear my mistress had been so merry, *Sir.*

FAULK. Nay, nay, nay — I'm not sorry that she has been happy — no, no, I am glad of that — I would not have had her sad or sick — yet surely a sympathetic heart would have shown itself even in the choice of a song — she might have been temperately healthy, and somehow, plaintively gay; — but she has been dancing too, I doubt not!

ACRES. What does the gentleman say about dancing?

ABS. He says the lady we speak of dances as well as she sings.

[1] RR: Odds Minnums. [2] R 3: Odds!

ACRES. Ay, truly, does she — there was at our last race ball ——

FAULK. Hell and the devil! — There! — there — I told you so![1] Oh! she thrives in my absence! — Dancing! But her whole feelings have been in opposition with mine! — I have been anxious, silent, pensive, sedentary — my days have been hours of care, my nights of watchfulness. — She has been all health! Spirit! Laugh! Song! Dance! — Oh! d—nd, d—e'd levity!

ABS. For Heaven's sake, Faulkland, don't expose yourself so! — Suppose she has danced, what then? — does not the ceremony of society often oblige ——

FAULK. Well, well, I'll contain myself — perhaps as you say — for form sake. — What, Mr. Acres, you were praising Miss Melville's manner of dancing a *minuet* — hey?

ACRES. O, I dare insure her for that — but what I was going to speak of was her *country dancing.* Odds swimmings! she has such an air with her!

FAULK. Now disappointment on her! — Defend this, Absolute; why don't you defend this? — Country-dances! jiggs and reels! am I to blame now? A Minuet I could have forgiven — I should not have minded that — I say I should not have regarded a Minuet — but *Country-dances!* — Z—ds! had she made one in a *Cotillon* — I believe I could have forgiven even that — but to be monkey-led for a night! — to run the gauntlet thro' a string of amorous palming puppies! — to show paces like a managed filly! — Oh, Jack, there never can be but *one* man in the world, whom a truly modest and delicate woman ought to pair with in a *country-dance;* and, even then, the rest of the couples should be her great-uncles and aunts!

ABS. Aye, to be sure! — grandfathers and grandmothers!

FAULK. If there be but one vicious mind in the Set, 'twill spread like a contagion — the action of their pulse beats to

[1] RR repeat "I told you so."

the lascivious movement of the jigg — their quivering, warm-breathed sighs impregnate the very air — the atmosphere becomes electrical to love, and each amorous spark darts thro' every link of the chain! — I must leave you — I own I am somewhat flurried — and that confounded looby has perceived it. [*Going.*

«ABS. Aye, aye, you are in a hurry to throw yourself at Julia's feet.

«FAULK. I'm not in a humour to be trifled with — I shall see her only to upbraid her.»

ABS. Nay, but stay, Faulkland, and thank Mr. Acres for his good news.

FAULK. D—n his news! [*Exit* FAULKLAND.

ABS. Ha! ha! ha! poor Faulkland five minutes since — "nothing on earth could give him a moment's uneasiness!"

ACRES. The gentleman wa'n't angry at my praising his mistress, was he?

ABS. A little jealous, I believe, Bob.

ACRES. You don't say so? Ha! ha! jealous of me — that's a good joke.

ABS. There's nothing strange in that, Bob: let me tell you, that sprightly grace and insinuating manner of your's will do some mischief among the girls here.

ACRES. Ah! you joke — ha! ha! mischief — ha! ha! but you know I am not my own property, my dear Lydia has forestalled me. She could never abide me in the country, because I used to dress so badly — but odds frogs and tambours! I shan't take matters so here, now ancient Madam has no voice in it — I'll make my old clothes know who's master. I shall straitway cashier the hunting-frock — and render my leather breeches incapable. My hair has been in training some time.

ABS. Indeed!

ACRES. Ay — and tho'ff the side curls are a little restive, my hind-part takes to it very kindly.

ABS. O, you'll polish, I doubt not.

ACRES. Absolutely I propose so — then if I can find out this Ensign Beverley, odds triggers and flints! I'll make him know the difference o't.

ABS. Spoke like a man! But pray, Bob, I observe you have got an odd kind of a new method of swearing ——

ACRES. Ha! ha! you've taken notice of it — 'tis genteel, isn't it? — I didn't invent it myself though; but a commander in our militia — a great scholar, I assure you — says that there is no meaning in the common oaths, and that nothing but their antiquity makes them respectable; because, he says, the ancients would never stick to an oath or two, but would say, by Jove! or by Bacchus! or by Mars! or by Venus! or by Pallus,[1] according to the sentiment — so that to swear with propriety, says my little Major, the 'oath should be an echo to the sense'; and this we call the *oath referential*, or *sentimental swearing* — ha! ha! ha! 'tis genteel, isn't it.

ABS. Very genteel, and very new, indeed — and I dare say will supplant all other figures of imprecation.

ACRES. Aye, aye, the best terms will grow obsolete. —D—ns have had their day.

Enter FAG

FAG. Sir, there is a gentleman below desires to see you. — Shall I show him into the parlour?

ABS. Aye — you may.

ACRES. Well, I must be gone ——

ABS. Stay; who is it, Fag?

FAG. Your father, sir.

ABS. You puppy, why didn't you show him up directly?

[*Exit* FAG.

ACRES. You have business with Sir Anthony. — I expect a message from Mrs. Malaprop at my lodgings. I have sent also to my dear friend, Sir Lucius O'Trigger. Adieu, Jack!

[1] RR: Pallas.

we must meet at night. Odds bottles and glasses![1] you shall give me a dozen bumpers to little Lydia.

ABS. That I will with all my heart. — [*Exit* ACRES.] Now for a parental lecture — I hope he has heard nothing of the business that brought[2] me here — I wish the gout had held him fast in Devonshire, with all my soul!

Enter SIR ANTHONY

ABS. Sir I am delighted to see you here; looking[3] so well! your sudden arrival at Bath made me apprehensive for your health.

SIR ANTH. Very apprehensive, I dare say, Jack. — What, you are recruiting here, hey?

ABS. Yes, Sir, I am on duty.

SIR ANTH. Well, Jack, I am glad to see you, tho' I did not expect it, for I was going to write to you on a little matter of business. — Jack, I have been considering that I grow old and infirm, and shall probably not trouble you long.

ABS. Pardon me, Sir, I never saw you look more strong and hearty; and I pray frequently that you may continue so.

SIR ANTH. I hope your prayers may be heard with all my heart. Well, then, Jack, I have been considering that I am so strong and hearty, I may continue to plague you a long time. Now, Jack, I am sensible that the income of your commission, and what I have hitherto allowed you, is but a small pittance for a lad of your spirit.

ABS. Sir, you are very good.

SIR ANTH. And it is my wish, while yet I live, to have my Boy make some figure in the world. — I have resolved, therefore, to fix you at once in a noble independence.

ABS. Sir, your kindness overpowers me — such generosity makes the gratitude of reason more lively than the sensations even of filial affection.

[1] R 3: we must meet at night, when you.
[2] RR: has brought. [3] RR: and looking.

SIR ANTH. I am glad you are so sensible of my attention — and you shall be master of a large estate in a few weeks.

ABS. Let my future life, Sir, speak my gratitude: I cannot express the sense I have of your munificence. — Yet, sir, I presume you would not wish me to quit the army?

SIR ANTH. Oh, that shall be as your wife chooses.

ABS. My wife, Sir!

SIR ANTH. Aye, aye, settle that between you — settle that between you.

ABS. A *wife*, Sir, did you say?

SIR ANTH. Aye, a wife — why; did not I mention her before?

ABS. Not a word of it, Sir.

SIR ANTH. Odd so! — I mus'n't forget *her* tho'. — Yes, Jack, the independence I was talking of is by a marriage — the fortune is saddled with a wife — but I suppose that makes no difference.

ABS. Sir! Sir! — you amaze me!

SIR ANTH. Why, what the d—l's the matter with the fool? Just now you were all gratitude and duty.

ABS. I was, Sir — you talked to me of independence and a fortune, but not a word of a wife.

SIR ANTH. Why — what difference does that make? Odds life, Sir! if you have the estate, you must take it with the live stock on it, as it stands.

ABS. If my happiness is to be the price, I must beg leave to decline the purchase. — Pray, Sir, who is the lady?

SIR ANTH. What's that to you, Sir? — Come, give me your promise to love, and to marry her directly.

ABS. Sure, Sir, this is not very reasonable, to summon my affections for a lady I know nothing of!

SIR ANTH. I am sure, Sir, 'tis more unreasonable in you *to object* to a lady you know nothing of.

ABS. Then, Sir, I must tell you plainly that my inclinations are fix'd on another.

«SIR ANTH. They are, are they? Well that's lucky — because you will have more merit in your obedience to me.

«ABS. Sir,» my heart is engaged to an Angel.

SIR ANTH. Then pray let it send an excuse. It is very sorry — but *business* prevents its waiting on her.

ABS. But my vows are pledged to her.

SIR ANTH. Let her foreclose, Jack; let her foreclose; they are not worth redeeming: besides, you have the Angel's vows in exchange, I suppose; so there can be no loss there.

ABS. You must excuse me, Sir, if I tell you, once for all, that in this point I cannot obey you.

SIR ANTH. Hark'ee, Jack; — I have heard you for some time with patience — I have been cool — quite cool; but take care — you know I am compliance itself — when I am not thwarted; — no one more easily led — when I have my own way; — but don't put me in a frenzy.

ABS. Sir, I must repeat — in this I cannot obey you.

SIR ANTH. Now d—n me! if ever I call you *Jack* again while I live!

ABS. Nay, Sir, but hear me.

SIR ANTH. Sir, I won't hear a word — not a word! not one word! so give me your promise by a nod — and I'll tell you what, Jack — I mean, you Dog — if you don't by ——

ABS. What, Sir, promise to link myself to some mass of ugliness! to ——

SIR ANTH. Zounds! sirrah! the lady shall be as ugly as I choose: she shall have a hump on each shoulder; she shall be as crooked as the Crescent; her one eye shall roll like the Bull's in Cox's Museum; she shall have a skin like a mummy, and the beard of a Jew — she shall be all this, sirrah! — yet I'll make you ogle her all day, and sit up all night to write sonnets on her beauty.

ABS. This is reason and moderation indeed!

Sir Anth. None of your sneering, puppy! no grinning, jackanapes!

Abs. Indeed, Sir, I never was in a worse humour for mirth in my life.

Sir Anth. 'Tis false, Sir! I know you are laughing in your sleeve: I know you will grin when I am gone, sirrah!

Abs. Sir, I hope I know my duty better.

Sir Anth. None of your passion, Sir! none of your violence, if you please! — It won't do with me, I promise you.

Abs. Indeed, Sir, I never was cooler in my life.

Sir Anth. 'Tis a confounded lie! — I know you are in a passion in your heart; I know you are, you hypocritical young dog! but it won't do.

Abs. Nay, Sir, upon my word.

Sir Anth. So you will fly out! can't you be cool, like me? What the devil good can *Passion* do? — *Passion* is of no service, you impudent, insolent, overbearing Reprobate! — There, you sneer again! don't provoke me! — but you rely upon the mildness of my temper — you do, you Dog! you play upon the weakness of my disposition! — Yet take care — the patience of a saint may be overcome at last! — but mark! I give you six hours and a half to consider of this: if you then agree, without any condition, to do everything on earth that I choose, why — confound you! I may in time forgive you. — If not, z—ds! don't enter the same hemisphere with me! don't dare to breathe the same air, or use the same light with me; but get an atmosphere and a sun of your own! I'll strip you of your commission; I'll lodge a five-and-threepence in the hands of trustees, and you shall live on the interest. — I'll disown you, I'll disinherit you, I'll unget you! and d—n me, if ever I call you Jack again! [*Exit* Sir Anthony.

Absolute *solus*

Abs. Mild, gentle, considerate father — I kiss your hands! — What a tender method of giving his opinion in these matters

Sir Anthony has! I dare not trust him with the truth. — I wonder what old wealthy Hag it is that he wants to bestow on me! — Yet he married himself for love! and was in his youth a bold Intriguer, and a gay Companion!

Enter FAG

FAG. Assuredly, Sir, our Father is wrath to a degree; he comes down stairs eight or ten steps at a time — muttering, growling, and thumping the bannisters all the way: I, and the Cook's dog stand bowing at the door — rap! he gives me a stroke on the head with his cane; bids me carry that to my master, then kicking the poor Turnspit into the area, d—ns us all, for a puppy triumvirate! — Upon my credit, Sir, were I in your place, and found my father such very bad company, I should certainly drop his acquaintance.

ABS. Cease your impertinence, Sir, at present. — Did you come in for nothing more? — Stand out of the way!

[*Pushes him aside, and Exit.*

FAG, *solus*

FAG. Soh! Sir Anthony trims my Master; He is afraid to reply to his Father — then vents his spleen on poor Fag! — When one is vexed by one person, to revenge one's self on another, who happens to come in the way, is the vilest injustice! Ah! it shows the worst temper — the basest ——

Enter ERRAND-BOY

BOY. Mr. Fag! Mr. Fag! your Master calls you.

FAG. Well, you little dirty puppy, you need not baul so! — The meanest disposition! the ——

BOY. Quick, quick, Mr. Fag!

FAG. *Quick! quick!* you impudent Jackanapes! am I to be commanded by you too? you little, impertinent, insolent, kitchenbred —— [*Exit, kicking and beating him.*

SCENE II. — *The North Parade*

Enter LUCY

LUCY. So — I shall have another Rival to add to my mistress's list — Captain Absolute. However, I shall not enter his name till my purse has received notice in form. Poor Acres is dismissed! — Well, I have done him a last friendly office, in letting him know that Beverley was here before him. — Sir Lucius is generally more punctual, when he expects to hear from his *dear Dalia*, as he calls her: I wonder he's not here! — I have a little scruple of conscience from this deceit; tho' I should not be paid so well, if my hero knew that Delia was near fifty, and her own mistress. «—I could not have thought he would have been so nice, when there's a golden egg in the case, as to care whether he has it from a pullet or an old hen.»

Enter SIR LUCIUS O'TRIGGER

SIR LUC. Hah! my little ambassadress — upon my conscience, I have been looking for you; I have been on the South Parade this half hour.

LUCY. [*Speaking simply.*] O gemini! and I have been waiting for your worship here on the North.

SIR LUC. Faith! — may be, that was the reason we did not meet; and it is very comical too, how you could go out and I not see you — for I was only taking a nap at the Parade Coffee-house, and I chose the *window* on purpose that I might not miss you.

LUCY. My stars! Now I'd wager a sixpence I went by while you were asleep.

SIR LUC. Sure enough it must have been so — and I never dreamt it was so late, till I waked. Well, but my little girl, have you got nothing for me?

LUCY. Yes, but I have: — I've got a letter for you in my pocket.

SIR LUC. O faith! I guessed you weren't come empty handed. — Well — let me see what the dear creature says.

LUCY. There, Sir Lucius. [*Gives him a letter*

SIR LUC. [Reads.] *Sir — there is often a sudden incentive impulse in love, that has a greater induction than years of domestic combination: such was the commotion I felt at the first superfluous view of Sir Lucius O'Trigger.* — Very pretty, upon my word. — «*As my motive is interested, you may be assured my love shall never be miscellaneous.* Very well.»

Female punctuation forbids me to say more; yet let me add that it will give me joy infallible to find Sir Lucius worthy the last criterion of my affections. «*Yours, while meretricious.* — DELIA. Upon my conscience! Lucy, your lady is a great mistress of language. — Faith, she's quite the queen of the dictionary! — for the devil a word dare refuse coming at her call — though one would think it was quite out of hearing.

LUCY. Aye, Sir, a lady of her experience ——

SIR LUC. Experience! what, at seventeen?

LUCY. O true, Sir — but then she reads so — my stars! how she will read off-hand!

SIR LUC. Faith, she must be very deep read to write this way — tho' she is rather an arbitrary writer too — for here are a great many poor words pressed into the service of this note, that would get their *habeas corpus* from any court in Christendom. «— However, when affection guides the pen, Lucy, he must be a brute who finds fault with the style.»

LUCY. Ah! Sir Lucius, if you were to hear how she talks of you!

SIR LUC. Oh, tell her, I'll make her the best husband in the world, and Lady O'Trigger into the bargain! — But we must get the old gentlewoman's consent — and do everything fairly.

LUCY. Nay, Sir Lucius, I thought you wa'n't rich enough to be so nice.

SIR LUC. Upon my word, young woman, you have hit it: —

I am so poor, that I can't afford to do a dirty action. — If I did not want money, I'd steal your mistress and her fortune with a great deal of pleasure. — However, my pretty girl, [*gives her money*,] here's a little something to buy you a ribband; and meet me in the evening, and I'll give you an answer to this. So, hussy, take a kiss beforehand to put you in mind. [*Kisses her.*

LUCY. O lud! Sir Lucius — I never seed such a gemman! My lady won't like you if you're so impudent.

SIR LUC. Faith she will, Lucy! — That same — pho! what's the name of it? — *Modesty* — is a quality in a lover more praised by the women than liked; so, if your mistress asks you whether Sir Lucius ever gave you a kiss, tell her *fifty* — my dear.

LUCY. What, would you have me tell her a lie?

SIR LUC. Ah, then, you baggage! I'll make it a truth presently.

LUCY. For shame now; here is some one coming.

SIR LUC. Oh, faith, I'll quiet your conscience!

[*Sees* FAG. — *Exit, humming a tune.*

Enter FAG

FAG. So, so, Ma'am! I humbly beg pardon.

LUCY. O lud! now, Mr. Fag, you flurry one so.

FAG. Come, come, Lucy, here's no one bye — so a little less simplicity, with a grain or two more sincerity, if you please. — You play false with us, Madam. — I saw you give the baronet a letter. — My master shall know this — and if he don't call him out, I will.

LUCY. Ha! ha! ha! you gentlemen's gentlemen are so hasty. — That letter was from Mrs. Malaprop, simpleton. — She is taken with Sir Lucius's address.

FAG. [1]What tastes some people have! — Why, I suppose I

[1] R 3 inserts "How!"

have walked by her window an hundred times. — But what says our young lady? any message to my master?

Lucy. Sad news. Mr. Fag. — A worse Rival than Acres! Sir Anthony Absolute has proposed his son.

Fag. What, Captain Absolute?

Lucy. Even so — I overheard it all.

Fag. Ha! ha! ha! very good, faith. Good bye, Lucy, I must away with this news.

Lucy. Well, . . . you may laugh . . . but it is true, I assure you. — [*Going.*] But . . . Mr. Fag . . . tell your master not to be cast down by this.

Fag. O he'll be so disconsolate!

Lucy. And charge him not to think of quarrelling with young Absolute.

Fag. Never fear! . . . never fear!

Lucy. Be sure . . . bid him keep up his spirits.

Fag. We will . . . we will. [*Exeunt severally.*

END OF THE SECOND ACT

ACT III

Scene I. — *The North Parade*

Enter Absolute

'Tis just as Fag told me, indeed . . . Whimsical enough, faith! My Father wants to *force* me to marry the very girl I am plotting to run away with! — He must not know of my connection with her yet a-while. — He has too summary a method of proceeding in these matters . . . «and Lydia shall not yet lose her hopes of an elopement.» — However, I'll read my recantation instantly. — My conversion is something sudden, indeed . . . but I can assure him it is very *sincere.* So, so . . . here he comes. He looks plaguy gruff. [*Steps aside.*

Enter SIR ANTHONY

No . . . I'll die sooner than forgive him . . . *Die*, did I say! I'll live these fifty years to plague him. — At our last meeting, his impudence had almost put me out of temper . . . An obstinate, passionate, self-willed boy! . . . Who can he take after? This is my return for getting him before all his brothers and sisters! . . . for putting him at twelve years old, into a marching regiment, and allowing him fifty pounds a year, beside his pay, ever since! . . . But I have done with him; . . . he's anybody's son for me. — I never will see him more, never . . . never . . . never . . . never.

ABS. Now for a penitential face.

SIR ANTH. Fellow, get out of my way.

ABS. Sir, you see a penitent before you.

SIR ANTH. I see an impudent scoundrel before me.

ABS. A sincere penitent. — I am come, Sir, to acknowledge my error, and to submit entirely to your will.

SIR ANTH. What's that?

ABS. I have been revolving, and reflecting, and considering on your past goodness, and kindness, and condescension to me.

SIR ANTH. Well, sir?

ABS. I have been likewise weighing and balancing what you were pleased to mention concerning duty, and obedience, and authority.

SIR ANTH. Well, Puppy?

ABS. Why then, Sir, the result of my reflections is . . . a resolution to sacrifice every inclination of my own to your satisfaction.

SIR ANTH. Why now you talk sense . . . absolute sense . . . I never heard anything more sensible in my life . . . Confound you; you shall be *Jack* again.

ABS. I am happy in the appellation.

SIR ANTH. Why, then, Jack, my dear Jack, I will now

inform you . . . who the lady really is. — Nothing but your passion and violence, you silly fellow, prevented my telling you at first. Prepare, Jack, for wonder and rapture — prepare. — What think you of Miss Lydia Languish?

ABS. Languish! What, the Languishes of Worcestershire?

SIR ANTH. Worcestershire! no. Did you never meet Mrs. Malaprop and her Niece, Miss Languish, who came into our country just before you were last ordered to your regiment?

ABS. Malaprop! Languish! I don't remember ever to have heard the names before. Yet, stay — I think I do recollect something. — *Languish! Languish!* She squints, don't she? — A little, red-haired girl?

SIR ANTH. Squints? — A red-haired girl! — Z—ds! no.

ABS. Then I must have forgot; it can't be the same person.

SIR ANTH. Jack! Jack! what think you of blooming, love-breathing seventeen?

ABS. As to that, Sir, I am quite indifferent. — If I can please you in the matter, 'tis all I desire.

SIR ANTH. Nay, but Jack, such eyes! such eyes! so innocently wild! so bashfully irresolute! not a glance but speaks and kindles some thought of love! Then, Jack, her cheeks! her cheeks, Jack! so deeply blushing at the insinuations of her tell-tale eyes! Then, Jack, her lips! — O, Jack, lips smiling at their own discretion; and if not smiling, more sweetly pouting; more lovely in sullenness.

ABS. That's she, indeed. . . . Well done, old gentleman.

SIR ANTH. Then, Jack, her neck! — O Jack! Jack!

ABS. And which is to be mine, Sir; the Niece or the Aunt?

SIR ANTH. Why, you unfeeling, insensible Puppy, I despise you! When I was of your age, such a description would have made me fly like a rocket! The *Aunt*, indeed! Odds life! when I ran away with your mother, I would not have touched anything old or ugly to gain an empire.

ABS. Not to please your father, sir?

Sir Anth. To please my father! z—ds! not to please — Oh, my father — odd so! — yes — yes; if my father indeed had desired — that's quite another matter. Tho' he wa'n't the indulgent father that I am, Jack.

Abs. I dare say not, Sir.

Sir Anth. But, Jack, you are not sorry to find your mistress is so beautiful?

Abs.[1] Sir, I repeat it; if I please you in this affair, 'tis all I desire. Not that I think a woman the worse for being handsome; but, Sir, if you please to recollect, you before hinted something about a hump or two, one eye, and a few more graces of that kind — now, without being very nice, I own I should rather chuse a wife of mine to have the usual number of limbs, and a limited quantity of back: and tho' *one* eye may be very agreeable, yet as the prejudice has always run in favour of *two*, I would not wish to affect a singularity in that article.

Sir Anth. What a phlegmatic sot it is! Why, sirrah, you're an anchorite! — a vile, insensible stock. You a soldier! — you're a walking block, fit only to dust the company's regimentals on! — Odds life! I have[2] a great mind to marry the girl myself!

Abs. I am entirely at your disposal, sir: if you should think of addressing Miss Languish yourself, I suppose you would have me marry the *Aunt;* or if you should change your mind, and take the old lady — 'tis the same to me — I'll marry the *Niece.*

Sir Anth. Upon my word, Jack, thou'rt either a very great hypocrite, or — but, come, I know your indifference on such a subject must be all a lie — I'm sure it must — come, now — d—n your demure face! — come, confess Jack — you have been lying, ha'n't you! «You have been lying, hey? — I'll never forgive you, if you ha'n't: — So now, own, my dear

[1] R 1, 2: *Sir Anth.* — An obvious misprint. [2] RR: I've.

Jack,» you have been playing the hypocrite, hey! I'll never forgive you, if you ha'n't been lying and playing the hypocrite.

Abs. I'm sorry, sir, that the respect and duty which I bear to you should be so mistaken.

Sir Anth. Hang your respect and duty! But come along with me, I'll write a note to Mrs. Malaprop, and you shall visit the lady directly.

«Abs. Where does she lodge, Sir?

«Sir Anth. What a dull question! Only on the Grove here.

«Abs. O! then I can call on her in my way to the coffee-house.

«Sir Anth. In your way to the coffee-house! You'll set your heart down in your way to the coffee-house, hey? Ah! you leaden-nerv'd, wooden-hearted dolt! But come along, you shall see her directly;» her eyes shall be the Promethean torch to you — come along, I'll never forgive you, if you don't come back, stark mad with rapture and impatience — if you don't, egad, I'll marry the girl myself! [*Exeunt.*

Scene II. — Julia's *Dressing-room*

Faulkland *solus*

Faulk. They told me Julia would return directly; I wonder[1] she is not yet come! — How mean does this captious, unsatisfied temper of mine appear to my cooler judgment! Yet I know not that I indulge it in any other point: but on this one subject, and to this one object,[2] whom I think I love beyond my life, I am ever ungenerously fretful, and madly capricious! I am conscious of it — yet I cannot correct myself! What tender, honest joy sparkled in her eyes when we met! How delicate was the warmth of her expression! — I was ashamed to appear less happy — though I had come resolved to wear a face of coolness and upbraiding. Sir Anthony's presence prevented my proposed expostulations; yet I must be satisfied that she

[1] R 1, 2, omit "I". [2] R 3: subject.

has not been so *very* happy in my absence. She is coming! Yes! — I know the nimbleness of her tread, when she thinks her impatient Faulkland counts the moments of her stay.

Enter JULIA

JUL. I had not hop'd to see you again so soon.

FAULK. Could I, Julia, be contented with my first welcome — restrained as we were by the presence of a third person?

JUL. O Faulkland, when your kindness can make me thus happy, let me not think that I discovered more coolness in your first salutation than my long-hoarded joy could have presaged.[1]

FAULK. 'Twas but your fancy, Julia. I *was* rejoiced to see you — to see you in such health. Sure I had no cause for coldness?

JUL. Nay then, I see you have taken something ill. You must not conceal from me what it is.

FAULK. Well, then — shall I own to you « — but you will despise me, Julia — nay, I despise myself for it. — Yet I *will* own» that my joy at hearing of your health and arrival here, by your neighbour Acres, was somewhat damped by his dwelling much on the high spirits you had enjoyed in Devonshire — on your mirth — your singing — dancing, and I know not what! For such is my temper, Julia, that I should regard every mirthful moment in your absence as a treason to constancy: — The mutual tear that steals down the cheek of parting lovers is a compact, that no smile shall live there till they meet again.

JUL. Must I never cease to tax my Faulkland with this teasing minute caprice? Can the idle reports of a silly boor weigh in your breast against my tried affection?

FAULK. They have no weight with me, Julia: No, no — I am happy if you have been so — yet only say, that you did

[1] R 3: discovered something of coldness in your first salutation.

not sing with *mirth* — say that you *thought* of Faulkland in the dance.

JUL. I never can be happy in your absence. — If I wear a countenance of content, it is to shew that my mind holds no doubt of my Faulkland's truth. If I seemed sad, it were to make malice triumph; and say, that I fixed[1] my heart on one, who left me to lament his roving, and my own credulity. — Believe me, Faulkland, I mean not to upbraid you, when I say, that I have often dressed sorrow in smiles, lest my friends should guess whose unkindness had caused my tears.

FAULK. You were ever all goodness to me. O, I am a brute, when I but admit a doubt of your true constancy!

JUL. If ever, without such cause from you, as I will not suppose possible, you find my affections veering but a point, may I become a proverbial scoff for levity, and base ingratitude.

FAULK. Ah! Julia, that *last* word is grating to me. I would I had no title to your *gratitude!* Search your heart, Julia; perhaps what you have mistaken for Love, is but the warm effusion of a too thankful heart.

JUL. For what quality must I love you?

FAULK. For no quality! To regard me for any quality of mind or understanding, were only to *esteem* me. And for person — I have often wish'd myself deformed, to be convinced that I owed no obligation *there* for any part of your affection.

JUL. Where Nature has bestowed a shew of nice attention in the features of a man, he should laugh at it, as misplaced. I have seen men, who in this vain article perhaps might rank above you; but my heart has never asked my eyes if it were so or not.

FAULK. Now this is not well from *you*, Julia — I despise person in a man — yet if you loved me as I wish, though I were an Æthiop, you'd think none so fair.

JUL. I see you are determined to be unkind! The *contract*

[1] RR: had fixed.

which my poor father bound us in gives you more than a lover's privilege.

FAULK. Again, Julia, you raise ideas that feed and justify my doubts. I would not have been more free — no — I am proud of my restraint. Yet — yet — perhaps your high respect alone for this solemn compact has fettered your inclinations, which else had made a[1] worthier choice. How shall I be sure, had you remained unbound in thought and promise, that I should still have been the object of your persevering love?

JUL. Then try me now. Let us be free as strangers as to what is past: — *my* heart will not feel more liberty!

FAULK. There now! so hasty, Julia! so anxious to be free! If your love for me were fixed and ardent, you would not lose[2] your hold, even tho' I wish'd it!

JUL. Oh! you torture me to the heart! I cannot bear it.

FAULK. I do not mean to distress you. If I loved you less I should never give you an uneasy moment. — But hear me. — All my fretful doubts arise from this — Women are not used to weigh, and separate the motives of their affections: — the cold dictates of prudence, gratitude, or filial duty, may sometimes be mistaken for the pleadings of the heart. I would not boast — yet let me say, that I have neither age, person, or character, to found dislike on; my fortune such as few ladies could be charged with *indiscretion* in the match. O Julia! when *Love* receives such countenance from *Prudence*, nice minds will be suspicious of its *birth*.

JUL. I know not whither your insinuations would tend: — but[3] as they seem pressing to insult me, I will spare you the regret of having done so. — I have given you no cause for this! [*Exit in tears.*

FAULK. In Tears! stay, Julia: stay but for a moment. — The door is fastened! — Julia! — my soul — but for one

[1] R 1, 2, omit "a." [2] R 1, 2: loose. [3] R 1, 2, omit "but."

moment! — I hear her sobbing! — 'Sdeath! what a brute am I to use her thus! Yet stay! Aye — she is coming now: — how little resolution there is in women![1] — how a few soft words can turn them! — No, faith, — she is *not* coming either! — Why, Julia — my love — say but that you forgive me — come but to tell me that — now this is being *too* resentful. Stay! she *is* coming too — I thought she would — no *steadiness* in anything! her going away must have been a mere trick then — she sha'n't see that I was hurt by it. — I'll affect indifference — [*Hums a tune; then listens.*] No z—ds! she's *not* coming! — nor don't intend it, I suppose. — This is not *steadiness*, but *obstinacy!* Yet I deserve it. — What, after so long an absence to quarrel with her tenderness! — 'twas barbarous and unmanly! — I should be ashamed to see her now. — I'll wait till her just resentment is abated — and when I distress her so again, may I lose her for ever! and be linked instead to some antique virago, whose gnawing passions, and long-hoarded spleen, shall make me curse my folly half the day, and all the night. [*Exit.*

SCENE III. — MRS. MALAPROP'S *Lodgings*

MRS. MALAPROP *and* CAPTAIN ABSOLUTE

MRS. MAL. Your being Sir Anthony's son, Captain, would itself be a sufficient accommodation; but from the ingenuity of your appearance, I am convinced you deserve the character here given of you.

ABS. Permit me to say, madam, that as I never yet have had the pleasure of seeing Miss Languish, my principal inducement in this affair at present is the honour of being allied to Mrs. Malaprop; of whose intellectual accomplishments, elegant manners, and unaffected learning, no tongue is silent.

MRS. MAL. Sir, you do me infinite honour! I beg, Captain, you'll be seated. — [*Sit.*] Ah! few gentlemen, now a

[1] RR: woman.

days, know how to value the ineffectual qualities in a woman! — few think how a little knowledge become [1] a gentlewoman. — Men have no sense now but for the worthless flower, beauty!

ABS. It is but too true, indeed, Ma'am; — yet I fear our ladies should share the blame — they think our admiration of *beauty* so great, that *knowledge* in *them* would be superfluous. Thus, like garden-trees, they seldom show fruits till time has robb'd them of [2] more specious blossom. — Few, like Mrs. Malaprop and the Orange-tree, are rich in both at once!

MRS. MAL. Sir, you overpower me with good-breeding. — He is the very Pine-apple of politeness! — You are not ignorant, Captain, that this giddy girl has somehow contrived to fix her affections on a beggarly, strolling, eves-dropping ensign, whom none of us have seen, and nobody knows anything of.

ABS. Oh, I have heard the silly affair before. — I'm not at all prejudiced against her on *that* account.

MRS. MAL. You are very good and very considerate, Captain. I am sure I have done everything in my power since I exploded the affair; long ago I laid my positive conjunction [3] on her, never to think on the fellow again; — I have since laid Sir Anthony's preposition before her; but, I am sorry to say, she seems resolved to decline every particle that I enjoin her.

ABS. It must be very distressing, indeed, Ma'am.

MRS. MAL. Oh! [4] it gives me the hydrostatics to such a degree. — I thought she had persisted from corresponding with him; but behold this very day, I have interceded another letter from the fellow! I believe I have it in my pocket.

ABS. Oh, the devil! my last note. [*Aside.*

MRS. MAL. Ay, here it is.

ABS. Ay, my note indeed! Oh, the little traitress Lucy. [*Aside.*

[1] R 3: becomes.
[2] RR: of the.
[3] R 3: conjunctions.
[4] R 1, 2: omit "Oh!"

MRS. MAL. There, perhaps you may know the writing.

[*Gives him the letter.*

ABS. I think I have seen the hand before — yes, I *certainly must* have seen this hand before: —

MRS. MAL. Nay, but read it, Captain.

ABS. [*Reads*] "*My soul's idol, my adored Lydia!*" — Very tender, indeed!

MRS. MAL. Tender! aye, and prophane too, o' my conscience.

ABS. [*Reads*] "*I am excessively alarmed at the intelligence you send me, the more so as my new rival*" —

MRS. MAL. That's *you*, sir.

ABS. "*Has universally the character of being an accomplished gentleman, and a man of honour.*" — Well, that's handsome enough.

MRS. MAL. Oh, the fellow has some design in writing so.

ABS. That he had, I'll answer for him, Ma'am.

MRS. MAL. But go on, Sir — you'll see presently.

ABS. "*As for the old weather-beaten she-dragon who guards you.*" — Who can he mean by that?

MRS. MAL. *Me*, Sir! — *me!* — he means *me* there — what do you think now? — but go on a little further.

ABS. Impudent scoundrel! — "*it shall go hard but I will elude her vigilance, as I am told that the same ridiculous vanity, which makes her dress up her coarse features, and deck her dull chat with hard words which she don't understand*" ——

MRS. MAL. There, Sir! an attack upon my language! what do you think of that? — an aspersion upon my parts of speech! was ever such a brute! save[1] if I reprehend any thing in this world, it is the use of my oracular tongue, and a nice derangement of epitaphs!

ABS. He deserves to be hang'd and quartered! let me see — "*same ridiculous vanity*" ——

[1] R 3: sure.

MRS. MAL. You need not read it again, Sir.

ABS. I beg pardon, Ma'am — "*does also lay her open to the grossest deceptions from flattery and pretended admiration*" — an impudent coxcomb! — "*so that I have a scheme to see you shortly with the old Harridan's consent, and even to make her a go-between in our interviews.*" — Was ever such assurance!

MRS. MAL. Did you ever hear anything like it? — he'll elude my vigilance, will he? — Yes, yes! ha! ha! he's very likely to enter these floors;[1] — we'll try who can plot best!

ABS.[2] Ha! ha! ha! a conceited puppy, ha! ha! ha! — Well, but Mrs. Malaprop, as the girl seems so infatuated by this fellow, suppose you were to wink at her corresponding with him for a little time — let her even plot an elopement with him — then do you connive at her escape — while *I*, just in the nick, will have the fellow laid by the heels, and fairly contrive to carry her off in his stead.

MRS. MAL. I am delighted with the scheme; never was anything better perpetrated!

ABS. But, pray, could not I see the lady for a few minutes now? — I should like to try her temper a little.

MRS. MAL. Why, I don't know — I doubt she is not prepared for a first visit[3] of this kind. There is a decorum in these matters.

ABS. O Lord! she won't mind *me* — only tell her Beverley ——

MRS. MAL. Sir!

ABS. Gently, good tongue. [*Aside.*

MRS. MAL. What did you say of Beverley?

ABS. Oh, I was going to propose that you should tell her, by way of jest, that it was Beverley who was below! she'd come down fast enough then — ha! ha! ha!

MRS. MAL. 'Twould be a trick she well deserves; besides,

[1] R 3: doors. [2] R 3 inserts: So we will Ma'am — so we will.
[3] R 3: for a visit.

you know the fellow tells her he'll get my consent to see her — ha! ha! Let him if he can, I say again. Lydia, come down here! — [*Calling.*] He'll make me a *go-between in their interviews!* — ha! ha! ha! Come down, I say, Lydia! I don't wonder at your laughing, ha! ha! ha! his impudence is truly ridiculous.

ABS. 'Tis very ridiculous, upon my soul, Ma'am, ha! ha! ha!

MRS. MAL. The little hussy won't hear. Well, I'll go and tell her at once who it is — she shall know that Captain Absolute is come to wait on her. And I'll make her behave as becomes a young woman.

ABS. As you please, Ma'am.

MRS. MAL. For the present, captain, your servant. Ah! you've not done laughing yet, I see — *elude my vigilance;* yes, yes; ha! ha! ha! [*Exit.*

ABS. Ha! ha! ha! one would think now that I might throw off all disguise at once, and seize my prize with security; but such is Lydia's caprice, that to undeceive were probably to lose her. I'll see whether she knows me.

[*Walks aside, and seems engaged in looking at the pictures.*

Enter LYDIA

LYD. What a scene am I now to go through! surely nothing can be more dreadful than to be obliged to listen to the loathsome addresses of a stranger to one's heart. I have heard of girls persecuted as I am, who have appealed in behalf of their favoured lover to the generosity of his rival: suppose I were to try it — there stands the hated rival — an officer too! — but O, how unlike my Beverley! I wonder he don't begin — truly he seems a very negligent wooer! — quite at his ease, upon my word! — I'll speak first — Mr. Absolute.

ABS. Madam. [*Turns round.*

LYD. O Heav'ns! Beverley!

ABS. Hush! — hush, my life! softly! be not surprised!

LYD. I am so astonished! and so terrified! and so overjoy'd! — for Heav'n's sake! how came you here?

ABS. Briefly, I have deceived your Aunt — I was informed that my new rival was to visit here this evening, and contriving to have him kept away, have passed myself on *her* for Capt. Absolute.

LYD. O, charming! And she really takes you for young Absolute.

ABS. O, she's convinced of it.

LYD. Ha! ha! ha! I can't forbear laughing to think how her sagacity is overreached!

ABS. But we trifle with our precious moments — such another opportunity may not occur; then let me conjure[1] my kind, my condescending angel, to fix the time when I may rescue her from undeserved persecution, and with a licensed warmth plead for my reward.

LYD. Will you then, Beverley, consent to forfeit that portion of my paltry wealth? — that burden on the wings of love?

ABS. Oh, come to me — rich only thus — in loveliness! Bring no portion to me but thy love — 'twill be generous in you, Lydia, — for well you know it is the only dower your poor Beverley can repay.

LYD. How persuasive are his words! — how charming will poverty be with him!

ABS. Ah! my soul, what a life will we then live! Love shall be our idol and support! we will worship him with a monastic strictness; abjuring all worldly toys, to center every thought and action there. — Proud of calamity, we will enjoy the wreck of wealth; while the surrounding gloom of adversity shall make the flame of our pure love show doubly bright. By Heav'ns! I would fling all goods of fortune from me with a prodigal hand, to enjoy the scene where I might clasp my Lydia to my bosom, and say, the world affords no smile to me — but

[1] RR: now conjure.

here — [*Embracing her.*] If she holds out now, the [illegible] is in it! [*Aside.*

LYD. Now could I fly with him to the Antipodes! but my persecution is not yet come to a crisis. [*Aside.*

Re-enter MRS. MALAPROP, *listening*

MRS. MAL. I am impatient to know how the little huzzy deports herself. [*Aside.*

ABS. So pensive, Lydia! — is then your warmth abated?

MRS. MAL. *Warmth abated!* — so! — she has been in a passion, I suppose. [*Aside.*[1]

LYD. No — nor ever can while I have life.

MRS. MAL. An ill-temper'd little devil! She'll be *in a passion all her life* — will she? [*Aside.*

LYD. Think not the idle threats of my ridiculous aunt can ever have any weight with me.

MRS. MAL. Very dutiful, upon my word! [*Aside.*

LYD. Let her choice be *Capt. Absolute*, but Beverley is mine.

MRS. MAL. I am astonished at her assurance! — *to his face — this to his face!*[2] [*Aside.*

ABS. Thus then let me enforce my suit. [*Kneeling.*

MRS. MAL. [*Aside*] Aye, poor young man! — down on his knees entreating for pity! — I can contain no longer. — Why, huzzy! huzzy![3] — I have overheard you.

ABS. Oh, confound her vigilance! [*Aside.*

MRS. MAL. Capt. Absolute, — I know not how to apologize for her shocking rudeness.

ABS. [*Aside*] So — all's safe, I find. — [*Aside*] I have hopes, Madam, that time will bring the young lady ——

MRS. MAL. Oh, there's nothing to be hoped for from her! she's as headstrong as an allegory on the banks of Nile.

LYD. Nay, Madam, what do you charge me with now?

MRS. MAL. Why, thou unblushing rebel — didn't you tell

[1] RR omit the stage directions down to "*Kneeling.*"

[2] R 3: this is to his face.

[3] R 3: why, thou vixen!

this gentleman to his face that you loved another better? — didn't you say you never would be his?

LYD. No, Madam — I did not.

MRS. MAL. Good Heav'ns! what assurance! — Lydia, Lydia, you ought to know that lying don't become a young woman! — Didn't you boast that Beverley, that stroller Beverley, possessed your heart? — Tell me that, I say.

LYD. 'Tis true, Ma'am, and none but Beverley ——

MRS. MAL. Hold; — hold, Assurance! — you shall not be so rude.

ABS. Nay, pray, Mrs. Malaprop, don't stop the young lady's speech: she's very welcome to talk thus — it does not hurt *me* in the least, I assure you.

MRS. MAL. You are *too* good, captain — *too* amiably patient — but come with me, Miss. — Let us see you again soon, Captain — remember what we have fixed.

ABS. I shall, Ma'am.

MRS. MAL. Come, take a graceful leave of the gentleman.

LYD. May every blessing wait on my Beverley, my lov'd Bev ——

MRS. MAL. Huzzy! I'll choke the word in your throat! — come along — come along.

[*Exeunt severally;* CAPTAIN ABSOLUTE *kissing his hand to* LYDIA — MRS. MALAPROP *stopping her from speaking.*]

SCENE IV. — ACRES' *Lodgings*

ACRES *and* DAVID

ACRES, *as just dress'd*

ACRES. Indeed, David — do you think I become it so?

DAV. You are quite another creature, believe me, Master, by the Mass! an' we've any luck we shall see the Devon monkeyrony in all the print-shops in Bath!

ACRES. Dress *does* make a difference, David.

DAV. 'Tis all in all, I think — difference! why, an' you were to go now to Clod Hall, I am certain the old lady wouldn't know you: Master Butler wouldn't believe his own eyes, and Mrs. Pickle would cry, "Lard presarve me!" our dairy-maid would come giggling to the door, and I warrant Dolly Tester, your Honour's favourite, would blush like my waistcoat. — Oons! I'll hold a gallon, there an't a dog in the house but would bark, and I question whether *Phillis* would wag a hair of her tail!

ACRES. Aye, David, there's nothing like *polishing*.

DAV. So I says of your Honour's boots; but the boy never heeds me!

ACRES. But, David, has Mr. De-la-Grace been here? I must rub up my balancing, and chasing, and boring.

DAV. I'll call again, Sir.

ACRES. Do — and see if there are any letters for me at the post-office.

DAV. I will. — By the Mass, I can't help looking at your head! — if I hadn't been by at the cooking, I wish I may die if I should have known the dish again myself. [*Exit.*

[ACRES *comes forward, practising a dancing-step.*] ACRES. Sink, slide — coupee. — Confound the first inventors of cotillons! say I — they are as bad as algebra to us country gentlemen. — I can walk a Minuet easy enough when I am[1] forced! — and I have been accounted a good stick in a Country-dance. — Odds jigs and tabors! I never valued your cross-over two couple — figure in — right and left — and I'd foot it with e'er a captain in the county! — but these outlandish heathen Allemandes and Cotillons are quite beyond me! — I shall never prosper at 'em, that's sure — mine are true-born English legs — they don't understand their curst French lingo! — their *Pas* this, and *Pas* that, and *Pas* t'other! — d—n me! my feet don't like to be called Paws! no, 'tis certain I have most Antigallican Toes!

[1] RR: I'm.

Enter SERVANT

SERV. Here is Sir Lucius O'Trigger to wait on you, Sir.

ACRES. Show him in.

Enter SIR LUCIUS

SIR LUC. Mr. Acres, I am delighted to embrace you.

ACRES. My dear Sir Lucius, I kiss your hands.

SIR LUC. Pray, my friend, what has brought you so suddenly to Bath?

ACRES. Faith! I have followed Cupid's Jack-a-lantern, and find myself in a quagmire at last. — In short, I have been very ill used, Sir Lucius. — I don't choose to mention names, but look on me as on a very ill-used gentleman.

SIR LUC. Pray what is the case? — I ask no names.

ACRES. Mark me, Sir Lucius, I falls[1] as deep as need be in love with a young lady — her friends take my part — I follow her to Bath — send word of my arrival; and receive answer, that the lady is to be otherwise disposed of. — This, Sir Lucius, I call being ill-used.

SIR LUC. Very ill, upon my conscience. — Pray, can you divine the cause of it?

ACRES. Why, there's the matter; she has another lover, *one* Beverley, who, I am told, is now in Bath. — Odds slanders and lies! he must be at the bottom of it.

SIR LUC. A rival in the case, is there? — and you think he has supplanted you unfairly?

ACRES. *Unfairly!* to be sure he has. — He never could have done it fairly.

SIR LUC. Then sure you know what is to be done!

ACRES. Not I, upon my soul!

SIR LUC. We wear no swords here, but you understand me.

ACRES. What! fight him.

SIR LUC. Aye, to be sure: what can I mean else?

[1] R 3: fall.

ACRES. But he has given me no provocation.

SIR LUC. Now, I think he has given you the greatest provocation in the world. — Can a man commit a more heinous offence against another than to fall in love with the same woman? O, by my soul! it is the most unpardonable breach of friendship.

ACRES. Breach of *friendship!* aye, aye; but I have no acquaintance with this man. I never saw him in my life.

SIR LUC. That's no argument at all — he has the less right then to take such a liberty.

ACRES. 'Gad, that's true — I grow full of anger, Sir Lucius! — I fire apace! Odds hilts and blades! I find a man may have a deal of valour in him, and not know it! But couldn't I contrive to have a little right of my side?

SIR LUC. What the d—l signifies *right*, when your *honour* is concerned? Do you think *Achilles*, or my little *Alexander the Great*, ever inquired where the right lay? No, by my soul, they drew their broad-swords, and left the lazy sons of peace to settle the justice of it.

ACRES. Your words are a grenadier's march to my heart! I believe courage must be catching! — I certainly do feel a kind of valour rising as it were — a kind of courage, as I may say. — Odds flints, pans, and triggers! I'll challenge him directly.

SIR LUC. Ah, my little friend, if I had[1] *Blunderbuss Hall* here, I could show you a range of ancestry, in the old[2] O'Trigger line, that would furnish the new room; every one of whom had killed his man! — For though the mansion-house and dirty acres have slipt through my fingers, I thank God our honour and the family-pictures are as fresh as ever.

ACRES. O, Sir Lucius! I have had ancestors too! — every man of 'em colonel or captain in the militia! — Odds balls and barrels! say no more — I'm brac'd for it — «my nerves are become catgut! my sinews wire! and my heart Pinchbeck!»

[1] RR: we had. [2] RR omit "old."

The thunder of your words has soured the milk of human kindness in my breast: — Z—ds! as the man in the play says, "I could do such deeds!"

SIR LUC. Come, come, there must be no passion at all in the case — these things should always be done civilly.

ACRES. I must be in a passion, Sir Lucius — I must be in a rage. — Dear Sir Lucius, let me be in a rage, if you love me. Come, here's pen and paper. — [*Sits down to write.*] I would the ink were red! — Indite, I say, indite! — How shall I begin? Odds bullets and blades! I'll write a good *bold hand*, however.

SIR LUC. Pray compose yourself.

ACRES. Come — now shall I begin with an oath? Do, Sir Lucius, let me begin with a damme.

SIR LUC. Pho! pho! do the thing *decently*, and like a Christian. Begin now — "*Sir*" ——

ACRES. That's too civil by half.

SIR LUC. "*To prevent the confusion that might arise.*"

ACRES. Well ——

SIR LUC. "*From our both addressing the same lady.*"

ACRES. Aye, there's the reason — "*same lady*" — Well ——

SIR LUC. "*I shall expect the honour of your company.*"

ACRES. Z—ds! I'm not asking him to dinner.

SIR LUC. Pray be easy.

ACRES. Well, then, "honour of your company."

SIR LUC. "*To settle our pretensions.*"

ACRES. Well.

SIR LUC. Let me see, aye, *King's-Mead-fields* will do — "*In King's-Mead fields.*"

ACRES. So, that's done — Well, I'll fold it up presently; my own crest — a hand and dagger — shall be the seal.

SIR LUC. You see now this little explanation will put a stop at once to all confusion or misunderstanding that might arise between you.

ACRES. Aye, we fight to prevent any misunderstanding.

SIR LUC. Now, I'll leave you to fix your own time. — Take my advice, and you'll decide it this evening if you can; then let the worst come of it, 'twill be off your mind to-morrow.

ACRES. Very true.

SIR LUC. So I shall see nothing[1] of you, unless it be by letter, till the evening. — I would do myself the honour to carry your message; but, to tell you a secret, I believe I shall have just such another affair on my own hands. There is a gay captain here, who put a jest on me lately, at the expence of my country, and I only want to fall in with the gentleman, to call him out.

ACRES. By my valour, I should like to see you fight first! Odds life! I should like to see you kill him, if it was only to get a little lesson.

SIR LUC. I shall be very proud of instructing you. — Well for the present — but remember now, when you meet your antagonist, do every thing in a mild and agreeable manner. — Let your courage be as keen, but at the same time as polished as your sword. [*Exeunt severally.*

END OF THE THIRD ACT

ACT IV

SCENE I. — ACRES' *Lodgings.*

ACRES *and* DAVID

DAVID. Then, by the Mass, Sir! I would do no such thing — ne'er a St.[2] Lucius O'Trigger in the kingdom should make me fight, when I wa'n't so minded. Oons! what will the old lady say, when she hears o't?

ACRES. Ah! David, if you had heard Sir Lucius! — Odds sparks and flames! he would have roused your valour.

DAVID. Not he, indeed. I hates such bloodthirsty cormo-

[1] RR add "more." [2] RR: Sir.

rants. Look'ee, Master, if you'd wanted a bout at boxing, quarter-staff, or short-staff, I should never be the man to bid you cry off: but for your curst sharps and snaps, I never knew any good come of 'em.

ACRES. But my *honour*, David, my *honour!* I must be very careful of my honour.

DAVID. Aye, by the Mass! and I would be very careful of it; and I think in return my *honour* couldn't do less than to be very careful of *me*.

ACRES. Odds blades! David, no gentleman will ever risk the loss of his honour!

DAVID. I say then, it would be but civil in *honour* never to risk the loss of the *gentleman*. — Look'ee, Master, this *honour* seems to me to be a marvellous false friend: aye, truly, a very courtier-like servant. — Put the case, I was a gentleman (which, thank God, no one can say of me;) well — my honour makes me quarrel with another gentleman of my acquaintance. — So — we fight. (Pleasant enough that!) Boh; — I kill him — (the more's my luck!) now, pray who gets the profit of it? — Why, my *honour*. But put the case that he kills me! — by the Mass! I go to the worms, and my honour whips over to my enemy.

ACRES. No, David — in that case! — Odds crowns and laurels! your honour follows you to the grave.

DAVID. Now, that's just the place where I could make a shift to do without it.

ACRES. Z—ds! David, you are a coward! — It doesn't become my valour to listen to you. — What, shall I disgrace my ancestors? — Think of that, David — think what it would be to disgrace my ancestors!

DAVID. Under favour, the surest way of not disgracing them, is to keep as long as you can out of their company. Look'ee now, Master, to go to them in such haste — with an ounce of lead in your brains — I should think might as well be let alone.

Our ancestors are very good kind of folks; but they are the last people I should choose to have a visiting acquaintance with.

Acres. But, David, now, you don't think there is such very, very, *very* great danger, hey? — Odds life! people often fight without any mischief done!

David. By the Mass, I think 'tis ten to one against you! — Oons! here to meet some lion-headed fellow, I warrant, with his d—n'd double-barrelled swords, and cut-and-thrust pistols! Lord bless us! it makes me tremble to think o't — Those be such desperate bloody-minded weapons! Well, I never could abide 'em! — from a child I never could fancy 'em! — I suppose there an't so merciless a beast in the world as your loaded pistol!

Acres. Z—ds! I *won't* be afraid! — Odds fire and fury! you shan't make me afraid. — Here is the challenge, and I have sent for my dear friend Jack Absolute to carry it for me.

David. Aye, i' the name of mi[s]chief, let *him* be the messenger. — For my part, I wouldn't lend a hand to it for the best horse in your stable. By the Mass! it don't look like another letter! It is, as I may say, a designing and malicious-looking letter! and I warrant smells of gunpowder like a soldier's pouch! — Oons! I wouldn't swear it mayn't go off!

Acres. Out, you poltroon! you han't the valour of a grass-hopper.

David. Well, I say no more — 'twill be sad news, to be sure, at Clod Hall! but I ha' done. How Phillis will howl when she hears of it! — Aye, poor bitch, she little thinks what shooting her Master's going after! And I warrant old Crop, who has carried your honour, field and road, these ten years, will curse the hour he was born. [*Whimpering.*

Acres. It won't do, David — I am determined to fight — so get along, you Coward, while I'm in the mind.

Enter SERVANT

SER. Captain Absolute, Sir.

ACRES. O! show him up. [*Exit* SERVANT.

DAVID. Well, Heaven send we be all alive this time to-morrow.

ACRES. What's that! — Don't provoke me, David!

DAVID. Good-bye, Master. [*Whimpering.*

ACRES. Get along, you cowardly, dastardly, croaking raven!

[*Exit* DAVID.

Enter CAPTAIN ABSOLUTE

ABS. What's the matter, Bob?

ACRES. A vile, sheep-hearted blockhead! If I hadn't the valour of St. George and the dragon to boot ——

ABS. But what did you want with me, Bob?

ACRES. Oh! — There —— [*Gives him the challenge.*

ABS. *To Ensign Beverley.* — So — what's going on now? [*Aside*] — [*Aloud.*][1] Well, what's this?

ACRES. A challenge!

ABS. Indeed! Why, you won't fight him; will you, Bob?

ACRES. 'Egad, but I will, Jack. Sir Lucius has wrought me to it. He has left me full of rage — and I'll fight this evening, that so much good passion mayn't be wasted.

ABS. But what have I to do with this?

ACRES. Why, as I think you know something of this fellow, I want you to find him out for me, and give him this mortal *defiance.*

ABS. Well, give it to me, and trust me he gets it.

ACRES. Thank you, my dear friend, my dear Jack; but it is giving you a great deal of trouble.

ABS. Not in the least — I beg you won't mention it. — No trouble in the world, I assure you.

ACRES. You are very kind. — What it is to have a friend! — You couldn't be my second, could you, Jack?

[1] RR omit.

ABS. Why no, Bob — not in *this* affair — it would not be quite so proper.

ACRES. Well, then, I must fix on my friend Sir Lucius. I shall have your good wishes, however, Jack?

ABS. Whenever he meets you, believe me.

Enter SERVANT

SER. Sir Anthony Absolute is below, inquiring for the Captain.

ABS. I'll come instantly. — Well, my little hero, success attend you. [*Going.*

ACRES. Stay — stay, Jack. — If Beverley should ask you what kind of a man your friend Acres is, do tell him I am a devil of a fellow — will you, Jack?

ABS. To be sure I shall. I'll say you are a determined dog — hey, Bob?

ACRES. Aye, do, do — and if that frightens him, 'egad, perhaps he mayn't come. So tell him I generally kill a man a week; will you, Jack?

[illegible] will, I will; I'll say you are called in the country [illegible] *b.*"

[illegible] ght — right — 'tis all to prevent mischief; for I [illegible] o take his life if I clear my honour.

[illegible] — that's very kind of you.

ACRES. Why, you don't wish me to kill him — do you, Jack?

ABS. No, upon my soul, I do not. But a devil of a fellow, hey? [*Going.*

ACRES. True, true — but stay — stay Jack, — you may add, that you never saw me in such a rage before — a most devouring rage!

ABS. I will, I will.

ACRES. Remember, Jack — a determined dog!

ABS. Aye, aye, "*Fighting Bob!*" [*Exeunt severally.*

SCENE II. — *Mrs.* MALAPROP'S *Lodgings*

MRS. MALAPROP *and* LYDIA

MRS. MAL. Why, thou perverse one! — tell me what you can object to him? Isn't he a handsome man? — tell me that. A genteel man? a pretty figure of a man?

LYD. [*Aside*] She little thinks whom she is praising! — [*Aloud.*] So is Beverley, Ma'am.

MRS. MAL. No caparisons, Miss, if you please. Caparisons don't become a young woman. No! Captain Absolute is indeed a fine gentleman!

LYD. Aye, the Captain Absolute *you* have seen. [*Aside.*

MRS. MAL. Then he's *so* well bred; — *so* full of alacrity, and adulation! — and has *so much* to say for himself: — in such good language, too! His physiognomy so grammatical! Then his presence is so noble! I protest, when I saw him, I thought of what Hamlet says in the play: — "Hesperian curls — the front of *Job* himself! — An eye, like March, to threaten at command! — A Station, like Harry Mercury, new —" Something about kissing — on a hill — however, the similitude struck me directly.

LYD. How enraged she'll be presently, when she discovers her mistake! [*Aside.*

Enter SERVANT

SER. Sir Anthony, and Captain Absolute are below, Ma'am.

MRS. MAL. Show them up here. — [*Exit* SERV.] Now, Lydia, I insist on your behaving as becomes a young woman. Shew your good breeding, at least, though you have forgot your duty.

LYD. Madam, I have told you my resolution; — I shall not only give him no encouragement, but I won't even speak to, or look at him.

[*Flings herself into a chair, with her face from the door.*

Enter SIR ANTHONY *and* ABSOLUTE

SIR ANTH. Here we are, Mrs. Malaprop; come to mitigate the frowns of unrelenting beauty, — and difficulty enough I had to bring this fellow. — I don't know what's the matter; but if I hadn't held him by force, he'd have given me the slip.

MRS. MAL. You have infinite trouble, Sir Anthony, in the affair. I am ashamed for the cause! Lydia, Lydia, rise, I beseech you! — pay your respects! [*Aside to her.*]

SIR ANTH. I hope, madam, that Miss Languish has reflected on the worth of this gentleman, and the regard due to her aunt's choice, and *my* alliance. — Now, Jack, speak to her! [*Aside to him.*]

ABS. What the d—l shall I do! [*Aside.*] — [*Aside*][1] You see, Sir, she won't even look at me, whilst you are here. I knew she wouldn't! I told you so. Let me entreat you, Sir, to leave us together!

[ABSOLUTE *seems to expostulate with his father.*

LYD. [*Aside.*] I wonder I han't heard my Aunt exclaim yet! sure she can't have looked at him! — perhaps their regimentals are alike, and she is something blind.

SIR ANTH. I say, Sir, I won't stir a foot yet!

MRS. MAL. I am sorry to say, Sir Anthony, that my affluence over my Niece is very small. — Turn round, Lydia: I blush for you! [*Aside to her.*]

SIR ANTH. May I not flatter myself that Miss Languish will assign what cause of dislike she can have to my son! — Why don't you begin, Jack? — Speak, you puppy — speak! [*Aside to him.*]

MRS. MAL. It is impossible, Sir Anthony, she can have any. She will not *say* she has. — Answer, hussy! why don't you answer? [*Aside to her.*]

SIR ANTH. Then, Madam, I trust that a childish and hasty

[1] RR omit, but Sheridan obviously intended the first *aside* to indicate soliloquy, the second to indicate *aside* to Absolute's father.

predilection will be no bar to Jack's happiness. — Z—ds! sirrah! why don't you speak? [*Aside to him.*]

LYD. [*Aside.*] I think my lover seems as little inclined to conversation as myself. — How strangely blind my Aunt must be![1]

ABS. Hem! hem! Madam — hem! — [ABSOLUTE *attempts to speak, then returns to* SIR ANTHONY.] Faith! Sir, I am so confounded! — and — so — so — confused! — I told you I should be so, Sir — I knew it. — The — the — tremor of my passion entirely takes away my presence of mind.

SIR ANTH. But it don't take away your voice, fool, does it? — Go up, and speak to her directly!

[ABSOLUTE *makes signs to* MRS. MAL. *to leave them together.*

MRS. MAL. Sir Anthony, shall we leave them together? — Ah! you stubborn, little vixen! [*Aside to her.*]

SIR ANTH. Not yet, Ma'am, not yet! — What the d—l are you at? unlock your jaws, sirrah, or —— [*Aside to him.*] [ABSOLUTE *draws near* LYDIA.]

ABS. Now Heav'n send she may be too sullen to look round! — I must disguise my voice. — [2][*Speaks in a low hoarse tone.*] Will not Miss Languish lend an ear to the mild accents of true love? Will not ——

SIR ANTH. What the d—l ails the fellow? why don't you speak out? — not stand croaking like a frog in a quinsey!

ABS. The — the — excess of my awe, and my — my — modesty quite choak me!

SIR ANTH. Ah! your *modesty* again! — I'll tell you what, Jack, if you don't speak out directly, and glibly too, I shall be in such a rage! — Mrs. Malaprop, I wish the lady would favour us with something more than a side-front.

[MRS. MALAPROP *seems to chide* LYDIA.

ABS. So! — all will out, I see! — [*Goes up to* LYDIA, *speaks softly.*] Be not surprised, my Lydia, suppress all surprise at present.

[1] R 1, 2: is.

[2] RR insert "(*Aside*)."

LYD. [*Aside.*] Heav'ns! 'tis Beverley's voice! Sure he can't have imposed on Sir Anthony too! — [*Looks round by degrees, then starts up.*] Is this possible! — my Beverley! — how can this be? — my Beverley?

ABS. Ah! 'tis all over. [*Aside.*

SIR ANTH. Beverley! — the devil — Beverley! — What can the girl mean? — this is my son, Jack Absolute.

MRS. MAL. For shame, hussy! for shame! your head runs so on that fellow, that you have him always in your eyes! — beg Captain Absolute's pardon directly.

LYD. I see no Captain Absolute, but my loved Beverley!

SIR ANTH. Z—ds! the girl's mad! — her brain's turned by reading.

MRS. MAL. O' my conscience, I believe so! — What do you mean by Beverley, hussey? — You saw Captain Absolute before to-day; there he is — your husband that shall be.

LYD. With all my soul, Ma'am — when I refuse my Beverley ——

SIR ANTH. Oh! she's as mad as Bedlam! — or has this fellow been playing us a rogue's trick! — Come here, sirrah, who the d—l are you!

ABS. Faith, Sir, I am not quite clear myself; but I'll endeavour to recollect.

SIR ANTH. Are you my son or not? — answer for your mother, you dog, if you won't for me.

MRS. MAL. Aye, Sir, who are you? O mercy! I begin to suspect! ——

ABS. Ye Powers of Impudence, befriend me! — [*Aside.*] Sir Anthony, most assuredly I am your wife's son; and that I sincerely believe myself to be *your's* also, I hope my duty has always shewn. — Mrs. Malaprop, I am your most respectful admirer, and shall be proud to add *affectionate nephew.* — I need not tell my Lydia, that she sees her faithful Beverley, who, knowing the singular generosity of her temper, assum'd that name, and a station, which has proved a test of the most disinterested love, which he now hopes to enjoy in a more elevated character.

LYD. So! — there will be no elopement after all! [*Sullenly.*

SIR ANTH. Upon my soul, Jack, thou art a very impudent fellow! to do you justice, I think I never saw a piece of more consummate assurance!

ABS. Oh, you flatter me, sir — you compliment — 'tis my *modesty*, you know, sir — my *modesty* that has stood in my way.

SIR ANTH. Well, I am glad you are not the dull, insensible varlet you pretended to be, however! — I'm glad you have made a fool of your father, you dog — I am. So this was your *penitence*, your *duty* and *obedience!* — I thought it was d—n'd sudden! — *You never heard their names before*, not you! — *what, Languishes of Worcestershire*, hey? — *if you could please me in the affair, 'twas all you desired!* — Ah! you dissembling villain! — What! — [*pointing to* LYDIA] *she squints don't she?* — *a little red-haired girl!* — hey? — Why, you hypocritical young rascal! — I wonder you a'n't ashamed to hold up your head!

ABS. 'Tis with difficulty, Sir. — I *am* confus'd — very much confus'd, as you must perceive.

MRS. MAL. O Lud! Sir Anthony! — a new light breaks in upon me! — hey! — how! what! Captain, did *you* write the Letters then? — What — I am to thank *you* for the elegant compilation of '*an old weather-beaten she-dragon*' — hey? — O mercy! — was it *you* that reflected on my parts of speech?

ABS. Dear Sir! my modesty will be overpower'd at last, if you don't assist me. — I shall certainly not be able to stand it!

SIR ANTH. Come, come, Mrs. Malaprop, we must forget and forgive; — odds life! matters have taken so clever a turn all of a sudden, that I could find in my heart to be so good-humoured! and so gallant! hey! Mrs. Malaprop!

[illegible]. MAL. Well, Sir Anthony, since *you* desire it, we will [illegible] anticipate the past; — so mind, young people — our retrospection will[1] be all to the future.

SIR ANTH. Come, we must leave them together; Mrs. Malaprop, they long to fly into each other's arms, I warrant! — Jack, isn't the *cheek* as I said, hey? — and the eye, you dog[2]? — and the lip — hey? Come, Mrs. Malaprop, we'll not disturb their tenderness — theirs is the time of life for happiness! — "*Youth's the season made for joy*" — [*Sings*] — hey! — Odds life! I'm in such spirits, — I don't know what I couldn't do! — Permit me, Ma'am — [*Gives his hand to* MRS. MALAPROP.] (*Sings*) Tol-de-rol — 'gad, I should like to have[3] a little fooling myself — Tol-de-rol! de-rol.

[*Exit singing, and handing* MRS. MAL.

LYDIA *sits sullenly in her chair*

ABS. So much thought bodes me no good. — [*Aside.*] So grave, Lydia!

LYD. Sir!

ABS [illegible] ught as much! — that d—n'd [illegible] — [*Aside.*] What, Lydia, now [illegible] riends consent*, as in our *mutual* [illegible]

[illegible] consent*, indeed! [*Peevishly.*

ABS. Come, come, we must lay aside some of our romance — a little *wealth* and *comfort* may be endur'd after all. And for your fortune, the lawyers shall make such settlements as ——

LYD. *Lawyers!* I *hate* lawyers!

ABS. Nay then, we will not wait for their lingering forms, but instantly procure the licence, and ——

LYD. The *licence!* — I *hate* licence!

ABS. Oh my Love! *be* not so unkind! — thus let me intreat —— [*Kneeling.*

[1] RR insert "now." [2] R 3: rogue. [3] RR omit "to have."

Lyd. Pshaw! — what signifies kneeling, when you know I *must* have you?

Abs. [*Rising.*] Nay, Madam, there shall be no constraint upon your inclinations, I promise you. — If I have lost your *heart* — I resign the rest — 'Gad, I must try what a little *spirit* will do. [*Aside.*]

Lyd. [*Rising.*] Then, Sir, let me tell you, the interest you had there was acquired by a mean, unmanly imposition, and deserves the punishment of fraud. — What, you have been treating *me* like a *child!* — humouring my romance! and laughing, I suppose, at your success!

Abs. You wrong me, Lydia, you wrong me — only hear ——

Lyd. So, while *I* fondly imagined we were deceiving my relations, and flatter'd myself that I should outwit and incense them *all* — behold! my hopes are to be crush'd at once, by my Aunt's consent and approbation — and *I* am *myself* the only dupe at last! — [*Walking about in heat.*]

«Abs. Nay, but hear me ——

«Lyd. No, Sir, you could not think that such paltry artifices could please me, when the mask was thrown off! But I suppose since your tricks have made you secure of my *fortune*, you are little solicitous about my *affections*. —» But here, Sir, here is the picture — Beverley's picture! [*taking a miniature from her bosom*] which I have worn, night and day, in spite of threats and entreaties! — There, Sir; [*flings it to him*] and be assured I throw the original from my heart as easily!

Abs. Nay, nay, Ma'am, we will not differ as to that. — Here [*taking out a picture*] *here* is Miss Lydia Languish. — What a difference! — aye, *there* is the heav'nly assenting smile, that first gave soul and spirit to my hopes! — those are the lips which seal'd a vow, as yet scarce dry in Cupid's calendar! and *there* the *half* resentful blush, that *would* have check'd the ardour of my thanks! — Well, all that's past? — all over indeed! — There, Madam — in *beauty*, that copy is not equal to you, but in my mind it's merit over the original, in being still the same, is such — that — I cannot find in my heart to *part with it.* [*Puts it up again.*

LYD. [*Softening.*] 'Tis *your own* doing, Sir — I, I, I suppose you are perfectly satisfied.

ABS. O, most certainly — sure, now this is much better than being in love! — ha! ha! ha! — there's some spirit in *this!* — What signifies breaking some scores of solemn promises, «half an hundred vows, under one's hand, with the marks of a dozen or two angels to witness» — all that's of no consequence, you know. To be sure people will say, that Miss don't[1] know her own mind — but never mind that: — Or, perhaps, they may be ill-natured enough to hint, that the gentleman grew tired of the lady and forsook her — but don't let that fret you.

LYD. There is no bearing his insolence. [*Bursts into tears.*

Enter MRS. MALAPROP *and* SIR ANTHONY

MRS. MAL. [*Entering.*] Come, we must interrupt your billing and cooing a while.

LYD. *This* is *worse* than your treachery and deceit, you base ingrate! [*Sobbing.*

SIR ANTH. What the devil's the matter now? — Z—ds! Mrs. Malaprop, this is the *oddest billing* and *cooing* I ever heard! — but what the deuce is the meaning of it? — I am quite astonished!

ABS. Ask the lady, Sir.

MRS. MAL. O mercy! — I'm quite analyzed for my part! — Why, Lydia, what is the reason of this?

LYD. Ask the *gentleman*, Ma'am.

SIR ANTH. Z—ds! I shall be in a phrenzy! — Why, Jack, you scoundrel,[2] you are not come out to be any one else, are you?

MRS. MAL. Aye, Sir, there's no more *trick*, is there? —

[1] RR: didn't. [2] R 3 omits "you scoundrel."

you are not like Cerberus, *three* Gentlemen at once, are you?

Abs. You'll not let me speak — I say the *lady* can account for *this* much better than I can.

Lyd. Ma'am, you once commanded me never to think of Beverley again — *there* is the man — I now obey you: for, from this moment, I renounce him for ever. [*Exit* Lydia.

Mrs. Mal. O mercy! and miracles! what a turn here is — why, sure Captain, you haven't behaved disrespectfully to my Niece?

Sir Anth. Ha! ha! ha! — ha! ha! ha! — now I see it. Ha! ha! ha! — now I see it — you have been too lively, Jack.

Abs. Nay, sir, upon my word ——

Sir Anth. Come, no lying, Jack — I'm sure *'twas* so.

Mrs Mal. O Lud! Sir Anthony! — O fie, Captain!

Abs. Upon my soul, Ma'am ——

Sir Anth. Come, no excuse, Jack; why, your father, you rogue, was so before you! — the blood of the Absolutes was always impatient. — Ha! ha! ha! poor little Lydia! why, you've frightened her, you Dog, you have.

Abs. By all that's good, sir ——

Sir Anth. Z—ds! say no more, I tell you. Mrs. Malaprop shall make your peace. You must make his peace, Mrs. Malaprop: — you must tell her 'tis Jack's way — tell her 'tis all our ways — it runs in the blood of our family! Come, get on, Jack.[1] Ha! ha! ha! — Mrs. Malaprop — a young villain! [*Pushing him out.*

Mrs. Mal. O! Sir Anthony! — O fie, Captain! [*Exeunt severally.*

[1] R 3: Come, away Jack.

Scene III. — *The North Parade*

Enter Sir Lucius O'Trigger

Sir Luc. [I] wonder[1] where this Capt. Absolute hides himself! Upon my conscience! these officers are always in one's way in love affairs: — I remember I might have married Lady Dorothy Carmine, if it had not been for a little rogue of a major, who ran away with her before she could get a sight of me! And I wonder too what it is the ladies can see in them to be so fond of them — unless it be a touch of the old serpent in 'em, that makes the little creatures be caught, like vipers with a bit of red cloth. Hah! isn't this the Captain coming? — faith it is! — There is a probability of succeeding about that fellow, that is mighty provoking! Who the devil is he talking to?

[*Steps aside.*

Enter Captain Absolute

Abs. To what fine purpose I have been plotting! a noble reward for all my schemes, upon my soul! — a little gypsey! — I did not think her romance could have made her so d—n'd absurd either. 'Sdeath, I never was in a worse humour in my life! — I could cut my own throat, or any other person's with the greatest pleasure in the world!

Sir Luc. O, faith! I'm in the luck of it. I never could have found him in a sweeter temper for my purpose — to be sure I'm just come in the nick! Now to enter into conversation with him, and so quarrel genteelly. — [Sir Lucius *goes up to* Absolute. With regard to that matter, Captain, I must beg leave to differ in opinion with you.

Abs. Upon my word, then, you must be a very subtle disputant: — because, Sir, I happened just then to be giving no opinion at all.

Sir Luc. That's no reason. For give me leave to tell you, a man may *think* an untruth as well as *speak* one.

[1] RR: I wonder.

Abs. Very true, Sir; but if a man never utters his thoughts, I should think they *might* stand a *chance* of escaping controversy.

Sir Luc. Then, sir, you differ in opinion with me, which amounts to the same thing.

Abs. Hark'ee, Sir Lucius; if I had not before known you to be a gentleman, upon my soul, I should not have discovered it at this interview: for what you can drive at, unless you mean to quarrel with me, I cannot conceive!

Sir Luc. I humbly thank you, Sir, for the quickness of your apprehension. — [*Bowing.*] — you have named the very thing I would be at.

Abs. Very well, Sir; I shall certainly not baulk your inclinations. — But I should be glad you would please to explain your motives.

Sir Luc. Pray, Sir, be easy — the quarrel is a very pretty quarrel as it stands — we should only spoil it, by trying to explain it. — However, your memory is very short, or you could not have forgot an affront you pass'd on me within this week. So no more, but name your time and place.

Abs. Well, Sir, since you are so bent on it, the sooner the better; let it be this evening — here, by the Spring Gardens. — We shall scarcely be interrupted.

Sir Luc. Faith! that same interruption in affairs of this nature shows very great ill-breeding. I don't know what's the reason, but in England, if a thing of this kind gets wind, people make such a pother, that a gentleman can never fight in peace and quietness. However, if it's the same to you, Captain, I should take it as a particular kindness, if you'd let us meet in King's-Mead-Fields, as a little business will call me there about six o'clock, and I may despatch both matters at once.

Abs. 'Tis the same to me exactly. A little after six, then we will discuss this matter more seriously.

SIR LUC. If you please, Sir; there will be very pretty small-sword light, though it won't do for a long shot. So that matter's settled, and my mind's at ease! [*Exit.*

Enter FAULKLAND *meeting* ABSOLUTE

ABS. Well met — I was going to look for you. O Faulkland! all the Dæmons of spite and disappointment have conspired against me! I'm so vex'd, that if I had not the prospect of a resource in being knock'd o' the head by and bye, I should scarce have spirits to tell you the cause.

FAULK. What can you mean? — Has Lydia changed her mind? — I should have thought her duty and inclination would now have pointed to the same object.

ABS. Aye, just as the eyes do of a person who squints: when her *love-eye* was fixed on *me*, t'other, her *eye* of *duty*, was finely obliqued: but when duty bid her point *that* the same way, off t'other turned on a swivel, and secured its retreat with a frown!

FAULK. But what's the resource you ——

ABS. O, to wind up the whole, a good-natured Irishman here has — [*Mimicking* SIR LUCIUS] beg'd leave to have the pleasure of cutting my throat — and I mean to indulge him — that's all.

FAULK. Prithee, be serious!

ABS. 'Tis fact, upon my soul! Sir Lucius O'Trigger — you know him by sight — for some affront, which I am sure I never intended, has obliged me to meet him this evening at six o'clock: 'tis on that account I wished to see you — you must go with me.

FAULK. Nay, there must be some mistake, sure. — Sir Lucius shall explain himself — and I dare say matters may be accommodated: but this evening did you say? I wish it had been any other time.

ABS. Why? there will be light enough: — there will (as Sir Lucius says) "be very pretty small-sword light, tho' it won't do for a long shot." Confound his long shots!

FAULK. But I am myself a good deal ruffled by a difference I have had with Julia — my vile tormenting temper has made me treat her so cruelly, that I shall not be myself till we are reconciled.

ABS. By Heav'ns! Faulkland, you don't deserve her!

Enter SERVANT, *gives* FAULKLAND *a letter*

FAULK. Oh, Jack! this is from Julia — I dread to open it — I fear it may be to take a last leave — perhaps to bid me return her letters — and restore —— O, how I suffer for my folly!

ABS. Here, let me see. — [*Takes the letter and opens it.*] Ay, a final sentence, indeed! — 'tis all over with you, faith!

FAULK. Nay, Jack, don't keep me in suspense!

ABS. Hear then — *As "I am convinced that my dear Faulkland's own reflections have already upbraided him for his last unkindness to me, I will not add a word on the subject. I wish to speak with you as soon as possible. Your's ever and truly,* JULIA." There's stubbornness and resentment for you! — [*Gives him the letter.*] Why, man, you don't seem one whit happier at this!

FAULK. O yes, I am; but — but ——

ABS. Confound your *buts.* — You never hear anything that would make another man bless himself, but you immediately d—n it with a *but.*

FAULK. Now, Jack, as you are my friend, own honestly — don't you think there is something forward — something indelicate in this haste to forgive? Women should never sue for reconciliation: *that* should *always* come from us. *They* should retain their coldness till *woo'd* to kindness; and their *pardon*, like their love, should "not unsought be won."

ABS. I have not patience to listen to you: — thou'rt incorrigible! so say no more on the subject. — I must go to settle a few matters. Let me see you before six — remember — at my lodgings. — A poor industrious devil like me, who have toil'd, and drudg'd, and plotted to gain my ends, and am at last disappointed by other people's folly — may in pity be allowed to swear and grumble a little; — but a captious sceptic in love — a slave to fretfulness and whim — who has no difficulties but of *his own* creating — is a subject more fit for ridicule than compassion! [*Exit* ABSOLUTE.

FAULK. I feel his reproaches! — yet I would not change this too exquisite nicety for the gross content with which *he* tramples on the thorns of love. — His engaging me in this duel, has started an idea in my head, which I will instantly pursue. — I'll use it as the touchstone of Julia's sincerity and disinterestedness — if her love prove pure and sterling ore — my name will rest on it with honour! and once I've stamped it there, I lay aside my doubts for ever: — but if the dross of selfishness, the allay of pride predominate, 'twill be best to leave her as a toy for some less cautious Fool to sigh for!

[*Exit* FAULKLAND.

END OF THE FOURTH ACT

ACT V

SCENE I. — JULIA'S *Dressing-Room*

JULIA, *sola*

How this message has alarmed me! what dreadful accident can he mean! why such charge to be alone? — O Faulkland! — how many unhappy moments! — how many tears have you cost me!

Enter FAULKLAND, *muffled up in a Riding-coat*

JUL. What means this? — why this caution, Faulkland?

FAULK. Alas! Julia, I am come to take a long farewell.

JUL. Heav'ns! what do you mean?

FAULK. You see before you a wretch, whose life is forfeited. Nay, start not! — the infirmity of my temper has drawn all this misery on me. — I left you fretful and passionate — an untoward accident drew me into a quarrel — the event is, that I must fly this kingdom instantly. O Julia, had I been so fortunate as to have called you mine intirely, before this mischance had fallen on me, I should not so deeply dread my banishment! «— But no more of that — your heart and promise were given to one happy in friends, character and station! They are not bound to wait upon a solitary, guilty exile.»

JUL. My soul is oppresst with sorrow at the *nature* of your misfortune: had these adverse circumstances arisen from a less fatal cause I should have felt strong comfort in the thought that I could *now* chase from your bosom every doubt of the warm sincerity of my love. — My heart has long known no other guardian — I now entrust my person to your honour — we will fly together. — When safe from pursuit, my Father's will may be fulfilled — and I receive a legal claim to be the partner of your sorrows, and tenderest comforter. Then on the bosom of your wedded Julia, you may lull your keen regret to slumbering; while virtuous love, with a Cherub's hand, shall smoothe the brow of upbraiding thought, and pluck the thorn from compunction.

FAULK. O Julia! I am bankrupt in gratitude! but the time is so pressing, it calls on you for so hasty a resolution. — Would you not wish some hours to weigh the advantages you forego, and what little compensation poor Faulkland can make you beside his solitary love?

JUL. I ask not a moment. No, Faulkland, I have lov'd you for yourself: and if I now, more than ever, prize the solemn engagement which so long has pledged us to each other, it is because it leaves no room for hard aspersions on my fame, and puts the seal of duty to an act of love. — But let us not linger. — Perhaps this delay ——

FAULK. 'Twill be better I should not venture out again till dark. — Yet am I grieved to think what numberless distresses will press heavy on your gentle disposition!

JUL. Perhaps your fortune may be forfeited by this unhappy act. — I know not whether 'tis so; but sure that alone can never make us unhappy. The little I have will be sufficient to *support* us; and *exile* never should be splendid.

FAULK. Aye, but in such an abject state of life, my wounded pride perhaps may increase the natural fretfulness of my temper, till I become a rude, morose companion, beyond your patience to endure. Perhaps the recollection of a deed, my conscience cannot justify, may haunt me in such gloomy and unsocial fits, that I shall hate the tenderness that would relieve me, break from your arms, and quarrel with your fondness!

JUL. If your thoughts should assume so unhappy a bent, you will the more want some mild and affectionate spirit to watch over and console you! one who can,[1] by bearing *your* infirmities with gentleness and resignation, may teach you *so* to bear the evils of your fortune.

FAULK. O Julia,[2] I have proved you to the quick! and with this useless device I throw away all my doubts. How shall I plead to be forgiven this last unworthy effect of my restless, unsatisfied disposition?

JUL. Has no such disaster happened as you related?

FAULK. I am ashamed to own that it was[3] pretended; yet in pity, Julia, do not kill me with resenting a fault which never can be repeated: But sealing, this once, my pardon, let me to-morrow, in the face of Heaven, receive my future guide and monitress, and expiate my past folly, by years of tender adoration.

JUL. Hold, Faulkland! — that you are free from a crime, which I before feared to name, Heaven knows how sincerely I rejoice! — These are tears of thankfulness for that! But that your cruel doubts should have urged you to an imposition that has wrung my heart, gives me now a pang more keen than I can express.

[1] RR omit "can." [2] R 3 omits "O." [3] RR insert "all."

FAULK. By Heav'ns! Julia ——

JUL. Yet hear me, — My Father loved you,·Faulkland! and you preserv'd the life that tender parent gave me; in his presence I pledged my hand — *joyfully* pledged it — where before I had given my heart. When, soon after, I lost that parent, it seemed to me that Providence had, in Faulkland, shown me whither to transfer without a pause, my grateful duty, as well as my affection: hence I have been content to bear from you what pride and delicacy would have forbid me from another. I will not upbraid you, by repeating how you have trifled with my sincerity ——

FAULK. I confess it all! yet hear ——

JUL. After such a year of trial — I might have flattered myself that I should not have been insulted with a new probation of my sincerity, as cruel as unnecessary! «A trick of such a nature, as to shew me plainly, that when I thought you lov'd me best, you even then regarded me as a mean dissembler; an artful, prudent hypocrite.

«FAULK. Never! never!»

JUL. I now see it is not in your nature to be content or confident in love. With this conviction — I never will be yours. While I had hopes that my persevering attention, and unreproaching kindness might in time reform your temper, I should have been happy to have gain'd a dearer influence over you; but I will not furnish you with a licensed power to keep alive an incorrigible fault, at the expense of one who never would contend with you.

FAULK. Nay, but, Julia, by my soul and honour, if after this ——

JUL. But one word more. — As my faith has once been given to you, I never will barter it with another. — I shall pray for your happiness with the truest sincerity; and the dearest blessing I can ask of Heaven to send you, will be to charm you from that unhappy temper, which alone has prevented the performance of our solemn engagement. — All I request of *you* is, that you will yourself reflect upon this infirmity, and when you number up the many true delights it has deprived you of, let it not be your *least* regret, that it lost you the love of one who would have follow'd you in beggary through the world! [*Exit.*

FAULK. She's gone! — for ever! — There was an awful resolution in her manner, that rivetted me to my place. — O Fool! — Dolt! — Barbarian! Cursed as I am, with more imperfections than my fellow-wretches, kind Fortune sent a heaven-gifted cherub to my aid, and, like a ruffian, I have driven her from my side! — I must now haste to my appointment. Well my mind is tuned for such a scene. I shall wish only to become a principal in it, and reverse the tale my cursed folly put me upon forging here. — O Love! — Tormenter! — Fiend! — whose influence, like the Moon's, acting on men of dull souls, makes idiots of them, but meeting subtler spirits, betrays their course, and urges sensibility to madness! [*Exit.*

Enter MAID *and* LYDIA

MAID. My Mistress, Ma'am, I know, was here just now — perhaps she is only in the next room. [*Exit* MAID.

LYD. Heigh ho! Though he has used me so, this fellow runs strangely in my head. I believe one lecture from my grave Cousin will make me recall him.

Enter JULIA

LYD. O Julia, I have come to you with such an appetite for consolation. — Lud! Child, what's the matter with you? You have been crying! — I'll be hanged, if that Faulkland has not been tormenting you.

JUL. You mistake the cause of my uneasiness! — Something *has* flurried me a little. Nothing that you can guess at. — I would not accuse Faulkland to a Sister! [*Aside.*]

Lyd. Ah! whatever vexations you may have, I can assure you mine surpass them. You know who Beverley proves to be?

Jul. I will now own to you, Lydia, that Mr. Faulkland had before informed me of the whole affair. Had young Absolute been the person you took him for, I should not have accepted your confidence on the subject, without a serious endeavour to counteract your caprice.

Lyd. So, then, I see I have been deceived by every one! But I don't care — I'll never have him.

Jul. Nay, Lydia ——

Lyd. Why, is it not provoking; when I thought we were coming to the prettiest distress imaginable, to find myself made a mere Smithfield bargain of at last! There had I projected one of the most sentimental elopements! — so becoming a disguise! — so amiable a ladder of Ropes! — Conscious Moon — four horses — Scotch parson — with such surprise to Mrs. Malaprop — and such paragraphs in the News-papers! — Oh, I shall die with disappointment!

Jul. I don't wonder at it? [!]

Lyd. Now — sad reverse! — what have I to expect, but, after a deal of flimsy preparation with a bishop's licence, and my Aunt's blessing, to go simpering up to the Altar; or perhaps be cried three times in a country-church, and have an unmannerly fat clerk ask the consent of every butcher in the parish to join John Absolute and Lydia Languish, *Spinster!* O, that I should live to hear myself called Spinster!

Jul. Melancholy, indeed!

Lyd. How mortifying, to remember the dear delicious shifts I used to be put to, to gain half a minute's conversation with this fellow! — How often have I stole forth, in the coldest night in January, and found him in the garden, stuck like a dripping statue! There would he kneel to me in the snow, and sneeze and cough so pathetically! he shivering with cold, and I with apprehension! and while the freezing blast numb'd our joints, how warmly would he press me to pity his flame, and glow with mutual ardour! — Ah, Julia, that was something like being in love.

JUL. If I were in spirits, Lydia, I should chide you only by laughing heartily at you: but it suits more the situation of my mind, at present, earnestly to entreat you not to let a man, who loves you with sincerity, suffer that unhappiness from your *caprice*, which I know too well caprice can inflict.

LYD. O Lud! what has brought my Aunt here?

Enter MRS. MALAPROP, FAG, *and* DAVID

MRS. MAL. So! so! here's fine work! — here's fine suicide, paracide, and salivation[1] going on in the fields! and Sir Anthony not to be found to prevent the antistrophe!

JUL. For Heaven's sake, Madam, what's the meaning of this?

MRS. MAL. That gentleman can tell you — 'twas he enveloped the affair to me.

LYD. Do, Sir, will you, inform us? [*To* FAG.

FAG. Ma'am, I should hold myself very deficient in every requisite that forms the man of breeding, if I delay'd a moment to give all the information in my power to a lady so deeply interested in the affair as you are.

LYD. But quick! quick, sir!

FAG. True, Ma'am, as you say, one should be quick in divulging matters of this nature; for should we be tedious, perhaps while we are flourishing on the subject, two or three lives may be lost!

LYD. O patience! — do, Ma'am, for Heaven's sake! tell us what is the matter?

MRS. MAL. Why, murder's the matter! slaughter's the matter! killing's the matter! — but he can tell you the perpendiculars.

[1] R 3: simulation.

LYD. Then, prythee, Sir, be brief.

FAG. Why, then, Ma'am, as to murder — I cannot take upon me to say — and as to slaughter, or man-slaughter, that will be as the jury finds it.

LYD. But who, Sir — who are engaged in this?

FAG. Faith, Ma'am, one is a young gentleman whom I should be very sorry anything was to happen to — a very pretty behaved gentleman! We have lived much together, and always on terms.

LYD. But who is this? who? who? who?

FAG. My Master, Ma'am — my Master — I speak of my Master.

LYD. Heavens! What, Captain Absolute!

MRS. MAL. Oh, to be sure, you are frightened now!

JUL. But who are with him, Sir?

FAG. As to the rest, Ma'am, his gentleman can inform you better than I? [.]

JUL. Do speak, friend. [*To* DAVID.

DAV. Look'ee, my Lady — by the Mass! there's mischief going on. Folks don't use to meet for amusement with firearms, firelocks, fire-engines, fire-screens, fire-office, and the devil knows what other crackers beside! — This, my Lady, I say, has an angry savour.[1]

JUL. But who is there beside Captain Absolute, friend?

DAV. My poor Master — under favour for mentioning him first. You know me, my Lady — I am David — and my Master of course is, or *was*, Squire Acres. — Then comes Squire Faulkland.

JUL. Do, Ma'am, let us instantly endeavour to prevent mischief.

MRS. MAL. O fie! it would be very inelegant in us: — we should only participate things.

DAV. Ah! do, Mrs. Aunt, save a few lives — they are

[1] RR: favour.

desperately given, believe me. — Above all, there is that bloodthirsty Philistine, Sir Lucius O'Trigger.

MRS. MAL. Sir Lucius O'Trigger? O mercy! have they drawn poor little dear Sir Lucius into the scrape? — Why, how you stand, girl! you have no more feeling than one of the Derbyshire Putrifactions!

LYD. What are we to do, Madam?

MRS. MAL. Why, fly with the utmost felicity, to be sure, to prevent mischief! — Here, friend, you can show us the place?

FAG. If you please, Ma'am! I will conduct you. — David, do you look for Sir Anthony. [*Exit* DAVID.

MRS. MAL. Come, girls! this gentleman will exhort us. — Come, Sir, you're our envoy — lead the way, and we'll precede.

FAG. Not a step before the ladies for the world!

MRS. MAL. You're sure you know the spot?

FAG. I think I can find it, Ma'am; and one good thing is, we shall hear the report of the pistols as we draw near, so we can't well miss them; — never fear, Ma'am, never fear.

[*Exeunt*,[1] *he talking*.

SCENE II. — *South-Parade*

Enter ABSOLUTE, *putting his sword under his great-coat*

ABS. A sword seen in the streets of Bath would raise as great an alarm as a mad-dog. — How provoking this is in Faulkland! — never punctual! I shall be obliged to go without him at last. — O, the devil! here's Sir Anthony! how shall I escape him? [*Muffles up his face, and takes a circle to go off*.

Enter SIR ANTHONY

SIR ANTH. How one may be deceived at a little distance! Only that I see he don't know me, I could have sworn that was Jack! — Hey! 'Gad's life! it is. — Why, Jack, you Dog! —

[1] R 3: *Exit*.

what are you afraid of? hey — sure I'm right. Why Jack, Jack Absolute! [*Goes up to him.*

Abs. Really, sir, you have the advantage of me: — I don't remember ever to have had the honour — my name is Saunderson, at your service.

Sir Anth. Sir, I beg your pardon — I took you — hey! — why, z—ds! it is — Stay — [*Looks up to his face.*] So, so — your humble servant, Mr. Saunderson! Why, you scoundrel, what tricks are you after now?

Abs. Oh, a joke, Sir, a joke! I came here on purpose to look for you, Sir.

Sir Anth. You did! well, I am glad you were so lucky: — but what are you muffled up so for? — what's this for? — hey?

Abs. 'Tis cool, Sir, isn't it? — rather chilly somehow: — but I shall be late — I have a particular engagement.

Sir Anth. Stay! — Why, I thought you were looking for me? — Pray, Jack, where is't you are going?

Abs. Going, sir?

Sir Anth. Ay, where are you going?

Abs. Where am I going?

Sir Anth. You unmannerly puppy!

Abs. I was going, sir, to — to — to — to Lydia — Sir, to Lydia — to make matters up if I could; — and I was looking for you, Sir, to — to —

Sir Anth. To go with you, I suppose. — Well, come along.

Abs. Oh! z—ds! no, Sir, not for the world! — I wished to meet with you, Sir, — to — to — to — You find it cool, I'm sure, Sir — you'd better not stay out.

Sir Anth. Cool! — not at all. — Well, Jack — and what will you say to Lydia?

Abs. Oh, Sir, beg her pardon, humour her — promise and vow: but I detain you, Sir — consider the cold air on your gout.

Sir Anth. Oh, not at all! — not at all! I'm in no hurry. —

Ah! Jack, you youngsters, when once you are wounded here [*Putting his hand to* ABSOLUTE'S *breast.*] Hey! what the deuce have you got here?

ABS. Nothing, Sir — nothing.

SIR ANTH. What's this? — here's something d—d hard.

ABS. Oh, trinkets, Sir! trinkets! — a bauble for Lydia.

SIR ANTH. Nay, let me see your taste. — [*Pulls his coat open, the sword falls.*] Trinkets! a bauble for Lydia! — z—ds! sirrah, you are not going to cut her throat, are you?

ABS. Ha! ha! ha! — I thought it would divert you, Sir, tho' I didn't mean to tell you till afterwards.

SIR ANTH. You didn't? — Yes, this is a very diverting trinket, truly!

ABS. Sir, I'll explain to you. — You know, Sir, Lydia is romantic, dev'lish romantic, and very absurd of course: — now, Sir, I intend, if she refuses to forgive me, to unsheath this sword, and swear — I'll fall upon its point, and expire at her feet!

SIR ANTH. Fall upon fiddlestick's end![1] — why, I suppose it is the very thing that would please her. — Get along, you Fool!

ABS. Well, Sir, you shall hear of my success — you shall hear. — "O Lydia! — forgive me, or this pointed steel" — says I.

SIR ANTH. "O, booby! stab away and welcome" — says she. — Get along! and damn your trinkets!

[*Exit* ABSOLUTE.

Enter DAVID, *running*

DAV. Stop him! stop him! Murder! Thief! Fire! — Stop fire! Stop fire! — O Sir Anthony — call! call! bid 'em stop! Murder! Fire!

SIR ANTH. Fire! Murder! — Where?

DAV. Oons! he's out of sight, and I'm out of breath for my part, O Sir Anthony, why didn't you stop him? why didn't you stop him?

[1] R 3: a fiddle-stick's end!

SIR ANTH. Z—ds! the fellow's mad! — Stop whom? stop Jack?

DAV. Ay, the Captain, Sir! — there's murder and slaughter ——

SIR ANTH. Murder!

DAV. Ay, please you, Sir Anthony, there's all kinds of murder, all sorts of slaughter to be seen in the fields: there's fighting going on, Sir — bloody sword-and-gun fighting!

SIR ANTH. Who are going to fight, Dunce?

DAV. Everybody that I know of, Sir Anthony: — everybody is going to fight, my poor Master, Sir Lucius O'Trigger, your son, the Captain ——

SIR ANTH. Oh, the Dog! I see his tricks. — Do you know the place?

DAV. King's-Mead-Fields.

SIR ANTH. You know the way?

DAV. Not an inch; but I'll call the mayor — aldermen — constables — churchwardens — and beadles — we can't be too many to part them.

SIR ANTH. Come along — give me your shoulder! we'll get assistance as we go — the lying villain! — Well, I shall be in such a frenzy! — So — this was the history of his d—d[1] trinkets! I'll bauble him! [*Exeunt.*

SCENE III. — *King's-Mead-Fields*

Enter SIR LUCIUS *and* ACRES, *with pistols*

ACRES. By my valour! then, Sir Lucius, forty yards is a good distance. Odds levels and aims! — I say it is a good distance.

SIR LUC. Is it for muskets or small field-pieces? Upon my conscience, Mr. Acres, you must leave those things to me. — Stay now — I'll show you. — [*Measures paces along the stage.*]

[1] R 3 omits "d—d."

There now, that is a very pretty distance — a pretty gentleman's distance.

ACRES. Z—ds! we might as well fight in a centry-[sentry] box! I tell you Sir Lucius, the farther he is off, the cooler I shall take my aim.

SIR LUC. Faith! then I suppose you would aim at him best of all if he was out of sight!

ACRES. No, Sir Lucius; but I should think forty or eight and thirty yards ——

SIR LUC. Pho! pho! nonsense! three or four feet between the mouths of your pistols is as good as a mile.

ACRES. Odds bullets, no! — by my valour! there is no merit in killing him so near: do, my dear Sir Lucius, let me bring him down at a long shot: — a long shot, Sir Lucius, if you love me!

SIR LUC. Well — the gentleman's friend and I must settle that. — But tell me now, Mr. Acres, in case of an accident, is there any little will or commission I could execute for you?

ACRES. I am much obliged to you, Sir Lucius, but I don't understand ——

SIR LUC. Why, you may think there's no being shot at without a little risk — and if an unlucky bullet should carry a *Quietus* with it — I say it will be no time then to be bothering you about family matters.

ACRES. A *Quietus!*

SIR LUC. For instance, now — if that should be the case — would you chuse to be pickled and sent home? — or would it be the same to you to lie here in the Abbey? I'm told there is very snug lying in the Abbey.

ACRES. Pickled! — Snug lying in the Abbey! — Odds tremors! Sir Lucius, don't talk so!

SIR LUC. I suppose, Mr. Acres, you never were engaged in an affair of this kind before?

ACRES. No, Sir Lucius, never before.

Sir Luc. Ah! that's a pity! — there's nothing like being used to a thing. Pray now, how would you receive the gentleman's shot?

Acres. Odds files! — I've practised that — there, Sir Lucius — there. [*Puts himself in an attitude.*] A side-front, hey? Odd! I'll make myself small enough? I'll stand edge-ways.

Sir Luc. Now — you're quite out — for if you stand so when I take my aim —— [*Levelling at him.*

Acres. Z—ds! Sir Lucius — are you sure it is not cocked?

Sir Luc. Never fear.

Acres. But — but — you don't know — it may go off of its own head!

Sir Luc. Pho! be easy. — Well, now if I hit you in the body, my bullet has a double chance — for if it misses a vital part of your right side — 'twill be very hard if it don't succeed on the left!

Acres. A vital part! O, my poor vitals![1]

Sir Luc. But, there — fix yourself so — [*Placing him*] — let him see the broad-side of your full front — there — now a ball or two may pass clean[2] through your body, and never do any harm at all.

Acres. Clean through me! — a ball or two clean through me!

Sir Luc. Aye — may they — and it is much the genteelest attitude into the bargain.

Acres. Look'ee! Sir Lucius — I'd just as lieve be shot in an awkward posture as a genteel one; so, by my valour! I will stand edge-ways.

Sir Luc. [*Looking at his watch.*] Sure they don't mean to disappoint us — Hah? — no [,] faith — I think I see them coming.

Acres. Hey! — what! — coming! ——

[1] R 3 omits "O, my poor vitals!"

[2] R 1, 2: clear.

SIR LUC. Aye. — Who are those yonder getting over the stile?

ACRES. There are two of them indeed! — well — let them come — hey, Sir Lucius! — we — we — we — we — won't run.

SIR LUC. Run!

ACRES. No — I say — we *won't* run, by my valour!

SIR LUC. What the devil's the matter with you?

ACRES. Nothing — nothing — my dear friend — my dear Sir Lucius — but I — I — I don't feel quite so bold, somehow, as I did.

SIR LUC. O fie! — consider your honour.

ACRES. Aye — true — my honour. Do, Sir Lucius, hedge[1] in a word or two every now and then about my honour.

SIR LUC. Well, here they're coming. [*Looking.*

ACRES. Sir Lucius — if I wa'n't with you, I should almost think I was afraid. — If my valour should leave me! — Valour will come and go.

SIR LUC. Then pray keep it fast, while you have it.

ACRES. Sir Lucius — I doubt it is going — yes — my valour is certainly going! — it is sneaking off! — I feel it oozing out as it were at the palms of my hands!

SIR LUC. Your honour — your honour. — Here they are.

ACRES. O mercy! — now — that I was[2] safe at Clod-Hall! or could be shot before I was aware!

Enter FAULKLAND *and* ABSOLUTE

SIR LUC. Gentlemen, your most obedient. — Hah! — what, Captain Absolute! — So, I suppose, sir, you are come here, just like myself — to do a kind office, first for your friend — then to proceed to business on your own account.

ACRES. What, Jack! — my dear Jack! — my dear friend!

ABS. Hark'ee, Bob, Beverley's at hand.

SIR LUC. Well, Mr. Acres — I don't blame your saluting

[1] R 3: edge. [2] RR: were.

the gentleman civilly. — So, Mr. Beverley, [*To* FAULKLAND] if you'll chuse your weapons, the Captain and I will measure the ground.

FAULK. *My* weapons, Sir!

ACRES. Odds life! Sir Lucius, I'm not going to fight Mr. Faulkland; these are my particular friends.

SIR LUC. What, Sir, did you not come here to fight Mr. Acres?

FAULK. Not I, upon my word, Sir.

SIR LUC. Well, now, that's mighty provoking! But I hope, Mr. Faulkland, as there are three of us come on purpose for the game — you won't be so cantanckerous as to spoil the party by sitting out.

ABS. O pray, Faulkland, fight to oblige Sir Lucius.

FAULK. Nay, if Mr. Acres is so bent on the matter ——

ACRES. No, no, Mr. Faulkland; I'll bear my disappointment like a Christian. — Look'ee, Sir Lucius, there's no occasion at all for me to fight; and if it is the same to you, I'd as lieve let it alone.

SIR LUC. Observe me, Mr. Acres — I must not be trifled with. You have certainly challenged somebody — and you came here to fight him. Now, if that gentleman is willing to represent him — I can't see, for my soul, why it isn't just the same thing.

ACRES. Z—nds,[1] — Sir Lucius — I tell you, 'tis one Beverley I've challenged — a fellow, you see, that dare not show his face! — if *he* were here, I'd make him give up his pretensions directly!

ABS. Hold, Bob — let me set you right — there is no such man as Beverley in the case. — The person who assumed that name is before you; and as his pretensions are the same in both characters, he is ready to support them in whatever way you please.

[1] R 3: Why no.

Sir Luc. Well, this is lucky. — Now you have an opportunity ——

Acres. What, quarrel with my dear friend, Jack Absolute? — not if he were fifty Beverleys! Z—ds! Sir Lucius, you would not have me be so unnatural.

Sir Luc. Upon my conscience, Mr. Acres, your valour has *oozed* away with a vengeance!

Acres. Not in the least! Odds Backs and Abettors! I'll be your second with all my heart — and if you should get a *Quietus*, you may command me entirely. I'll get you a *snug lying* in the *Abbey here;* or *pickle* you, and send you over to Blunderbuss-hall, or any[1] of the kind, with the greatest pleasure.

Sir Luc. Pho! pho! you are little better than a coward.

Acres. Mind, gentlemen, he calls me a *Coward;* Coward was the word, by my valour!

Sir Luc. Well, Sir?

Acres. Look'ee, Sir Lucius, 'tisn't that I mind the word Coward — *Coward* may be said in joke — But if you had called me a *Poltroon*, odds Daggers and Balls ——

Sir Luc. Well, sir?

Acres. I should have thought you a very ill-bred man.

Sir Luc. Pho! you are beneath my notice.

Abs. Nay, Sir Lucius, you can't have a better second than my friend Acres. — He is a most *determined dog* — called in the country, *Fighting Bob.* — He generally *kills a man a week* — don't you Bob?

Acres. Aye — at home!

Sir Luc. Well, then, Captain, 'tis we must begin — so come out, my little counsellor — [*Draws his sword*] — and ask the gentleman, whether he will resign the lady, without forcing you to proceed against him?

Abs. Come on then, sir — [*Draws*]; since you won't let it be an amicable suit, here's *my reply.*

[1] R 3: any thing.

Enter SIR ANTHONY, DAVID, *and the* WOMEN

DAVID. Knock 'em all down, sweet Sir Anthony; knock down my Master in particular; and bind his hands over to their good behaviour.

SIR ANTH. Put up, Jack, put up, or I shall be in a frenzy — how came you in a duel, Sir?

ABS. Faith, Sir, that gentleman can tell you better than I; 'twas he call'd on me, and you know, Sir, I serve his Majesty.

SIR ANTH. Here's a pretty fellow; I catch him going to cut a man's throat, and he tells me he serves his Majesty! — Zounds! sirrah, then how durst you draw the King's sword against one of his subjects?

ABS. Sir! I tell you, that gentleman called me out, without explaining his reasons.

SIR ANTH. Gad! Sir, how came you to call my son out, without explaining your reasons!

SIR LUC. Your son, Sir, insulted me in a manner which my honour could not brook.

SIR ANTH. Zounds! Jack, how durst you insult the gentleman in a manner which his honour could not brook?

MRS. MAL. Come, come, let's have no Honour before ladies — Captain Absolute, come here — How could you intimidate us so? — Here's Lydia has been terrified to death for you.

ABS. For fear I should be kill'd, or escape, Ma'am?

MRS. MAL. Nay, no delusions to the past — Lydia is convinc'd; speak, child.

SIR LUC. With your leave, Ma'am, I must put in a word here — I believe I could interpret the young lady's silence — Now mark ——

LYD. What is it you mean, Sir?

SIR LUC. Come, come, Delia, we must be serious now — this is no time for trifling.

LYD. 'Tis true, Sir; and your reproof bids me offer this gentleman my hand, and solicit the return of his affections.

ABS. O! my little angel, say you so? — Sir Lucius — I perceive there must be some mistake here — with regard to the affront which you affirm I have given you — I can only say, that it could not have been intentional. And as you must be convinced, that I should not fear to support a real injury — you shall now see that I am not ashamed to atone for an inadvertency — I ask your pardon. — But for this lady, while honour'd with her approbation, I will support my claim against any man whatever.

SIR ANTH. Well said, Jack, and I'll stand by you, my Boy.

ACRES. Mind, I give up all my claim — I make no pretensions to anything in the world; and if I can't get a wife, without fighting for her, by my Valour! I'll live a bachelor.

SIR LUC. Captain, give me your hand — an affront handsomely acknowledged becomes an obligation — and as for the Lady, if she chuses to deny her own handwriting here —— [*Takes out letters.*

MRS. MAL. O, he will disolve my mystery! — Sir Lucius, perhaps there's some mistake — perhaps, I can illuminate ——

SIR LUC. Pray, old gentlewoman, don't interfere where you have no business. — Miss Languish, are you my Delia, or not?

LYD. Indeed, Sir Lucius, I am not.

[LYDIA *and* ABSOLUTE *walk aside.*

MRS. MAL. Sir Lucius O'Trigger — ungrateful as you are — I own the soft impeachment — pardon my blushes, I am Delia.

SIR LUC. You Delia — pho! pho! be easy.

MRS. MAL. Why, thou barbarous Vandyke — those letters are mine. — When you are more sensible of my benignity — perhaps I may be brought to encourage your addresses.

SIR LUC. Mrs. Malaprop, I am extremely sensible of your condescension; and whether you or Lucy have put this trick on me, I am equally beholden to you. — And to show you I am not ungrateful, Captain Absolute! since you have taken that lady from me, I'll give you my Delia into the bargain.

ABS. I am much obliged to you, Sir Lucius; but here's our friend, fighting Bob, unprovided for.

SIR LUC. Hah! little Valour — here, will you make your fortune?

ACRES. Odds Wrinkles! No. — But give me[1] your hand, Sir Lucius, forget and forgive; but if ever I give you a chance of *pickling* me again, say Bob Acres is a Dunce, that's all.

SIR ANTH. Come, Mrs. Malaprop, don't be cast down — you are in your bloom yet.

MRS. MAL. O Sir Anthony — men are all barbarians.

[*All retire but* JULIA *and* FAULKLAND.

JUL. [*Aside*] He seems dejected and unhappy — not sullen; there was some foundation, however, for the tale he told me — O woman! how true should be your judgment, when your resolution is so weak!

FAULK. Julia! — how can I sue for what I so little deserve? I dare not presume — yet Hope is the child of Penitence.

JUL. Oh! Faulkland, you have not been more faulty in your unkind treatment of me, than I am now in wanting inclination to resent it. As my heart honestly bids me place my weakness to the account of love, I should be ungenerous not to admit the same plea for yours.

FAULK. Now I shall be blest indeed!

[*Sir Anthony comes forward.*

SIR ANTH. What's going on here? — So you have been quarrelling too, I warrant? Come, Julia, I never interfered before; but let me have a hand in the matter at last. — All the faults I have ever seen in my friend Faulkland, seemed to proceed from what he calls the *delicacy* and *warmth* of his affection for you. — There, marry him directly, Julia, you'll find he'll mend surprisingly! [*The rest come forward.*

SIR LUC. Come, now, I hope there is no dissatisfied person,

[1] R 1, 2: us.

but what is content; for as I have been disappointed myself, it will be very hard if I have not the satisfaction of seeing other people succeed better ——

ACRES. You are right, Sir Lucius. — So Jack, I wish you joy. — Mr. Faulkland the same. — Ladies, — come now, to show you I'm neither vex'd nor angry, Odds Tabors and Pipes! I'll order the fiddles in half an hour to the New Rooms — and I insist on your all meeting me there.

SIR ANTH. 'Gad! Sir, I like your spirit; and at night we single lads will drink a health to the young couples, and a husband to Mrs. Malaprop.

FAULK. Our partners are stolen from us, Jack — I hope to be congratulated by each other — yours for having checked in time the errors of an ill-directed Imagination, which might have betray'd an innocent heart; and mine, for having, by her gentleness and candour, reformed the unhappy temper of one, who by it made wretched whom he loved most, and tortured the heart he ought to have ador'd.

ABS. Well, Jack, [Faulkland?][1] we have both tasted the Bitters, as well as the Sweets of Love; with this difference only, that *you* always prepared the bitter cup for yourself, while I ——

LYD. Was always obliged to *me* for it, hey! Mr. Modesty? —— But come, no more of that — our happiness is now as unallay'd[2] as general.

JUL. Then let us study to preserve it so: and while Hope pictures to us a flattering scene of future Bliss, let us deny its pencil those colours which are too bright to be lasting. — When Hearts deserving Happiness would unite their fortunes, Virtue would crown them with an unfading garland of modest, hurtless flowers; but ill-judging Passion will force the gaudier Rose into the wreath, whose thorn offends them, when its Leaves are dropped! [*Exeunt omnes.*

[1] This is Fraser Rae's pertinent query, since in Act II, Scene 1, Absolute calls his friend "Faulkland."

[2] Modern eds.: unalloyed.

EPILOGUE

BY THE AUTHOR

SPOKEN BY MRS. BULKLEY

LADIES, for *You* — I heard our Poet say —
He'd try to coax some *Moral* from his Play:
'One moral's plain — cried I — without more fuss;
Man's social happiness all rests on Us —
Thro' all the Drama — whether d—n'd or not —
Love gilds the *Scene*, and *Women* guide the *plot.*
From every rank — obedience is our due —
D'ye doubt? — The world's great stage shall prove it true.'
  The Cit — well skill'd to shun domestic strife —
Will sup abroad; — but first — he'll ask his *wife:*
John Trot, his friend — for once, will do the same,
But then — he'll just *step home to tell my dame.*
  The *surly Squire* — at noon resolves to rule,
And half the day — zounds! Madam is a fool!
Convinced at night, the vanquish'd Victor says,
Ah, Kate! *you women have such coaxing ways.*
  The *jolly Toper* chides each tardy blade, —
Till reeling Bacchus calls on Love for aid:
Then with each Toast he sees fair bumpers swim,
And kisses Chloe on the sparkling Brim!
  Nay, I have heard that Statesmen — great and wise —
Will *sometimes* counsel with a Lady's eyes!
The servile suitors — watch her various face,
She smiles preferment — or she frowns disgrace,
Curtsies a pension here — there nods a place.
  Nor with less awe, in scenes of humbler life,
Is *view'd* the *mistress*, or is *heard* the *wife.*
The poorest Peasant of the poorest soil,
The child of Poverty, and heir to Toil,

Early from radiant Love's impartial light
Steals one small spark, to cheer his world of night:
Dear spark! — that oft through winter's chilling woes
Is all the warmth his little cottage knows!
The wandering *Tar* — who, not for *years* has press'd,
The widow'd Partner of his *day* of rest,
On the cold deck — far from her arms remov'd, —
Still hums the ditty which his Susan loved:
And while around the cadence rude is blown,
The Boatswain whistles in a softer tone.
The *Soldier*, fairly proud of wounds and toil,
Pants for the *triumph* of his Nancy's smile!
But ere the battle should he list' her cries,
The Lover trembles — and the Hero dies!
That heart, by war and honour steel'd to fear,
Droops on a sigh, and sickens at a tear!
But ye more cautious — ye nice judging few,
Who give to Beauty only Beauty's due,
Tho' friends to Love — *Ye* view with deep regret
Our conquests marr'd — our triumphs incomplete,
'Till polish'd wit more lasting charms disclose,
And Judgment fix the darts which Beauty throws!
In female breasts did Sense and Merit rule,
The Lover's mind would ask no other school;
Sham'd into sense — the Scholars of our eyes,
Our Beaux from *Gallantry* would soon be wise;
Would gladly light, their homage to improve,
The Lamp of Knowledge at the Torch of Love!

THE SCHOOL FOR SCANDAL

THE TEXT OF THE SCHOOL FOR SCANDAL

THE text of *The School for Scandal* in this edition is taken, by Mr. Fraser Rae's generous permission, from his *Sheridan's Plays now printed as he wrote them.* In his Prefatory Notes (xxxvii), Mr. Rae writes: "The manuscript of it [*The School for Scandal*] in Sheridan's own handwriting is preserved at Frampton Court and is now printed in this volume. This version differs in many respects from that which is generally known, and I think it is even better than that which has hitherto been read and acted. As I have endeavoured to reproduce the works of Sheridan as he wrote them, I may be told that he was a bad hand at punctuating and very bad at spelling. . . . But Sheridan's shortcomings as a speller have been exaggerated." Lest "Sheridan's shortcomings" either in spelling or in punctuation should obscure the text, I have, in this edition, inserted in brackets some explanatory suggestions. It has seemed best, also, to adopt a uniform method for indicating stage-directions and abbreviations of the names of characters. There can be no gain to the reader in reproducing, for example, Sheridan's different indications for the part of Lady Sneerwell — *Lady Sneerwell, Lady Sneer., Lady Sn.*, and *Lady S.* — or his varying use of *Exit* and *Ex.*, or his inconsistencies in the use of italics in the stage-directions. Since, however, Sheridan's biographers, from Moore to Fraser Rae, have shown that no authorised or correct edition of *The School for Scandal* was published in Sheridan's lifetime, there seems unusual justification for reproducing the text of the play itself with absolute fidelity to the original manuscript. Mr. Ridgway, who repeatedly sought to obtain a copy corrected by the author, according to Moore's account (*Life of Sheridan*, I. p. 260), "was told by Mr. Sheridan, as an excuse for keeping it back, that he had been nineteen years endeavouring to satisfy himself with the style of The School for Scandal, but had not yet succeeded." Mr. Rae (*Sheridan*, I. p. 332) recorded his discovery of the manuscript of "two acts of The School for Scandal prepared by Sheridan for publication," and hoped, before his death, to publish this partial revision. Numberless unauthorized changes in the play have been made for histrionic purposes, from the first undated Dublin edition to that of Mr. Augustin Daly. Current texts may usually be traced, directly or indirectly, to the two-volume Murray edition of Sheridan's plays, in 1821. Some of the changes from the original manuscript, such as the blending of the parts of Miss Verjuice and Snake, are doubtless effective for reasons of dramatic economy, but many of the "cuts" are to be regretted from the reader's standpoint. The student of English drama will prefer Sheridan's own text to editorial emendations, however clever or effective for dramatic ends.

THE SCHOOL FOR SCANDAL

A COMEDY

A PORTRAIT[1]

ADDRESSED TO MRS. CREWE, WITH THE COMEDY OF THE SCHOOL FOR SCANDAL

BY R. B. SHERIDAN, ESQ.

TELL me, ye prim adepts in Scandal's school,
Who rail by precept, and detract by rule,
Lives there no character, so tried, so known,
So deck'd with grace, and so unlike your own,
That even you assist her fame to raise,
Approve by envy, and by silence praise! —
Attend! — a model shall attract your view —
Daughters of calumny, I summon you!
You shall decide if this a portrait prove,
Or fond creation of the Muse and Love. —
Attend, ye virgin critics, shrewd and sage,
Ye matron censors of this childish age,
Whose peering eye and wrinkled front declare
A fixt antipathy to young and fair;
By cunning, cautious; or by nature, cold,
In maiden madness, virulently bold! —
Attend! ye skilled to coin the precious tale,
Creating proof, where innuendos fail!
Whose practised memories, cruelly exact,
Omit no circumstance, except the fact! —

[1] This *Portrait* and Garrick's *Prologue* are not included in Fraser Rae's text.

Attend, all ye who boast, — or old or young, —
The living libel of a slanderous tongue!
So shall my theme as far contrasted be,
As saints by fiends, or hymns by calumny.
Come, gentle Amoret (for 'neath that name,
In worthier verse is sung thy beauty's fame);
Come — for but thee who seeks the Muse? and while
Celestial blushes check thy conscious smile,
With timid grace, and hesitating eye,
The perfect model, which I boast, supply: —
Vain Muse! couldst thou the humblest sketch create
Of her, or slightest charm couldst imitate —
Could thy blest strain in kindred colours trace
The faintest wonder of her form and face —
Poets would study the immortal line,
And *Reynolds* own *his* art subdued by thine;
That art, which well might added lustre give
To Nature's best and Heaven's superlative:
On *Granby's* cheek might bid new glories rise,
Or point a purer beam from *Devon's* eyes!
Hard is the task to shape that beauty's praise,
Whose judgment scorns the homage flattery pays!
But praising Amoret we cannot err,
No tongue o'ervalues Heaven, or flatters her!
Yet she, by Fate's perverseness — she alone
Would doubt our truth, nor deem such praise her own!
Adorning Fashion, unadorn'd by dress,
Simple from taste, and not from carelessness;
Discreet in gesture, in deportment mild,
Not stiff with prudence, nor uncouthly wild:
No state has *Amoret!* no studied mien;
She frowns no *goddess*, and she moves no *queen*.
The softer charm that in her manner lies
Is framed to captivate, yet not surprise;
It justly suits th' expression of her face, —
'Tis less than dignity, and more than grace!
On her pure cheek the native hue is such,

That, form'd by Heav'n to be admired so much,
The hand divine, with a less partial care,
Might well have fix'd a fainter crimson there,
And bade the gentle inmate of her breast, —
Inshrined Modesty! — supply the rest.
But who the peril of her lips shall paint?
Strip them of smiles — still, still all words are faint!
But moving Love himself appears to teach
Their action, though denied to rule her speech;
And thou who seest her speak and dost not hear,
Mourn not her distant accents 'scape thine ear;
Viewing those lips, thou still may'st make pretence
To judge of what she says, and swear 'tis sense:
Cloth'd with such grace, with such expression fraught,
They move in meaning, and they pause in thought!
But dost thou farther watch, with charm'd surprise,
The mild irresolution of her eyes,
Curious to mark how frequent they repose,
In brief eclipse and momentary close —
Ah! seest thou not an ambush'd Cupid there,
Too tim'rous of his charge, with jealous care
Veils and unveils those beams of heav'nly light,
Too full, too fatal else, for mortal sight?
Nor yet, such pleasing vengeance fond to meet,
In pard'ning dimples hope a safe retreat.
What though her peaceful breast should ne'er allow
Subduing frowns to arm her altered brow,
By Love, I swear, and by his gentle wiles,
More fatal still the mercy of her smiles!
Thus lovely, thus adorn'd, possessing all
Of bright or fair that can to woman fall,
The height of vanity might well be thought
Prerogative in her, and Nature's fault.
Yet gentle *Amoret*, in mind supreme
As well as charms, rejects the vainer theme;
And, half mistrustful of her beauty's store,
She barbs with wit those darts too keen before: —

Read in all knowledge that her sex should reach,
Though *Greville*, or the *Muse*, should deign to teach,
Fond to improve, nor tim'rous to discern
How far it is a woman's grace to learn;
In *Millar's* dialect she would not prove
Apollo's priestess, but Apollo's love,
Graced by those signs which truth delights to own,
The timid blush, and mild submitted tone:
Whate'er she says, though sense appear throughout,
Displays the tender hue of female doubt;
Deck'd with that charm, how lovely wit appears,
How graceful *science*, when that robe she wears!
Such too her talents, and her bent of mind,
As speak a sprightly heart by thought refined:
A taste for mirth, by contemplation school'd,
A turn for ridicule, by candour ruled,
A scorn of folly, which she tries to hide;
An awe of talent, which she owns with pride!
  Peace, idle Muse! no more thy strain prolong,
But yield a theme thy warmest praises wrong;
Just to her merit, though thou canst not raise
Thy feeble verse, behold th' acknowledged praise
Has spread conviction through the envious train,
And cast a fatal gloom o'er Scandal's reign!
And lo! each pallid hag, with blister'd tongue,
Mutters assent to all thy zeal has sung —
Owns all the colours just — the outline true;
Thee my inspirer, and my *model* — CREWE!

DRAMATIS PERSONÆ[1]

SIR PETER TEAZLE	*Mr. King*
SIR OLIVER SURFACE	*Mr. Yates*
YOUNG SURFACE .	*Mr. Palmer*
CHARLES (his *Brother*) .	*Mr. Smith*
CRABTREE . . .	*Mr. Parsons*
SIR BENJAMIN BACKBITE . .	*Mr. Dodd*
ROWLEY . . .	*Mr. Aikin*
SPUNGE	

MOSES . . . . .
SNAKE . . . . .
CARELESS — and other companions to CHARLES

LADY TEAZLE . . .
MARIA . . . . .
LADY SNEERWELL . .
MRS. CANDOUR . .
MISS VERJUICE . .

PROLOGUE

WRITTEN BY MR. GARRICK

A SCHOOL for Scandal! tell me, I beseech you,
Needs there a school this modish art to teach you?
No need of lessons now, the knowing think;
We might as well be taught to eat and drink.
Caused by a dearth of scandal, should the vapours
Distress our fair ones — let them read the papers;
Their powerful mixtures such disorders hit;
Crave what you will — there's *quantum sufficit.*
"Lord!" cries my Lady Wormwood (who loves tattle,
And puts much salt and pepper in her prattle),
Just risen at noon, all night at cards when threshing
Strong tea and scandal — "Bless me, how refreshing!
Give me the papers, Lisp — how bold and free! [*Sips.*
Last night Lord L. [*Sips*] *was caught with Lady D.*
For aching heads what charming sal volatile! [*Sips.*
If Mrs. B. will still continue flirting,

[1] From Sheridan's manuscript.

We hope she'll DRAW, *or we'll* UNDRAW *the curtain.*
Fine satire, poz — in public all abuse it,
But, by ourselves [*Sips*], our praise we can't refuse it.
Now, Lisp, read you — there, at that dash and star:"
"Yes, ma'am — *A certain lord had best beware,*
Who lives not twenty miles from Grosvenor Square;
For, should he Lady W. find willing,
Wormwood is bitter" —— "Oh! that's me! the villain!
Throw it behind the fire, and never more
Let that vile paper come within my door."
Thus at our friends we laugh, who feel the dart;
To reach our feelings, we ourselves must smart.
Is our young bard so young, to think that he
Can stop the full spring-tide of calumny?
Knows he the world so little, and its trade?
Alas! the devil's sooner raised than laid.
So strong, so swift, the monster there's no gagging:
Cut Scandal's head off, still the tongue is wagging.
Proud of your smiles once lavishly bestow'd,
Again our young Don Quixote takes the road;
To show his gratitude he draws his pen,
And seeks his hydra, Scandal, in his den.
For your applause all perils he would through —
He'll fight — that's write — a cavalliero true,
Till every drop of blood — that's ink — is spilt for you.

ACT I

Scene I. — Lady Sneerwell's *House*

Lady Sneerwell *at her dressing table with* Lappet; Miss Verjuice *drinking chocolate*

Lady Sneer. The Paragraphs you say were all inserted:

Verj. They were Madam — and as I copied them myself in a feigned Hand there can be no suspicion whence they came.

LADY SNEER. Did you circulate the Report of Lady Brittle's Intrigue with Captain Boastall?

VERJ. Madam by this Time Lady Brittle is the Talk of half the Town — and I doubt not in a week the Men will toast her as a Demirep.

LADY SNEER. What have you done as to the insinuation as to a certain Baronet's Lady and a certain Cook.

VERJ. That is in as fine a Train as your Ladyship could wish. I told the story yesterday to my own maid with directions to communicate it directly to my Hairdresser. He I am informed has a Brother who courts a Milliners' Prentice in Pallmall whose mistress has a first cousin whose sister is Feme [Femme] de Chambre to Mrs. Clackit — so that in the common course of Things it must reach Mrs. Clackit's Ears within four-and-twenty hours and then you know the Business is as good as done.

LADY SNEER. Why truly Mrs. Clackit has a very pretty Talent — a great deal of industry — yet — yes — been tolerably successful in her way — To my knowledge she has been the cause of breaking off six matches [,] of three sons being disinherited and four Daughters being turned out of Doors. Of three several Elopements, as many close confinements — nine separate maintenances and two Divorces. — nay I have more than once traced her causing a *Tête-à-Tête* in the Town and Country Magazine — when the Parties perhaps had never seen each other's Faces before in the course of their Lives.

VERJ. She certainly has Talents.

LADY SNEER. But her manner is gross.

VERJ. 'Tis very true. She generally designs well [,] has a free tongue and a bold invention — but her colouring is too dark and her outline often extravagant — She wants that delicacy of Tint — and mellowness of sneer — which distinguish your Ladyship's Scandal.

LADY SNEER. Ah you are Partial Verjuice.

VERJ. Not in the least — everybody allows that Lady Sneerwell can do more with a word or a Look than many can with the most laboured Detail even when they happen to have a little truth on their side to support it.

LADY SNEER. Yes my dear Verjuice. I am no Hypocrite to deny the satisfaction I reap from the Success of my Efforts. Wounded myself, in the early part of my Life by the envenomed Tongue of Slander I confess I have since known no Pleasure equal to the reducing others to the Level of my own injured Reputation.

VERJ. Nothing can be more natural — But my dear Lady Sneerwell There is one affair in which you have lately employed me, wherein, I confess I am at a Loss to guess your motives.

LADY SNEER. I conceive you mean with respect to my neighbour, Sir Peter Teazle, and his Family — Lappet. — And has my conduct in this matter really appeared to you so mysterious? [*Exit* MAID.

VERJ. Entirely so.

LADY SNEER. [VERJ.?] An old Batchelor as Sir Peter was[,] having taken a young wife from out of the Country — as Lady Teazle is — are certainly fair subjects for a little mischievous raillery — but here are two young men — to whom Sir Peter has acted as a kind of Guardian since their Father's death, the eldest possessing the most amiable Character and universally well spoken of[,] the youngest the most dissipated and extravagant young Fellow in the Kingdom, without Friends or caracter — the former one an avowed admirer of yours and apparently your Favourite[,] the latter attached to Maria Sir Peter's ward — and confessedly beloved by her. Now on the face of these circumstances it is utterly unaccountable to me why you a young Widow with no great jointure — should not close with the passion of a man of such character and expectations as Mr. Surface — and more so why you should be so uncommonly earnest to destroy the mutual Attachment subsisting between his Brother Charles and Maria.

LADY SNEER. Then at once to unravel this mistery — I must inform you that Love has no share whatever in the intercourse between Mr. Surface and me.

VERJ. No!

LADY SNEER. His real attachment is to Maria or her Fortune — but finding in his Brother a favoured Rival, He has been obliged to mask his Pretensions — and profit by my Assistance.

VERJ. Yet still I am more puzzled why you should interest yourself in his success.

LADY SNEER. Heavens! how dull you are! cannot you surmise the weakness which I hitherto, thro' shame have concealed even from you — must I confess that Charles — that Libertine, that extravagant, that Bankrupt in Fortune and Reputation — that He it is for whom I am thus anxious and malicious and to gain whom I would sacrifice — everything ——

VERJ. Now indeed — your conduct appears consistent and I no longer wonder at your enmity to Maria, but how came you and Surface so confidential?

LADY SNEER. For our mutual interest — but I have found out him a long time since [,] altho' He has contrived to deceive everybody beside — I know him to be artful selfish and malicious — while with Sir Peter, and indeed with all his acquaintance, He passes for a youthful Miracle of Prudence — good sense and Benevolence.

VERJ. Yes yes — I know Sir Peter vows He has not his equal in England; and, above all, He praises him as a *man of sentiment.*

LADY SNEER. True and with the assistance of his sentiments and hypocrisy he has brought Sir Peter entirely in his interests with respect to Maria and is now I believe attempting to flatter Lady Teazle into the same good opinion towards him — while poor Charles has no Friend in the House — though I fear he has a powerful one in Maria's Heart, against whom we must direct our schemes.

SERV. Mr. Surface.

LADY SNEER. Shew him up. He generally calls about this Time. I don't wonder at People's giving him to me for a Lover.

Enter SURFACE

SURF. My dear Lady Sneerwell, how do you do to-day — your most obedient.

LADY SNEER. Miss Verjuice has just been arraigning me on our mutual attachment now; but I have informed her of our real views and the Purposes for which our Geniuses at present co-operate. You know how useful she has been to us — and believe me the confidence is not ill-placed.

SURF. Madam, it is impossible for me to suspect that a Lady of Miss Verjuice's sensibility and discernment ——

LADY SNEER. Well — well — no compliments now — but tell me when you saw your mistress or what is more material to me your Brother.

SURF. I have not seen either since I saw you — but I can inform you that they are at present at Variance — some of your stories have taken good effect on Maria.

LADY SNEER. Ah! my dear Verjuice the merit of this belongs to you. But do your Brother's Distresses encrease?

SURF. Every hour. I am told He had another execution in his house yesterday — in short his Dissipation and extravagance exceed anything I have ever heard of.

LADY SNEER. Poor Charles!

SURF. True Madam — notwithstanding his Vices one can't help feeling for him — ah poor Charles! I'm sure I wish it was in my Power to be of any essential Service to him — for the man who does not share in the Distresses of a Brother — even though merited by his own misconduct — deserves ——

Lady Sneer. O Lud you are going to be moral, and forget that you are among Friends.

Surf. Egad, that's true — I'll keep that sentiment till I see Sir Peter. However it is certainly a charity to rescue Maria from such a Libertine who — if He is to be reclaim'd, can be so only by a Person of your Ladyship's superior accomplishments and understanding.

Verj. 'Twould be a Hazardous experiment.

Surf. But — Madam — let me caution you to place no more confidence in our Friend Snake the Libeller — I have lately detected him in frequent conference with old Rowland [Rowley] who was formerly my Father's Steward and has never been a friend of mine.

Lady Sneer. I'm not disappointed in Snake, I never suspected the fellow to have virtue enough to be faithful even to his own Villany.

Enter Maria

Maria my dear — how do you do — what's the matter?

Mar. O here is that disagreeable lover of mine, Sir Benjamin Backbite, has just call'd at my guardian's with his odious Uncle Crabtree — so I slipt out and ran hither to avoid them.

Lady Sneer. Is that all?

Verj. Lady Sneerwell — I'll go and write the Letter I mention'd to you.

Surf. If my Brother Charles had been of the Party, madam, perhaps you would not have been so much alarmed.

Lady Sneer. Nay now — you are severe for I dare swear the Truth of the matter is Maria heard *you* were here — but my dear — what has Sir Benjamin done that you should avoid him so ——

Mar. Oh He has done nothing — but his conversation is a perpetual Libel on all his Acquaintance.

Surf. Aye and the worst of it is there is no advantage in

not knowing Them, for He'll abuse a stranger just as soon as his best Friend — and Crabtree is as bad.

LADY SNEER. Nay but we should make allowance [—] Sir Benjamin is a wit and a poet.

MAR. For my Part — I own madam — wit loses its respect with me, when I see it in company with malice. — What do you think, Mr. Surface?

SURF. Certainly, Madam, to smile at the jest which plants a Thorn on another's Breast is to become a principal in the mischief.

LADY SNEER. Pshaw — there's no possibility of being witty without a little [ill] nature — the malice of a good thing is the Barb that makes it stick. — What's your opinion, Mr. Surface?

SURF. Certainly madam — that conversation where the Spirit of Raillery is suppressed will ever appear tedious and insipid —

MAR. Well I'll not debate how far Scandal may be allowable — but in a man I am sure it is always contemtable. — We have Pride, envy, Rivalship, and a Thousand motives to depreciate each other — but the male-slanderer must have the cowardice of a woman before He can traduce one.

LADY SNEER. I wish my Cousin Verjuice hadn't left us — she should embrace you.

SURF. Ah! she's an old maid and is privileged of course.

Enter SERVANT

Madam Mrs. Candour is below and if your Ladyship's at leisure will leave her carriage.

LADY SNEER. Beg her to walk in. Now, Maria [,] however here is a Character to your Taste, for tho' Mrs. Candour is a little talkative everybody allows her to be the best-natured and best sort of woman.

MAR. Yes with a very gross affectation of good Nature and

Benevolence — she does more mischief than the Direct malice of old Crabtree.

SURF. Efaith 'tis very true Lady Sneerwell — Whenever I hear the current running again the characters of my Friends, I never think them in such Danger as when Candour undertakes their Defence.

LADY SNEER. Hush here she is ——

Enter MRS. CANDOUR

MRS. CAN. My dear Lady Sneerwell how have you been this Century. I have never seen you tho' I have heard of you very often. — Mr. Surface — the World says scandalous things of you — but indeed it is no matter what the world says, for I think one hears nothing else but scandal.

SURF. Just so, indeed, Ma'am.

MRS. CAN. Ah Maria Child — what [!] is the whole affair off between you and Charles? His extravagance, I presume — The Town talks of nothing else ——

MAR. I am very sorry, Ma'am, the Town has so little to do.

MRS. CAN. True, true, Child; but there's no stopping people's Tongues. I own I was hurt to hear it — as I indeed was to learn from the same quarter that your guardian, Sir Peter [,] and Lady Teazle have not agreed lately so well as could be wish'd.

MAR. 'Tis strangely impertinent for people to busy themselves so.

MRS. CAN. Very true, Child; but what's to be done? People will talk — there's no preventing it. — why it was but yesterday I was told that Miss Gadabout had eloped with Sir Filagree Flirt. But, Lord! there is no minding what one hears; tho' to be sure I had this from very good authority.

MAR. Such reports are highly scandalous.

MRS. CAN. So they are Child — shameful! shameful! but the world is so censorious no character escapes. Lord, now!

who would have suspected your friend, Miss Prim, of an indiscretion Yet such is the ill-nature of people, that they say her unkle stopped her last week just as she was stepping into a Postchaise with her Dancing-master.

MAR. I'll answer for't there are no grounds for the Report.

MRS. CAN. Oh, no foundation in the world I dare swear [;] no more probably than for the story circulated last month, of Mrs. Festino's affair with Colonel Cassino — tho' to be sure that matter was never rightly clear'd up.

SURF. The license of invention some people take is monstrous indeed.

MAR. 'Tis so but in my opinion, those who report such things are equally culpable.

MRS. CAN. To be sure they are [;] Tale Bearers are as bad as the Tale makers — 'tis an old observation and a very true one — but what's to be done as I said before — how will you prevent People from talking — to-day, Mrs. Clackitt assured me, Mr. and Mrs. Honeymoon were at last become mere man and wife — like [the rest of their] acquaintance — she likewise hinted that a certain widow in the next street had got rid of her Dropsy and recovered her shape in a most surprising manner — at the same [time] Miss Tattle, who was by affirm'd, that Lord Boffalo had discover'd his Lady at a house of no extraordinary Fame — and that Sir Harry Bouquet and Tom Saunter were to measure swords on a similar Provocation. but — Lord! do you think I would report these Things — No, no [!] Tale Bearers as I said before are just as bad as the tale-makers.

SURF. Ah! Mrs. Candour, if everybody had your Forbearance and good nature —

MRS. CAN. I confess Mr. Surface I cannot bear to hear People traduced behind their Backs [;] and when ugly circumstances come out against our acquaintances I own I always love to think the best — by the bye I hope 'tis not true that your Brother is absolutely ruin'd —

SURF. I am afraid his circumstances are very bad indeed, Ma'am —

MRS. CAN. Ah! I heard so — but you must tell him to keep up his Spirits — everybody almost is in the same way — Lord Spindle, Sir Thomas Splint, Captain Quinze, and Mr. Nickit — all up, I hear, within this week; so, if Charles is undone, He'll find half his Acquaintance ruin'd too, and that, you know, is a consolation —

SURF. Doubtless, Ma'am — a very great one.

Enter SERVANT

SERV. Mr. Crabtree and Sir Benjamin Backbite.

LADY SNEER. Soh! Maria, you see your lover pursues you — Positively you shan't escape.

Enter CRABTREE *and* SIR BENJAMIN BACKBITE

CRAB. Lady Sneerwell, I kiss your hand. Mrs. Candour I don't believe you are acquainted with my Nephew Sir Benjamin Backbite — Egad, Ma'am, He has a pretty wit — and is a pretty Poet too isn't He Lady Sneerwell?

SIR BEN. O fie, Uncle!

CRAB. Nay egad it's true — I back him at a Rebus or a Charade against the best Rhymer in the Kingdom — has your Ladyship heard the Epigram he wrote last week on Lady Frizzle's Feather catching Fire — Do Benjamin repeat it — or the Charade you made last Night extempore at Mrs. Drowzie's conversazione — Come now your first is the Name of a Fish, your second a great naval commander — and

SIR BEN. Dear Uncle — now — prithee ——

CRAB. Efaith, Ma'am — 'twould surprise you to hear how ready he is at all these Things.

LADY SNEER. I wonder Sir Benjamin you never publish anything.

SIR BEN. To say truth, Ma'am, 'tis very vulgar to Print and as my little Productions are mostly Satires and Lampoons I find they circulate more by giving copies in confidence to the Friends of the Parties — however I have some love-Elegies, which, when favoured with this lady's smile I mean to give to the Public. [*Pointing to* MARIA.

CRAB. 'Fore Heaven, ma'am, they'll immortalize you — you'll be handed down to Posterity, like Petrarch's Laura, or Waller's Sacharissa.

SIR BEN. Yes Madam I think you will like them — when you shall see in a beautiful Quarto Page how a neat rivulet of Text shall meander thro' a meadow of margin — 'fore Gad, they will be the most elegant Things of their kind —

CRAB. But Ladies, have you heard the news?

MRS. CAN. What, Sir, do you mean the Report of ——

CRAB. No ma'am that's not it. — Miss Nicely is going to be married to her own Footman.

MRS. CAN. Impossible!

CRAB. Ask Sir Benjamin.

SIR BEN. 'Tis very true, Ma'am — everything is fixed and the wedding Livery bespoke.

CRAB. Yes and they say there were pressing reasons for't.

MRS. CAN. It cannot be — and I wonder any one should believe such a story of so prudent a Lady as Miss Nicely.

SIR BEN. O Lud! ma'am, that's the very reason 'twas believed at once. She has always been so cautious and so reserved, that everybody was sure there was some reason for it at bottom.

LADY SNEER. Yes a Tale of Scandal is as fatal to the Reputation of a prudent Lady of her stamp as a Fever is generally to those of the strongest Constitutions, but there is a sort of puny sickly Reputation, that is always ailing yet will outlive the robuster characters of a hundred Prudes.

SIR BEN. True Madam there are Valetudinarians in Reputation as well as constitution — who being conscious of their weak Part, avoid the least breath of air, and supply their want of Stamina by care and circumspection —

Mrs. Can. Well but this may be all mistake — You know, Sir Benjamin very trifling circumstances often give rise to the most injurious Tales.

Crab. That they do I'll be sworn Ma'am — did you ever hear how Miss Shepherd came to lose her Lover and her Character last summer at Tunbridge — Sir Benjamin you remember it —

Sir Ben. O to be sure the most whimsical circumstance —

Lady Sneer. How was it Pray —

Crab. Why one evening at Mrs. Ponto's Assembly — the conversation happened to turn on the difficulty of breeding Nova-Scotia Sheep in this country — says a young Lady in company [, "] I have known instances of it [—]for Miss Letitia Shepherd, a first cousin of mine, had a Nova-Scotia Sheep that produced her Twins. [" — "] What! ["] cries the old Dowager Lady Dundizzy (who you know is as deaf as a Post), ["] has Miss Letitia Shepherd had twins ["] — This Mistake — as you may imagine, threw the whole company into a fit of Laughing — However 'twas the next morning everywhere reported and in a few Days believed by the whole Town, that Miss Letitia Shepherd had actually been brought to Bed of a fine Boy and Girl — and in less than a week there were People who could name the Father, and the Farm House where the Babies were put out to Nurse.

Lady Sneer. Strange indeed!

Crab. Matter of Fact, I assure you — O Lud! Mr. Surface pray is it true that your uncle Sir Oliver is coming home —

Surf. Not that I know of indeed Sir.

Crab. He has been in the East Indies a long time — you can scarcely remember him — I believe — sad comfort on his arrival to hear how your Brother has gone on!

Surf. Charles has been imprudent Sir to be sure [;] but I

hope no Busy people have already prejudiced Sir Oliver against him — He may reform —

SIR BEN. To be sure He may — for my Part I never believed him to be so utterly void of Principle as People say — and tho' he has lost all his Friends I am told nobody is better spoken of — by the Jews.

CRAB. That's true egad nephew — if the Old Jewry was a Ward I believe Charles would be an alderman — no man more popular there, 'fore Gad I hear He pays as many annuities as the Irish Tontine and that whenever He's sick they have Prayers for the recovery of his Health in the synagogue —

SIR BEN. Yet no man lives in greater Splendour: — they tell me when He entertains his Friends — He can sit down to dinner with a dozen of his own Securities, have a score Tradesmen waiting in the Anti-Chamber, and an officer behind every guest's Chair.

SURF. This may be entertainment to you Gentlemen but you pay very little regard to the Feelings of a Brother.

MAR. Their malice is intolerable — Lady Sneerwell I must wish you a good morning — I'm not very well. [*Exit* MAR.

MRS. CAN. O dear she chang'd colour very much!

LADY SNEER. Do Mrs. Candour follow her — she may want assistance.

MRS. CAN. That I will with all my soul ma'am. — Poor dear Girl — who knows — what her situation may be!

[*Exit* MRS. CAN.

LADY SNEER. 'Twas nothing but that she could not bear to hear Charles reflected on notwithstanding their difference.

SIR BEN. The young Lady's Penchant is obvious.

CRAB. But Benjamin — you mustn't give up the Pursuit for that — follow her and put her into good humour — repeat her some of your verses — come, I'll assist you —

SIR BEN. Mr. Surface I did not mean to hurt you — but depend on't your Brother is utterly undone — [*Going.*

CRAB. O Lud! aye — undone — as ever man was — can't raise a guinea.

SIR BEN. And everything sold — I'm told — that was movable — [*Going.*

CRAB. I was at his house — not a thing left but some empty Bottles that were overlooked and the Family Pictures, which I believe are framed in the Wainscot. [*Going.*

SIR BEN. And I'm very sorry to hear also some bad stories against him. [*Going.*

CRAB. O He has done many mean things — that's certain!

SIR BEN. But however as He is your Brother —— [*Going.*

CRAB. We'll tell you all another opportunity. [*Exeunt.*

LADY SNEER. Ha! ha! ha! 'tis very hard for them to leave a subject they have not quite run down.

SURF. And I believe the Abuse was no more acceptable to your Ladyship than Maria.

LADY SNEER. I doubt her Affections are farther engaged than we imagin'd but the Family are to be here this Evening so you may as well dine where you are and we shall have an opportunity of observing farther — in the meantime, I'll go and plot Mischief and you shall study Sentiments. [*Exeunt.*

SCENE II. — SIR PETER'S *House*

Enter SIR PETER

SIR PET. When an old Bachelor takes a young Wife — what is He to expect — 'Tis now six months since Lady Teazle made me the happiest of men — and I have been the most miserable Dog ever since that ever committed wedlock. We tift a little going to church — and came to a Quarrel before the Bells had done ringing — I was more than once nearly chok'd with gall during the Honeymoon — and had lost all comfort in Life before my Friends had done wishing me Joy — yet I chose with caution — a girl bred wholly in the country

— who never knew luxury beyond one silk gown — nor dissipation above the annual Gala of a Race-Ball — Yet she now plays her Part in all the extravagant Fopperies of the Fashion and the Town, with as ready a Grace as if she had never seen a Bush nor a grass Plot out of Grosvenor-Square! I am sneered at by my old acquaintance — paragraphed — in the news Papers — She dissipates my Fortune, and contradicts all my Humours — yet the worst of it is I doubt I love her or I should never bear all this. However I'll never be weak enough to own it.

Enter Rowley

Row. Sir Peter, your servant: — how is 't with you Sir —

Sir Pet. Very bad — Master Rowley — very bad[.] I meet with nothing but crosses and vexations —

Row. What can have happened to trouble you since yesterday?

Sir Pet. A good — question to a married man —

Row. Nay I'm sure your Lady Sir Peter can't be the cause of your uneasiness.

Sir Pet. Why has anybody told you she was dead[?]

Row. Come, come, Sir Peter, you love her, notwithstanding your tempers do not exactly agree.

Sir Pet. But the Fault is entirely hers, Master Rowley — I am myself, the sweetest temper'd man alive, and hate a teasing temper; and so I tell her a hundred Times a day —

Row. Indeed!

Sir Pet. Aye and what is very extraordinary in all our disputes she is always in the wrong! But Lady Sneerwell, and the Set she meets at her House, encourage the perverseness of her Disposition — then to complete my vexations — Maria — my Ward — whom I ought to have the Power of a Father over, is determined to turn Rebel too and absolutely refuses the man whom I have long resolved on for her husband — meaning I suppose, to bestow herself on his profligate Brother.

Row. You know Sir Peter I have always taken the Liberty to differ with you on the subject of these two young Gentlemen — I only wish you may not be deceived in your opinion of the elder. For Charles, my life on't! He will retrieve his errors yet — their worthy Father, once my honour'd master, was at his years nearly as wild a spark.

Sir Pet. You are wrong, Master Rowley — on their Father's Death you know I acted as a kind of Guardian to them both — till their uncle Sir Oliver's Eastern Bounty gave them an early independence. Of course no person could have more opportunities of judging of their Hearts — and I was never mistaken in my life. Joseph is indeed a model for the young men of the Age — He is a man of Sentiment — and acts up to the Sentiments he professes — but for the other [,] take my word for't [if] he had any grain of Virtue by descent — he has dissipated it with the rest of his inheritance. Ah! my old Friend, Sir Oliver will be deeply mortified when he finds how Part of his Bounty has been misapplied.

Row. I am sorry to find you so violent against the young man because this may be the most critical Period of his Fortune. I came hither with news that will surprise you.

Sir Pet. What! let me hear —

Row. Sir Oliver is arrived and at this moment in Town.

Sir Pet. How! — you astonish me — I thought you did not expect him this month! —

Row. I did not — but his Passage has been remarkably quick.

Sir Pet. Egad I shall rejoice to see my old Friend — 'Tis sixteen years since we met — We have had many a Day together — but does he still enjoin us not to inform his Nephews of his Arrival?

Row. Most strictly — He means, before He makes it known to make some trial of their Dispositions and we have already planned something for the purpose.

SIR PET. Ah there needs no art to discover their merits — however he shall have his way — but pray does he know I am married!

ROW. Yes and will soon wish you joy.

SIR PET. You may tell him 'tis too late — ah Oliver will laugh at me — we used to rail at matrimony together — but He has been steady to his Text — well He must be at my house tho' — I'll instantly give orders for his Reception — but Master Rowley — don't drop a word that Lady Teazle and I ever disagree.

ROW. By no means.

SIR PET. For I should never be able to stand Noll's jokes; so I'd have him think that we are a very happy couple.

ROW. I understand you — but then you must be very careful not to differ while He's in the House with you.

SIR PET. Egad — and so we must — that's impossible. Ah! Master Rowley when an old Batchelor marries a young wife — He deserves — no the crime carries the Punishment along with it. [*Exeunt.*

END OF THE FIRST ACT

ACT II

SCENE I. — SIR PETER *and* LADY TEAZLE

SIR PET. Lady Teazle — Lady Teazle I'll not bear it.

LADY TEAZ. Sir Peter — Sir Peter you — may scold or smile, according to your Humour [,] but I ought to have my own way in everything, and what's more I will too — what! tho' I was educated in the country I know very well that women of Fashion in London are accountable to nobody after they are married.

SIR PET. Very well! ma'am very well! so a husband is to have no influence, no authority?

Lady Teaz. Authority! no, to be sure — if you wanted authority over me, you should have adopted me and not married me[:] I am sure you were old enough.

Sir Pet. Old enough — aye there it is — well — well — Lady Teazle, tho' my life may be made unhappy by your Temper — I'll not be ruined by your extravagance —

Lady Teaz. My extravagance! I'm sure I'm not more extravagant than a woman of Fashion ought to be.

Sir Pet. No no Madam, you shall throw away no more sums on such unmeaning Luxury — 'Slife to spend as much to furnish your Dressing Room with Flowers in winter as would suffice to turn the Pantheon into a Greenhouse, and give a *Fête Champêtre* at Christmas.

Lady Teaz. Lord! Sir Peter am I to blame because Flowers are dear in cold weather? You should find fault with the Climate, and not with me. For my Part I'm sure I wish it was spring all the year round — and that Roses grew under one's Feet!

Sir Pet. Oons! Madam — if you had been born to those Fopperies I shouldn't wonder at your talking thus; — but you forget what your situation was when I married you —

Lady Teaz. No, no, I don't — 'twas a very disagreeable one or I should never have married you.

Sir Pet. Yes, yes, madam, you were then in somewhat a humbler Style — the daughter of a plain country Squire. Recollect Lady Teazle when I saw you first — sitting at your tambour in a pretty figured linen gown — with a Bunch of Keys at your side, and your apartment hung round with Fruits in worsted, of your own working —

Lady Teaz. O horrible! — horrible! — don't put me in mind of it!

Sir Pet. Yes, yes Madam and your daily occupation to inspect the Dairy, superintend the Poultry, make extracts from the Family Receipt-book, and comb your aunt Deborah's Lap Dog.

Lady Teaz. Abominable!

Sir Pet. Yes Madam — and what were your evening amusements? to draw Patterns for Ruffles, which you hadn't the materials to make — play Pope Joan with the Curate — to read a sermon to your Aunt — or be stuck down to an old Spinet to strum your father to sleep after a Fox Chase.

Lady Teaz. Scandalous — Sir Peter not a word of it true —

Sir Pet. Yes, Madam — These were the recreations I took you from — and now — no one more extravagantly in the Fashion — Every Fopery adopted — a head-dress to o'er top Lady Pagoda with feathers pendant horizontal and perpendicular — you forget[,] Lady Teazle — when a little wired gauze with a few Beads made you a fly Cap not much bigger than a blew-bottle, and your Hair was comb'd smooth over a Roll —

Lady Teaz. Shocking! horrible Roll!!

Sir Pet. But now — you must have your coach — *Vis-à-vis*, and three powder'd Footmen before your Chair — and in the summer a pair of white cobs to draw you to Kensington Gardens — no recollection when you were content to ride double, behind the Butler, on a docked Coach-Horse?

Lady Teaz. Horrid! — I swear I never did.

Sir Pet. This, madam, was your situation — and what have I not done for you? I have made you woman of Fashion of Fortune of Rank — in short I have made you my wife.

Lady Teaz. Well then and there is but one thing more you can make me to add to the obligation.

Sir Pet. What's that pray?

Lady Teaz. Your widow. —

Sir Pet. Thank you Madam — but don't flatter yourself for though your ill-conduct may disturb my Peace it shall never break my Heart I promise you — however I am equally obliged to you for the Hint.

Lady Teaz. Then why will you endeavour to make yourself

so disagreeable to me — and thwart me in every little elegant expense.

SIR PET. 'Slife — Madam I pray, had you any of these elegant expenses when you married me?

LADY TEAZ. Lud Sir Peter would you have me be out of the Fashion?

SIR PET. The Fashion indeed! — what had you to do with the Fashion before you married me?

LADY TEAZ. For my Part — I should think you would like to have your wife thought a woman of Taste —

SIR PET. Aye there again — Taste! Zounds Madam you had no Taste when you married me —

LADY TEAZ. That's very true indeed Sir Peter! after having married you I should never pretend to Taste again I allow.

SIR PET. So — so then — Madam — if these are your Sentiments pray how came I to be honour'd with your Hand?

LADY TEAZ. Shall I tell you the Truth?

SIR PET. If it's not too great a Favour.

LADY TEAZ. Why the Fact is I was tired of all those agreeable Recreations which you have so good naturally [naturedly] Described — and having a Spirit to spend and enjoy a Fortune — I determined to marry the first rich man that would have me.

SIR PET. A very honest confession — truly — but pray madam was there no one else you might have tried to ensnare but me.

LADY TEAZ. O lud — I drew my net at several but you were the only one I could catch.

SIR PET. This is plain dealing indeed —

LADY TEAZ. But now Sir Peter if we have finish'd our daily Jangle I presume I may go to my engagement at Lady Sneerwell's?

SIR PET. Aye — there's another Precious circumstance — a charming set of acquaintance — you have made there!

LADY TEAZ. Nay Sir Peter they are People of Rank and Fortune — and remarkably tenacious of reputation.

SIR PET. Yes egad they are tenacious of Reputation with a vengeance, for they don't chuse anybody should have a Character but themselves! Such a crew! Ah! many a wretch has rid on hurdles who has done less mischief than these utterers of forged Tales, coiners of Scandal, and clippers of Reputation.

LADY TEAZ. What would you restrain the freedom of speech?

SIR PET. Aye they have made you just as bad [as] any one of the Society.

LADY TEAZ. Why — I believe I do bear a Part with a tolerable Grace — But I vow I bear no malice against the People I abuse, when I say an ill-natured thing, 'tis out of pure Good Humour — and I take it for granted they deal exactly in the same manner with me, but Sir Peter you know you promised to come to Lady Sneerwell's too.

SIR PET. Well well I'll call in, just to look after my own character.

LADY TEAZ. Then, indeed, you must make Haste after me, or you'll be too late — so good bye to ye.

SIR PET. So — I have gain'd much by my intended expostulation — yet with what a charming air she contradicts every thing I say — and how pleasingly she shows her contempt of my authority — Well tho' I can't make her love me, there is certainly a great satisfaction in quarrelling with her; and I think she never appears to such advantage as when she is doing everything in her Power to plague me. [*Exit.*

SCENE II. — *At* LADY SNEERWELL'S

LADY SNEERWELL, MRS. CANDOUR, CRABTREE, SIR BENJAMIN BACKBITE, *and* SURFACE

LADY SNEER. Nay, positively, we will hear it.

SURF. Yes — yes the Epigram by all means.

SIR BEN. O plague on't unkle — 'tis mere nonsense —

CRAB. No no; 'fore gad very clever for an extempore!

SIR BEN. But ladies you should be acquainted with the circumstances. You must know that one day last week as Lady Betty Curricle was taking the Dust in High Park, in a sort of duodecimo Phaeton — she desired me to write some verses on her Ponies — upon which I took out my Pocket-Book — and in one moment produced — the following: —

'Sure never were seen two such beautiful Ponies;
Other Horses are Clowns — and these macaronies,
Nay to give 'em this Title, I'm sure isn't wrong,
Their Legs are so slim — and their Tails are so long.

CRAB. There Ladies — done in the smack of a whip and on Horseback too.

SURF. A very Phœbus, mounted — indeed Sir Benjamin.

SIR BEN. Oh dear Sir — Trifles — Trifles.

Enter LADY TEAZLE *and* MARIA

MRS. CAN. I must have a Copy —

LADY SNEER. Lady Teazle — I hope we shall see Sir Peter?

LADY TEAZ. I believe He'll wait on your Ladyship presently.

LADY SNEER. Maria my love you look grave. Come, you shall sit down to Piquet with Mr. Surface.

MAR. I take very little Pleasure in cards — however, I'll do as you Please.

LADY TEAZ. I am surprised Mr. Surface should sit down with her — I thought He would have embraced this opportunity of speaking to me before Sir Peter came — [*Aside.*

MRS. CAN. Now, I'll die but you are so scandalous I'll forswear your society.

LADY TEAZ. What's the matter, Mrs. Candour?

MRS. CAN. They'll not allow our friend Miss Vermillion to be handsome.

LADY SNEER. Oh, surely she is a pretty woman. . . .

[CRAB.] I am very glad you think so ma'am.

MRS. CAN. She has a charming fresh Colour.

CRAB. Yes when it is fresh put on —

LADY TEAZ. O fie! I'll swear her colour is natural — I have seen it come and go —

CRAB. I dare swear you have, ma'am: it goes of a Night, and comes again in the morning.

SIR BEN. True, uncle, it not only comes and goes but what's more egad her maid can fetch and carry it —

MRS. CAN. Ha! ha! ha! how I hate to hear you talk so! But surely, now, her Sister, is or was very handsome.

CRAB. Who? Mrs. Stucco? O lud! she's six-and-fifty if she's an hour!

MRS. CAN. Now positively you wrong her[;] fifty-two, or fifty-three is the utmost — and I don't think she looks more.

SIR BEN. Ah! there's no judging by her looks, unless one was to see her Face.

LADY SNEER. Well — well — if she does take some pains to repair the ravages of Time — you must allow she effects it with great ingenuity — and surely that's better than the careless manner in which the widow Ocre chaulks her wrinkles.

SIR BEN. Nay now — you are severe upon the widow — come — come, it isn't that she paints so ill — but when she has finished her Face she joins it on so badly to her Neck, that she looks like a mended Statue, in which the Connoisseur sees at once that the Head's modern tho' the Trunk's antique ——

CRAB. Ha! ha! ha! well said, Nephew!

MRS. CAN. Ha! ha! ha! Well, you make me laugh but I vow I hate you for it — what do you think of Miss Simper?

SIR BEN. Why, she has very pretty Teeth.

LADY TEAZ. Yes and on that account, when she is neither speaking nor laughing (which very seldom happens) — she never absolutely shuts her mouth,. but leaves it always on a-Jar, as it were ——

MRS. CAN. How can you be so ill-natured!

LADY TEAZ. Nay, I allow even that's better than the Pains Mrs. Prim takes to conceal her losses in Front — she draws her mouth till it resembles the aperture of a Poor's-Box, and all her words appear to slide out edgewise.

LADY SNEER. Very well Lady Teazle I see you can be a little severe.

LADY TEAZ. In defence of a Friend it is but justice, but here comes Sir Peter to spoil our Pleasantry.

Enter SIR PETER

SIR PET. Ladies, your obedient — Mercy on me — here is the whole set! a character's dead at every word, I suppose.

MRS. CAN. I am rejoiced you are come, Sir Peter — they have been so censorious and Lady Teazle as bad as any one.

SIR PET. That must be very distressing to you, Mrs. Candour I dare swear.

MRS. CAN. O they will allow good Qualities to nobody — not even good nature to our Friend Mrs. Pursy.

LADY TEAZ. What, the fat dowager who was at Mrs. Codrille's [Quadrille's] last Night?

LADY SNEER. Nay — her bulk is her misfortune and when she takes such Pains to get rid of it you ought not to reflect on her.

MRS. CAN. 'Tis very true, indeed.

LADY TEAZ. Yes, I know she almost lives on acids and

small whey — laces herself by pulleys and often in the hottest noon of summer you may see her on a little squat Pony, with her hair plaited up behind like a Drummer's and puffing round the Ring on a full trot.

MRS. CAN. I thank you Lady Teazle for defending her.

SIR PET. Yes, a good Defence, truly!

MRS. CAN. But for Sir Benjamin, He is as censorious as Miss Sallow.

CRAB. Yes and she is a curious Being to pretend to be censorious — an awkward Gawky, without any one good Point under Heaven!

LADY SNEER. Positively you shall not be so very severe. Miss Sallow is a Relation of mine by marriage, and, as for her Person great allowance is to be made — for, let me tell you a woman labours under many disadvantages who tries to pass for a girl at six-and-thirty.

MRS. CAN. Tho', surely she is handsome still — and for the weakness in her eyes considering how much she reads by candle-light it is not to be wonder'd at.

LADY SNEER. True and then as to her manner — upon my word I think it is particularly graceful considering she never had the least Education[:] for you know her Mother was a Welch milliner, and her Father a sugar-Baker at Bristow. —

SIR BEN. Ah! you are both of you too good-natured!

SIR PET. Yes, damned good-natured! Her own relation! mercy on me! [*Aside.*

MRS. CAN. For my Part I own I cannot bear to hear a friend ill-spoken of?

SIR PET. No, to be sure!

SIR BEN. Ah you are of a moral turn Mrs. Candour and can sit for an hour to hear Lady Stucco talk sentiments.

LADY SNEER. Nay I vow Lady Stucco is very well with the Dessert after Dinner for she's just like the Spanish Fruit one cracks for mottoes — made up of Paint and Proverb.

Mrs. Can. Well, I never will join in ridiculing a Friend — and so I constantly tell my cousin Ogle — and you all know what pretensions she has to be critical in Beauty.

Lady Teaz. O to be sure she has herself the oddest countenance that ever was seen — 'tis a collection of Features from all the different Countries of the globe.

Sir Ben. So she has indeed — an Irish Front ——

Crab. Caledonian Locks ——

Sir Ben. Dutch Nose ——

Crab. Austrian Lips ——

Sir Ben. Complexion of a Spaniard ——

Crab. And Teeth *à la Chinoise* ——

Sir Ben. In short, her Face resembles a *table d'hôte* at Spa — where no two guests are of a nation ——

Crab. Or a Congress at the close of a general War — wherein all the members even to her eyes appear to have a different interest and her Nose and Chin are the only Parties likely to join issue.

Mrs. Can. Ha! ha! ha!

Sir Pet. Mercy on my Life [!] a Person they dine with twice a week! [*Aside.*

Lady Sneer. Go — go — you are a couple of provoking Toads.

Mrs. Can. Nay but I vow you shall not carry the Laugh off so — for give me leave to say, that Mrs. Ogle ——

Sir Pet. Madam — madam — I beg your Pardon — there's no stopping these good Gentlemen's Tongues — but when I tell you Mrs. Candour that the Lady they are abusing is a particular Friend of mine, I hope you'll not take her Part.

Lady Sneer. Ha! ha! ha! well said, Sir Peter — but you are a cruel creature — too Phlegmatic yourself for a jest and too peevish to allow wit in others.

Sir Pet. Ah Madam true wit is more nearly allow'd [allied?] to good Nature than your Ladyship is aware of.

LADY SNEER. True Sir Peter — I believe they are so near akin that they can never be united.

SIR BEN. O rather Madam suppose them man and wife because one seldom sees them together.

LADY TEAZ. But Sir Peter is such an Enemy to Scandal I believe He would have it put down by Parliament.

SIR PET. 'Fore heaven! Madam if they were to consider the Sporting with Reputation of as much importance as poaching on manors — and pass an Act for the Preservation of Fame — there are many would thank them for the Bill.

LADY SNEER. O Lud! Sir Peter would you deprive us of our Privileges —

SIR PET. Aye Madam — and then no person should be permitted to kill characters or run down reputations, but qualified old Maids and disappointed Widows. —

LADY SNEER. Go, you monster —

MRS. CAN. But sure you would not be quite so severe on those who only report what they hear?

SIR PET. Yes Madam, I would have Law Merchant for that too — and in all cases of slander currency, whenever the Drawer of the Lie was not to be found, the injured Party should have a right to come on any of the indorsers.

CRAB. Well for my Part I believe there never was a Scandalous Tale without some foundation.[1]

[1] The story in Act I. Scene I., told by Crabtree about Miss Letitia Piper, is repeated here, the speaker being Sir Peter:

SIR PETER. O nine out of ten malicious inventions are founded on some ridiculous misrepresentation — Mrs. Candour you remember how poor Miss Shepherd lost her Lover and her Character one Summer at Tunbridge.

MRS. C. To be sure that was a very ridiculous affair.

CRAB. Pray tell us Sir Peter how it was.

SIR P. Why madam — [The story follows.]

MRS. C. Ha ha strange indeed —

SIR P. Matter of Fact I assure you. . . .

LADY T. As sure as can be — Sir Peter will grow scandalous himself — if you encourage him to tell stories. [Fraser Rae's footnote — *Ed.*]

LADY SNEER. Come Ladies shall we sit down to Cards in the next Room?

Enter SERVANT, *whispers* SIR PETER

SIR PET. I'll be with them directly. — [*Exit* SERVANT.] I'll get away unperceived.

LADY SNEER. Sir Peter you are not leaving us?

SIR PET. Your Ladyship must excuse me — I'm called away by particular Business — but I leave my Character behind me — [*Exit.*

SIR BEN. Well certainly Lady Teazle that lord of yours is a strange being — I could tell you some stories of him would make you laugh heartily if He wern't your Husband.

LADY TEAZ. O pray don't mind that — come do let's hear 'em. [*join the rest of the Company going into the Next Room.*

SURF. Maria I see you have no satisfaction in this society.

MAR. How is it possible I should? If to raise malicious smiles at the infirmities or misfortunes of those who have never injured us be the province of wit or Humour, Heaven grant me a double Portion of Dullness —

SURF. Yet they appear more ill-natured than they are — they have no malice at heart —

MAR. Then is their conduct still more contemptible [;] for in my opinion — nothing could excuse the intemperance of their tongues but a natural and ungovernable bitterness of Mind.

SURF. Undoubtedly Madam — and it has always been a sentiment of mine — that to propagate a malicious Truth wantonly — is more despicable than to falsify from Revenge, but can you Maria feel thus [f]or others and be unkind to me alone — nay is hope to be denied the tenderest Passion. —

MAR. Why will you distress me by renewing this subject —

SURF. Ah! Maria! you would not treat me thus and oppose your guardian's Sir Peter's wishes — but that I see that my profligate Brother is still a favour'd Rival.

MAR. Ungenerously urged — but whatever my sentiments

of that unfortunate young man are, be assured I shall not feel more bound to give him up because his Distresses have sunk him so low as to deprive him of the regard even of a Brother.

SURF. Nay but Maria do not leave me with a Frown — by all that's honest, I swear ——Gad's Life here's Lady Teazle — you must not — no you shall — for tho' I have the greatest Regard for Lady Teazle ——

MAR. Lady Teazle!

SURF. Yet were Sir Peter to suspect ——

[*Enter* LADY TEAZLE, *and comes forward*]

LADY TEAZ. What's this, Pray — do you take her for me! — Child you are wanted in the next Room. — What's all this, pray —

SURF. O the most unlucky circumstance in Nature. Maria has somehow suspected the tender concern I have for your happiness, and threaten'd to acquaint Sir Peter with her suspicions — and I was just endeavouring to reason with her when you came.

LADY TEAZ. Indeed but you seem'd to adopt — a very tender mode of reasoning — do you usually argue on your knees?

SURF. O she's a Child — and I thought a little Bombast —— but Lady Teazle when are you to give me your judgment on my Library as you promised ——

LADY TEAZ. No — no I begin to think it would be imprudent — and you know I admit you as a Lover no farther than Fashion requires.

SURF. True — a mere Platonic Cicisbeo, what every London wife is entitled to.

LADY TEAZ. Certainly one must not be out of the Fashion — however, I have so much of my country Prejudices left — that — though Sir Peter's ill humour may vex me ever so, it never shall provoke me to ——

SURF. The only revenge in your Power — well I applaud your moderation.

LADY TEAZ. Go — you are an insinuating Hypocrite — but we shall be miss'd — let us join the company.

SURF. True, but we had best not return together.

LADY TEAZ. Well don't stay — for Maria shan't come to hear any more of your Reasoning, I promise you — [*Exit.*

SURF. A curious Dilemma truly my Politics have run me into. I wanted at first only to ingratiate myself with Lady Teazle that she might not be my enemy with Maria — and I have I don't know how — become her serious Lover, so that I stand a chance of Committing a Crime I never meditated — and probably of losing Maria by the Pursuit! — Sincerely I begin to wish I had never made such a Point of gaining so very good a character, for it has led me into so many curst Rogueries that I doubt I shall be exposed at last. [*Exit.*

SCENE III. — *At* SIR PETER'S

— ROWLEY *and* SIR OLIVER —

SIR OLIV. Ha! ha! ha! and so my old Friend is married, hey? — a young wife out of the country! — ha! ha! that he should have stood Bluff to old Bachelor so long and sink into a Husband at last!

ROW. But you must not rally him on the subject Sir Oliver — 'tis a tender Point I assure you though He has been married only seven months.

SIR OLIV. Ah then he has been just half a year on the stool of Repentance — Poor Peter! But you say he has entirely given up Charles — never sees him, hey?

ROW. His Prejudice against him is astonishing — and I am sure greatly increased by a jealousy of him with Lady Teazle — which he has been industriously led into by a scandalous Society — in the neighbourhood — who have contributed not a little to Charles's ill name. Whereas the truth is [,] I believe [,] if the lady is partial to either of them his Brother is the Favourite.

SIR OLIV. Aye — I know — there are a set of malicious prating prudent Gossips both male and Female, who murder characters to kill time, and will rob a young Fellow of his good name before He has years to know the value of it . . . but I am not to be prejudiced against my nephew by such I promise you! No! no — if Charles has done nothing false or mean, I shall compound for his extravagance.

ROW. Then my life on't, you will reclaim him. Ah, Sir, it gives me new vigour to find that your heart is not turned against him — and that the son of my good old master has one friend however left —

SIR OLIV. What! shall I forget Master Rowley — when I was at his house myself — egad my Brother and I were neither of us very prudent youths — and yet I believe you have not seen many better men than your old master was [.]

ROW. 'Tis this Reflection gives me assurance that Charles may yet be a credit to his Family — but here comes Sir Peter ——

SIR OLIV. Egad so He does — mercy on me — He's greatly altered — and seems to have a settled married look — one may read Husband in his Face at this Distance. —

Enter SIR PETER

SIR PET. Ha! Sir Oliver — my old Friend — welcome to England — a thousand Times!

SIR OLIV. Thank you — thank you — Sir Peter — and Efaith I am as glad to find you well [,] believe me —

SIR PET. Ah! 'tis a long time since we met — sixteen year I doubt Sir Oliver — and many a cross accident in the Time —

SIR OLIV. Aye I have had my share — but, what [!] I find you are married — hey my old Boy — well — well it can't be help'd — and so I wish you joy with all my heart —

Sir Pet. Thank you — thanks Sir Oliver. — Yes, I have entered into the happy state but we'll not talk of that now.

Sir Oliv. True true Sir Peter old Friends shouldn't begin on grievances at first meeting. No, no —

Row. Take care pray Sir ——

Sir Oliv. Well — so one of my nephews I find is a wild Rogue — hey?

Sir Pet. Wild! — oh! my old Friend — I grieve for your disappointment there — He's a lost young man indeed — however his Brother will make you amends; Joseph is indeed what a youth should be — everybody in the world speaks well of him —

Sir Oliv. I am sorry to hear it — he has too good a character to be an honest Fellow. Everybody speaks well of him! Psha! then He has bow'd as low to Knaves and Fools as to the honest dignity of Virtue.

Sir Pet. What Sir Oliver do you blame him for not making Enemies?

Sir Oliv. Yes — if He has merit enough to deserve them.

Sir Pet. Well — well — you'll be convinced when you know him — 'tis edification to hear him converse — he professes the noblest Sentiments.

Sir Oliv. Ah plague on his Sentiments — if he salutes me with a scrap sentence of morality in his mouth I shall be sick directly — but however don't mistake me Sir Peter I don't mean to defend Charles's Errors — but before I form my judgment of either of them, I intend to make a trial of their Hearts — and my Friend Rowley and I have planned something for the Purpose.

Row. And Sir Peter shall own he has been for once mistaken.

Sir. Pet. My life on Joseph's Honour ——

Sir Oliv. Well come give us a bottle of good wine — and we'll drink the Lads' Healths and tell you our scheme.

SIR PET. *Alons* [*Allons*], then ——

SIR OLIV. But don't Sir Peter be so severe against your old Friend's son.

SIR PET. 'Tis his Vices and Follies have made me his Enemy. —

ROW. Come — come — Sir Peter consider how early He was left to his own guidance.

SIR OLIV. ,Odds my Life — I am not sorry that He has run out of the course a little — for my Part, I hate to see dry Prudence clinging to the green Juices of youth — 'tis like ivy round a sapling and spoils the growth of the Tree.

END OF THE SECOND ACT

ACT III

SCENE I. — *At* SIR PETER'S

SIR PETER, SIR OLIVER, *and* ROWLEY

SIR PET. Well, then, we will see the Fellows first and have our wine afterwards. — but how is this, Master Rowley — I don't see the Jet of your scheme.

ROW. Why Sir — this Mr. Stanley whom I was speaking of, is nearly related to them by their mother. He was once a merchant in Dublin — but has been ruined by a series of undeserved misfortunes — and now lately coming over to solicit the assistance of his friends here — has been flyng [flung] into prison by some of his Creditors — where he is now with two helpless Boys. —

SIR OLIV. Aye and a worthy Fellow too I remember him. But what is this to lead to — ?

ROW. You shall hear — He has applied by letter both to Mr. Surface and Charles — from the former he has received nothing but evasive promises of future service, while Charles has done all that his extravagance has left him power to do —

and He is at this time endeavouring to raise a sum of money — part of which, in the midst of his own distresses, I know He intends for the service of poor Stanley.

SIR OLIV. Ah! he is my Brother's Son.

SIR PET. Well, but how is Sir Oliver personally to ——

ROW. Why Sir I will inform Charles and his Brother that Stanley has obtain'd permission to apply in person to his Friends — and as they have neither of them ever seen him [,] let Sir Oliver assume his character — and he will have a fair opportunity of judging at least of the Benevolence of their Dispositions.

SIR PET. Pshaw! this will prove nothing — I make no doubt Charles is Coxcomb and thoughtless enough to give money to poor relations if he had it —

SIR OLIV. Then He shall never want it —. I have brought a few Rupees home with me Sir Peter — and I only want to be sure of bestowing them rightly. —

ROW. Then Sir believe me you will find in the youngest Brother one who in the midst of Folly and dissipation — has still, as our immortal Bard expresses it, —

"a Tear for Pity and a Hand open as the day for melting Charity."

SIR PET. Pish! What signifies his having an open Hand or Purse either when He has nothing left to give! — but if you talk of humane Sentiments — Joseph is the man — Well, well, make the trial, if you please. But where is the fellow whom you brought for Sir Oliver to examine, relative to Charles's affairs?

ROW. Below waiting his commands, and no one can give him better intelligence — This, Sir Oliver, is a friendly Jew, who to do him justice, has done everything in his power to bring your nephew to a proper sense of his extravagance.

SIR PET. Pray let us have him in.

ROW. Desire Mr. Moses to walk upstairs.

[*Calls to* SERVANT.

Sir Pet. But Pray why should you suppose he will speak the truth?

Row. Oh, I have convinced him that he has no chance of recovering certain Sums advanced to Charles but through the bounty of Sir Oliver, who He knows is arrived; so that you may depend on his Fidelity to his interest. I have also another evidence in my Power, one Snake, whom I shall shortly produce to remove some of *your* Prejudices[,] Sir Peter[,] relative to Charles and Lady Teazle.

Sir Pet. I have heard too much on that subject.

Row. Here comes the honest Israelite.

Enter Moses

— This is Sir Oliver.

Sir Oliv. Sir — I understand you have lately had great dealings with my Nephew Charles.

Mos. Yes Sir Oliver — I have done all I could for him, but He was ruined before He came to me for Assistance.

Sir Oliv. That was unlucky truly — for you have had no opportunity of showing your Talents.

Mos. None at all — I hadn't the Pleasure of knowing his Distresses till he was some thousands worse than nothing, till it was impossible to add to them.

Sir Oliv. Unfortunate indeed! but I suppose you have done all in your Power for him honest Moses?

Mos. Yes he knows that — This very evening I was to have brought him a gentleman from the city who does not know him and will I believe advance some money.

Sir Pet. What[!] one Charles has never had money from before?

Mos. Yes [—] Mr. Premium, of Crutched Friars.

Sir Pet. Egad, Sir Oliver a Thought strikes me! — Charles you say does'nt know Mr. Premium?

Mos. Not at all.

Sir Pet. Now then Sir Oliver you may have a better opportunity of satisfying yourself than by an old romancing tale of a poor Relation — go with my friend Moses and represent Mr. Premium and then I'll answer for't you'll see your Nephew in all his glory.

Sir Oliv. Egad I like this Idea better than the other, and I may visit Joseph afterwards as old Stanley.

Sir Pet. True so you may.

Row. Well this is taking Charles rather at a disadvantage, to be sure — however Moses — you understand Sir Peter and will be faithful ——

Mos. You may depend upon me — and this is near the Time I was to have gone.

Sir Oliv. I'll accompany you as soon as you please, Moses —— but hold — I have forgot one thing — how the plague shall I be able to pass for a Jew?

Mos. There's no need — the Principal is Christian.

Sir Oliv. Is He — I'm very sorry to hear it — but then again — an't I rather too smartly dressed to look like a money-Lender?

Sir Pet. Not at all; 'twould not be out of character, if you went in your own carriage — would it, Moses!

Mos. Not in the least.

Sir Oliv. Well — but — how must I talk [?] there's certainly some cant of usury and mode of treating that I ought to know.

Sir Pet. Oh, there's not much to learn — the great point as I take it is to be exorbitant enough in your Demands hey Moses?

Mos. Yes that's very great Point.

Sir Oliv. I'll answer for't I'll not be wanting in that — I'll ask him eight or ten per cent. on the loan — at least.

Mos. You'll be found out directly — if you ask him no more than that, you'll be discovered immediately.

Sir Oliv. Hey! — what the Plague! — how much then?

Mos. That depends upon the Circumstances — if he appears not very anxious for the supply, you should require only forty or fifty per cent. — but if you find him in great Distress, and want the monies very bad — you may ask double.

Sir Pet. A good — [h]onest Trade you're learning, Sir Oliver —

Sir Oliv. Truly, I think so — and not unprofitable —

Mos. Then you know — you haven't the monies yourself, but are forced to borrow them for him of a Friend.

Sir Oliv. O I borrow it of a Friend do I?

Mos. And your friend is an unconscion'd Dog — but you can't help it.

Sir Oliv. My Friend's an unconscionable Dog, is he?

Mos. Yes — and He himself hasn't the monies by him — but is forced to sell stock — at a great loss —

Sir Oliv. He is forced to sell stock is he — at a great loss, is he — well that's very kind of him —

Sir Pet. Efaith, Sir Oliver — Mr. Premium I mean — you'll soon be master of the Trade — but, Moses would have him inquire if the borrower is a minor —

Mos. O yes —

Sir Pet. And in that case his Conscience will direct him —

Mos. To have the Bond in another Name to be sure.

Sir Oliv. Well — well I shall be perfect —

Sir Pet. But hearkee wouldn't you have him also run out a little against the annuity Bill — that would be in character I should think —

Mos. Very much —

Row. And lament that a young man now must be at years of discretion before He is suffered to ruin himself!

Mos. Aye, great Pity!

Sir Pet. And abuse the Public for allowing merit to an act whose only object is to snatch misfortune and imprudence from the rapacious Relief of usury! and give the minor a chance of inheriting his estate without being undone by coming into Possession.

SIR OLIV. So — so — Moses shall give me further instructions as we go together.

SIR PET. You will not have much time [,] for your Nephew lives hard bye —

SIR OLIV. Oh Never — fear [:] my Tutor appears so able that tho' Charles lived in the next street it must be my own Fault if I am not a compleat Rogue before I turn the Corner —

[*Exeunt* SIR OLIVER *and* MOSES.

SIR PET. So — now I think Sir Oliver will be convinced — you shan't follow them Rowley. You are partial and would have prepared Charles for 'tother plot.

ROW. No upon my word Sir Peter —

SIR PET. Well, go bring me this Snake, and I'll hear what he has to say presently. I see Maria, and want to speak with her. — [*Exit* ROWLEY.] I should be glad to be convinced my suspicions of Lady Teazle and Charles were unjust — I have never yet opened my mind on this subject to my Friend Joseph. . . . I am determined. I will do it — He will give me his opinion sincerely. —

Enter MARIA

So Child — has Mr. Surface returned with you —

MAR. No Sir — He was engaged.

SIR PET. Well — Maria — do you not reflect [,] the more you converse with that amiable young man [,] what return his Partiality for you deserves?

MAR. Indeed Sir Peter — your frequent importunity on this subject distresses me extremely — you compell me to Declare that I know no man who has ever paid me a particular Attention whom I would not prefer to Mr. Surface —

SIR PET. Soh! Here's Perverseness — no — no — Maria,

'tis Charles only whom you would prefer — 'tis evident his Vices and Follies have won your Heart.

MAR. This is unkind Sir — You know I have obey'd you in neither seeing nor corresponding with him — I have heard enough to convince me that He is unworthy my regard — Yet I cannot think it culpable — if while my understanding severely condemns his Vices, my Heart suggests some Pity for his Distresses.

SIR PET. Well well pity him as much as you please, but give your Heart and Hand to a worthier object.

MAR. Never to his Brother!

SIR PET. Go — perverse and obstinate! but take care, Madam — you have never yet known what the authority of a Guardian is — don't compel me to inform you of it. —

MAR. I can only say, you shall not have just Reason — 'tis true, by my Father's will I am for a short period bound to regard you as his substitute, but I must cease to think you so when you would compel me to be miserable. [*Exit.*

SIR PET. Was ever man so crossed as I am [?] everything conspiring to fret me! I had not been involved in matrimony a fortnight [,] before her Father — a hale and hearty man, died on purpose, I believe — for the Pleasure of plaguing me with the care of his Daughter . . . but here comes my Helpmate! — She appears in great good humour —— how happy I should be if I could teaze her into loving me tho' but a little ——

Enter LADY TEAZLE

LADY TEAZ. Lud! Sir Peter I hope you haven't been quarrelling with Maria? It isn't using me well to be ill humour'd when I am not bye —!

SIR PET. Ah! Lady Teazle you might have the Power to make me good humour'd at all times —

LADY TEAZ. I am sure — I wish I had — for I want you to be in a charming sweet temper at this moment — do be good humour'd now — and let me have two hundred Pounds will you?

SIR PET. Two hundred Pounds! what can't I be in a good humour without paying for it — but speak to me thus — and Efaith there's nothing I could refuse you. You shall have it — but seal me a bond for the repayment.

LADY TEAZ. O no — there — my Note of Hand will do as well —

SIR PET. And you shall no longer reproach me with not giving you an independent settlement — I shall shortly surprise you — and you'll not call me ungenerous — but shall we always live thus — hey?

LADY TEAZ. If you — please — I'm sure I don't care how soon we leave off quarrelling provided you'll own you were tired first —

SIR PET. Well — then let our future contest be who shall be most obliging.

LADY TEAZ. I assure you Sir Peter Good Nature becomes you — you look now as you did before we were married — when you used to walk with me under the Elms, and tell me stories of what a Gallant you were in your youth — and chuck me under the chin you would — and ask me if I thought I could love an old Fellow who would deny me nothing — didn't you?

SIR PET. Yes — yes — and you were as kind and attentive ——

LADY TEAZ. Aye so I was — and would always take your Part, when my acquaintance used to abuse you and turn you into ridicule —

SIR PET. Indeed!

LADY TEAZ. Aye — and when my cousin Sophy has called you a stiff peevish old batchelor and laugh'd at me for thinking of marrying one who might be my Father — I have always defended you — and said I didn't think you so ugly by any means, and that you'd make a very good sort of a husband —

SIR PET. And you prophesied right — and we shall certainly now be the happiest couple ——

LADY TEAZ. And never differ again.

SIR PET. No never — tho' at the same time indeed — my dear Lady Teazle — you must watch your Temper very narrowly — for in all our little Quarrels — my dear — if you recollect my Love you always began first —

LADY TEAZ. I beg your Pardon — my dear Sir Peter — indeed — you always gave the provocation.

SIR PET. Now — see, my Love take care — contradicting isn't the way to keep Friends.

LADY TEAZ. Then don't you begin it my Love!

SIR PET. There now — you are going on — you don't perceive [,] my Life, that you are just doing the very thing my Love which you know always makes me angry.

LADY TEAZ. Nay — you know if you will be angry without any reason — my Dear ——

SIR PET. There now you want to quarrel again.

LADY TEAZ. No — I am sure I don't — but if you will be so peevish ——

SIR PET. There — now who begins first?

LADY TEAZ. Why you to be sure — I said nothing[—]but there's no bearing your Temper.

SIR PET. No — no — my dear — the fault's in your own temper.

LADY TEAZ. Aye you are just what my Cousin Sophy said you would be —

SIR PET. Your Cousin Sophy — is a forward impertinent Gipsey —

LADY TEAZ. Go you great Bear — how dare you abuse my Relations —

SIR PET. Now may all the Plagues of marriage be doubled on me, if ever I try to be Friends with you any more ——

LADY TEAZ. So much the Better.

Sir Pet. No — no Madam 'tis evident you never cared a pin for me — I was a madman to marry you —

Lady Teaz. And I am sure I was a Fooll to marry you — an old dangling Batchelor, who was single of [at] fifty — only because He never could meet with any one who would have him.

Sir Pet. Aye — aye — Madam — but you were pleased enough to listen to me — you never had such an offer before —

Lady Teaz. No — didn't I refuse Sir. Jeremy Terrier — who everybody said would have been a better Match — for his estate is just as good as yours — and he has broke his Neck since we have been married!

Sir Pet. I have done with you Madam! You are an unfeeling — ungrateful — but there's an end of everything — I believe you capable of anything that's bad — Yes, Madam — I now believe the Reports relative to you and Charles — Madam — yes — Madam — you and Charles are — not without grounds ——

Lady Teaz. Take — care Sir Peter — you had better not insinuate any such thing! I'll not be suspected without cause I promise you ——

Sir Pet. Very — well — Madam — very well! a separate maintenance — as soon as you Please. Yes Madam or a Divorce — I'll make an example of myself for the Benefit of all old Batchelors — Let us separate, Madam.

Lady Teaz. Agreed — agreed — and now — my dear Sir Peter we are of a mind again, we may be the happiest couple — and never differ again, you know — ha! ha! — Well you are going to be in a Passion I see — and I shall only interrupt you — so, bye! bye! hey — young Jockey try'd and countered. [*Exit.*

Sir Pet. Plagues and tortures! She pretends to keep her temper, can't I make her angry neither! O! I am the miserable fellow! But I'll not bear her presuming to keep her

Temper — No she may break my Heart — but she shan't keep her Temper. [*Exit.*

SCENE II. — *At* CHARLES'S *House*

Enter TRIP, MOSES, *and* SIR OLIVER

TRIP. Here Master Moses — if you'll stay a moment — I'll try whether Mr. —— what's the Gentleman's Name?

SIR OLIV. Mr. —— Moses — what *is* my name ——

MOS. Mr. Premium ——

TRIP. Premium — very well. [*Exit* TRIP — *taking snuff.*

SIR OLIV. To judge by the Servants — one wouldn't believe the master was ruin'd — but what — sure this was my Brother's House ——

MOS. Yes Sir Mr. Charles bought it of Mr. Joseph with the Furniture, Pictures, &c. — just as the old Gentleman left it — Sir Peter thought it a great peice of extravagance in him.

SIR OLIV. In my mind the other's economy in selling it to him was more reprehensible by half. ——

Enter TRIP

TRIP. My Master [,] Gentlemen [,] says you must wait, he has company, and can't speak with you yet.

SIR OLIV. If he knew who it was wanted to see him, perhaps he wouldn't have sent such a Message.

TRIP. Yes — yes — Sir — He knows you are here — I didn't forget little Premium — no — no ——

SIR OLIV. Very well — and pray Sir what may be your Name?

TRIP. Trip Sir — my Name is Trip, at your Service.

SIR OLIV. Well then Mr. Trip — I presume your master is seldom without company ——

TRIP. Very seldom Sir — the world says ill-natured things of him but 'tis all malice — no man was ever better beloved —

Sir he seldom sits down to dinner without a dozen particular Friends ——

SIR OLIV. He's very happy indeed — you have a pleasant sort of Place here I guess?

TRIP. Why yes — here are three or four of us pass our time agreeably enough — but then our wages are sometimes a little in arrear — and not very great either — but fifty Pounds a year and find our own Bags and Bouquets ——

SIR OLIV. Bags and Bouquets! — Halters and Bastinadoes! [*Aside.*

TRIP. But *à propos* Moses — have you been able to get me that little Bill discounted?

SIR OLIV. Wants to raise money too! — mercy on me! has his distresses, I warrant[,] like a Lord—and affects Creditors and Duns! [*Aside.*

MOS. 'Twas not be done, indeed ——

TRIP. Good lack — you surprise me — My Friend Brush has indorsed it and I thought when he put his name at the Back of a Bill 'twas as good as cash.

MOS. No 'twouldn't do.

TRIP. A small sum — but twenty Pound — harkee, Moses do you think you could get it me by way of annuity?

SIR OLIV. An annuity! ha! ha! a Footman raise money by annuity — Well done Luxury egad! [*Aside.*

MOS. Who would you get to join with you?

TRIP. You know my Lord Applice — you have seen him however ——

MOS. Yes ——

TRIP. You must have observed what an appearance he makes — nobody dresses better, nobody throws off faster — very well this Gentleman will stand my security.

MOS. Well — but you must insure your Place.

TRIP. O with all my Heart — I'll insure my Place, and my Life too, if you please.

SIR OLIV. It's more than I would your neck ——

MOS. But is there nothing you could deposit?

TRIP. Why nothing capital of my master's wardrobe has drop'd lately — but I could give you a mortgage on some of his winter Cloaths with equity of redemption before November or — you shall have the reversion — of the French velvet, or a post obit on the Blue and Silver — these I should think Moses — with a few Pair of Point Ruffles as a collateral security — hey, my little Fellow?

MOS. Well well — we'll talk presently — we detain the Gentlemen ——

SIR OLIV. O pray don't let mė interrupt Mr. Trip's Negotiation.

TRIP. Harkee — I heard the Bell — I believe,Gentlemen I can now introduce you — don't forget the annuity little Moses.

SIR OLIV. If the man be a shadow of his Master this is the Temple of Dissipation indeed! [*Exeunt.*

SCENE III. — CHARLES, CARELESS, *etc.*, *etc.*

At Table with Wine

CHAS. 'Fore Heaven, 'tis true! — there is the great Degeneracy of the age — many of our acquaintance have Taste — Spirit, and Politeness — but plague on't they won't drink ——

CARE. It is so indeed — Charles — they give into all the substantial Luxuries of the Table — and abstain from nothing but wine and wit — Oh, certainly society suffers by it intolerably — for now instead of the social spirit of Raillery that used to mantle over a glass of bright Burgundy their conversation is become just like the Spa water they drink which has all the Pertness and flatulence of champaine without its spirit or Flavour.

1ST GENT. But what are they to do who love Play better than wine ——

CARE. True — there's Harry diets himself — for gaming and is now under a hazard Regimen.

CHAS. Then He'll have the worst of it — what you wouldn't train a horse for the course by keeping him from corn — For my Part egad I am never so successful as when I'm a little — merry — let me throw on a Bottle of Champaine and I never lose — at least I never feel my losses which is exactly the same thing.

2D GENT. Aye that may be — but it is as impossible to follow wine and play as to unite Love and Politics.

CHAS. Pshaw — you may do both — Caesar made Love and Laws in a Breath — and was liked by the Senate as well as the Ladies — but no man can pretend to be a Believer in Love, who is an abjurer of wine — 'tis the Test by which a Lover knows his own Heart — fill a dozen Bumpers to a dozen Beauties, and she that floats atop is the maid that has bewitched you.

CARE. Now then Charles — be honest and give us yours ——

CHAS. Why I have withheld her only in compassion to you — if I toast her you should give a round of her Peers, which is impossible! on earth!

CARE. O, then we'll find some canonized Vestals or heathen Goddesses that will do I warrant ——

CHAS. Here then — Bumpers — you Rogues — Bumpers! Maria — Maria ——

1ST GENT. Maria who?

CHAS. Oh, damn the Surname 'tis too formal to be register'd in Love's calendar — but now Careless beware — beware — we must have Beauty's superlative.

1ST GENT. Nay Never study [,] Careless — we'll stand to the Toast — tho' your mistress should want an eye — and you know you have a song will excuse you ——

CARE. Egad so I have — and I'll give him the song instead of the Lady. ——

SONG. — AND CHORUS — [1]

Here's to the maiden of bashful fifteen;
  Here's to the widow of fifty;
Here's to the flaunting extravagant quean,
  And here's to the housewife that's thrifty.
Chorus. Let the toast pass, —
    Drink to the lass,
I'll warrant she'll prove an excuse for a glass.

Here's to the charmer whose dimples we prize;
  Now to the maid who has none, sir;
Here's to the girl with a pair of blue eyes,
  And here's to the nymph with but one, sir.
Chorus. Let the toast pass, &c.

Here's to the maid with a bosom of snow:
  Now to her that's as brown as a berry:
Here's to the wife with a face full of woe,
  And now to the damsel that's merry.
Chorus. Let the toast pass, &c.

For let 'em be clumsy, or let 'em be slim,
  Young or ancient, I care not a feather;
So fill a pint bumper quite up to the brim,
So fill up your glasses, nay, fill to the brim,
  And let us e'en toast them together.
Chorus. Let the toast pass, &c.

[*Enter* TRIP *whispers* CHARLES

2D GENT. Bravo Careless — Ther's Toast and Sentiment too.

1ST GENT. E' faith there's infinite charity in that song. ——

CHAS. Gentlemen, you must excuse me a little. — Careless, take the Chair, will you?

CARE. Nay prithee, Charles — what now — this is one of your Peerless Beauties I suppose — has dropped in by chance?

CHAS. No — Faith — to tell you the Truth 'tis a Jew and a Broker who are come by appointment.

[1] The words which follow this title are not inserted in the manuscript of the play. [Fraser Rae's footnote. — *Ed.*]

CARE. O dam it let's have the Jew in.

1ST GENT. Aye and the Broker too by all means ——

2D GENT. Yes yes the Jew and the Broker.

CHAS. Egad with all my Heart — Trip — bid the Gentlemen walk in — tho' there's one of them a Stranger I can tell you ——

TRIP. What Sir — would you chuse Mr. Premium to come up with ——

1ST GENT. Yes — yes Mr. Premium certainly.

CARE. To be sure — Mr. Premium — by all means Charles, let us give them some generous Burgundy, and perhaps they'll grow conscientious ——

CHAS. O, Hang 'em — no — wine does but draw forth a man's natural qualities; and to make them drink would only be to whet their Knavery.

Enter TRIP, SIR OLIVER, *and* MOSES

CHAS. So — honest Moses — walk in — walk in pray Mr. Premium — that's the Gentleman's name isn't it Moses.

MOS. Yes Sir.

CHAS. Set chairs — Trim. — Sit down, Mr Premium. — Glasses Trim. — sit down Moses. — Come, Mr. Premium I'll give you a sentiment — Here's Success to Usury — Moses fill the Gentleman a bumper.

MOS. Success to Usury!

CARE. Right Moses — Usury is Prudence and industry and deserves to succeed ——

SIR OLIV. Then Here is — all the success it deserves! [*Drinks.*

CHAS. Mr. Premium you and I are but strangers yet — but I hope we shall be better acquainted by and bye ——

SIR OLIV. Yes Sir hope we shall — more intimately perhaps than you'll wish. [*Aside.*[1]

[1] From this place to Scene ii. Act IV. several sheets are missing. [Fraser Rae's footnote. — *Ed.*]

CARE. No, no, that won't do! Mr. Premium, you have demurred at the toast, and must drink it in a pint bumper.

1ST. GENT. A pint bumper, at least.

MOS. Oh, pray, sir, consider — Mr. Premium's a gentleman.

CARE. And therefore loves good wine.

2D GENT. Give Moses a quart glass — this is mutiny, and a high contempt for the chair.

CARE. Here, now for't! I'll see justice done, to the last drop of my bottle.

SIR OLIV. Nay, pray, gentlemen — I did not expect this usage.

CHAS. No, hang it, you shan't; Mr. Premium's a stranger.

SIR OLIV. Odd! I wish I was well out of their company. [*Aside.*

CARE. Plague on 'em then! if they won't drink, we'll not sit down with them. Come, Harry, the dice are in the next room. — Charles, you'll join us when you have finished your business with the gentlemen?

CHAS. I will! I will! — [*Exeunt* SIR HARRY BUMPER *and* GENTLEMEN; CARELESS *following.*] Careless.

CARE. [*Returning.*] Well!

CHAS. Perhaps I may want you.

CARE. Oh, you know I am always ready: word, note, or bond, 'tis all the same to me. [*Exit.*

MOS. Sir, this is Mr. Premium, a gentleman of the strictest honour and secrecy; and always performs what he undertakes. Mr. Premium, this is ——

CHAS. Psha! have done. Sir, my friend Moses is a very honest fellow, but a little slow at expression: he'll be an hour giving us our titles. Mr. Premium, the plain state of the matter is this: I am an extravagant young fellow who wants to borrow money; you I take to be a prudent old fellow, who have got money to lend. I am blockhead enough to give fifty per cent. sooner than not have it! and you, I presume, are rogue enough to take a hundred if you can get it. Now, sir, you see we are acquainted at once, and may proceed to business without further ceremony.

SIR OLIV. Exceeding frank, upon my word. I see, sir, you are not a man of many compliments.

CHAS. Oh, no, sir! plain dealing in business I always think best.

SIR OLIV. Sir, I like you the better for it. However, you are mistaken in one thing; I have no money to lend, but I believe I could procure some of a friend; but then he's an unconscionable dog. Isn't he, Moses? And must sell stock to accommodate you. Mustn't he, Moses!

MOS. Yes, indeed! You know I always speak the truth, and scorn to tell a lie!

CHAS. Right. People that speak truth generally do. But these are trifles, Mr. Premium. What! I know money isn't to be bought without paying for't!

SIR OLIV. Well, but what security could you give? You have no land, I suppose?

CHAS. Not a mole-hill, nor a twig, but what's in the bough-pots out of the window!

SIR OLIV. Nor any stock, I presume?

CHAS. Nothing but live stock — and that's only a few pointers and ponies. But pray, Mr. Premium, are you acquainted at all with any of my connections?

SIR OLIV. Why, to say the truth, I am.

CHAS. Then you must know that I have a devilish rich uncle in the East Indies, Sir Oliver Surface, from whom I have the greatest expectations?

SIR OLIV. That you have a wealthy uncle, I have heard; but how your expectations will turn out is more, I believe, than you can tell.

CHAS. Oh, no! — there can be no doubt. They tell me

I'm a prodigious favourite, and that he talks of leaving me everything.

SIR OLIV. Indeed! this is the first I've heard of it.

CHAS. Yes, yes, 'tis just so. Moses knows 'tis true; don't you, Moses?

MOS. Oh, yes! I'll swear to't.

SIR OLIV. Egad, they'll persuade me presently I'm at Bengal. [*Aside.*

CHAS. Now I propose, Mr. Premium, if it's agreeable to you, a post-obit on Sir Oliver's life: though at the same time the old fellow has been so liberal to me, that I give you my word, I should be very sorry to hear that anything had happened to him.

SIR OLIV. Not more than I should, I assure you. But the bond you mention happens to be just the worst security you could offer me — for I might live to a hundred and never see the principal.

CHAS. Oh, yes, you would! the moment Sir Oliver dies, you know, you would come on me for the money.

SIR OLIV. Then I believe I should be the most unwelcome dun you ever had in your life.

CHAS. What! I suppose you're afraid that Sir Oliver is too good a life?

SIR OLIV. No, indeed I am not; though I have heard he is as hale and healthy as any man of his years in Christendom.

CHAS. There again, now, you are misinformed. No, no, the climate has hurt him considerably, poor uncle Oliver. Yes, yes, he breaks apace, I'm told — and is so much altered lately that his nearest relations would not know him.

SIR OLIV. No! Ha! ha! ha! so much altered lately that his nearest relations would not know him! Ha! ha! ha! egad — ha! ha! ha!

CHAS. Ha! ha! — you're glad to hear that, little Premium?

SIR OLIV. No, no, I'm not.

CHAS. Yes, yes, you are — ha! ha! ha! — you know that mends your chance.

SIR OLIV. But I'm told Sir Oliver is coming over; nay, some say he is actually arrived.

CHAS. Psha! sure I must know better than you whether he's come or not. No, no, rely on't he's at this moment at Calcutta. Isn't he, Moses?

MOS. Oh, yes, certainly.

SIR OLIV. Very true, as you say, you must know better than I, though I have it from pretty good authority. Haven't I, Moses?

MOS. Yes, most undoubted!

SIR OLIV. But, sir, as I understand you want a few hundreds immediately, is there nothing you could dispose of?

CHAS. How do you mean?

SIR OLIV. For instance, now, I have heard that your father left behind him a great quantity of massy old plate.

CHAS. O Lud! that's gone long ago. Moses can tell you how better than I can.

SIR OLIV. [*Aside.*] Good lack! all the family race-cups and corporation-bowls! — [*Aloud.*] Then it was also supposed that his library was one of the most valuable and compact.

CHAS. Yes, yes, so it was — vastly too much so for a private gentleman. For my part, I was always of a communicative disposition, so I thought it a shame to keep so much knowledge to myself.

SIR OLIV. [*Aside.*] Mercy upon me! learning that had run in the family like an heir-loom! — [*Aloud.*] Pray, what has become of the books?

CHAS. You must inquire of the auctioneer, Master Premium, for I don't believe even Moses can direct you.

MOS. I know nothing of books.

SIR OLIV. So, so, nothing of the family property left, I suppose?

CHAS. Not much, indeed; unless you have a mind to the family pictures. I have got a room full of ancestors above: and if you have a taste for old paintings, egad, you shall have 'em a bargain!

SIR OLIV. Hey! what the devil! sure, you wouldn't sell your forefathers, would you?

CHAS. Every man of them, to the best bidder.

SIR OLIV. What! your great-uncles and aunts?

CHAS. Ay, and my great-grandfathers and grandmothers too.

SIR OLIV. [*Aside.*] Now I give him up! — [*Aloud.*] What the plague, have you no bowels for your own kindred? Odd's life! do you take me for Shylock in the play, that you would raise money of me on your own flesh and blood?

CHAS. Nay, my little broker, don't be angry: what need you care, if you have your money's worth?

SIR OLIV. Well, I'll be the purchaser: I think I can dispose of the family canvas. — [*Aside.*] Oh, I'll never forgive him this! never!

Re-enter CARELESS

CARE. Come, Charles, what keeps you?

CHAS. I can't come yet. I'faith, we are going to have a sale above stairs; here's little Premium will buy all my ancestors!

CARE. Oh, burn your ancestors!

CHAS. No, he may do that afterwards, if he pleases. Stay, Careless, we want you: egad, you shall be auctioneer — so come along with us.

CARE. Oh, have with you, if that's the case. I can handle a hammer as well as a dice box! Going! going!

SIR OLIV. Oh, the profligates! [*Aside.*

CHAS. Come, Moses, you shall be appraiser, if we want one. Gad's life, little Premium, you don't seem to like the business?

SIR OLIV. Oh, yes, I do, vastly! Ha! ha! ha! yes, yes, I

think it a rare joke to sell one's family by auction — ha! ha! — [*Aside.*] Oh, the prodigal!

CHAS. To be sure! when a man wants money, where the plague should he get assistance, if he can't make free with his own relations? [*Exeunt.*

SIR OLIV. I'll never forgive him; never! never!

END OF THE THIRD ACT

ACT IV

SCENE I. — *A Picture Room in* CHARLES SURFACE'S *House*

Enter CHARLES, SIR OLIVER, MOSES, *and* CARELESS

CHAS. Walk in, gentlemen, pray walk in; — here they are, the family of the Surfaces, up to the Conquest.

SIR OLIV. And, in my opinion, a goodly collection.

CHAS. Ay, ay, these are done in the true spirit of portrait-painting; no *volontière grace* or expression. Not like the works of your modern Raphaels, who give you the strongest resemblance, yet contrive to make your portrait independent of you; so that you may sink the original and not hurt the picture. No, no; the merit of these is the inveterate likeness — all stiff and awkward as the originals, and like nothing in human nature besides.

SIR OLIV. Ah! we shall never see such figures of men again.

CHAS. I hope not. Well, you see, Master Premium, what a domestic character I am; here I sit of an evening surrounded by my family. But come, get to your pulpit, Mr. Auctioneer; here's an old gouty chair of my grandfather's will answer the purpose.

CARE. Ay, ay, this will do. But, Charles, I haven't a hammer; and what's an auctioneer without his hammer?

CHAS. Egad, that's true. What parchment have we here? Oh, our genealogy in full. [*Taking pedigree down.*] Here,

Careless, you shall have no common bit of mahogany, here's the family tree for you, you rogue! This shall be your hammer, and now you may knock down my ancestors with their own pedigree.

SIR OLIV. What an unnatural rogue! — an *ex post facto* parricide! [*Aside.*

CARE. Yes, yes, here's a list of your generation indeed; — faith, Charles, this is the most convenient thing you could have found for the business, for 'twill not only serve as a hammer, but a catalogue into the bargain. Come, begin — A-going, a-going, a-going!

CHAS. Bravo, Careless! Well, here's my great uncle, Sir Richard Ravelin, a marvellous good general in his day, I assure you. He served in all the Duke of Marlborough's wars, and got that cut over his eye at the battle of Malplaquet. What say you, Mr. Premium? look at him — there's a hero! not cut out of his feathers, as your modern clipped captains are, but enveloped in wig and regimentals, as a general should be. What do you bid?

SIR OLIV. [*Aside to Moses.*] Bid him speak.

MOS. Mr. Premium would have you speak.

CHAS. Why, then, he shall have him for ten pounds, and I'm sure that's not dear for a staff-officer.

SIR OLIV. [*Aside.*] Heaven deliver me! his famous uncle Richard for ten pounds! — [*Aloud.*] Very well, sir, I take him at that.

CHAS. Careless, knock down my uncle Richard. — Here, now, is a maiden sister of his, my great-aunt Deborah, done by Kneller, in his best manner, and esteemed a very formidable likeness. There she is, you see, a shepherdess feeding her flock. You shall have her for five pounds ten — the sheep are worth the money.

SIR OLIV. [*Aside.*] Ah! poor Deborah! a woman who set such a value on herself! — [*Aloud.*] Five pounds ten — she's mine.

CHAS. Knock down my aunt Deborah! Here, now, are two that were a sort of cousins of theirs. — You see, Moses, these pictures were done some time ago, when beaux wore wigs, and the ladies their own hair.

SIR OLIV. Yes, truly, head-dresses appear to have been a little lower in those days.

CHAS. Well, take that couple for the same.

MOS. 'Tis a good bargain.

CHAS. Careless! — This, now, is a grandfather of my mother's, a learned judge, well known on the western circuit, — What do you rate him at, Moses?

MOS. Four guineas.

CHAS. Four guineas! Gad's life, you don't bid me the price of his wig. — Mr. Premium, you have more respect for the woolsack; do let us knock his lordship down at fifteen.

SIR OLIV. By all means.

CARE. Gone!

CHAS. And there are two brothers of his, William and Walter Blunt, Esquires, both members of Parliament, and noted speakers; and, what's very extraordinary, I believe, this is the first time they were ever bought or sold.

SIR OLIV. That is very extraordinary, indeed! I'll take them at your own price, for the honour of Parliament.

CARE. Well said, little Premium! I'll knock them down at forty.

CHAS. Here's a jolly fellow — I don't know what relation, but he was mayor of Norwich: take him at eight pounds.

SIR OLIV. No, no; six will do for the mayor.

CHAS. Come, make it guineas, and I'll throw you the two aldermen here into the bargain.

SIR OLIV. They're mine.

CHAS. Careless, knock down the mayor and aldermen. But, plague on't! we shall be all day retailing in this manner; do let us deal wholesale: what say you, little Premium?

Give me three hundred pounds for the rest of the family in the lump.

CARE. Ay, ay, that will be the best way.

SIR OLIV. Well, well, anything to accommodate you; they are mine. But there is one portrait which you have always passed over.

CARE. What, that ill-looking little fellow over the settee?

SIR OLIV. Yes, sir, I mean that; though I don't think him so ill-looking a little fellow, by any means.

CHAS. What, that? Oh; that's my uncle Oliver! 'Twas done before he went to India.

CARE. Your uncle Oliver! Gad, then you'll never be friends, Charles. That, now, to me, is as stern a looking rogue as ever I saw; an unforgiving eye, and a damned disinheriting countenance! an inveterate knave, depend on't. Don't you think so, little Premium?

SIR OLIV. Upon my soul, sir, I do not; I think it is as honest a looking face as any in the room, dead or alive. But I suppose uncle Oliver goes with the rest of the lumber?

CHAS. No, hang it! I'll not part with poor Noll. The old fellow has been very good to me, and, egad, I'll keep his picture while I've a room to put it in.

SIR OLIV. [*Aside.*] The rogue's my nephew after all! — [*Aloud.*] But, sir, I have somehow taken a fancy to that picture.

CHAS. I'm sorry for't, for you certainly will not have it. Oons, haven't you got enough of them?

SIR OLIV. [*Aside.*] I forgive him everything! — [*Aloud.*] But, sir, when I take a whim in my head, I don't value money. I'll give you as much for that as for all the rest.

CHAS. Don't tease me, master broker; I tell you I'll not part with it, and there's an end of it.

SIR OLIV. [*Aside.*] How like his father the dog is. — [*Aloud.*] Well, well, I have done. — [*Aside.*] I did not perceive it before, but I think I never saw such a striking resemblance. — [*Aloud.*] Here is a draught for your sum.

CHAS. Why, 'tis for eight hundred pounds!

SIR OLIV. You will not let Sir Oliver go?

CHAS. Zounds! no! I tell you, once more.

SIR OLIV. Then never mind the difference, we'll balance that another time. But give me your hand on the bargain; you are an honest fellow, Charles — I beg pardon, sir, for being so free. — Come, Moses.

CHAS. Egad, this is a whimsical old fellow! — But hark'ee, Premium, you'll prepare lodgings for these gentlemen.

SIR OLIV. Yes, yes, I'll send for them in a day or two.

CHAS. But, hold; do now send a genteel conveyance for them, for, I assure you, they were most of them used to ride in their own carriages.

SIR OLIV. I will, I will — for all but Oliver.

CHAS. Ay, all but the little nabob.

SIR OLIV. You're fixed on that?

CHAS. Peremptorily.

SIR OLIV. [*Aside.*] A dear extravagant rogue! — [*Aloud.*] Good day! Come, Moses. — [*Aside.*] Let me hear now who dares call him profligate! [*Exit with* MOSES.

CARE. Why, this is the oddest genius of the sort I ever met with!

CHAS. Egad, he's the prince of brokers, I think. I wonder how the devil Moses got acquainted with so honest a fellow. — Ha! here's Rowley. — Do, Careless, say I'll join the company in a few moments.

CARE. I will — but don't let that old blockhead persuade you to squander any of that money on old musty debts, or any such nonsense; for tradesmen, Charles, are the most exorbitant fellows.

CHAS. Very true, and paying them is only encouraging them.

CARE. Nothing else.

CHAS. Ay, ay, never fear. — [*Exit* CARELESS.] So! this was an odd old fellow, indeed. Let me see, two-thirds of these five hundred and thirty odd pounds are mine by right. Fore Heaven! I find one's ancestors are more valuable relations than I took them for! — Ladies and gentlemen, your most obedient and very grateful servant.

[*Bows ceremoniously to the pictures.*

Enter ROWLEY

Ha! old Rowley! egad, you are just come in time to take leave of your old acquaintance.

ROW. Yes, I heard they were a-going. But I wonder you can have such spirits under so many distresses.

CHAS. Why, there's the point! my distresses are so many, that I can't affort to part with my spirits; but I shall be rich and splenetic, all in good time. However, I suppose you are surprised that I am not more sorrowful at parting with so many near relations; to be sure, 'tis very affecting; but you see they never move a muscle, so why should I?

ROW. There's no making you serious a moment.

CHAS. Yes, faith, I am so now. Here, my honest Rowley, here, get me this changed directly, and take a hundred pounds of it immediately to old Stanley.

ROW. A hundred pounds! Consider only ——

CHAS. Gad's life, don't talk about it! poor Stanley's wants are pressing, and, if you don't make haste, we shall have some one call that has a better right to the money.

ROW. Ah! there's the point! I never will cease dunning you with the old proverb ——

CHAS. *Be just before you're generous.* — Why, so I would if I could; but Justice is an old hobbling beldame, and I can't get her to keep pace with Generosity, for the soul of me.

ROW. Yet, Charles, believe me, one hour's reflection ——

CHAS. Ay, ay, it's very true; but, hark'ee, Rowley, while I have, by Heaven I'll give; so, damn your economy! and now for hazard. [*Exeunt.*

SCENE II. — *The Parlour*

Enter SIR OLIVER *and* MOSES

MOS. Well sir, I think as Sir Peter said you have seen Mr. Charles in high Glory — 'tis great Pity He's so extravagant.

SIR OLIV. True — but he would not sell my Picture —

MOS. And loves wine and women so much —

SIR OLIV. But He wouldn't sell my Picture.

MOS. And game so deep —

SIR OLIV. But He wouldn't sell my Picture. O — here's Rowley!

Enter ROWLEY

ROW. So — Sir Oliver — I find you have made a Purchase ——

SIR OLIV. Yes — yes — our young Rake has parted with his Ancestors like old Tapestry — sold Judges and Generals by the foot — and maiden Aunts as cheap as broken China. —

ROW. And here has he commissioned me to re-deliver you Part of the purchase-money — I mean tho' in your necessitous character of old Stanley ——

MOS. Ah! there is the Pity of all! He is so damned charitable.

ROW. And I left a Hosier and two Tailors in the Hall — who I'm sure won't be paid, and this hundred would satisfy 'em.

SIR OLIV. Well — well — I'll pay his debts and his Benevolences too — I'll take care of old Stanley — myself — But now I am no more a Broker, and you shall introduce me to the elder Brother as Stanley ——

ROW. Not yet a while — Sir Peter I know means to call there about this time.

Enter TRIP

TRIP. O Gentlemen — I beg Pardon for not showing you out — this way — Moses, a word. [*Exit* TRIP *with* MOSES.

SIR OLIV. There's a Fellow for you — Would you believe it that Puppy intercepted the Jew, on our coming, and wanted to raise money before he got to his master!

ROW. Indeed!

SIR OLIV. Yes — they are now planning an annuity Business — Ah Master Rowley [,] in my Day Servants were content with the Follies of their Masters when they were worn a little Thread Bare but now they have their Vices like their Birth Day cloaths with the gloss on. [*Exeunt.*

SCENE III. — *A Library*

SURFACE *and* SERVANT

SURF. No letter from Lady Teazle?

SERV. No Sir —

SURF. I am surprised she hasn't sent if she is prevented from coming —! Sir Peter certainly does not suspect me — yet I wish I may not lose the Heiress, thro' the scrape I have drawn myself in with the wife — However, Charles's imprudence and bad character are great Points in my Favour.

SERV. Sir — I believe that must be Lady Teazle —

SURF. Hold [!] see — whether it is or not before you go to the Door — I have a particular Message for you if it should be my Brother.

SERV. 'Tis her ladyship Sir — She always leaves her Chair at the milliner's in the next Street.

SURF. Stay — stay — draw that Screen before the Window — that will do — my opposite Neighbour is a maiden Lady of so curious a temper! — [SERVANT *draws the screen and exit.*] I have a difficult Hand to play in this Affair — Lady Teazle has lately suspected my Views on Maria — but She must by no means be let into that secret, at least till I have her more in my Power.

Enter Lady Teazle

Lady Teaz. What[!] Sentiment in soliloquy — have you been very impatient now? — O Lud! don't pretend to look grave — I vow I couldn't come before ——

Surf. O Madam[,] Punctuality is a species of Constancy, a very unfashionable quality in a Lady.

Lady Teaz. Upon my word you ought to pity me, do you know Sir Peter is grown so ill-tempered to me of Late! and so jealous! of Charles too that's the best of the story isn't it?

Surf. I am glad my scandalous Friends keep that up. [*Aside.*

Lady Teaz. I am sure I wish He would let Maria marry him — and then perhaps He would be convinced — don't you — Mr. Surface?

Surf. Indeed I do not. — [*Aside.*] O certainly I do — for then my dear Lady Teazle would also be convinced how wrong her suspicions were of my having any design on the silly Girl ——

Lady Teaz. Well — well I'm inclined to believe you — besides I really never could perceive why she should have so many admirers.

Surf. O for her Fortune — nothing else —

Lady Teaz. I believe so for tho' she is certainly very pretty — yet she has no conversation in the world — and is so grave and reserved — that I declare I think she'd have made an excellent wife for Sir Peter. —

Surf. So she would.

Lady Teaz. Then — one never hears her speak ill of anybody — which you know is mighty dull —

Surf. Yet she doesn't want understanding —

Lady Teaz. No more she does — yet one is always disappointed when one hears [her] speak — For though her Eyes have no kind of meaning in them — she very seldom talks Nonsense.

SURF. Nay — nay surely — she has very fine eyes —

LADY TEAZ. Why so she has — tho' sometimes one fancies there's a little sort of a squint —

SURF. A squint — O fie — Lady Teazle.

LADY TEAZ. Yes yes — I vow now — come there is a left-handed Cupid in one eye — that's the Truth on't.

SURF. Well — his aim is very direct however — but Lady Sneerwell has quite corrupted you.

LADY TEAZ. No indeed — I have not opinion enough of her to be taught by her, and I know that she has lately rais'd many scandalous hints of me — which you know one always hears from one common Friend, or other.

SURF. Why to say truth I believe you are not more obliged to her than others of her acquaintance.

LADY TEAZ. But isn't [it] provoking to hear the most ill-natured Things said to one and there's my friend Lady Sneerwell has circulated I don't know how many scandalous tales of me, and all without any foundation, too; that's what vexes me.

SURF. Aye Madam to be sure that is the Provoking circumstance — without Foundation — yes yes — there's the mortification indeed — for when a slanderous story is believed against one — there certainly is no comfort like the consciousness of having deserved it ——

LADY TEAZ. No to be sure — then I'd forgive their malice — but to attack me, who am really so innocent — and who never say an ill-natured thing of anybody — that is, of any Friend —! and then Sir Peter too — to have him so peevish — and so suspicious — when I know the integrity of my own Heart — indeed 'tis monstrous.

SURF. But my dear Lady Teazle 'tis your own fault if you suffer it — when a Husband entertains a groundless suspicion of his Wife and withdraws his confidence from her — the original compact is broke and she owes it to the Honour of her sex to endeavour to outwit him —

LADY TEAZ. Indeed — So that if He suspects me without cause it follows that the best way of curing his Jealousy is to give him reason for't —

SURF. Undoubtedly — for your Husband [should] never be deceived in you — and in that case it becomes you to be frail in compliment to his discernment —

LADY TEAZ. To be sure what you say is very reasonable — and when the consciousness of my own Innocence ——

SURF. Ah: my dear — Madam there is the great mistake — 'tis this very conscious Innocence that is of the greatest Prejudice to you — what is it makes you negligent of Forms and careless of the world's opinion — why the consciousness of your Innocence — what makes you thoughtless in your Conduct and apt to run into a thousand little imprudences — why the consciousness of your Innocence — what makes you impatient of Sir Peter's temper, and outrageous at his suspicions — why the consciousness of your own Innocence —

LADY TEAZ. 'Tis very true.

SURF. Now my dear Lady Teazle if you but once make a trifling *Faux Pas* you can't conceive how cautious you would grow, and how ready to humour and agree with your Husband.

LADY TEAZ. Do you think so —

SURF. O I'm sure on't; and then you'd find all scandal would cease at once — for in short your Character at Present is like a Person in a Plethora, absolutely dying of too much Health —

LADY TEAZ. So — so — then I perceive your Prescription is that I must sin in my own Defence — and part with my virtue to preserve my Reputation. —

SURF. Exactly so upon my credit Ma'am [.]

LADY TEAZ. Well certainly this is the oddest Doctrine — and the newest Receipt for avoiding calumny.

SURF. An infallible one believe me — Prudence like experience must be paid for —

LADY TEAZ. Why if my understanding were once convinced ——

SURF. Oh, certainly Madam, your understanding *should* be convinced — yes — yes — Heaven forbid I should persuade you to do anything you *thought* wrong — no — no — I have too much honor to desire it —

LADY TEAZ. Don't — you think we may as well leave Honor out of the Argument? [*Rises.*

SURF. Ah — the ill effects of your country education I see still remain with you.

LADY TEAZ. I doubt they do indeed — and I will fairly own to you, that If I could be persuaded to do wrong it would be by Sir Peter's ill-usage — sooner than your honourable Logic, after all.

SURF. Then by this Hand, which He is unworthy of ——

Enter SERVANT

Sdeath, you Blockhead — what do you want?

SERV. I beg your Pardon Sir, but I thought you wouldn't chuse Sir Peter to come up without announcing him?

SURF. Sir Peter — Oons — the Devil!

LADY TEAZ. Sir Peter! O Lud! I'm ruined! I'm ruin'd!

SERV. Sir, 'twasn't I let him in.

LADY TEAZ. O I'm undone — what will become of me now Mr. Logick. — Oh! mercy, He's on the Stairs — I'll get behind here — and if ever I'm so imprudent again ——

[*Goes behind the screen* —

SURF. Give me that — Book! ——

[*Sits down* — SERVANT *pretends to adjust his Hair* —

Enter SIR PETER

SIR PET. Aye — ever improving himself! — Mr. Surface —

SURF. Oh! my dear Sir Peter — I beg your Pardon — [*Gap-*

ing and throws away the Book.] I have been dosing [dozing] over a stupid Book! well — I am much obliged to you for this Call — You haven't been here I believe since I fitted up this Room — Books you know are the only Things I am a Coxcomb in —

SIR PET. 'Tis very neat indeed — well well that's proper — and you make even your Screen a source of knowledge — hung I perceive with Maps —

SURF. O yes — I find great use in that Screen.

SIR PET. I dare say you must — certainly — when you want to find out anything in a Hurry.

SURF. Aye or to hide anything in a Hurry either —

SIR PET. Well I have a little private Business — if we were alone —

SURF. You needn't stay.

SERV. No — Sir —— [*Exit* SERVANT.

SURF. Here's a Chair — Sir Peter — I beg ——

SIR PET. Well — now we are alone — there *is* a subject — my dear Friend — on which I wish to unburthen my Mind to you — a Point of the greatest moment to my Peace — in short, my good Friend — Lady Teazle's conduct of late has made me very unhappy.

SURF. Indeed I'm very sorry to hear it —

SIR PET. Yes 'tis but too plain she has not the least regard for me — but what's worse, I have pretty good Authority to suspect that she must have formed an attachment to another.

SURF. Indeed! you astonish me.

SIR PET. Yes — and between ourselves — I think I have discover'd the Person.

SURF. How — you alarm me exceedingly!

SIR PET. Ah: my dear Friend I knew you would sympathize with me. —

SURF. Yes — believe me Sir Peter — such a discovery would hurt me just as much as it would you —

SIR PET. I am convinced of it — ah — it is a happiness to have a Friend whom one can trust even with one's Family secrets — but have you no guess who I mean?

SURF. I haven't the most distant Idea — it can't be Sir Benjamin Backbite.

SIR PET. O — No. What say you to Charles?

SURF. My Brother — impossible! — O no Sir Peter you mustn't credit the scandalous insinuations you hear — no no — Charles to be sure has been charged with many things but I can never think He would meditate so gross an injury —

SIR PET. Ah! my dear Friend — the goodness of your own Heart misleads you — you judge of others by yourself.

SURF. Certainly Sir Peter — the Heart that is conscious of its own integrity is ever slowest to credit another's Treachery.—

SIR PET. True — but your Brother has no sentiment [—] you never hear him talk so. —

SURF. Well there certainly is no knowing what men are capable of — no — there is no knowing — yet I can't but think Lady Teazle herself has too much Principle ——

SIR PET. Aye but what's Principle against the Flattery of a handsome — lively young Fellow —

SURF. That's very true —

SIR PET. And then you know the difference of our ages makes it very improbable that she should have any great affection for me — and if she were to be frail and I were to make it Public — why the Town would only laugh at the foolish old Batchelor, who had married a girl ——

SURF. That's true — to be sure People would laugh.

SIR PET. Laugh — aye and make Ballads — and Paragraphs and the Devil knows what of me —

SURF. No — you must never make it public —

SIR PET. But then again that the Nephew of my old Friend, Sir Oliver[,] should be the Person to attempt such an injury — hurts me more nearly —

SURF. Undoubtedly — when Ingratitude barbs the Dart of Injury — the wound has double danger in it —

SIR PET. Aye — I that was in a manner left his Guardian — in his House he had been so often entertain'd — who never in my Life denied him my advice —

SURF. O 'tis not to be credited — There may be a man capable of such Baseness, to be sure — but for my Part till you can give me positive Proofs you must excuse me withholding my Belief. However, if this should be proved on him He is no longer a brother of mine I disclaim kindred with him — for the man who can break thro' the Laws of Hospitality — and attempt the wife of his Friend deserves to be branded as the Pest of Society.

SIR PET. What a difference there is between you — what noble sentiments! —

SURF. But I cannot suspect Lady Teazle's honor.

SIR PET. I'm sure I wish to think well of her — and to remove all ground of Quarrel between us — She has lately reproach'd me more than once with having made no settlement on her — and, in our last Quarrel, she almost hinted that she should not break her Heart if I was dead. — now as we seem to differ in our Ideas of Expense I have resolved she shall be her own Mistress in that Respect for the future — and if I were to die — she shall find that I have not been inattentive to her Interests while living — Here my Friend are the Draughts of two Deeds which I wish to have your opinion on — by one she will enjoy eight hundred a year independent while I live — and by the other the bulk of my Fortune after my Death.

SURF. This conduct Sir Peter is indeed truly Generous! I wish it may not corrupt my pupil. — [*Aside.*]

SIR PET. Yes I am determined she shall have no cause to complain — tho' I would not have her acquainted with the latter instance of my affection yet awhile.

SURF. Nor I — if I could help it.

SIR PET. And now my dear Friend if you please we will talk over the situation of your Hopes with Maria.

SURF. No — no — Sir Peter — another Time if you Please — [*softly*].

SIR PET. I am sensibly chagrined at the little Progress you seem to make in her affection.

SURF. I beg you will not mention it — What are my Disappointments when your Happiness is in Debate [*softly*]. 'Sdeath I shall be ruined every way.

SIR PET. And tho' you are so averse to my acquainting Lady Teazle with *your* passion, I am sure she's not your Enemy in the Affair.

SURF. Pray Sir Peter, now oblige me. — I am really too much affected by the subject we have been speaking of to bestow a thought on my own concerns — The Man who is entrusted with his Friend's Distresses can never ——

Enter SERVANT

Well, Sir?

SERV. Your Brother Sir, is — speaking to a Gentleman in the Street, and says He knows you're within.

SURF. 'Sdeath, Blockhead — I'm *not* within — I'm out for the Day.

SIR PET. Stay — hold — a thought has struck me — you shall be at home.

SURF. Well — well — let him up. — [*Exit* SERV.] He'll interrupt Sir Peter, however. [*Aside.*

SIR PET. Now, my good Friend — oblige me I Intreat you — before Charles comes — let me conceal myself somewhere — Then do you tax him on the Point we have been talking on — and his answers may satisfy me at once. —

SURF. O Fie — Sir Peter — would you have *me* join in so mean a Trick? to trepan my Brother too?

SIR PET. Nay you tell me you are *sure* He is innocent — if

so you do him the greatest service in giving him an opportunity to clear himself — and — you will set my Heart at rest — come you shall not refuse me — here behind this Screen will be — hey! what the Devil — there seems to be one listener here already — I'll swear I saw a Petticoat. —

SURF. Ha! ha! ha! Well this is ridiculous enough — I'll tell you, Sir Peter — tho' I hold a man of Intrigue to be a most despicable Character — yet you know it doesn't follow that a man is to be an absolute Joseph either — hark'ee — 'tis a little French Milliner — a silly Rogue that plagues me — and having some character, on your coming she ran behind the Screen. —

SIR PET. Ah a Rogue — but 'egad she has overheard all I have been saying of my Wife.

SURF. O 'twill never go any farther, you may depend on't.

SIR PET. No! — then efaith let her hear it out. — Here's a Closet will do as well. —

SURF. Well, go in there. —

SIR PET. Sly rogue — sly Rogue. —

SURF. Gad's my Life what an Escape —! and a curious situation I'm in! — to part man and wife in this manner. —

LADY TEAZ. [*peeps out.*] Couldn't I steal off —

SURF. Keep close, my Angel!

SIR PET. [*Peeping out.*] Joseph — tax him home.

SURF. Back — my dear Friend

LADY TEAZ. [*Peeping out.*] Couldn't you lock Sir Peter in? —

SURF. Be still — my Life!

SIR PET. [*Peeping.*] You're sure the little Milliner won't blab?

SURF. In! in! my good Sir Peter — 'Fore Gad, I wish I had a key to the Door.

Enter CHARLES

CHAS. Hollo! Brother — what has been the matter? your

Fellow wouldn't let me up at first — What [!] have you had a Jew or a wench with you. —

SURF. Neither Brother I assure you.

CHAS. But — what has made Sir Peter steal off? I thought He had been with you —

SURF. He *was* Brother — but hearing you were coming He didn't chuse to stay —

CHAS. What [!] was the old Gentleman afraid I wanted to borrow money of him?

SURF. No Sir — but I am sorry to find [,] Charles — you have lately given that worthy man grounds for great Uneasiness.

CHAS. Yes they tell me I do that to a great many worthy men — but how so Pray?

SURF. To be plain with you Brother He thinks you are endeavouring to gain Lady Teazle's Affections from him.

CHAS. Who I — O Lud! not I upon my word. — Ha! ha! ha! so the old Fellow has found out that He has got a young wife has He? or what's worse she has discover'd that she has an old Husband?

SURF. This is no subject to jest on Brother — He who can laugh ——

CHAS. True true as you were going to say — then seriously I never had the least idea of what you charge me with, upon my honour.

SURF. Well it will give Sir Peter great satisfaction to hear this.

CHAS. [*Aloud.*] To be sure, I once thought the lady seemed to have taken a fancy — but upon my soul I never gave her the least encouragement. — Beside you know my Attachment to Maria —

SURF. But sure Brother even if Lady Teazle had betray'd the fondest Partiality for you ——

CHAS. Why — look'ee Joseph — I hope I shall never deliberately do a dishonourable Action — but if a pretty woman was purposely to throw herself in my way — and that pretty woman married to a man old enough to be her Father ——

SURF. Well?

CHAS. Why I believe I should be obliged to borrow a little of your Morality, that's all. — but, Brother do you know now that you surprize me exceedingly by naming me with Lady Teazle — for faith I always understood *you* were her Favourite —

SURF. O for shame! Charles — This retort is Foolish.

CHAS. Nay I swear I have seen you exchange such significant Glances ——

SURF. Nay — nay — Sir — this is no jest —

CHAS. Egad — I'm serious — Don't you remember — one Day, when I called here ——

SURF. Nay — prithee — Charles

CHAS. And found you together ——

SURF. Zounds, Sir — I insist ——

CHAS. And another time when your Servant ——

SURF. Brother — brother a word with you — Gad I must stop him — [*Aside.*

CHAS. Informed — me that ——

SURF. Hush! — I beg your Pardon but Sir Peter has overheard all we have been saying — I knew you would clear yourself, or I shouldn't have consented —

CHAS. How Sir Peter — Where is He —

SURF. Softly, there! [*Points to the closet.*

CHAS. [*In the Closet!*] O 'fore Heaven I'll have him out — Sir Peter come forth!

SURF. No — no ——

CHAS. I say Sir Peter — come into court. — [*Pulls in* SIR PETER.] What — my old Guardian — what [!] turn inquisitor and take evidence incog. —

SIR PET. Give me your hand — Charles — I believe I have suspected you wrongfully; but you mustn't be angry with Joseph — 'twas my Plan —

CHAS. Indeed! —

SIR PET. But I acquit you — I promise you I don't think near so ill of you as I did — what I have heard has given me great satisfaction.

CHAS. Egad then 'twas lucky you didn't hear any more. Wasn't it Joseph?

SIR PET. Ah! you would have retorted on him.

CHAS. Aye — aye — that was a Joke.

SIR PET. Yes, yes, I know his honor too well.

CHAS. Yet you might as well have suspected him as me in this matter, for all that — mightn't He, Joseph?

SIR PET. Well well I believe you —

SURF. Would they were both out of the Room!

Enter SERVANT, *whispers* SURFACE

SIR PET. And in future perhaps we may not be such Strangers.

SURF. Gentlemen — I beg Pardon — I must wait on you downstairs — Here is a Person come on particular Business ——

CHAS. Well you can see him in another Room — Sir Peter and I haven't met a long time and I have something to say [to] him.

SURF. They must not be left together. — I'll send this man away and return directly — [SURFACE *goes out.*

SIR PET. Ah — Charles if you associated more with your Brother, one might indeed hope for your reformation — He is a man of Sentiment — Well! there is nothing in the world so noble as a man of Sentiment!

CHAS. Pshaw! He is too moral by half — and so apprehensive of his good Name, as he calls it, that I suppose He would as soon let a Priest in his House as a Girl —

SIR PET. No — no — come come, — you wrong him — no, Joseph is no Rake but he is no such Saint in that either. I have a great mind to tell him — we should have such a Laugh!

CHAS. Oh, hang him? He's a very Anchorite — a young Hermit!

SIR PET. Harkee — you must not abuse him, he may chance to hear of it again I promise you.

CHAS. Why you won't tell him?

SIR PET. No — but — this way. Egad, I'll tell him — Harkee, have you a mind to have a good laugh against Joseph?

CHAS. I should like it of all things —

SIR PET. Then, E'faith, we will — I'll be quit with him for discovering me. — He had a girl with him when I called. [*Whispers.*

CHAS. What[!] Joseph[!] you jest —

SIR PET. Hush! — a little French Milliner — and the best of the Jest is — she's in the room now.

CHAS. The devil she is —

SIR PET. Hush! I tell you. [*Points.*

CHAS. Behind the screen! Odds Life, let's unveil her!

SIR PET. No — no! He's coming — you shan't indeed!

CHAS. Oh, egad, we'll have a peep at the little milliner!

SIR PET. Not for the world — Joseph will never forgive me.

CHAS. I'll stand by you ——

SIR PET. Odds Life! Here He's coming —

[SURFACE *enters just as* CHARLES *throws down the Screen.*

Re-enter JOSEPH SURFACE

CHAS. Lady Teazle! by all that's wonderful!

SIR PET. Lady Teazle! by all that's Horrible!

CHAS. Sir Peter — This is one of the smartest French Milliners I ever saw! — Egad, you seem all to have been diverting yourselves here at Hide and Seek — and I don't see who is out of the Secret! — Shall I beg your Ladyship to inform me! — Not a word! — Brother! — will you please to explain this matter? What! is Honesty Dumb too? — Sir Peter, though I found you in the Dark — perhaps you are not so now — all mute! Well tho' I can make nothing of the Affair, I make no doubt but you perfectly understand one another — so I'll leave you to yourselves. — [*Going.*] Brother I'm sorry to find you have given that worthy man grounds for so much uneasiness! — Sir Peter — there's nothing in the world so noble as a man of Sentiment! —

[*Stand for some time looking at one another. Exit* CHARLES.

SURF. Sir Peter — notwithstanding I confess that appearances are against me. If you will afford me your Patience I make no doubt but I shall explain everything to your satisfaction. —

SIR PET. If you please — Sir —

SURF. The Fact is Sir — that Lady Teazle knowing my Pretensions to your ward Maria — I say Sir Lady Teazle — being apprehensive of the Jealousy of your Temper — and knowing my Friendship to the Family. She Sir — I say call'd here — in order that I might explain those Pretensions — but on your coming being apprehensive — as I said of your Jealousy — she withdrew — and this, you may depend on't is the whole truth of the Matter.

SIR PET. A very clear account upon the [my] word and I dare swear the Lady will vouch for every article of it.

LADY TEAZ. For not one word of it Sir Peter —

SIR PET. How[!] don't you think it worth while to agree in the lie.

LADY TEAZ. There is not one Syllable of Truth in what that Gentleman has told you.

SIR PET. I believe you upon my soul Ma'am —

SURF. 'Sdeath, madam, will you betray me! [*Aside.*

LADY TEAZ. Good Mr. Hypocrite by your leave I will speak for myself —

SIR PET. Aye let her alone Sir — you'll find she'll make out a better story than you without Prompting.

Lady Teaz. Hear me Sir Peter — I came hither on no matter relating to your ward and even ignorant of this Gentleman's pretensions to her — but I came — seduced by his insidious arguments — and pretended Passion [—] at least to listen to his dishonourable Love if not to sacrifice your Honour to his Baseness.

Sir Pet. Now, I believe, the Truth is coming indeed[.]

Surf. The Woman's mad —

Lady Teaz. No Sir — she has recovered her Senses. Your own Arts have furnished her with the means. Sir Peter — I do not expect you to credit me — but the Tenderness you express'd for me, when I am sure you could not think I was a witness to it, has penetrated so to my Heart that had I left the Place without the Shame of this discovery — my future life should have spoken the sincerity of my Gratitude — as for that smooth-tongued Hypocrite — who would have seduced the wife of his too credulous Friend while he pretended honourable addresses to his ward — I behold him now in a light so truly despicable that I shall never again Respect myself for having Listened to him. [*Exit.*

Surf. Notwithstanding all this Sir Peter — Heaven knows ——

Sir Pet. That you are a Villain! — and so I leave you to your conscience —

Surf. You are too Rash Sir Peter — you *shall* hear me — The man who shuts out conviction by refusing to ——

[*Exeunt,* Surface *following and speaking.*

END OF THE FOURTH

ACT V

Scene. I — *The Library*

Enter Surface *and* Servant

Surf. Mr. Stanley! and why should you think I would see him? — you must know he came to ask something!

Serv. Sir — I shouldn't have let him in but that Mr. Rowley came to the Door with him.

Surf. Pshaw! — Blockhead to suppose that I should now be in a Temper to receive visits from poor Relations! — well why don't you show the Fellow up?

Serv. I will — Sir — Why, Sir — it was not my Fault that Sir Peter discover'd my Lady ——

Surf. Go, fool! — [*Exit* Serv.] Sure Fortune never play'd a man of my policy such a Trick before — my character with Sir Peter! — my Hopes with Maria! — destroy'd in a moment! — I'm in a rare Humour to listen to other People's Distresses! — I shan't be able to bestow even a benevolent sentiment on Stanley — So! here — He comes and Rowley with him — I *must* try to recover myself, and put a little Charity into my Face however. —— [*Exit.*

Enter Sir Oliver *and* Rowley

Sir Oliv. What! does He avoid us? that was He — was it not?

Row. It was Sir — but I doubt you are come a little too abruptly — his Nerves are so weak that the sight of a poor Relation may be too much for him — I should have gone first to break you to him.

Sir Oliv. A Plague of his Nerves — yet this is He whom Sir Peter extolls as a Man of the most Benevolent way of thinking! —

Row. As to his way of thinking —I can't pretend to decide[,] for, to do him justice He appears to have as much speculative Benevolence as any private Gentleman in the Kingdom — though he is seldom so sensual as to indulge himself in the exercise of it ——

SIR OLIV. Yet [he] has a string of charitable Sentiments I suppose at his Fingers' ends! —

ROW. Or, rather at his Tongue's end Sir Oliver; for I believe there is no sentiment he has more faith in than that 'Charity begins at Home.'

SIR OLIV. And his I presume is of that domestic sort which never stirs abroad at all.

ROW. I doubt you'll find it so — but He's coming — I mustn't seem to interrupt you — and you know immediately — as you leave him — I come in to announce — your arrival in your real Character.

SIR OLIV. True — and afterwards you'll meet me at Sir Peter's ——

ROW. Without losing a moment. [*Exit.*

SIR OLIV. So — I see he has premeditated a Denial by the Complaisance of his Features.

Enter SURFACE

SURF. Sir — I beg you ten thousand Pardons for keeping — you a moment waiting — Mr. Stanley — I presume ——

SIR OLIV. At your Service.

SURF. Sir — I beg you will do me the honour to sit down — I entreat you Sir.

SIR OLIV. Dear Sir there's no occasion — too civil by half!

SURF. I have not the Pleasure of knowing you, Mr. Stanley — but I am extremely happy to see you look so well — you were nearly related to my mother — I think Mr. Stanley ——

SIR OLIV. I was Sir — so nearly that my present Poverty I fear may do discredit to her Wealthy Children — else I should not have presumed to trouble you. —

SURF. Dear Sir — there needs no apology — He that is in Distress tho' a stranger has a right to claim kindred with the wealthy — I am sure I wish I was of that class, and had it in my power to offer you even a small relief.

SIR OLIV. If your Unkle, Sir Oliver were here — I should have a Friend ——

SURF. I wish He was Sir, with all my Heart — you should not want an advocate with him — believe me Sir.

SIR OLIV. I should not need one — my Distresses would recommend me. — but I imagined — his Bounty had enabled you to become the agent of his Charity.

SURF. My dear Sir — you are strangely misinformed — Sir Oliver is a worthy Man, a worthy man — a very worthy sort of Man — but avarice Mr. Stanley is the vice of age — I will tell you my good Sir in confidence: — what he has done for me has been a mere — nothing [;] tho' People I know have thought otherwise and for my Part I never chose to contradict the Report.

SIR OLIV. What! — has he never transmitted — you — Bullion — Rupees — Pagodas!

SURF. O Dear Sir — Nothing of the kind — no — no — a few Presents now and then — china, shawls, congo Tea, Avadavats — and indian Crackers — little more, believe me.

SIR OLIV. Here's Gratitude for twelve thousand pounds! — Avadavats and indian Crackers.

SURF. Then my dear — Sir — you have heard, I doubt not, of the extravagance of my Brother — Sir — there are very few would credit what I have done for that unfortunate young man.

SIR OLIV. Not I for one!

SURF. The sums I have lent him! indeed — I have been exceedingly to blame — it was an amiable weakness! however I don't pretend to defend it — and now I feel it doubly culpable — since it has deprived me of the power of serving *you* Mr. Stanley as my Heart directs ——

SIR OLIV. Dissembler! Then Sir — you cannot assist me?

SURF. At Present it grieves me to say I cannot — but whenever I have the ability, you may depend upon hearing from me.

SIR OLIV. I am extremely sorry ——

SURF. Not more than I am believe me — to pity without the Power to relieve is still more painful than to ask and be denied ——

SIR OLIV. Kind Sir — your most obedient humble servant.

SURF. You leave me deeply affected Mr. Stanley — William — be ready to open the door ——

SIR OLIV. O, Dear Sir, no ceremony ——

SURF. Your very obedient ——

SIR OLIV. Your most obsequious ——

SURF. You may depend on hearing from me whenever I can be of service ——

SIR OLIV. Sweet Sir — you are too good ——

SURF. In the mean time I wish you Health and Spirits ——

SIR OLIV. Your ever grateful and perpetual humble Servant ——

SURF. Sir — yours as sincerely ——

SIR OLIV. Charles! — you are my Heir. [*Exit.*

SURFACE, *solus*

Soh! — This is one bad effect of a good Character — it invites applications from the unfortunate and there needs no small degree of address to gain the reputation of Benevolence without incurring the expence. — The silver ore of pure Charity is an expensive article in the catalogue of a man's good Qualities — whereas the sentimental French Plate I use instead of it makes just as good a shew — and pays no tax.

Enter ROWLEY

ROW. Mr. Surface — your Servant: I was apprehensive of interrupting you, tho' my Business demands immediate attention — as this Note will inform you ——

Surf. Always Happy to see Mr. Rowley — how — Oliver — Surface! — My Unkle arrived!

Row. He is indeed — we have just parted — quite well — after a speedy voyage — and impatient to embrace his worthy Nephew.

Surf. I am astonished! — William[!] stop Mr. Stanley, if He's not gone ——

Row. O — He's out of reach — I believe.

Surf. Why didn't you let me know this when you came in together. —

Row. I thought you had particular — Business — but I must be gone to inform your Brother, and appoint him here to meet his Uncle. He will be with you in a quarter of an hour ——

Surf. So he says. Well — I am strangely overjoy'd at his coming — never to be sure was anything so damn'd unlucky!

Row. You will be delighted to see how well He looks.

Surf. O — I'm rejoiced to hear it — just at this time ——

Row. I'll tell him how impatiently you expect him ——

Surf. Do — do — pray — give my best duty and affection — indeed, I cannot express the sensations I feel at the thought of seeing him! — certainly his coming just at this Time is the cruellest piece of ill Fortune —— [*Exeunt.*

Scene II. — *At* Sir Peter's *House*

Enter Mrs. Candour *and* Servant

Serv. Indeed Ma'am, my Lady will see nobody at Present.

Mrs. Can. Did you tell her it was her Friend Mrs. Candour ——

Serv. Yes Ma'am but she begs you will excuse her ——

Mrs. Can. Do go again — I shall be glad to see her if it be only for a moment — for I am sure she must be in great Distress [*exit* Maid] — Dear Heart — how provoking! — I'm not mistress of half the circumstances! — We shall have the whole affair in the newspapers with the Names of the Parties at length before I have dropt the story at a dozen houses.

Enter SIR BENJAMIN

Sir Benjamin you have heard, I suppose ——

SIR BEN. Of Lady Teazle and Mr. Surface ——

MRS. CAN. And Sir Peter's Discovery ——

SIR BEN. O the strangest Piece of Business to be sure ——

MRS. CAN. Well I never was so surprised in my life! — I am so sorry for all Parties — indeed,

SIR BEN. Now I don't Pity Sir Peter at all — he was so extravagant — partial to Mr. Surface ——

MRS. CAN. Mr. Surface! — why 'twas with Charles Lady Teazle was detected.

SIR BEN. No such thing Mr. Surface is the gallant.

MRS. CAN. No — no — Charles is the man — 'twas Mr. Surface brought Sir Peter on purpose to discover them ——

SIR BEN. I tell you I have it from one ——

MRS. CAN. And I have it from one ——

SIR BEN. Who had it from one who had it ——

MRS. CAN. From one immediately — but here comes Lady Sneerwell — perhaps she knows the whole affair.

Enter LADY SNEERWELL

LADY SNEER. So — my dear Mrs. Candour Here's a sad affair of our Friend Teazle ——

MRS. CAN. Aye my dear Friend, who could have thought it.

LADY SNEER. Well there is no trusting to appearances [;] tho' — indeed she was always too lively for me.

MRS. CAN. To be sure, her manners were a little too — free — but she was very young ——

LADY SNEER. And had indeed some good Qualities.

MRS. CAN. So she had indeed — but have you heard the Particulars?

LADY SNEER. No — but everybody says that Mr. Surface ——

SIR BEN. Aye there I told you — Mr. Surface was the Man.

MRS. CAN. No — no — indeed the assignation was with Charles ——

LADY SNEER. With Charles! — You alarm me Mrs. Candour!

MRS. CAN. Yes — yes He was the Lover — Mr. Surface — do him justice — was only the Informer.

SIR BEN. Well I'll not dispute with you Mrs. Candour — but be it which it may — I hope that Sir Peter's wound will not ——

MRS. CAN. Sir Peter's wound! O mercy! I didn't hear a word of their Fighting ——

LADY SNEER. Nor I a syllable!

SIR BEN. No — what no mention of the Duel ——

MRS. CAN. Not a word —

SIR BEN. O, Lord — yes — yes — they fought before they left the Room.

LADY SNEER. Pray let us hear.

MRS. CAN. Aye — do oblige — us with the Duel ——

SIR BEN. 'Sir' — says Sir Peter — immediately after the Discovery, 'you are a most ungrateful Fellow.'

MRS. CAN. Aye to Charles ——

SIR BEN. No, no — to Mr. Surface — 'a most ungrateful Fellow; and old as I am, Sir,' says He, 'I insist on immediate satisfaction.'

MRS. CAN. Aye that must have been to Charles for 'tis very unlikely Mr. Surface should go to fight in his own House.

SIR BEN. Gad's Life, Ma'am, not at all — giving me immediate satisfaction — on this, Madam — Lady Teazle seeing Sir Peter in such Danger — ran out of the Room in strong Hysterics — and Charles after her calling out for Hartshorn and Water! Then Madam — they began to fight with Swords ——

Enter Crabtree

Crab. With Pistols — Nephew — I have it from undoubted authority.

Mrs. Can. Oh, Mr. Crabtree then it is all true ——

Crab. Too true indeed Ma'am, and Sir Peter Dangerously wounded ——

Sir Ben. By a thrust in second — quite thro' his left side

Crab. By a Bullet lodged in the Thorax ——

Mrs. Can. Mercy — on me[!] Poor Sir Peter ——

Crab. Yes, ma'am tho' Charles would have avoided the matter if he could ——

Mrs. Can. I knew Charles was the Person ——

Sir Ben. O my Unkle I see knows nothing of the matter ——

Crab. But Sir Peter tax'd him with the basest ingratitude ——

Sir Ben. That I told you, you know ——

Crab. Do Nephew let me speak — and insisted on immediate ——

Sir Ben. Just as I said ——

Crab. Odds life! Nephew allow others to know something too — A Pair of Pistols lay on the Bureau — for Mr. Surface — it seems, had come home the Night before late from Salt-Hill where He had been to see the Montem with a Friend, who has a Son at Eton — so unluckily the Pistols were left Charged ——

Sir Ben. I heard nothing of this ——

Crab. Sir Peter forced Charles to take one and they fired — it seems pretty nearly together — Charles's shot took Place as I tell you — and Sir Peter's miss'd — but what is very extraordinary the Ball struck against a little Bronze Pliny that stood over the Fire Place — grazed out of the window at a right angle — and wounded the Postman, who was just coming to the Door with a double letter from Northamptonshire.

Sir Ben. My Unkle's account is more circumstantial I must confess — but I believe mine is the true one for all that.

LADY SNEER. I am more interested in this Affair than they imagine — and must have better information. — [*Exit.*

SIR BEN. Ah! Lady Sneerwell's alarm is very easily accounted for. —

CRAB. Yes yes, they certainly *do* say — but that's neither here nor there.

MRS. CAN. But pray where is Sir Peter at present ——

CRAB. Oh! they — brought him home and He is now in the House, tho' the Servants are order'd to deny it ——

MRS. CAN. I believe so — and Lady Teazle — I suppose attending him ——

CRAB. Yes yes — and I saw one of the Faculty enter just before me ——

SIR BEN. Hey — who comes here ——

CRAB. Oh, this is He — the Physician depend on't.

MRS. CAN. O certainly it must be the Physician and now we shall know ——

Enter SIR OLIVER

CRAB. Well, Doctor — what Hopes?

MRS. CAN. Aye Doctor how's your Patient?

SIR BEN. Now Doctor isn't it a wound with a small sword ——

CRAB. A bullet lodged in the Thorax — for a hundred!

SIR OLIV. Doctor! — a wound with a small sword! and a Bullet in the Thorax! — oon's are you mad, good People?

SIR BEN. Perhaps, Sir, you are not a Doctor.

SIR OLIV. Truly Sir I am to thank you for my degree If I am.

CRAB. Only a Friend of Sir Peter's then I presume — but, sir, you must have heard of this accident —

SIR OLIV. Not a word!

CRAB. Not of his being dangerously wounded?

SIR OLIV. The Devil he is!

SIR BEN. Run thro' the Body ——

CRAB. Shot in the breast ——

SIR BEN. By one Mr. Surface ——

CRAB. Aye the younger.

SIR OLIV. Hey! what the plague! you seem to differ strangely in your accounts — however you agree that Sir Peter is dangerously wounded.

SIR BEN. Oh yes, we agree in that.

CRAB. Yes, yes, I believe there can be no doubt in that.

SIR OLIV. Then, upon my word, for a person in that Situation, he is the most imprudent man alive — For here he comes walking as if nothing at all was the matter.

Enter SIR PETER

Odd's heart, sir Peter! you are come in good time I promise you, for we had just given you over!

SIR BEN. 'Egad, Uncle this is the most sudden Recovery!

SIR OLIV. Why, man, what do you do out of Bed with a Small Sword through your Body, and a Bullet lodg'd in your Thorax?

SIR PET. A Small Sword and a Bullet —

SIR OLIV. Aye these Gentlemen would have kill'd you without Law or Physic, and wanted to dub me a Doctor to make me an accomplice.

SIR PET. Why! what is all this?

SIR BEN. We rejoice, Sir Peter, that the Story of the Duel is not true — and are sincerely sorry for your other Misfortune.

SIR PET. So — so — all over the Town already! [*Aside.*

CRAB. Tho', Sir Peter, you were certainly vastly to blame to marry at all at your years.

SIR PET. Sir, what Business is that of yours?

MRS. CAN. Tho' Indeed, as Sir Peter made so good a Husband, he's very much to be pitied.

SIR PET. Plague on your pity, Ma'am, I desire none of it.

SIR BEN. However Sir Peter, you must not mind the Laughing and Jests you will meet with on the occasion.

SIR PET. Sir, I desire to be master in my own house.

CRAB. 'Tis no Uncommon Case, that's one comfort.

SIR PET. I insist on being left to myself, without ceremony, — I insist on your leaving my house directly!

MRS. CAN. Well, well, we are going and depend on't, we'll make the best report of you we can.

SIR PET. Leave my house!

CRAB. And tell how hardly you have been treated.

SIR PET. Leave my House —

SIR BEN. And how patiently you bear it.

SIR PET. Friends! Vipers! Furies! Oh that their own Venom would choke them!

SIR OLIV. They are very provoking indeed, Sir Peter.

Enter ROWLEY

ROW. I heard high words: what has ruffled you Sir Peter —

SIR PET. Pshaw what signifies asking — do I ever pass a Day without my Vexations?

SIR OLIV. Well I'm not Inquisitive — I come only to tell you, that I have seen both my Nephews in the manner we proposed.

SIR PET. A Precious Couple they are!

ROW. Yes and Sir Oliver — is convinced that your judgment was right Sir Peter.

SIR OLIV. Yes I find Joseph is Indeed the Man after all.

ROW. Aye as Sir Peter says, He's a man of Sentiment.

SIR OLIV. And acts up to the Sentiments he professes.

ROW. It certainly is Edification to hear him talk.

SIR OLIV. Oh, He's a model for the young men of the age! But how's this, Sir Peter? you don't Join us in your Friend Joseph's Praise as I expected.

SIR PET. Sir Oliver, we live in a damned wicked world, and the fewer we praise the better.

ROW. What do *you* say so, Sir Peter — who were never mistaken in your Life?

SIR PET. Pshaw — Plague on you both — I see by your sneering you have heard — the whole affair — I shall go mad among you!

ROW. Then to fret you no longer Sir Peter — we are indeed acquainted with it all — I met Lady Teazle coming from Mr. Surface's so humbled, that she deigned to request *me* to be her advocate with you —

SIR PET. And does Sir Oliver know all too?

SIR OLIV. Every circumstance!

SIR PET. What of the closet and the screen — hey[?]

SIR OLIV. Yes yes — and the little French Milliner. Oh, I have been vastly diverted with the story! ha! ha! ha!

SIR PET. 'Twas very pleasant!

SIR OLIV. I never laugh'd more in my life, I assure you: ha! ha!

SIR PET. O vastly diverting! ha! ha!

ROW. To be sure Joseph with his Sentiments! ha! ha!

SIR PET. Yes his sentiments! ha! ha! a hypocritical Villain!

SIR OLIV. Aye and that Rogue Charles — to pull Sir Peter out of the closet: ha! ha!

SIR PET. Ha! ha! 'twas devilish entertaining to be sure —

SIR OLIV. Ha! ha! Egad, Sir Peter I should like to have seen your Face when the screen was thrown down — ha! ha!

SIR PET. Yes, my face when the Screen was thrown down: ha! ha! ha! O I must never show my head again!

SIR OLIV. But come — come it isn't fair to laugh at you neither my old Friend — tho' upon my soul I can't help it —

SIR PET. O pray don't restrain your mirth on my account: it does not hurt me at all — I laugh at the whole affair myself — Yes — yes — I think being a standing Jest for all one's acquaintance a very happy situation — O yes — and then of a morning to read the Paragraphs about Mr. S——, Lady T——, and Sir P——, will be so entertaining! — I shall certainly leave town tomorrow and never look mankind in the Face again!

Row. Without affectation Sir Peter, you may despise the ridicule of Fools — but I see Lady Teazle going towards the next Room — I am sure you must desire a Reconciliation as earnestly as she does.

Sir Oliv. Perhaps *my* being here prevents her coming to you — well I'll leave honest Rowley to mediate between you; but he must bring you all presently to Mr. Surface's — where I am now returning — if not to reclaim a Libertine, at least to expose Hypocrisy.

Sir Pet. Ah! I'll be present at your discovering yourself there with all my heart; though 'tis a vile unlucky Place for discoveries.

Sir Oliv. However it is very convenient to the carrying on of my Plot that you all live so near one another! [*Exit* Sir Oliver.

Row. We'll follow —

Sir Pet. She is not coming here you see, Rowley —

Row. No but she has left the Door of that Room open you perceive. — see she is in Tears —!

Sir Pet. She seems indeed to wish I should go to her. — how dejected she appears —

Row. And will you refrain from comforting her —

Sir Pet. Certainly a little mortification appears very becoming in a wife — don't you think it will do her good to let her Pine a little.

Row. O this is ungenerous in you —

Sir Pet. Well I know not what to think — you remember Rowley the Letter I found of her's — evidently intended for Charles?

Row. A mere forgery, Sir Peter — laid in your way on Purpose — this is one of the Points which I intend Snake shall give you conviction on —

Sir Pet. I wish I were once satisfied of that — She looks this way —— what a remarkably elegant Turn of the Head she has! Rowley I'll go to her —

Row. Certainly —

Sir Pet. Tho' when it is known that we are reconciled, People will laugh at me ten times more!

Row. Let — them laugh — and retort their malice only by showing them you are happy in spite of it.

Sir Pet. Efaith so I will — and, if I'm not mistaken we may yet be the happiest couple in the country —

Row. Nay Sir Peter — He who once lays aside suspicion ——

Sir Pet. Hold Master Rowley — if you have any Regard for me — never let me hear you utter anything like a Sentiment. I have had enough of *them* to serve me the rest of my Life.

[*Exeunt.*

Scene the Last. — *The Library*

Surface *and* Lady Sneerwell

Lady Sneer. Impossible! will not Sir Peter immediately be reconciled to *Charles?* and of consequence no longer oppose his union with *Maria?* the thought is Distraction to me!

Surf. Can Passion — furnish a Remedy?

Lady Sneer. No — nor cunning either. O I was a Fool, an Ideot — to league with such a Blunderer!

Surf. Surely Lady Sneerwell I am the greatest Sufferer — yet you see I bear the accident with Calmness.

Lady Sneer. Because the Disappointment hasn't reached your *Heart* — your interest only attached you to Maria — had you felt for her — what I have for that ungrateful Libertine — neither your Temper nor Hypocrisy could prevent your showing the sharpness of your Vexation.

Surf. But why should your Reproaches fall on me for this Disappointment?

Lady Sneer. Are not you the cause of it? what had you to bate in your Pursuit of Maria to pervert Lady Teazle by the way. — had you not a sufficient field for your Roguery in blinding Sir Peter and supplanting your Brother — I hate such an avarice of crimes — 'tis an unfair monopoly and never prospers.

SURF. Well I admit I have been to blame — I confess I deviated from the direct Road of wrong but I don't think we're so totally defeated neither.

LADY SNEER. No!

SURF. You tell me you have made a trial of Snake since we met — and that you still believe him faithful to us —

LADY SNEER. I do believe so.

SURF. And that he has undertaken should it be necessary — to swear and prove that Charles is at this Time contracted by vows and Honour to your Ladyship — which some of his former letters to you will serve to support —

LADY SNEER. This, indeed, might have assisted —

SURF. Come — come it is not too late yet — but hark! this is probably my Unkle Sir Oliver — retire to that Room — we'll consult further when He's gone. —

LADY SNEER. Well but if *He* should find you out to —

SURF. O I have no fear of that — Sir Peter will hold his tongue for his own credit sake — and you may depend on't I shall soon Discover Sir Oliver's weak side! —

LADY SNEER. I have no diffidence of your abilities — only be constant to one roguery at a time — [*Exit.*

SURF. I will — I will — So 'tis confounded hard after such bad Fortune, to be baited by one's confederate in evil — well at all events my character is so much better than Charles's, that I certainly — hey — what! — this is not Sir Oliver — but old Stanley again! — Plague on't that He should return to teaze me just now — I shall have Sir Oliver come and find him here — and ——

Enter SIR OLIVER

Gad's life, Mr. Stanley — why have you come back to plague me at this time? you must not stay now upon my word!

SIR OLIV. Sir — I hear your Unkle Oliver is expected here — and tho' He has been so penurious to you, I'll try what He'll do for me —

SURF. Sir! 'tis impossible for you to stay now — so I must beg —— come any other time and I promise you you shall be assisted.

SIR OLIV. No — Sir Oliver and I must be acquainted —

SURF. Zounds Sir then [I] insist on your qüitting the — Room directly —

SIR OLIV. Nay Sir ——

SURF. Sir — I insist on't — here William show this Gentleman out. Since you compel me Sir — not one moment — this is such insolence. [*Going to push him out.*

Enter CHARLES

CHAS. Heyday! what's the matter now? — what the Devil have you got hold of my little Broker here! Zounds — Brother, don't hurt little Premium. What's the matter — my little Fellow?

SURF. So! He has been with you, too, has He —

CHAS. To be sure He has! Why, 'tis as honest a little —— But sure Joseph you have not been borrowing money too have you?

SURF. Borrowing — no! — But, Brother — you know sure we expect Sir Oliver every ——

CHAS. O Gad, that's true — Noll mustn't find the little Broker here to be sure —

SURF. Yet Mr. Stanley insists ——

CHAS. Stanley — why his name's Premium —

SURF. No no Stanley.

CHAS. No, no — Premium.

SURF. Well no matter which — but ——

CHAS. Aye aye Stanley or Premium, 'tis the same thing as you say — for I suppose He goes by half a hundred Names, besides A. B's at the Coffee-House. [*Knock.*

SURF. 'Sdeath — here's Sir Oliver at the Door ——Now I beg — Mr. Stanley ——

CHAS. Aye aye and I beg Mr. Premium ——

SIR OLIV. Gentlemen ——

SURF. Sir, by Heaven you shall go —

CHAS. Aye out with him certainly ——

SIR OLIV. This violence ——

SURF. 'Tis your own Fault.

CHAS. Out with him to be sure.

[*Both forcing* SIR OLIVER *out.*

Enter SIR PETER TEAZLE, LADY TEAZLE, MARIA, *and* ROWLEY

SIR PET. My old Friend, Sir Oliver! — hey! what in the name of wonder! — Here are dutiful Nephews! — assault their Unkle at his first Visit!

LADY TEAZ. Indeed Sir Oliver 'twas well we came in to rescue you.

ROW. Truly it was — for I perceive Sir Oliver the character of old Stanley was no Protection to you.

SIR OLIV. Nor of Premium either — the necessities of the former could not extort a shilling from that benevolent Gentleman; and with the other I stood a chance of faring worse than my Ancestors, and being knocked down without being bid for.

SURF. Charles!

CHAS. Joseph!

SURF. 'Tis compleat!

CHAS. Very!

SIR OLIV. Sir Peter — my Friend and Rowley too — look on that elder Nephew of mine — You know what He has already received from my Bounty and you know also how gladly I would have look'd on half my Fortune as held in trust for him — judge then my Disappointment in discovering him to be destitute of Truth — Charity — and Gratitude —

SIR PET. Sir Oliver — I should be more surprized at this

Declaration, if I had not myself found him to be selfish — treacherous and Hypocritical.

Lady Teaz. And if the Gentleman pleads not guilty to these pray let him call *me* to his Character.

Sir Pet. Then I believe we need add no more — if He knows himself He will consider it as the most perfect Punishment that He is known to the world —

Chas. If they talk this way to Honesty — what will they say to *me* by and bye!

Sir Oliv. As for that Prodigal — his Brother there ——

Chas. Aye now comes my Turn — the damn'd Family Pictures will ruin me —

Surf. Sir Oliver — Unkle — will you honour me with a hearing —

Chas. I wish Joseph now would make one of his long speeches and I might recollect myself a little —

Sir Oliv. And I suppose you would undertake to vindicate yourself entirely —

Surf. I trust I could —

Sir Oliv. Nay — if you desert your Roguery in its Distress and try to be justified — you have even less principle than I thought you had. — [*To* Charles Surface] Well, Sir — and *you* could *justify* yourself too I suppose —

Chas. Not that I know of, Sir Oliver.

Sir Oliv. What[!] little Premium has been let too much into the secret I presume.

Chas. True — Sir — but they were Family Secrets, and should not be mentioned again you know.

Row. Come Sir Oliver I know you cannot speak of Charles's Follies with anger.

Sir Oliv. Odd's heart no more I can — nor with gravity either — Sir Peter do you know the Rogue bargain'd with me for all his Ancestors — sold me Judges and Generals by the Foot, and Maiden Aunts as cheap as broken China!

CHAS. To be sure, Sir Oliver, I did make a little free with the Family Canvas that's the truth on't: — my Ancestors may certainly rise in judgment against me there's no denying it — but believe me sincere when I tell you, and upon my soul I would not say so if I was not — that if I do not appear mortified at the exposure of my Follies, it is because I feel at this moment the warmest satisfaction in seeing you, my liberal benefactor.

SIR OLIV. Charles — I believe you — give me your hand again: the ill-looking little fellow over the Couch has made your Peace.

CHAS. Then Sir — my Gratitude to the original is still encreased.

LADY TEAZ. [*Advancing.*] Yet I believe, Sir Oliver, here is one whom Charles is still more anxious to be reconciled to.

SIR OLIV. O I have heard of his Attachment there — and, with the young Lady's Pardon if I construe right that Blush ——

SIR PET. Well — Child — speak your sentiments — you know — we are going to be reconciled to Charles —

MAR. Sir — I have little to say — but that I shall rejoice to hear that He is happy — For me — whatever claim I had to his Affection — I willing resign to one who has a better title.

CHAS. How Maria!

SIR PET. Heyday — what's the mystery now? while he appeared an incorrigible Rake, you would give your hand to no one else and now that He's likely to reform I'll warrant you won't have him!

MAR. His own Heart — and Lady Sneerwell know the cause.

[CHAS.] Lady Sneerwell!

SURF. Brother it is with great concern — I am obliged to speak on this Point, but my Regard to Justice obliges me — and Lady Sneerwell's injuries can no longer — be concealed —

[*Goes to the Door.*

Enter LADY SNEERWELL

SIR PET. Soh! another French milliner egad! He has one in every Room in the House I suppose —

LADY SNEER. Ungrateful Charles! Well may you be surprised and feel for the indelicate situation which your Perfidy has forced me into.

CHAS. Pray Unkle, is this another Plot of yours? for as I have Life I don't understand it.

SURF. I believe Sir there is but the evidence of one Person more necessary to make it extremely clear.

SIR PET. And that Person — I imagine, is Mr. Snake — Rowley — you were perfectly right to bring him with us — and pray let him appear.

ROW. Walk in, Mr. Snake —

Enter SNAKE

I thought his Testimony might be wanted — however it happens unluckily that He comes to confront Lady Sneerwell and not to support her —

LADY SNEER. A Villain! — Treacherous to me at last! Speak, Fellow, have you too conspired against me?

SNAKE. I beg your Ladyship — ten thousand Pardons — you paid me extremely Liberally for the Lie in question — but I unfortunately have been offer'd double to speak the Truth.

LADY SNEER. The Torments of Shame and Disappointment on you all!

LADY TEAZ. Hold — Lady Sneerwell — before you go let me thank you for the trouble you and that Gentleman have taken in writing Letters from me to Charles and answering them yourself — and let me also request you to make my Respects to the Scandalous College — of which you are President — and inform them that Lady Teazle, Licentiate, begs leave to return the diploma they granted her — as she leaves of[f] Practice and kills Characters no longer.

LADY SNEER. Provoking — insolent! — may your Husband live these fifty years! [*Exit.*

SIR PET. Oons what a Fury ——

LADY TEAZ. A malicious Creature indeed!

SIR PET. Hey — not for her last wish? —

LADY TEAZ. O No —

SIR OLIV. Well Sir, and what have you to say now?

SURF. Sir, I am so confounded, to find that Lady Sneerwell could be guilty of suborning Mr. Snake in this manner to impose on us all that I know not what to say —— however, lest her Revengeful Spirit should prompt her to injure my Brother I had certainly better follow her directly. [*Exit.*

SIR PET. Moral to the last drop!

SIR OLIV. Aye and marry her Joseph if you can. — Oil and Vinegar egad: — you'll do very well together.

ROW. I believe we have no more occasion for Mr. Snake at Present —

SNAKE. Before I go — I beg Pardon once for all for whatever uneasiness I have been the humble instrument of causing to the Parties present.

SIR PET. Well — well you have made atonement by a good Deed at last —

SNAKE. But I must Request of the Company that it shall never be known —

SIR PET. Hey! — what the Plague — are you ashamed of having done a right thing once in your life?

SNAKE. Ah: Sir — consider I live by the Badness of my Character! — I have nothing but my Infamy to depend on! — and, if it were once known that I had been betray'd into an honest Action, I should lose every Friend I have in the world.

SIR OLIV. Well — well we'll not traduce you by saying anything to your Praise never fear. [*Exit* SNAKE.

SIR PET. There's a precious Rogue — Yet that fellow is a Writer and a Critic.

LADY TEAZ. See[,] Sir Oliver[,] there needs no persuasion now to reconcile your Nephew and Maria —

SIR OLIV. Aye — aye — that's as it should be and egad we'll have the wedding to-morrow morning —

CHAS. Thank you, dear Unkle!

SIR PET. What! you rogue don't you ask the Girl's consent first —

CHAS. Oh, I have done that a long time — above a minute ago — and She has look'd yes —

MAR. For Shame — Charles — I protest Sir Peter, there has not been a word ——

SIR OLIV. Well then the fewer the Better — may your love for each other never know — abatement.

SIR PET. And may you live as happily together as Lady Teazle and I — intend to do —

CHAS. Rowley my old Friend — I am sure you congratulate me and I suspect too that I owe you much.

SIR OLIV. You do, indeed, Charles —

ROW. If my Efforts to serve you had not succeeded you would have been in my debt for the attempt — but deserve to be happy — and you over-repay me.

SIR PET. Aye honest Rowley always said you would reform.

CHAS. Why as to reforming Sir Peter I'll make no promises — and that I take to be a proof that I intend to set about it — But here shall be my Monitor — my gentle Guide. — ah! can I leave the Virtuous path those Eyes illumine?

Tho' thou, dear Maid, should'st wave [waive] thy Beauty's Sway,
— Thou still must Rule — because I will obey:
An humbled fugitive from Folly View,
No sanctuary near but Love and *You:*
You can indeed each anxious Fear remove,
For even Scandal dies if you approve. [*To the audience.*

EPILOGUE

BY MR. COLMAN

SPOKEN BY LADY TEAZLE

I, WHO was late so volatile and gay,
Like a trade-wind must now blow all one way,
Bend all my cares, my studies, and my vows,
To one dull rusty weathercock — my spouse!
So wills our virtuous bard — the motley Bayes
Of crying epilogues and laughing plays!
Old bachelors, who marry smart young wives,
Learn from our play to regulate your lives:
Each bring his dear to town, all faults upon her —
London will prove the very source of honour.
Plunged fairly in, like a cold bath it serves,
When principles relax, to brace the nerves:
Such is my case; and yet I must deplore
That the gay dream of dissipation's o'er.
And say, ye fair! was ever lively wife,
Born with a genius for the highest life,
Like me untimely blasted in her bloom,
Like me condemn'd to such a dismal doom?
Save money — when I just knew how to waste it!
Leave London — just as I began to taste it!
Must I then watch the early crowing cock,
The melancholy ticking of a clock;
In a lone rustic hall for ever pounded,
With dogs, cats, rats, and squalling brats surrounded?
With humble curate can I now retire,
(While good Sir Peter boozes with the squire,)
And at backgammon mortify my soul,
That pants for loo, or flutters at a vole?

Seven's the main! Dear sound that must expire,
Lost at hot cockles round a Christmas fire;
The transient hour of fashion too soon spent,
Farewell the tranquil mind, farewell content!
Farewell the plumèd head, the cushion'd tête,
That takes the cushion from its proper seat!
That spirit-stirring drum! — card drums I mean,
Spadille — odd trick — pam — basto — king and queen!
And you, ye knockers, that, with brazen throat,
The welcome visitors' approach denote;
Farewell all quality of high renown,
Pride, pomp, and circumstance of glorious town!
Farewell! your revels I partake no more,
And Lady Teazle's occupation's o'er!
All this I told our bard; he smiled, and said 'twas clear,
I ought to play deep tragedy next year.
Meanwhile he drew wise morals from his play,
And in these solemn periods stalk'd away: —
"Bless'd were the fair like you; her faults who stopp'd,
And closed her follies when the curtain dropp'd!
No more in vice or error to engage,
Or play the fool at large on life's great stage."

THE CRITIC

THE TEXT OF THE CRITIC

The text of *The Critic* in this edition is taken, by Mr. Fraser Rae's generous permission, from his *Sheridan's Plays now printed as he wrote them*. Those parts of the first act which are missing from Sheridan's manuscript, Mr. Rae supplied from the current text of the play, indicating such passages by foot-notes. With Sheridan's text I have collated the first edition of *The Critic* (1781), referred to in my foot-notes as C 1. Save in cases that involve the meaning of the text, I have disregarded the numerous variants in spelling and punctuation. In one noticeable matter of detail, Sheridan's text seems decidedly preferable to C 1 — in the frequent use of such colloquial abbreviations as "that's," "she's," "it's," "you'll," and "didn't." To illustrate more striking differences between the texts, C 1, at the end of Act II, scene 2, "cuts" the entire passage introducing the Lamplighter who "does one of the River Gods in the Procession," and whose consequent mixing of oil and water gives whimsical zest to Puff's remarks. The printers have been "so devilish free with their cutting here," that the reader echoes Puff's earlier words: "Hey, what the Plague! — what a cut is here?" On the other hand, C 1 contains some additions of considerable length. Possibly the changes in C 1 from Sheridan's manuscript represent alterations for histrionic purposes during the year and more that elapsed between the first performance of *The Critic* and its appearance in print. Even if, as two at least of Sheridan's editors have asserted, though without supplying proof, the 1781 edition was printed with Sheridan's sanction, this does not necessarily involve personal editorial supervision. Mr. Rae says positively: "With the exception of 'The Rivals,' none of these plays [*Rivals*, *Duenna*, *School for Scandal*, *Critic*] was given to the world by Sheridan himself. All the other published copies were reproductions of those used on the stage. Many changes had been made in them for histrionic purposes." In view of Sheridan's attitude toward the publication of *The School for Scandal*, and of the fact that the printed edition of the one play actually prepared by him for publication closely follows his manuscript, it is hard to believe that the numerous changes in C 1 represent the author's own revision of *The Critic*. Sheridan's own manuscript contains the only indisputably authentic text of *The Critic*.

THE CRITIC;

OR, A TRAGEDY REHEARSED

A DRAMATIC PIECE IN THREE ACTS

TO MRS. GREVILLE

MADAM, — In requesting your permission to address the following pages to you, which, as they aim themselves to be critical, require every protection and allowance that approving taste or friendly prejudice can give them, I yet ventured to mention no other motive than the gratification of private friendship and esteem. Had I suggested a hope that your implied approbation would give a sanction to their defects, your particular reserve, and dislike to the reputation of critical taste, as well as of poetical talent, would have made you refuse the protection of your name to such a purpose. However, I am not so ungrateful as now to attempt to combat this disposition in you. I shall not here presume to argue that the present state of poetry claims and expects every assistance that taste and example can afford it; nor endeavour to prove that a fastidious concealment of the most elegant productions of judgment and fancy is an ill return for the possession of those endowments. Continue to deceive yourself in the idea that you are known only to be eminently admired and regarded for the valuable qualities that attach private friendships, and the graceful talents that adorn conversation. Enough of what you have written has stolen into full public notice to answer my purpose, and you will, perhaps, be the only person, conversant in elegant literature, who shall read this address and not perceive that by publishing your particular approbation of the following drama, I have a more interested object than to boast the true respect and regard with which I have the honour to be, Madam, your very sincere and obedient humble servant, R. B. SHERIDAN.

DRAMATIS PERSONÆ

AS ORIGINALLY ACTED AT DRURY LANE THEATRE IN 1779

SIR FRETFUL PLAGIARY . .	*Mr. Parsons*
PUFF	*Mr. King*
DANGLE . . .	*Mr. Dodd*
SNEER. . . .	*Mr. Palmer*
SIGNOR PASTICCIO RITORNELLO .	*Mr. Delpini*
INTERPETER . .	*Mr. Baddeley*
UNDER PROMPTER	*Mr. Phillimore*
MR. HOPKINS .	*Mr. Hopkins*
MRS. DANGLE .	*Mrs. Hopkins*
SIGNORE PASTICCIO RITORNELLO . . .	*Miss Field and the Miss Abrams*

Scenemen, Musicians, and Servants

CHARACTERS OF THE TRAGEDY

LORD BURLEIGH.	*Mr. Moody*
GOVERNOR OF TILBURY FORT .	*Mr. Wrighten*
EARL OF LEICESTER	*Mr. Farren*
SIR WALTER RALEIGH . . .	*Mr. Burton*
SIR CHRISTOPHER HATTON . .	*Mr. Waldron*
MASTER OF THE HORSE . .	*Mr. Kenny*
DON FEROLO WHISKERANDOS	*Mr. Bannister, jun.*
BEEFEATER . .	*Mr. Wright*
JUSTICE . . .	*Mr. Packer*
SON	*Mr. Lamash*
CONSTABLE . .	*Mr. Fawcett*
THAMES . . .	*Mr. Gawdry*
TILBURINA . .	*Miss Pope*
CONFIDANT . .	*Mrs. Bradshaw*
JUSTICE'S LADY	*Mrs. Johnston*
FIRST NIECE .	*Miss Collett*
SECOND NIECE .	*Miss Kirby*

Knights, Guards, Constables, Sentinels, Servants, Chorus; Rivers, Attendants, &c., &c.

SCENE. — LONDON: *in* DANGLE'S *House during the First Act, and throughout the rest of the Play in* DRURY LANE THEATRE.

PROLOGUE

BY THE HONOURABLE RICHARD FITZPATRICK

The sister Muses, whom these realms obey,
Who o'er the drama hold divided sway,
Sometimes by evil counsellors, 'tis said,
Like earth-born potentates have been misled.
In those gay days of wickedness and wit,
When Villiers criticised what Dryden writ,
The tragic queen, to please a tasteless crowd,
Had learn'd to bellow, rant, and roar so loud,
That frighten'd Nature, her best friend before,
The blustering beldam's company foreswore;
Her comic sister, who had wit 'tis true,
With all her merits, had her failings too:
And would sometimes in mirthful moments use
A style too flippant for a well-bred muse;
Then female modesty abash'd began
To seek the friendly refuge of the fan,
Awhile behind that slight intrenchment stood,
Till driven from thence, she left the stage for good.
In our more pious, and far chaster times,
These sure no longer are the Muse's crimes!
But some complain that, former faults to shun,
The reformation to extremes has run.
The frantic hero's wild delirium past,
Now insipidity succeeds bombast:
So slow Melpomene's cold numbers creep,
Here dulness seems her drowsy court to keep,
And we are scarce awake, whilst you are fast asleep.
Thalia, once so ill-behaved and rude,
Reform'd, is now become an arrant prude;

Retailing nightly to the yawning pit
The purest morals, undefiled by wit!
Our author offers, in these motley scenes,
A slight remonstrance to the drama's queens:
Nor let the goddesses be over nice;
Free-spoken subjects give the best advice.
Although not quite a novice in his trade,
His cause to-night requires no common aid.
To this, a friendly, just, and powerful court,
I come ambassador to beg support.
Can he undaunted brave the critic's rage?
In civil broils with brother bards engage?
Hold forth their errors to the public eye,
Nay more, e'en newspapers themselves defy?
Say, must his single arm encounter all?
By number vanquish'd, e'en the brave may fall;
And though no leader should success distrust,
Whose troops are willing, and whose cause is just;
To bid such hosts of angry foes defiance,
His chief dependence must be, your alliance.

ACT I

SCENE I. — *A Room in* DANGLE'S *House*

MR. *and* MRS. DANGLE *discovered at breakfast, and reading newspapers*

DANG. [*Reading.*] *Brutus to Lord North. — Letter the second on the State of the Army* — Psha! *To the first L dash D of the A dash Y. — Genuine extract of a Letter from St. Kitt's. — Coxheath Intelligence. — It is now confidently asserted that Sir Charles Hardy* — Psha! nothing but about the fleet and the nation! — and I hate all politics but theatrical politics. — Where's the Morning Chronicle?

MRS. DANG. Yes, that's your Gazette.

DANG. So, here we have it. — [*Reads.*] *Theatrical intelligence extraordinary. — We hear there is a new tragedy in rehearsal at Drury Lane Theatre, called the Spanish Armada, said to be written by Mr. Puff, a gentleman well known in the theatrical world. If we may allow ourselves to give credit to the report of the performers, who, truth to say, are in general but indifferent judges, this piece abounds with the most striking and received beauties of modern composition.* — So! I am very glad my friend Puff's tragedy is in such forwardness. — Mrs. Dangle, my dear, you will be very glad to hear that Puff's tragedy ——

MRS. DANG. Lord, Mr Dangle, why will you plague me about such nonsense? — Now the plays are begun I shall have no peace. — Isn't it sufficient to make yourself ridiculous by your passion for the theatre, without continually teasing me to join you? Why can't you ride your hobby-horse without desiring to place me on a pillion behind you, Mr. Dangle?

DANG. Nay, my dear, I was only going to read ——

MRS. DANG. No, no; you will never read anything that's worth listening to. You hate to hear about your country; there are letters every day with Roman signatures, demonstrating the certainty of an invasion, and proving that the nation is utterly undone. But you never will read anything to entertain one.

DANG. What has a woman to do with politics, Mrs. Dangle?

MRS. DANG. And what have you to do with the theatre, Mr. Dangle? Why should you affect the character of a critic? I have no patience with you! — haven't you made yourself the jest of all your acquaintance by your interference in matters where you have no business? Are you not called a theatrical Quidnunc, and a mock Mæcenas to second-hand authors?

DANG. True; my power with the managers is pretty notorious. But is it no credit to have applications from all quarters for my interest — from lords to recommend fiddlers, from ladies to get boxes, from authors to get answers, and from actors to get engagements?

MRS. DANG. Yes, truly; you have contrived to get a share in all the plague and trouble of theatrical property, without the profit, or even the credit of the abuse that attends it.

DANG. I am sure, Mrs. Dangle, you are no loser by it, however; you have all the advantages of it. Mightn't you, last winter, have had the reading of the new pantomime a fortnight previous to its performance? And doesn't Mr. Fosbrook let you take places for a play before it is advertised, and set you down for a box for every new piece through the season? And didn't my friend, Mr. Smatter, dedicate his last farce to you at my particular request, Mrs. Dangle?

MRS. DANG. Yes; but wasn't the farce damned, Mr. Dangle? And to be sure it is extremely pleasant to have one's house made the motley rendezvous of all the lackeys of literature; the very high 'Change of trading authors and jobbing critics! — Yes, my drawing-room is an absolute register-office for candidate actors, and poets without character. — Then to be continually alarmed with misses and ma'ams piping hysteric changes on Juliets and Dorindas, Pollys and Ophelias; and the very furniture trembling at the probationary starts and unprovoked rants of would-be Richards and Hamlets! — And what is worse than all, now that the manager has monopolized the Opera House, haven't we the signors and signoras calling here, sliding their smooth semibreves, and gargling glib divisions in their outlandish throats — with foreign emissaries and French spies, for aught I know, disguised like fiddlers and figure dancers?

DANG. Mercy! Mrs. Dangle!

MRS. DANG. And to employ yourself so idly at such an alarming crisis as this too — when, if you had the least spirit, you would have been at the head of one of the Westminster associations — or trailing a volunteer pike in the Artillery

Ground! But you — o' my conscience, I believe, if the French were landed to-morrow, your first inquiry would be, whether they had brought a theatrical troop with them.

DANG. Mrs. Dangle, it does not signify — I say the stage is *the mirror of Nature*, and the actors are *the Abstract and brief Chronicles of the Time:* and pray what can a man of sense study better? — Besides, you will not easily persuade me that there is no credit or importance in being at the head of a band of critics, who take upon them to decide for the whole town, whose opinion and patronage all writers solicit, and whose recommendation no manager dares refuse.

MRS. DANG. Ridiculous! — Both managers and authors of the least merit laugh at your pretensions. — The public is their critic — without whose fair approbation they know no play can rest on the stage, and with whose applause they welcome such attacks as yours, and laugh at the malice of them, where they can't at the wit.

DANG. Very well, madam — very well!

Enter SERVANT

SER. Mr. Sneer, sir, to wait on you.

DANG. Oh, show Mr. Sneer up. — [*Exit* SERVANT.] — Plague on't, now we must appear loving and affectionate, or Sneer will hitch us into a story.

MRS. DANG. With all my heart; you can't be more ridiculous than you are.

DANG. You are enough to provoke ——

Enter SNEER

Ha! my dear Sneer, I am vastly glad to see you. — My dear, here's Mr. Sneer.

MRS. DANG. Good-morning to you, sir.

DANG. Mrs. Dangle and I have been diverting ourselves with the papers. Pray, Sneer, won't you go to Drury Lane Theatre the first night of Puff's tragedy?

SNEER. Yes; but I suppose one shan't be able to get in, for on the first night of a new piece they always fill the house with orders to support it. But here, Dangle, I have brought you two pieces, one of which you must exert yourself to make the managers accept, I can tell you that; for 'tis written by a person of consequence.

DANG. So! now my plagues are beginning.

SNEER. Ay, I am glad of it, for now you'll be happy. Why, my dear Dangle, it is a pleasure to see how you enjoy your volunteer fatigue, and your solicited solicitations.

DANG. It's a great trouble — yet, egad, it's pleasant too. — Why, sometimes of a morning I have a dozen people call on me at breakfast time, whose faces I never saw before, nor ever desire to see again.

SNEER. That must be very pleasant indeed!

DANG. And not a week but I receive fifty letters, and not a line in them about any business of my own.

SNEER. An amusing correspondence!

DANG. [*Reading.*] *Bursts into tears and exit.* — What, is this a tragedy?

SNEER. No, that's a genteel comedy, not a translation — only taken from the French: it is written in a style which they have lately tried to run down; the true sentimental, and nothing ridiculous in it from the beginning to the end.

MRS. DANG. Well, if they had kept to that, I should not have been such an enemy to the stage; there was some edification to be got from those pieces, Mr. Sneer!

SNEER. I am quite of your opinion, Mrs. Dangle: the theatre, in proper hands, might certainly be made the school of morality; but now, I am sorry to say it, people seem to go there principally for their entertainment!

MRS. DANG. It would have been more to the credit of the managers to have kept it in the other line.

SNEER. Undoubtedly, madam; and hereafter perhaps to

have had it recorded, that in the midst of a luxurious and dissipated age, they preserved two houses in the capital, where the conversation was always moral at least, if not entertaining!

DANG. Now, egad, I think the worst alteration is in the nicety of the audience! — No *double-entendre*, no smart innuendo admitted; even Vanbrugh and Congreve obliged to undergo a bungling reformation!

SNEER. Yes, and our prudery in this respect is just on a par with the artificial bashfulness of a courtesan, who increases the blush upon her cheek in an exact proportion to the diminution of her modesty.

DANG. Sneer can't even give the public a good word! But what have we here? — This seems a very odd ——

SNEER. Oh, that's a comedy, on a very new plan; replete with wit and mirth, yet of a most serious moral! You see it is called *The Reformed House-breaker;* where, by the mere force of humour, house-breaking is put in so ridiculous a light, that if the piece has its proper run, I have no doubt but that bolts and bars will be entirely useless by the end of the season.

DANG. Egad, this is new indeed!

SNEER. Yes; it is written by a particular friend of mine, who has discovered that the follies and foibles of society are subjects unworthy the notice of the comic muse, who should be taught to stoop only to the greater vices and blacker crimes of humanity — gibbeting capital offences in five acts, and pillorying petty larcencies in two. — In short, his idea is to dramatize the penal laws, and make the stage a court of ease to the Old Bailey.

DANG. It is truly moral.

Re-enter SERVANT

SER. Sir Fretful Plagiary, sir.

DANG. Beg him to walk up. — [*Exit* SERVANT.] Now, Mrs. Dangle, Sir Fretful Plagiary is an author to your own taste.

MRS. DANG. I confess he is a favourite of mine, because everybody else abuses him.

SNEER. Very much to the credit of your charity, madam, if not of your judgment.

DANG. But, egad, he allows no merit to any author but himself, that's the truth on't — though he's my friend.

SNEER. Never. — He is as envious as an old maid verging on the desperation of six and thirty; and then the insidious humility with which he seduces you to give a free opinion on any of his works, can be exceeded only by the petulant arrogance with which he is sure to reject your observations.

DANG. Very true, egad — though he's my friend.

SNEER. Then his affected contempt of all newspaper strictures; though, at the same time, he is the sorest man alive, and shrinks like scorched parchment from the fiery ordeal of true criticism: yet is he so covetous of popularity, that he had rather be abused than not mentioned at all.

DANG. There's no denying it — though he is my friend.

SNEER. You have read the tragedy he has just finished, haven't you?

DANG. Oh, yes; he sent it to me yesterday.

SNEER. Well, and you think it execrable, don't you?

DANG. Why, between ourselves, egad, I must own — though he is my friend — that it is one of the most — He's here —— [*Aside.*]— finished and most admirable perform ——

SIR FRET. [*Without.*] Mr. Sneer with him did you say?

Enter SIR FRETFUL PLAGIARY

DANG. Ah, my dear friend! — Egad, we were just speaking of your tragedy. — Admirable, Sir Fretful, admirable!

SNEER. You never did anything beyond it, Sir Fretful — never in your life.

SIR FRET. You make me extremely happy; for without a

compliment, my dear Sneer, there isn't a man in the world whose judgment I value as I do yours and Mr. Dangle's.

MRS. DANG. They are only laughing at you, Sir Fretful; for it was but just now that ——

DANG. Mrs. Dangle! — Ah, Sir Fretful, you know Mrs. Dangle. — My friend Sneer was rallying just now: — he knows how she admires you, and ——

SIR FRET. O Lord, I am sure Mr. Sneer has more taste and sincerity than to ——[*Aside.*] A damned double-faced fellow!

DANG. Yes, yes — Sneer will jest — but a better humoured ——

SIR FRET. Oh, I know ——

DANG. He has a ready turn for ridicule — his wit costs him nothing.

SIR FRET. No, egad — or I should wonder how he came by it. [*Aside.*

MRS. DANG. Because his jest is always at the expense of his friend. [*Aside.*

DANG. But, Sir Fretful, have you sent your play to the managers yet? — or can I be of any service to you?

SIR FRET. No, no, I thank you: I believe the piece had sufficient recommendation with it. — I thank you though. — I sent it to the manager of Covent Garden Theatre this morning.

SNEER. I should have thought now, that it might have been cast (as the actors call it) better at Drury Lane.

SIR FRET. O Lud! no — never send a play there while I live — hark'ee! [*Whispers* SNEER.

SNEER. Writes himself! — I know he does.

SIR FRET. I say nothing — I take away from no man's merit — am hurt at no man's good fortune — I say nothing. — But this I will say — through all my knowledge of life, I have observed — that there is not a passion so strongly rooted in the human heart as envy.

SNEER. I believe you have reason for what you say, indeed.

SIR FRET. Besides — I can tell you it is not always so safe to leave a play in the hands of those who write themselves.

SNEER. What, they may steal from them, hey, my dear Plagiary?

SIR FRET. Steal! — to be sure they may; and, egad, serve your best thoughts as gypsies do stolen children, disfigure them to make 'em pass for their own.

SNEER. But your present work is a sacrifice to Melpomene, and he, you know, never ——

SIR FRET. That's no security: a dexterous plagiarist may do anything. Why, sir, for aught I know, he might take out some of the best things in my tragedy, and put them into his own comedy.

SNEER. That might be done, I dare be sworn.

SIR FRET. And then, if such a person gives you the least hint or assistance, he is devilish apt to take the merit of the whole ——

DANG. If it succeeds.

SIR FRET. Ay, but with regard to this piece, I think I can hit that gentleman, for I can safely swear he never read it.

SNEER. I'll tell you how you may hurt him more.

SIR FRET. How?

SNEER. Swear he wrote it.

SIR FRET. Plague on't now, Sneer, I shall take it ill! — I believe you want to take away my character as an author.

SNEER. Then I am sure you ought to be very much obliged to me.

SIR FRET. Hey! — sir! ——

DANG. Oh, you know, he never means what he says.

SIR FRET. Sincerely then — do you like the piece?

SNEER. Wonderfully!

SIR FRET. But come, now, there must be something that you think might be mended, hey? — Mr. Dangle, has nothing struck you?

DANG. Why, faith, it is but an ungracious thing, for the most part, to ——

SIR FRET. With most authors it is just so, indeed; they are in general strangely tenacious! But, for my part, I am never so well pleased as when a judicious critic points out any defect to me; for what is the purpose of showing a work to a friend, if you don't mean to profit by his opinion?

SNEER. Very true. —[1] Why then though I seriously admire the piece upon the whole — yet there is one small objection which if you'll give me leave, I'll mention —

SIR FRET.[2] You can't oblige me more.

SNEER. I think it wants Incident.

SIR FRET. Good God! you surprise me — wants Incident —

SNEER. Yes I own I think the Incidents are too few.

SIR FRET.[3] Believe me there is no Person for whose Judgment I have a more implicit Deference. But I protest to you[4] I am only apprehensive myself[5] that the Incidents are too crowded — Mr. Dangle[6] how does it strike you?

DANG. Really I cannot[7] agree with Mr. Sneer[8]—I think the Plot quite sufficient — and the four first Acts by many Degrees the best I ever read or saw in my Life — If I might venture to suggest anything it is that the interest rather falls off in the Fifth Act.[9]

SIR FRET. Rises I believe you mean Sir.

DANG. No I don't, upon my word.

SIR FRET. Yes yes you do[10]—it certainly don't fall off — I assure you — no no it don't fall off.

DANG. Now Mrs. Dangle did[11] you say it struck you in the same light?[12]

[1] The sheets of manuscript which are preserved begin here. [Fraser Rae.]
[2] C 1 inserts "Sir." [3] C 1: Good God! — Believe me, Mr. Sneer, there is.
[4] C 1 inserts "Mr. Sneer." [5] C 1 omits "myself."
[6] C 1: My dear Dangle. [7] C 1: can't. [8] C 1: my friend Sneer.
[9] C 1 omits "Act." [10] C 1 inserts: "upon my soul."
[11] C 1: didn't you. [12] End of this part of the manuscript. [Fraser Rae.]

Mrs. Dang. No, indeed, I did not. — I did not see a fault in any part of the play, from the beginning to the end.

Sir Fret. Upon my soul, the women are the best judges after all!

Mrs. Dang. Or, if I made any objection, I am sure it was to nothing in the piece; but that I was afraid it was on the whole, a little too long.

Sir Fret. Pray, madam do you speak as to duration of time; or do you mean that the story is tediously spun out?

Mrs. Dang. O Lud! no — I speak only with reference to the usual length of acting plays.

Sir Fret. Then I am very happy — very happy indeed — because the play is a short play, a remarkably short play. I should not venture to differ with a lady on a point of taste; but on these occasions, the watch, you know, is the critic.

Mrs. Dang. Then, I suppose, it must have been Mr. Dangle's drawling manner of reading it to me.

Sir Fret. Oh, if Mr. Dangle read it, that's quite another affair! — But I assure you, Mrs. Dangle, the first evening you can spare me three hours and a half, I'll undertake to read you the whole, from beginning to end, with the prologue and epilogue, and allow time for the music between the acts.

Mrs. Dang. I hope to see it on the stage next.

Dang. Well, Sir Fretful, I wish you may be able to get rid as easily of the newspaper criticisms as you do of ours.

Sir Fret. The newspapers! Sir, they are the most villainous — licentious — abominable — infernal — Not that I ever read them — no — I make it a rule never to look into a newspaper.

Dang. You are quite right; for it certainly must hurt an author of delicate feelings to see the liberties they take.

Sir Fret. No, quite the contrary! their abuse is, in fact, the best panegyric — I like it of all things. An author's reputation is only in danger from their support.

SNEER. Why, that's true — and that attack, now, on you the other day ——

SIR FRET. What? where?

DANG. Ay, you mean in a paper of Thursday: it was completely ill-natured, to be sure.

SIR FRET. Oh, so much the better. — Ha! ha! ha! I wouldn't have it otherwise.

DANG. Certainly it is only to be laughed at; for ——

SIR FRET. You don't happen to recollect what the fellow said, do you?

SNEER. Pray, Dangle — Sir Fretful seems a little anxious —

SIR FRET. O Lud, no! — anxious! — not I — not the least. — I — but one may as well hear, you know.

DANG. Sneer, do you recollect? — [*Aside to* SNEER.] Make out something.

SNEER. [*Aside to* DANGLE.] I will. — [*Aloud.*] Yes, yes, I remember perfectly.

SIR FRET. Well, and pray now — not that it signifies — what might the gentleman say?

SNEER. Why, he roundly asserts that you have not the slightest invention or original genius whatever; though you are the greatest traducer of all other authors living.

SIR FRET. Ha! ha! ha! — very good!

SNEER. That as to comedy, you have not one idea of your own, he believes, even in your commonplace-book — where stray jokes and pilfered witticisms are kept with as much method as the ledger of the lost and stolen office.

SIR FRET. Ha! ha! ha! — very pleasant!

SNEER. Nay, that you are so unlucky as not to have the skill even to steal with taste: — but that you glean from the refuse of obscure volumes, where more judicious plagiarists have been before you; so that the body of your work is a composition of dregs and sentiments — like a bad tavern's worst wine.

SIR FRET. Ha! ha!

SNEER. In your more serious efforts, he says, your bombast would be less intolerable, if the thoughts were ever suited to the expression: but the homeliness of the sentiment stares through the fantastic encumbrance of its fine language, like a clown in one of the new uniforms!

SIR FRET. Ha! ha!

SNEER. That your occasional tropes and flowers suit the general coarseness of your style, as tambour sprigs would a ground of linsey-woolsey; while your imitations of Shakspeare resemble the mimicry of Falstaff's page, and are about as near the standard of the original.

SIR FRET. Ha!

SNEER. In short, that even the finest passages you steal are of no service to you; for the poverty of your own language prevents their assimilating; so that they lie on the surface like lumps of marl on a barren moor, encumbering what it is not in their power to fertilize!

SIR FRET. [*After great agitation.*] Now, another person would be vexed at this!

SNEER. Oh! but I wouldn't have told you — only to divert you.

SIR FRET. I know it — I am diverted. — Ha! ha! ha! — not the least invention! — Ha! ha! ha! — very good! — very good!

SNEER. Yes — no genius! ha! ha! ha!

DANG. A severe rogue! ha! ha! ha! But you are quite right, Sir Fretful, never to read such nonsense.

SIR FRET. To be sure — for if there is anything to one's praise, it is a foolish vanity to be gratified at it; and, if it is abuse — why one is always sure to hear of it from one damned good-natured friend or other!

Enter SERVANT

SER. Sir, there is an Italian gentleman, with a French

interpreter, and three young ladies, and a dozen musicians, who say they are sent by Lady Rondeau and Mrs. Fugue.

DANG. Gadso! they come by appointment! — Dear Mrs. Dangle, do let them know I'll see them directly.

MRS. DANG. You know, Mr. Dangle, I shan't understand a word they say.

DANG. But you hear there's an interpreter.

MRS. DANG. Well, I'll try to endure their complaisance till you come. [*Exit.*

SER. And Mr. Puff, sir, has sent word that the last rehearsal is to be this morning, and that he'll call on you presently.

DANG. That's true — I shall certainly be at home. — [*Exit* SERVANT.] — Now, Sir Fretful, if you have a mind to have justice done you in the way of answer, egad, Mr. Puff's your man.

SIR FRET. Psha! sir, why should I wish to have it answered, when I tell you I am pleased at it?

DANG. True, I had forgot that. But I hope you are not fretted at what Mr. Sneer ——

SIR FRET. Zounds! no, Mr. Dangle; don't I tell you these things never fret me in the least?

DANG. Nay, I only thought ——

SIR FRET. And let me tell you, Mr. Dangle, 'tis damned affronting in you to suppose that I am hurt when I tell you I am not.

SNEER. But why so warm, Sir Fretful?

SIR FRET. Gad's life! Mr. Sneer, you are as absurd as Dangle: how often must I repeat it to you, that nothing can vex me but your supposing it possible for me to mind the damned nonsense you have been repeating to me! — and, let me tell you, if you continue to believe this, you must mean to insult me, gentlemen — and, then, your disrespect will affect me no more than the newspaper criticisms — and I shall treat it with exactly the same calm indifference and philosophic contempt — and so your servant. [*Exit.*

SNEER. Ha! ha! ha! poor Sir Fretful! Now will he go and vent his philosophy in anonymous abuse of all modern critics and authors. — But, Dangle, you must get your friend Puff to take me to the rehearsal of his tragedy.

DANG. I'll answer for't, he'll thank you for desiring it. But come and help me to judge of this musical family: they are recommended by people of consequence, I assure you.

SNEER. I am at your disposal the whole morning! — but I thought you had been a decided critic in music as well as in literature.

DANG. So I am — but I have a bad ear. I' faith, Sneer, though, I am afraid we were a little too severe on Sir Fretful — though he is my friend.

SNEER. Why, 'tis certain, that unnecessarily to mortify the vanity of any writer is a cruelty which mere dulness never can deserve; but where a base and personal malignity usurps the place of literary emulation, the aggressor deserves neither quarter nor pity.

DANG. That's true, egad! — though he's my friend!

SCENE II. — *A Drawing-room in* DANGLE'S *House*

MRS. DANGLE, SIGNOR PASTICCIO RITORNELLO, SIGNORE PASTICCIO RITORNELLO, INTERPRETER, *and* MUSICIANS *discovered*

INTERP. Je dis, madame, j'ai l'honneur to introduce et de vous demander votre protection pour le Signor Pasticcio Ritornello et pour sa charmante famille.

SIGNOR PAST. Ah! vosignoria, noi vi preghiamo di favoritevi colla vostra protezione.

1 SIGNORA PAST. Vosignoria fatevi questi grazie.

2 SIGNORA PAST. Si, signora.

INTERP. Madame — me interpret. — C'est à dire — in English — qu'ils vous prient de leur faire l'honneur ——

Mrs. Dang. I say again, gentlemen, I don't understand a word you say.

Signor Past. Questo signore spiegherò ——

Interp.' Oui — me interpret. — Nous avons les lettres de recommendation pour Monsieur Dangle de ——

Mrs. Dang. Upon my word, sir, I don't understand you.

Signor Past. La Contessa Rondeau è nostra padrona.

3 Signora Past. Si, padre, et Miladi Fugue.

Interp. O! — me interpret. — Madame, ils disent — in English — Qu'ils ont l'honneur d'être protégés de ces dames. — You understand?

Mrs. Dang. No, sir, — no understand!

Enter Dangle *and* Sneer

Interp. Ah, voici, Monsieur Dangle!

All Italians. Ah! Signor Dangle!

Mrs. Dang. Mr. Dangle, here are two very civil gentlemen trying to make themselves understood, and I don't know which is the interpreter.

Dang. Eh, bien!

[*The* Interpreter *and* Signor Pasticcio *here speak at the same time.*]

Interp. Monsieur Dangle, le grand bruit de vos talens pour la critique, et de votre intérêt avec messieurs les directeurs à tous les théâtres ——

Signor Past. Vosignoria siete si famoso par la vostra conoscenza, e vostra interessa colla le direttore da ——

Dang. Egad, I think the interpreter is the hardest to be understood of the two!

Sneer. Why, I thought, Dangle, you had been an admirable linguist!

Dang. So I am, if they would not talk so damned fast.

Sneer. Well, I'll explain that — the less time we lose in

hearing them the better — for that, I suppose, is what they are brought here for.

[*Speaks to* SIGNOR PASTICCIO — *they sing trios, &c.,* DANGLE *beating out of time.*]

Enter SERVANT *and whispers* DANGLE

DANG. Show him up. — [*Exit* SERVANT.] Bravo! admirable! bravissimo! admirablissimo! — Ah! Sneer! where will you find voices such as these in England?

SNEER. Not easily.

DANG. But Puff is coming. — Signor and little signoras obligatissimo! — Sposa Signora Danglena — Mrs. Dangle, shall I beg you to offer them some refreshments, and take their address in the next room.

[*Exit* MRS. DANGLE *with* SIGNOR PASTICCIO, SIGNORE PASTICCIO, MUSICIANS, *and* INTERPRETER, *ceremoniously.*

Re-enter SERVANT

SER. Mr. Puff, sir. [*Exit.*

Enter PUFF [1]

DANG. My dear Puff!

PUFF. My dear Dangle, how is't [2] with you?

DANG. Mr. Sneer give me leave to introduce Mr. Puff to you.

PUFF. Mr. Sneer! [3] Sir he is a Gentleman whom I have long panted for the Honor of knowing — a Gentleman whose critical Talents and transcendent Judgment ——

SNEER. Dear sir ——

DANG. Nay don't be modest Sneer — my Friend Puff only talks to you in the style of his Profession.

SNEER. Of [4] his profession!

PUFF. Yes Sir — I make no Secret of the trade I follow — among Friends and Brother Authors — Dangle knows I love

[1] From this place to the end the manuscript has been followed. [Fraser Rae.]

[2] C 1: is it. [3] C 1: Mr. Sneer is this? [4] C 1 omits "Of."

to be Frank on the subject — and to advertise my self vivâ voce. — I am Sir — a Practitioner in Panegyric — or to speak more Plainly — a Professor of the Art of Puffing, at your service or anybody else's.

SNEER. Sir, you are very Obliging — I fancy[1] Mr. Puff I have often admired your Talents in the daily Prints.

PUFF. Yes[2] I flatter myself I do as much Business in that way as any six of the Fraternity in Town. — devilish hard work all the summer, friend Dangle, — never worked harder! But, hark'ee, — the winter managers were a little sore I believe.

DANG. O[3] no I believe they took it all in good part.

PUFF. Ah![4] then that must have been affectation in them — for egad there were some of the Attacks which there was no laughing at.

SNEER. Aye the humourous ones. — But I should think, Mr. Puff, that Authors would in general be able to do this sort of work for themselves.

PUFF. Aye[5] but in a clumsy way — besides we look on that as an encroachment — and so take the opposite side. I dare say now you conceive half the very civil Paragraphs and advertisements you see are[6] written by the Parties concerned or their Friends — no such thing — nine out of ten manufactured by me in the way of Business.

SNEER. Indeed!

PUFF. Even the auctioneers now — the auctioneers I say — tho' the rogues have lately got some credit for their Language — not an article of the merit theirs — take 'em[7] out of their pulpits, and they are as dull as catalogues! — No Sir; 'twas I first enrich'd their style — 'twas I first taught them to crowd their Advertisements with panegyrical superlatives, each epithet rising above the other like the Bidders in their own auction

[1] C 1: believe. [2] C 1: Yes, sir. [3] C 1 omits "O." [4] C 1: Aye!
[5] C 1: Why yes. [6] C 1: to be. [7] C 1: them.

Rooms! From me they learned to inlay their Phraseology with variegated Chips of Exotic metaphor: By me too their inventive faculties were called forth — yes Sir by me they were instructed to clothe ideal walls with gratuitous fruits — to insinuate obsequious Rivulets into visionary Groves — to teach courteous shrubs to nod their approbation of the grateful soil — or on emergencies to raise upstart oaks where there never had been an Acorn — to create a delightful Vicinage without the assistance of a Neighbour — waft salubrious Gales[1] or fix the temple of Hygeia in the fens of Lincolnshire!

DANG. I am sure you have done them infinite Service — for now when a Gentleman's[2] ruined, He parts with his House with some credit.

SNEER. Service! egad[3] if they had any gratitude they would erect a statue to him — they would figure you[4] as a presiding Mercury, the God of traffic and Fiction, with a Hammer in his Hand instead of a Caduceus. — But pray Mr. Puff what first put you on exercising your Talents in this way?

PUFF. Egad Sir — sheer Necessity — the proper Parent of an art so nearly allied to Invention — You must know Mr. Sneer that from the first Time I tried my hand at an Advertisement my success was such that for some time after I led a most extraordinary Life indeed!

SNEER. How Pray —

PUFF. Sir I supported myself two years entirely by my misfortunes.

SNEER. By your misfortunes!

PUFF. Yes Sir assisted by long sickness and other occasional Disorders! and a very comfortable Living I had of it.

SNEER. From Sickness and misfortunes! You practised as a Doctor and an Attorney at once?

PUFF. No egad both maladies and miseries were my own.

[1] C 1 omits "waft salubrious Gales."
[2] C 1: gentleman is.
[3] C 1 omits "egad."
[4] C 1: him.

SNEER. Hey — what the Plague!

DANG. 'Tis true, efaith.

PUFF. Hark'ee! — By Advertisements — *To the charitable and Humane! and to those whom Providence hath blessed with Affluence!*

SNEER. Oh! I understand you.

PUFF. And, in truth, I deserved what I got! for, I suppose never man went thro such a series of Calamities in the same space of time. Sir — I was five times made a bankrupt, and *reduced from a state of Affluence by a train of unavoidable misfortunes* — then Sir, tho a very *industrious Tradesman I was twice burned out and lost my little all both Times* — I lived upon those Fires a month — I soon after was confined by a most excruciating Disorder and *lost the use of my Limbs* — that told very well for I had the case strongly attested and went about to collect the subscriptions myself.

DANG. Egad — I believe that was when you first call'd on me.

PUFF. In November last — O no — I was at that Time *a close prisoner in the Marshalsea for a Debt benevolently contracted to serve a friend.* I was afterwards twice *tapp'd for a Dropsy* which declined into a very profitable *consumption.* I was then *reduced to* — O no — then I became *a widow with six helpless children* — after having had *eleven Husbands press'd and being left every time eight months gone with child, and without money to get me into an Hospital* —

DANG.[1] Mercy on me —

SNEER. And you bore all with Patience, I make no Doubt —

PUFF. Why yes — tho' I made some judicious[2] attempts at Felo de se — but as [I] did not find them[3] answer, I left off killing myself very soon — Well Sir at last what with Bankruptcies, Fires, Gout, Dropsies, Imprisonments and other

[1] C 1 omits this speech.
[2] C 1: occasional.
[3] C 1: those *rash actions.*

valuable calamities having got together a pretty handsome sum I determined to quit a Business which had always gone rather against my conscience — and in a more liberal way still to indulge my Talent[1] for Fiction and embellishment thro my favourite Channels of Diurnal Communication — and so Sir you have my History.

SNEER. Most obligingly communicative indeed[2] — but surely Mr. Puff there is no great mystery in your Present Profession?

PUFF. Mystery! Sir — I will take upon me to say the matter was never scientifically treated nor reduced to Rule before.

SNEER. Reduced to Rule!

PUFF. O Lud Sir, you are very ignorant, I am afraid — Yes Sir — Puffing is of various Sorts — the Principal are, *the Puff direct — the Puff oblique*[3] — *the Puff collateral, the Puff Preliminary*, and *the Puff Collusive*. These all[4] as circumstances require assume the varied[5] Forms of Letter to the Editor — occasional Anecdote — impartial Critique — observation from Correspondent, or Advertisement from the Party.

SNEER. The Puff direct, I can conceive ——

PUFF. O yes that's simple enough — for instance, — A new comedy or Farce is to be produced at one of the Theatres (though by-the-by they don't bring out half what they ought to do) — the author, suppose Mr. Smatter, or Mr. Flimsey[6] — or any particular Friend of mine — very well — the Day before it is performed I write an account of the manner in which it was received — I have the Plot from the Author — and only add — "characters strongly drawn — highly colour'd — hand of a master — fund of genuine humour — mine of

[1] C 1: talents.

[2] C 1 inserts: and your confession if published, might certainly serve the cause of true charity, by rescuing the most useful channels of appeal to benevolence from the cant of imposition.

[3] C 1 rearranges: the PUFF PRELIMINARY — the PUFF COLLATERAL — the PUFF COLLUSIVE, and the PUFF OBLIQUE, or PUFF by IMPLICATION.

[4] C 1: These all assume. [5] C 1: various. [6] C 1: Dapper.

Invention — neat Dialogue — Attic salt." Then for the performance — "Mr. Dodd was astonishingly great in the Character of young Mr. Something [1] — that universal and judicious Actor Mr. Palmer perhaps never appeared to more advantage [2] — but it is impossible for [3] language to do justice to Mr. King — indeed he more than merited those repeated Bursts of applause which he drew from a most brilliant and judicious Audience — as to the scenery — the miraculous Powers of Mr. Loutherbourg's [4] Pencil are universally acknowledged — in short we are at a loss which to admire most, the unrivall'd Genius of the Author — the great attention and Liberality of the Managers — The wonderful abilities of the Painter, or the incredible exertions of all the Performers."

SNEER. That's pretty well indeed — Sir.

PUFF. O cool — quite cool — to what I sometimes do.

SNEER. And you think [5] there are any who are influenced by this?

PUFF. O Lud yes Sir — the number of those who go thro' the fatigue of judging for themselves is very small indeed.

SNEER. Well Sir the Puff Preliminary?

PUFF. O that Sir does well in the Form of a caution — in a matter of Gallantry now — Sir Flimsy Gossimer wishes to be well with Lady Fanny Fete — he applies to me — I open trenches for him with a Paragraph in the Morning Post. — "It is recommended to the beautiful and accomplished Lady F four stars F dash E to be on her guard against that dangerous character, Sir F dash G; who, however pleasing and insinuating his manners may be, is certainly not remarkable for the *constancy of his Attachments!*" — in italics. Here you see Sir Flimsy Gossimer is introduced to the particular notice of Lady Fanny — who perhaps never thought of him before —

[1] C 1: of SIR HARRY. [2] C 1 adds: than in the COLONEL.
[3] C 1: but it is not in the power of.
[4] C 1: DE LOUTHERBOURG'S. [5] C 1: And do you think.

she finds herself publicly cautioned to avoid him which naturally makes her desirous to see[1] him — the observation of their Acquaintance causes a pretty kind of mutual embarrassment — this produces a sort of sympathy of interest, which if Sir Flimsy is unable to improve effectually He at least gains the credit of having their names mention'd together by a particular set, and in a particular way — which nine times out of ten is the full accomplishment of modern Gallantry.

DANG. Egad, Sneer, you will be quite an adept in the Business.

PUFF. Now Sir the *Puff Collateral* is much used as an appendage to advertisements, and may take the Form of Anecdote. — "Yesterday, as the celebrated George Bonmot was sauntering down St. James's Street, He met the lively Lady Mary Myrtle coming out of the Park: — 'Good God, Lady Mary,' said George,[2] 'I'm surprised to meet you in a white Jacket, — for I expected never to have seen you but in a full-trimmed uniform and a Light Horseman's Cap!' — 'Heavens, George, where could you have learned that?' — 'Why,' replied the wit, 'I just saw a Print of you in a new Publication called the Camp Magazine; which, by the bye, is a devilish clever thing and is sold at No. 3, on the right hand of the way two Doors from the Printing Office, the corner of Ivy Lane, Paternoster Row."[3]

SNEER. Ah! that's very ingenious indeed[4] —

PUFF. But the *puff collusive* is the newest of any — for it acts in the disguise of determined Hostility — it is much used by Bold book-sellers and enterprizing Poets. — "An indignant correspondent observes — that the New Poem call'd *Beelzebub's Cotillon, or Proserpine's Fête Champêtre*, is one of the most unjustifiable Performances He ever read. The severity with which certain characters are handled is quite shocking — and

[1] C 1: of seeing.
[2] C 1 omits "said George."
[3] C 1 adds: price only one shilling!
[4] C 1: Very ingenious indeed!

as there are many descriptions in it too warmly colour'd for female Delicacy the shameful avidity with which this Piece is bought by all People of Fashion is a reproach on the taste of the Times, and a disgrace to the Delicacy of the Age." Here you see the two strongest inducements are held forth — 1st, that nobody ought to read it — and secondly, that everybody buys it — on the strength of which the Publisher boldly prints the tenth Edition, before he had sold ten of the first — and then establishes it by threatening himself with the Pillory, or absolutely indicting himself for *Scan. Mag.*

DANG. Ha! ha! gad, I know it's so —[1]

PUFF. As to the Puff oblique, or Puff by Implication it is too various and extensive to be illustrated by an Instance — it attracts in Titles and Presumes in Patents — it lurks in the Limitation of a Subscription — and invites in the assurance of crowd and incommodation at Public Places, it delights to draw forth conceal'd merit, with a most disinterested assiduity — and often[2] wears a countenance of smiling censure and tender Reproach — it has a wonderful memory for Parliamentary Debates and will often give the whole speech of a favoured member with the most flattering accuracy. But above all it is a great Dealer in Reports and Suppositions — it has the earliest intelligence of intended Preferments that will reflect honour on the Patrons and embryo Promotions of modest Gentlemen who know nothing of the matter themselves — it can hint a Ribband for implied services in the air of a common Report — and with the carelessness of a casual Paragraph suggest officers into commands to which they have no pretension but their wishes. This — Sir is the last Principal Class of[3] the Art of Puffing — a Practice[4] which I hope you will now agree with me is of the highest Dignity — yielding a Tablature of Benevolence and Public Spirit; befriending equally Trade

[1] C 1: Ha! ha! ha! 'gad I know it is so.
[2] C 1: sometimes.
[3] C 1: in.
[4] C 1: An art.

Gallantry Criticism and Politics — The applause of Genius — The Register of Charity — The Triumph of Heroism — the self Defence of Contractors — the Fame of Patriots[1] — and the Gazette of Ministers.

SNEER. Sir, I am completely a convert both to the importance and ingenuity of your profession; and now, sir, there is but one thing which can possibly increase my respect for you, and that is, your permitting me to be present this morning at the rehearsal of your new trage ——

PUFF. Hush, for heaven's sake! — *My* tragedy! — Egad, Dangle, I take this very ill: you know how apprehensive I am of being known to be the author.

DANG. I' faith I would not have told — but it's in the papers, and your name at length in the Morning Chronicle.

PUFF. Ah! those damned editors never can keep a secret! — Well, Mr. Sneer, no doubt you will do me great honour — I shall be infinitely happy — highly flattered ——

DANG. I believe it must be near the time — shall we go together?

PUFF. No; it will not be yet this hour, for they are always late at that theatre: besides, I must meet you there, for I have some little matters here to send to the papers, and a few paragraphs to scribble before I go. — [*Looking at memorandums.*] Here is *A conscientious Baker, on the subject of the Army Bread; and a Detester of visible Brickwork, in favour of the new-invented Stucco;* both in the style of Junius, and promised for to-morrow. The Thames navigation too is at a stand. Misomud or Anti-shoal must go to work again directly. — Here too are some political memorandums — I see; ay — *To take Paul Jones, and get the Indiamen out of the Shannon — reinforce Byron — compel the Dutch — to* — so! — I must do that in the evening papers, or reserve it for the Morning

[1] C 1: orators.

Herald; for I know that I have undertaken to-morrow, besides, to establish the unanimity of the fleet in the Public Advertiser, and to shoot Charles Fox in the Morning Post. — So, egad, I ha'n't a moment to lose.

DANG. Well, we'll meet in the Green Room.

[*Exeunt severally.*

END OF THE FIRST ACT

ACT II

SCENE I. — DANGLE, PUFF, *and* SNEER[1]

PUFF. I say that[2] what Shakspeare says of the[3] Actors may be better applied to the Purpose of Plays — *They* ought to be "the abstract and brief Chronicle[4] of the Times." Therefore when History, and particularly the History of our own country furnishes anything like a case in Point to the time in which an Author writes [,] if he knows his own Interest, he'll[5] take advantage of it — so Sir — I call my Tragedy *The Spanish Armada;* and have laid the scene before Tilbury Fort.

SNEER. A most Happy Thought certainly!

DANG. Egad it was — I told you so — but pray now I don't understand how you have contrived to introduce any Love into it? and that you know is as necessary to a modern Tragedy as — to a Simile, and therefore you had better not try to make one on the subject.[6]

PUFF. Love! O nothing so easy — for it is a received Point among Poets, that where History gives you a good heroic out Line for a Play, you may fill up with a little love at your own Discretion: in doing which nine times out of Ten you only

[1] C I: SCENE I. The THEATRE. Enter DANGLE, PUFF, and SNEER, *as before the Curtain.*

[2] C I: No, no, sir. [3] C I omits "the." [4] C I: Chronicles.

[5] C I: he will. [6] C I omits from "and that you know."

make up a Deficiency in the private History of the Times. Now I rather think I have done this with some Address.[1]

SNEER. No scandal about Queen Elizabeth I hope —

PUFF. O Lud no — no — I only suppose the Governor of Tilbury Fort's Daughter to be in Love with the son of the Spanish Admiral.

SNEER. O is that all [?]

DANG. Excellent efaith — I see it at once — But won't this appear rather improbable?

PUFF. To be sure it will — but what the Plague! a Play is not to show occurrences that happen every Day — but things just so strange, that tho' they never did they might happen.

SNEER. Certainly nothing is unnatural that is not Physically impossible.

PUFF. Very true and for that matter Don,[2] for that's the Lover's Name, might have been over here in the train of the Spanish ambassador; or Tilburnia [Tilburina], for that is the lady's name, might have been in Love with him from having heard his character, or seen his Picture; or from knowing that he was the last man in the world she ought to be in Love [with] or for any other good female Reason — however Sir the Fact is that tho' she's[3] but a Knight's Daughter egad she is in Love like any Princess!

DANG. Poor young Lady — I feel for her already! for I can conceive how great the conflict must be between her Passion and her Duty — her Love for her country and her Love for Don.[4]

PUFF. O amazing — her poor susceptible Heart is swayed to and fro by contending Passions like ——

Enter UNDER PROMPTER

UND. PROMP. Sir the scene is set and everything is ready to begin if you please.

[1] C 1: success.
[2] C 1: DON FEROLO WISKERANDOS.
[3] C 1: she is.
[4] C 1: DON FEROLO WISKERANDOS.

PUFF. Egad then we'll lose no Time.

UND. PROMP. Tho, I believe Sir you will find it very short for all the Performers have profited by the kind Permission you granted them.

PUFF. Hey what!

UND. PROMP. You know Sir you gave them leave to cut out or omit whatever they found heavy or unnecessary to the Plot — and I must own they have taken very liberal advantage of your Indulgence.

PUFF. Well well they are in general very good Judges and I know I am luxuriant. — Now, Mr. Hopkins as soon as you please —

UND. PROMP. [*To the* Orchestra.[1]] Gentlemen will you play a few Bars of something to[2] ——

PUFF. Aye that's right — for as we have the Scenes and dresses egad, we'll go to 't as if it was the first Night's Performance — but you need not mind stopping between the acts[3] — Orchestra *Play*. Soh[!] stand clear Gentlemen — now you know there will be a cry of Down! Down! — Hats off! — Silence! — Then up curtain, and let us see what our Painters have done for us. [*Curtain rises.*

SCENE II. — *Before Tilbury Fort*

"SENTINELS[4] *asleep*

DANG. Tilbury Fort! — very fine indeed!

PUFF. Now what do you think I open with —

SNEER. Faith I can't guess.

PUFF. A clock. — Hark! — [*Clock strikes.*] I open with a clock striking[,] to beget an awful attention in the Audience — it also marks the time, which is four o'clock in the morning

[1] C 1: *Musick.* [2] C 1: just to.
[3] C 1: [*Exit Under Prompter.*] (*Orchestra play. Then the Bell rings.*)
[4] C 1: *Two Centinels.*

and saves a Description of the rising Sun and a great deal about gilding the eastern Hemisphere.

DANG. But pray are the Centinels to be asleep?

PUFF. Fast as Watchmen.

SNEER. Isn't that odd though at such an alarming crisis?

PUFF. Aye,[1] but smaller things must give way to a striking scene at the opening. And the case is that two great men are coming to this very spot to begin the Piece — it is not to be supposed now[2] they would open their Lips if these Fellows were watching them — so egad I must either have sent them off their Posts — or set them asleep.

SNEER. O that accounts for it — but tell us who are these coming?

PUFF. Those[3] are they — Sir Walter Raleigh, and Sir Christopher Hatton — you'll know Sir Christopher by his turning out his Toes — famous you know for his Dancing — I like to preserve all the little Traits of Character — now observe[4] —

"*Enter* SIR WALTER RALEIGH *and* SIR CHRISTOPHER HATTON

SIR CHRIST. True, gallant Raleigh!" —

DANG. What [!] they had been talking before [?]

PUFF. O yes all the way as they came along. — I beg Pardon Gentlemen[5] but these are Particular Friends of mine whose Remarks may be of great service to us. — don't mind interrupting them whenever anything strikes you.[6]

"SIR CHRIST. True, gallant Raleigh!
But O, thou champion of thy Country's fame,
There is a Question which I yet must ask:
A Question which I never ask'd before —
What mean these mighty Armaments?
This general muster and this Throng of Chiefs?

[1] C 1: To be sure it is.
[2] C 1: now, it is not to be supposed.
[3] C 1: These.
[4] C 1: attend.
[5] C 1 inserts [*to the Actors*].
[6] C 1 inserts [*To Sneer and Dangle*].

SNEER. Pray Mr. Puff, how came Sir Christopher Hatton never to ask that question before?

PUFF. What before the Play began! — how the plague could he?

DANG. That's true, efaith!

PUFF. But you will hear what he thinks of the Matter.

"SIR CHRIST. Alas, my noble Friend, when I behold
Yon tented Plains in martial Symmetry
Array'd; when I count o'er yon glittering lines
Of crested warriors, where the Proud Steeds Neigh,
And valour-breathing Trumpet's shrill Appeal,
Responsive vibrate on my listening ear;
When virgin Majesty herself I view,
Like her Protecting Pallas, veil'd in steel,
With graceful Confidence exhort to Arms!
When briefly all I hear — or see bears stamp
Of martial preparation[1] and of stern defence,
I cannot but surmise — forgive, my Friend,
If the Conjecture's rash — I cannot but
Surmise — the State some Danger apprehends!"

SNEER. A very cautious Conjecture that.

PUFF. Yes that's his Character — not to give an opinion but on good[2] Grounds. — now then.

"SIR WALT. O most accomplish'd Christopher!" ——

PUFF. He calls him by his Christian Name, to show that they are on the most familiar Terms.

"SIR WALT. O most accomplish'd Christopher — I find
Thy staunch Sagacity still tracks the future,
In the fresh Print of the o'ertaken Past."

PUFF. Figurative!

"SIR WALT. Thy Fears are just —
SIR CHRIST. But where? whence? when? and what
The Danger is — methinks I fain would learn.
SIR WALT. You know, my Friend, scarce two revolving suns,
And three revolving moons, have closed their course
Since Haughty Philip, in despight of Peace,
With hostile hand hath struck at England's Trade.

[1] C: vigilance. [2] C 1: secure.

SIR CHRIST. I know it well.
SIR WALT. Philip, you know, is proud Iberia's king!
SIR CHRIST. He is —
SIR WALT. His subjects in base Bigotry
And Catholic Oppression held — while we
You know the Protestant Persuasion own —
SIR CHRIST. We do —
SIR WALT. You know beside — his boasted Armament,
The famed Armada, by the Pope Baptized,
With Purpose to invade these Realms —
SIR CHRIST. Is sailed —
Our last advices so advise [1] —
SIR WALT. While the Spanish [2] Admiral's chief hope,
his darling son ——
SIR CHRIST. Don [3] ——
SIR WALT. The same — by chance a Prisoner hath been ta'en,
And in this fort of Tilbury ——
SIR CHRIST. Is now
Confined — 'tis true, and oft from yon tall turret's top
I've mark'd the youthful Spaniard's haughty mien —
Unconquer'd, tho' in chains.
SIR WALT. You also know — "

DANG. Mr. Puff, as he knows all this, why does Sir Walter go on telling him?

PUFF. But the Audience are'nt [4] supposed to know anything of the matter, are they?

SNEER. True; but I think you manage ill — for there certainly appears no reason why Sir Walter should be so communicative.

PUFF. Fore Gad now [5] that's [6] one of the most *ungrateful* observations I ever heard — for the less inducement *he* has to tell all this, the more I think you ought to be obliged to him — for I'm [7] sure you'd know nothing of the Plot [8] without it —

DANG. That's very true, upon my word!

[1] C 1: report.
[2] C 1: Iberian.
[3] C 1: Ferolo Wiskerandos hight.
[4] C 1: are not.
[5] C 1: For, egad now.
[6] C 1: that is.
[7] C 1: I am.
[8] C 1: matter.

PUFF. But you'll[1] find He was not going on.

"SIR CHRIST. Enough, enough — 'tis plain —
And I no more am in Amazement lost!" ——

PUFF. Here now you see Sir Christopher didn't[2] in Fact ask any one Question for his own Information.

SNEER. No, indeed his has been a most disinterested curiosity!

DANG. Really I find that we are very much obliged to them both.

PUFF. To be sure you are. Now then for the commander-in-chief, the Earl of Leicester, who, you know, was no favourite but of the queen's. — We left off — *in amazement lost!*

"SIR CHRIST. Am in amazement lost.
But see — where noble Leicester comes — supreme
In Honours and Command.
SIR WALT. And yet, methinks,
At such a time, so perilous, so fear'd,
That Staff might well become an abler Grasp.
SIR CHRIST. And so, by Heaven think I — but, soft He's Here!"

PUFF. Aye they envy him! —

SNEER. But who are these with him?

PUFF. O very valiant knights! one's[3] the Governor of the Fort, the other the master of the horse. And now, I think, you shall hear some better Language. I was obliged to be plain and intelligible in the first Scene, because there was so much matter of Fact in it; but now faith![4] you have trope, Figure and Metaphor, as Plenty as noun substantives.

"*Enter* EARL OF LEICESTER, GOVERNOR, MASTER OF THE HORSE, KNIGHTS, *etc.*

LEIC. How's this, my friends! is't thus your new-fledged zeal,
And plumèd valour moulds in roosted sloth?
Why dimly glimmers that Heroic Flame,

[1] C 1: you will. [2] C 1: did not.
[3] C 1: one is. [4] C 1: efaith.

Whose reddening Blaze, by patriot Spirit fed,
Should be the beacon of a kindling Realm?
Can the quick current of a Patriot Heart
Thus stagnate in a cold and pond-like[1] converse,
Or freeze in Tideless Inactivity?
No rather let the Fountain of your Valour
Spring through each stream of enterprise,
Each petty channel of conducive Daring,
Till the full torrent of your foaming Wrath
O'erwhelm the Flats of sunk Hostility!"

PUFF. There it is — followed up!

"SIR WALT. No more [!] the freshening Breath of thy Rebuke
Hath fill'd the swelling canvas of our Souls
And thus tho' fate should cut the cable of
[*All take hands.*
Our Hopes[2] — in Friendship's closing line
We'll grapple with despair, and if we fall,
We'll fall in glory's Wake!

LEIC. There spoke old England's Genius!
Then, are we all resolved?

ALL. We are — all resolved.

LEIC. To conquer — or be free?

ALL. To conquer, or be free.

LEIC. All?

ALL. All."

DANG. Nem. con! egad!

PUFF. O yes! — where they do agree on the Stage their unanimity is wonderful!

"LEIC. Then let's embrace — and now —— [*Kneels.*"

SNEER. What the Plague, is he going to Pray?

PUFF. Yes — hush: — in great emergencies, there is nothing like a Prayer.

"LEIC. O mighty Mars!"

DANG. But why should he pray to Mars?

PUFF. Hush!

[1] C 1: weedy. [2] C 1: Our topmost hopes.

"LEIC. If in thy Homagė bred,
Each Point of Discipline I've still observed;
Nor but by due Promotion and the right
Of Service to the Rank of major General
Have risen [,] assist thy Votary now!
GOV. Yet do not rise — hear me![1]
KNIGHT. And me!
SIR WALT. And me!
SIR CHRIST. And me![2]
ALL. Behold thy votaries submissive beg,
That thou wilt[3] deign to grant them, all they ask!
Assist them to accomplish all their ends,
And sanctify whatever means they use
To gain them!"

SNEER. A very orthodox Quintetto!

PUFF. Vastly well gentlemen — is that well managed or not? Have you such a prayer as that on the stage?

SNEER. Not exactly.

LEIC. [*To* PUFF.] But Sir — you haven't settled how we are to get off here.

PUFF. You couldn't[4] go off kneeling, could ye?[5]

SIR WALT. [*To* PUFF.] O no Sir impossible!

PUFF. It would have a good effect efaith! if you could exeunt praying! — Yes, and would vary the establish'd mode of springing off with a glance at the Pit.

SNEER. Oh, never mind — so as you get them off! — I'll answer for't[6] the Audience won't care how.

PUFF. Well then repeat the last Line Standing [,] and go off the old way.

"ALL. And sanctify whatever means we use
To gain them. [*Exeunt.*"

DANG. Bravo — a fine exit.

[1] C 1 inserts: MASTER OF HORSE. And me!
[2] C 1 inserts: PUFF. Now, pray all together.
[3] C 1: will.
[4] C 1: could not.
[5] C 1: you.
[6] C 1: for it.

SNEER. Well really Mr. Puff ——

PUFF. Stay a moment!

"*The* CENTINELS *get up.*

1 SENT. All this shall to Lord Burleigh's ear.

2 SENT. 'Tis meet it should — The General it seems is disaproved.[1]

[*Exeunt.*"

DANG. Hey! — why, I thought those Fellows had been asleep?

PUFF. Only a pretence there's the Art of it[2] — I mean it to mark Lord Burleigh's Character who you know was famous for his skill in procuring Intelligence and employ'd all sorts of People as spies.

SNEER. But isn't it odd they never were[3] taken Notice of — not even by the commander-in-chief?

PUFF. O Lud Sir — if people who want to listen or overhear were not always connived at in a Tragedy, there would be no carrying on any Plot in the World.

DANG. That's certain!

PUFF. But take care — my dear Dangle — the morning-gun is going to fire. [*Cannon fires.*

DANG. Hey[4] — Well, that will have a fine effect!

PUFF. I think so, and helps to realize the scene.[5] There are more cannon to fire.

UND. PROMP. [*Within.*] No Sir.

PUFF. Now then for soft music. (*Musick*)

SNEER. Pray what's that for?

PUFF. It shows that Tilburina is coming — nothing intro-

[1] C 1 omits "The General," etc.

[2] C 1 reads hereafter: they were spies of Lord Burleigh's.

[3] C 1: were never. [4] C 1 omits.

[5] C 1 reads hereafter: [*Cannon twice*]. What the plague! — *three* morning guns! — there never is but one! . . . aye, this is always the way at the Theatre — give these fellows a good thing, and they never know when to have done with it. You have no more cannon to fire?

duces you a Heroine like soft music. Here she comes — all in tune to the minuet in Ariadne.[1]

DANG. And her confidant, I suppose?

PUFF. To be sure![2]

"*Enter* TILBURINA *and* CONFIDANT

TILB. Now has the whispering breath of gentle morn
Bid[3] Nature's voice and Nature's beauty rise;
While orient Phœbus, with unborrow'd hues,
Clothes the waked loveliness which all night slept
In heavenly drapery! Darkness is fled.
Now Flowers unfold their Beauties to the Sun,
And blushing kiss the Beam he sends to wake them —
The strip'd Carnation, and the guarded Rose,
The vulgar Wall Flower, and smart Gillyflower,
The Polyanthus mean — the dapper Daisy,
Sweet William, and sweet Marjory[4] — and all
The Tribe of single and of double Pinks!
Now too the feather'd Warblers tune their Notes —
Around, and charm the listening Grove. The Lark!
The Linnet, Chaffinch, Bullfinch, Goldfinch, Greenfinch!
— But O to me no joy can they afford
Nor Rose, nor Wallflower, nor smart Gillyflow'r,
Nor Polyanthus mean, nor dapper Daisy,
Nor William sweet, nor marjory[5] — nor Lark,
Linnet, nor all the finches of the grove!

PUFF. Your white Handkerchief, Ma'am![6] ——

TILB. I thought, sir, I wasn't to use that till *heart-rending woe.*

PUFF. O yes, madam, at 'the Finches of the Grove,' if you please.

"TILB. Nor all the finches of the grove.[7] [*Weeps.*"

PUFF. Vastly well, Ma'am![8]

[1] C 1 omits this sentence.

[2] C 1 adds: here they are — inconsolable to the minuet in Ariadne! (*Soft musick.*)

[3] C 1: Bad.

[4] C 1: marjorum.

[5] C 1: marjoram.

[6] C 1: madam.

[7] C 1: Nor lark,
Linnet, nor all the finches of the grove. [*Weeps.*

[8] C 1: madam.

DANG. Vastly well Indeed!

"TILB. For, O, too sure, Heart-rending woe is now
The Lot of wretched Tilburina!"

DANG. Oh![1]

SNEER. Oh![2]

"CON. Be comforted, sweet Lady — who knows,[3]
But Heaven has yet some milk-white Day in store?
TILB. Alas! my gentle Nora,
Thy tender youth as yet hath never mourn'd
Love's fatal Dart — else wouldst thou know that when
The soul is sunk in comfortless Despair,
It cannot taste of merriment."

DANG. That's certain —

"CON. But — see where your stern father comes:
It is not meet that he should find you thus."

PUFF. Hey, what the Plague! — what a cut is here? Why, what's[4] become of the description of her first meeting with Don[5] — his gallant behaviour in the sea-fight — and the simile of the Canary Bird?

TILB. Indeed Sir, you'll find they will not be miss'd.

PUFF. Very well — very well!

TILB. [*To* CONFIDANT.] The cue, ma'am, if you please.

"CON. It is not meet that he should find you thus.
TILB. Thou counsel'st right — but 'tis no easy task
For barefaced Grief to wear a Mask of Joy.

Enter GOVERNOR

GOV. How's this — in Tears? — O Tilburina shame!
Is this a Time for maudling tenderness,
And Cupid's baby woes — hast thou not heard
That Haughty Spain's Pope — consecrated[6] fleet
Advances to our Shores, while England's fate,
Like a clipp'd Guinea, trembles in the scale?

[1] C 1: O! — 'tis too much.
[2] C 1: Oh! — it is indeed.
[3] C 1: for who knows.
[4] C 1: what is.
[5] C 1: Don Wiskerandos.
[6] C 1: Pope-consecrated.

TILB. Then is the crisis of *my* Fate at hand!
I see the fleets approach — I see ——"

PUFF. Now pray Gentlemen, mind. This is one of the most useful Figures we Tragedy writers have by which a Hero or Heroine, in consideration of their being often obliged to overlook Things that *are* on the Stage, is allowed to hear and see a number of things that are not.

SNEER. Yes — a kind of Poetical Second-sight!

PUFF. Yes. — Now then, ma'am.[1]

"TILB. I see their Decks
Are clear'd — I see the signal made
The Line is form'd — a cable's length asunder!
I see the frigates station'd in the rear;
And now I hear the Thunder of the guns!
I hear the victor's shouts — I also hear
The vanquish'd groan! — and now 'tis smoke — and now
I see the loose sails shiver in the wind
I see — I see — what soon you'll see ——

GOV. Hold Daughter Peace — this love hath turn'd thy Brain:
The Spanish Fleet thou *canst* not see — because
— It is not yet in Sight!"

DANG. Egad tho', the Governor seems to make no Allowance for this poetical Figure you talk of.

PUFF. No — a plain matter of Fact man — that's his Character.

"TILB. But will you then refuse his offer?
GOV. I must I will I can I ought I do.
TILB. Think what a noble Price.
GOV. No more you urge in vain —
TILB. His Liberty is all he asks."

SNEER. All who asks Mr. Puff?

PUFF. Egad Sir, I can't tell — Here has been such cutting and slashing I don't know where they have got to myself.

TILB. Indeed Sir, you will find it will connect very well.

"— And your reward secure."

[1] C 1: madam.

PUFF. O — if they hadn't been so devilish free with their cutting here, you'd [have] found that Don[1] has been tampering for his Liberty — and has persuaded Tilburina to make this Proposal to her Father — and now pray observe the conciseness with which the Argument is conducted — egad, the pro and con goes as smart as Hits in a Fencing-match. It is indeed a sort of small-sword-logic, which we have borrowed from the French.

"TILB. A Retreat in Spain!
GOV. Outlawry here!
TILB. Your Daughter's Prayer!
GOV. Your Father's Oath!
TILB. My Lover!
GOV. My Country!
TILB. Tilburina!
GOV. England!
TILB. A Title!
GOV. Honour!
TILB. A Pension!
GOV. A Conscience!
TILB. A Thousand Pounds!
GOV. Ha! thou hast touch'd me nearly ——"

PUFF. There you see — she threw in Tilburina. Quick parry Carte with England![2] thrust in tierce a Title! — parried by Honour. Ha! a Pension over the arm! — put by by conscience. Then flankonade with a thousand pounds — and a palpable Hit egad!

SNEER. Well Push'd indeed.[3]

"TILB. Canst thou —
Reject the suppliant, and the Daughter too?
GOV. No More — I would not hear thee plead in Vain:
The Father softens — but the Governor's resolved.[4] [*Exit.*"

[1] C 1: you would have found that Don Wiskerandos.
[2] C 1 inserts "Hah!"
[3] C 1 omits this speech.
[4] C 1: Is fix'd.

DANG. Aye that Antithesis of Persons, is a most established Figure.

"TILB. 'Tis well — hence then fond Hopes, — fond Passion hence;
Duty behold I am all over thine ——
WHISK. [*Without.*] Where is my love — my Tilb . . . Ha![1]
TILB. Ha!
DON. [*Without.*] Where is my Love — my ——
TILB. Ha!
WHISK. My beauteous Enemy! ——"

PUFF. O dear Ma'am, you must start a great deal more than that — Consider you had just determined in favour of Duty — when in a moment, the sound of his Voice revives your Passion — overthrows your resolution — destroys your obedience — if you don't express all that in your start — you do nothing at all.

TILB. Well — we'll try again.

DANG. Speaking from within has always a fine effect.

SNEER. Very.[2]

"TILB. Behold I am all — over thine.
DON. Where is my Love? my ——
TILB. Ha!
DON. My beauteous Enemy!
My conquering Tilburina! (enter) ha![3] is't thus
We meet — why are thy looks averse? what means —[4]

[1] C I omits this speech and the following.
[2] C I omits to "My conquering," etc.
[3] C I: How!
[4] C I continues: what means
That falling tear — that frown of boding woe?
Hah! now indeed I am a prisoner!
Yes, now I feel the galling weight of these
Disgraceful chains — which, cruel Tilburina!
Thy doating captive gloried in before. —
But thou art false, and Wiskerandos is undone!
TILB. O no; how little dost thou know thy Tilburina!
WISK. Art thou then true? Begone cares, doubts and fears,
I make you all a present to the winds;
And if the winds reject you — try the waves.

[OVER]

PUFF. Heyday — Here's a cut! — What are all the mutual Protestations out?

TILB. Now pray Sir, don't interrupt us here[1] — you ruin one's[2] feelings.[3]

SNEER. No, pray don't interrupt them.

"WHISK. One last embrace.
TILB. Now farewell — forever.
WHISK. For ever!
TILB. Aye for ever! [*Going*"

PUFF.[4] Gad's life! — Sir! Ma'am![5] if you go out without the Parting look, you might as well dance out. Here — here! —

CON. But pray Sir — How am I to get off here?

PUFF.[6] Pshaw! what the Devil signifies how *you* get off! edge away at the Top or where you will.[7] Now, Ma'am — you see ——

TILB. We understand you Sir.[8]

"BOTH. Oh! [*Turning back, and exeunt. — Scene closes.*"

DANG. O charming —

PUFF. The wind you know, is the established receiver of all stolen sighs, and cast off griefs and apprehensions.

TILB. Yet must we part? — stern duty seals our doom:
Though here I call yon conscious clouds to witness,
Could I pursue the bias of my soul,
All friends, all right of parents I'd disclaim,
And thou, my Wiskerandos, should'st be father,
And mother, brother, cousin, uncle, aunt,
And friend to me!

WISK. O matchless excellence! — and must we part?
Well, if — we must — we must — and in that case,
The less is said the better.

[1] C 1: just here.
[2] C 1: our.
[3] C 1 inserts: PUFF. *Your* feelings! — but zounds, *my* feelings, ma'am!
[4] C 1 inserts "S'death and fury!"
[5] C 1: Madam.
[6] C 1 inserts "*You.*"
[7] C 1: [*Pushes the confidant off*].
[8] C 1 adds: "Aye for ever."

PUFF. Hey! — 'tis pretty well I believe — you see I don't attempt to strike out anything new — but I take it I improve on the establish'd modes.

SNEER. You do indeed — but pray isn't Queen Elizabeth to appear?

PUFF. No — not once — but she is to be talked of for ever — so that egad you'll think a hundred Times that she is on the point of coming in.

SNEER. Hang it I think it's a pity to keep her in the Green-Room all the Night.

PUFF. O no, that always has a fine Effect — it keeps up Expectation.

DANG. But aren't we to have a Battle neither?[1]

PUFF. Yes yes, you will have a Battle at last but egad it's not to be by Land — but by Sea — and that's the only quite new thing in the Piece.

DANG. O — ho[2] — what Drake at the Armada hey.

PUFF. Yes efaith — Fire-Ships and all — then we shall end with a Procession. Hey that will do I think?

SNEER. No doubt on't.

PUFF. But come we must not lose Time — so now for the Underplot.

SNEER. Hey[3] what the Plague, have you another Plot?

PUFF. O Lud[4] yes — ever while you live have two Plots to your Tragedy. The grand Point in managing them is only to let your Under Plot have as little connection with your chief[5] Plot as possible. — I flatter myself nothing can be more distinct than mine, for as in my chief Plot the characters are all great People, I have laid my under Plot in low Life and — as the former is to end in deep Distress, I make the other end as happy as a Farce — Now Mr. Hopkins as soon as you please.

[1] C 1: But are we not to have a battle?
[2] C 1 omits "O — ho."
[3] C 1 omits "Hey."
[4] C 1: O lord.
[5] C 1: main.

Enter UNDER PROMPTER

UND. PROMP. Sir—the Carpenters say[1] it is impossible you can go to the Park Scene yet.

PUFF. The Park Scene! no — I mean the Description scene here in the wood.

UND. PROMP. Sir the Performers have cut it out.

PUFF. Cut it out!

UND. PROMP. Yes Sir.

PUFF. What! the whole account of Queen Elizabeth?

UND. PROMP. Yes Sir.

PUFF. And the Description of her Horse and Side-Saddle?

UND. PROMP. Yes Sir.

PUFF. So — so — this is very fine indeed! — Mr. Hopkins how the Devil[2] could you suffer this?

MR. HOP. [*From within.*] Sir indeed the Pruning Knife——

PUFF. The Pruning Knife — zounds! — the Axe! — why here has been such lopping and topping — I shan't have the bare Trunk of my Play left presently! — Very well Sir — the performers must do as they please — but upon my soul I'll print it every word.

SNEER. That I would indeed.

PUFF. Very well Sir — then we must go on. — Zounds I wouldn't have parted with the Description of the Horse! — Well Sir go on. — Sir it was one of the finest and most laboured Things. — Very well, sir; let them go on. — There you had him and his accoutrements, from the Bit to the Crupper. — Very well Sir; we must go to the Park Scene.

UND. PROMP. Sir — there's the point — the Carpenters say that unless there is some Business put in here before the Drop they sha'n't have time to clear away the Fort[3] —

[1] C 1: carpenter says.

[2] C 1: plague.

[3] C 1 adds: or sink Gravesend and the river.

PUFF. So! this is a pretty Dilemma, indeed — Do call the Head Carpenter to me.[1]

UND. PROMP. Mr. Butler — [*enter* CARPENTER *dress'd*]. Here he is Sir.

PUFF. Hey — this is the Head Carpenter!

UND. PROMP. Yes — Sir — He was to have walked as one of the Generals at the Review — For the truth is your Tragedy employs everybody in the company.

PUFF. *O* — then pray, Mr. General-Carpenter what is all this?

CARP. Why Sir, you only consider what my men have to do — they have to remove Tilbury Fort with the Cannon and to sink Gravesend and the River and I only desire three minutes to do it in.

PUFF. Hah! and they've cut the Scene.

CARP. Besides if I could manage in less, I question if the Lamplighter could clear away the Sun in the time.

PUFF. Do call one of them here.

CARP. Master Lamplighter! [*Without*] Mr. Langley! Here [*enter* LAMPLIGHTER *as a River God and a Page holding up his train*].

PUFF. Sir — your most obedient servant — Who the Devil's this!

UND. PROMP. The master Lamplighter, Sir. He does one of the River Gods in the Procession.

PUFF. O, a River God is he — well Sir you won't have time I understand —

L. Three minutes at least Sir — unless you have a mind to burn the Fort.

PUFF. Hah! and they've cut out the Scene!

[1] C I omits hereafter to Sneer's speech at the end of the scene, and alters Puff's speech as follows: So! this is a pretty dilemma truly! — Gentlemen — you must excuse me, these fellows will never be ready, unless I go and look after them myself.

CARP. Lord Sir, there only wants a little business to be put in here — just as long as while we have been speaking will do it —

PUFF. What then are you all ready now? [*From behind*] Yes all clear.

PUFF. O then I shall easily manage it —

UND. PROMP. Clear the Stage.

PUFF. And do General keep a sharp look out and beg the River God not to spare his Oyl in the last scene — it must be brilliant. Gentlemen I beg a thousand Pardons.

SNEER. O dear Sir — these little things will happen.[1]

[*Exeunt.*

ACT III

SCENE I. — *The Theatre, before the curtain*

Enter PUFF, SNEER, *and* DANGLE

PUFF. Well, we are ready; now then for the justices.

[*Curtain rises.*

"JUSTICES, CONSTABLES, *etc., discovered*"

SNEER. This I suppose is a sort of Senate Scene.[2]

DANG. It is the Under Plot, isn't it?

PUFF. Yes. — What, gentlemen, do you mean to go at once to the Discovery Scene?

JUST. If you please, sir.

PUFF. Oh, very well! — Hark'ee, I don't chuse to say anything more but efaith they have mangled my play in a most Shocking Manner.

DANG. It's a great pity!

PUFF. Now then Mr. Justice if you please.

[1] C I adds: PUFF. To cut out this scene! — but I'll print it — egad, I'll print it every word!

[2] C I inserts: PUFF. To be sure — there has not been one yet.

"JUST. Are all the Volunteers without?
CONST. They are.
Some ten in Fetters, and some twenty Drunk.
JUST. Attends the youth — whose most opprobrious Fame
And clear convicted Crimes have stamp'd for[1] soldier?
CONST. He waits your Pleasure — eager to repay
The best Reprieve that sends him to the Fields
Of Glory, there to raise his branded Hand
In Honour's cause.
JUST. 'Tis well — 'tis Justice arms him!
Oh! may he now defend his Country's Laws
With half the Spirit he has broke them all!
If 'tis your Worship's Pleasure — bid him enter.
CONST. I fly — the Herald of your will. [*Exit.*"

PUFF. Quick, Sir.

SNEER. But, Mr. Puff, I think not only the Justice, but the Clown seems to talk in as high a style as the first Hero among them.

PUFF. Heaven forbid they shouldnt[2] in a free country — Sir I'm[3] not for making slavish Distinctions — and giving all the fine Language to the upper Sort of People.

DANG. That's very noble in you indeed!

"*Enter the* JUSTICE'S LADY."

PUFF. Now, pray mark this Scene.

"LADY. Forgive this interruption, good my Love;
But as I just now pass'd a handcuff'd[4] youth,
Whom rude Hands hither lead — strange bodings seized
My flutt'ring Heart — and to myself I said,
An' if our Jack[5] had lived he'd surely been
This Stripling's Height!
JUST. Ha! sure some Powerful sympathy directs
Us both — for this youth.[6]

Enter SON *and* CONSTABLE

What is thy name?

[1] C 1: him. [2] C 1: should not. [3] C 1: I am.
[4] C 1: pris'ner. [5] C 1: Tom. [6] C 1 omits "for this youth."

SON. My Name's John Wilkins[1] — *Alias* have I none —
Though orphan'd, and without a Friend
JUST. Thy Parents?
SON. My Father dwelt in Rochester — and was,
As I have heard — a Fishmonger — no more."

PUFF. What Sir do you leave out the account of your Birth, Parentage, and Education?

SON. They have settled it so Sir.[2]

PUFF. O!

"LADY. How loudly Nature whispers to my Heart
Had He no other Name?
SON. I've seen a Bill
Of his sign'd Tomkins, creditor.
JUST. Ha! by Heavens! Our Boy is now before us.[3]
LADY. Has he his Ears?
SON. Lady — for three long winters have I mourned their Loss.
LADY. It is! it is!
JUST. This does indeed confirm
Each circumstance the Gipsy told [—] quick loose
Those ignominious [bonds?] prepare [!][4]
SON. I do.
JUST. No Orphan, nor without a Friend art thou —
I am thy Father; here's thy Mother; there
Your[5] uncle — this thy first cousin, and Those
Are all your near Relations!
LADY. O ecstasy of Bliss!
SON. O most unlook'd for Happiness!
LADY. O wonderful event! [*Faints.*]"

PUFF. There, you see Relationship like murder will out.

"JUST. See she revives — this joy's too much![6]
But come — and we'll unfold the rest within;
And thou[7] must needs want rest and food.
Hence may each orphan hope, as Chance directs,
To find a Father where he least expects! [*Exeunt.*"

[1] C 1: TOM JENKINS.
[2] C 1 adds "here."
[3] C 1 omits this speech and to "This does indeed confirm."
[4] C 1: Each circumstance The gypsey told! — Prepare!
[5] C 1: Thy.
[6] C 1: Now let's revive — else were this joy too much!
[7] C 1 inserts "my boy."

PUFF. What do you think of that?

DANG. One of the finest Discovery scenes I ever saw! — Why this Under Plot would have made a Tragedy in itself.

SNEER. Aye or a Comedy either.

PUFF. And keeps quite clear you see of the other.

"*Enter* SCENEMEN, *taking away the seats*"

PUFF. The scene remains does it?

SCENEMAN. Yes Sir.

PUFF. You are to leave one chair, you know. — But it's[1] always awkward in a Tragedy[2] you Fellows coming in in your Playhouse Liveries to remove things. I wish that could be managed better.[3]

"*Enter* BEEFEATER

BEEF. Perdition catch my soul but I *do* love thee!"

SNEER. Haven't I heard that line before?

PUFF. No, I fancy not. — Where, pray?

DANG. Yes, I think there's something like it in Othello.

PUFF. Gad! now you put me in mind on't I believe there is — but that's no consequence — all that can be said is that two People happen'd to hit upon the same thought — and Shakespeare made use of it first, that's all.

SNEER. Very true.

PUFF. Now Sir, your Soliloquy — but speak more to the Pit if you please[4] ——

"BEEF. Though hopeless Love finds comfort in Despair,
It never can endure a Rival's Bliss!
But soft — I am observed. [*Exit*."

DANG. That's a very short Soliloquy.

PUFF. Yes — but it would have been a great deal longer if He had not been observed.

[1] C 1: it is. [2] C 1 inserts "to have."
[3] C 1 adds: So now for my mysterious yeoman.
[4] C 1 adds: the soliloquy always to the pit — that's a rule.

Sneer. A most sentimental Beefeater That Mr. Puff!

Puff. Hark'ee — I wouldn't[1] have you be too sure that He is a Beefeater.

Sneer. O[2] what, a Hero in Disguise?

Puff. No matter — I only give you a hint — but now for my principal character. Here He comes — Lord Burleigh in Person! Pray Gentlemen, step this way — softly — I only hope He's perfect[3] — if He is but perfect! —

"*Enter* Lord Burleigh, *goes slowly to a chair and sits*"

Sneer. Mr. Puff!

Puff. Hush! — Vastly well![4]

Dang. What isn't he to speak at all?

Puff. Egad I thought you'd ask me that — yes it is a very likely thing — that a minister in his situation with the whole affairs of the Nation on his Head, should have time to talk! — but hush! or you'll put him out.

Sneer. Put him out! how the Plague can that be if He's not going to say anything?

Puff. There's a reason! why his Part is to *think* — and how the plague do you imagine he can *think* — if you keep talking —

Dang. That's very true, upon my word!

"Lord Burleigh *comes forward*, "*Shakes his head, and exit*"

Puff. Now — hush! — close![5]

Sneer. He is very perfect indeed! Now, pray what did he mean [by] that ——

Puff. You don't take it —

Sneer. No I don't upon my soul.

Puff. Why, by that shake of his Head, he gave you to Understand that even tho' everything was to be hoped from

[1] C 1: would not. [2] C 1 omits "O."

[3] C 1: the Lord High Treasurer is perfect.

[4] C 1 adds: Sir! vastly well! a most interesting gravity!

[5] C 1 omits this speech.

the Justice of their cause and wisdom of their measures[1] — yet, if there was not a greater spirit shown on the Part of the People, the country would at last fall a sacrifice to the hostile ambition of the Spanish monarchy.

SNEER. The Devil! did He mean all that by shaking his Head?

PUFF. Every word of it — if He shook his Head as I taught him.

DANG. Ah! there certainly is a vast deal to be done on the Stage by dumb show and expression of Face![2]

SNEER. Oh, here are some of our old acquaintance.

"*Enter* SIR CHRISTOPHER HATTON *and* SIR WALTER RALEIGH

SIR CHRIST. My niece and your niece too!
By Heaven! there's witchcraft in't. — He could not else
Have gain'd their hearts. — But see where they approach!
Some horrid purpose lowering on their brows!

SIR WALT. Let us withdraw and mark them. [*They withdraw*."

SNEER. What is all this?

PUFF. Ah! here has been more pruning! — but the fact is, these two young ladies are also in love with Don Whiskerandos. Now, Gentlemen — this scene goes entirely for what we call situation and *Stage Effect*, by which the greatest applause may be obtain'd, without the asistance of Language, Sentiment, or Character: pray mark!

"*Enter two* NIECES

1ST NIECE. Ellena here!
She is his Scorn as much[3] — that is
Some comfort still!"

PUFF. O dear — Ma'am[4] you are not to say that to her

[1] C 1: that even tho' they had more justice in their cause and wisdom in their measures.

[2] C 1 adds: and a judicious author knows how much he may trust to it.

[3] C 1: as much as I.

[4] C 1: madam.

face! — Aside — Ma'am — aside. — The whole scene is to be aside. Very true Sir.[1]

"1ST NIECE. She is his scorn as much as I —
That is some comfort still. [*Aside.*
2ND NIECE. He scorns I know Ellena's love;[2]
But Tilburina lords it o'er his Heart. [*Aside.*
1ST NIECE. But see the proud Destroyer of my Peace — In freedom too[3]
Revenge is all the good I've left. [*Aside.*
2ND NIECE. He comes the false Disturber of my Quiet.
By Tilburina feared.[4]
Now Vengeance do thy worst. [*Aside.*

Enter DON FEROLO WHISKERANDOS

WHISK. O hateful Liberty — if thus
In vain I seek my Tilburina!
BOTH NIECES. And ever shalt!

SIR CHRISTOPHER HATTON *and* SIR WALTER RALEIGH *come forward*

SIR CHRIST. *and* SIR WALT. Hold! we will avenge you.
WHISK. Hold you — or see your Nieces bleed!

[*The two nieces draw their two daggers to strike* WHISKERANDOS, *the two Uncles at the instant with their two swords drawn, catch their two nieces arms, and turn the points of their swords to* WHISKERANDOS, *who immediately draws two daggers, and holds them to the two nieces' bosoms.*][5]

PUFF. There's situation for you! there's an heroic Group! —You see I have them all at a dead Lock.[6] The Ladies can't stab Whiskerandos — he durst not strike them, for fear of their unkles — the unkles durst not kill him because of their Nieces. — and[7] every one of them is afraid to let go first.

SNEER. Why, then they must stand there for ever!

[1] C I omits "Very true Sir."
[2] C I: I know he prizes not Pollina's love.
[3] C I omits "In freedom too."
[4] C I omits this line.
[5] The stage-direction inserted above is from C I.
[6] C I reserves this sentence to follow "because of their Nieces."
[7] C I: for.

PUFF. So they would, if I hadn't a good[1] contrivance for't. — Now mind ——

"*Enter* BEEFEATER *with his halbert*,

BEEF. In the Queen's Name I charge you all to drop
Your Swords and Daggers!
[*They drop their swords and daggers.*"

SNEER. That is a contrivance indeed!

PUFF. Aye — in the queen's name.

"SIR CHRIST. Come, niece!
SIR WALT. Come, niece! [*Exeunt with the two* NIECES.
WHISK. What's he, who bids us thus renounce our guard?
BEEF. Thou must do more — renounce thy love!
WHISK. Thou liest — base Beefeater!
BEEF. Ha! hell! the lie!
By Heaven thou'st roused the lion in my heart!
Off, yeoman's habit! — base disguise! off! off!
[*Discovers himself by throwing off his upper dress, and appearing in a very fine waistcoat.*
Am I a Beefeater now?
Or beams my crest as terrible as when
In Biscay's Bay I took thy captive sloop?"

PUFF. There, egad! he comes out to be the very captain of the privateer who had taken Whiskerandos prisoner — and was himself an old lover of Tilburina's.

DANG. Admirably managed indeed!

PUFF. Now stand out of their way.

WHISK. I thank thee Fortune, that hast thus bestowed
A weapon to chastise this Insolent.
[*Takes up one of the swords.*
BEEF. I take thy challenge, Spaniard, and I thank thee,
Fortune, too! [*Takes up one of the swords.*"

DANG. That's excellently contrived! — It seems as if the two uncles had left their swords on purpose for them.

PUFF. No, egad, they could not help leaving them.

[1] C 1: very fine.

"WHISK. Vengeance and Tilburina!
BEEF. Exactly so ——
[*They fight — and after the usual number of wounds given*, WHISKERANDOS *falls.*
WHISK. O cursed parry! — that last thrust in tierce
Was fatal. — Captain, thou hast fenced well!
And Whiskerandos quits this bustling scene
For all eter ——
BEEF. —— nity — he would have added, but stern death
Cut short his being, and the noun at once!"

PUFF. O my dear sir, you are too slow: now mind me. — Sir, shall I trouble you to die again?

"WHISK. And Whiskerandos quits this bustling scene
For all eter ——
BEEF. —— nity — he would have added, ——

PUFF. No Sir — that's not it — once more, if you please Don Whiskerandos.[1]

WHISK. I wish Sir, you would Practise this without me — I can't stay dying here all Night.

PUFF. Very well — we'll go it over by-and-bye — [*Exit* WHISKERANDOS.] I must humour these gentlemen!

"BEEF. Farewell — brave Spaniard!"[2]

PUFF. Dear sir, you needn't speak that speech, as the Body's walked off.

BEEF. That's true, sir — then I'll join the Fleet.

PUFF. If you please. — [*Exit* BEEFEATER.] Now, who comes on?

"*Enter* GOVERNOR[3]

GOV. A Hemisphere of Evil Planets reign!
And every planet sheds contagious frenzy!
My Spanish prisoner is slain! my Daughter,
Meeting the dead corse Borne along, has gone
Distract! [*Trumpets.*

[1] C I omits "Don Whiskerandos." [2] C I adds: and when next —
[3] C I adds: *with his hair properly disordered.*

But Hark! I am summon'd to the Fort:
Perhaps the Fleets have met! amazing crisis!
O Tilburina! from thy aged father's beard
Thou'st pluck'd the few black[1] hairs which time had left!
[*Exit.*"[2]

PUFF. True. — Now enter Tilburina!

SNEER. Egad the Business comes on quick here.

PUFF. Yes Sir — now she comes in stark mad in white satin.

SNEER. Why in white satin?

PUFF. O Lud[3] Sir — when a Heroine goes mad she always goes into white Satin. — don't she, Dangle?

DANG. Always[4] —

Enter TILBURINA *and her* CONFIDANT *mad*[5]

SNEER. But, what the Deuce! is the confidante to be mad too?

PUFF. To be sure she is — the Confidante is always to do whatever her mistress does — weep when she weeps — smile when she smiles — go mad when she goes mad. — Now, Ma'am — but keep your madness in the background.[6]

"TILB.[7] The wind whistles — the moon rises — see, they have kill'd my squirrel in his cage — is this a Grasshopper? — Ah no; it is my Friend[8] — you shall not keep him — I know you have him in your Pocket — An oyster may be cross'd in Love! — who says A whale's a Bird? — ha! did you call my Love? — He's here! He's there! — He's everywhere! Ah me! he's nowhere. [*Exit.*"

PUFF. There, do you ever desire to see anybody madder than that?

[1] C 1: brown.

[2] C 1 inserts: SNEER. Poor gentleman!
PUFF. Yes — and no one to blame but his daughter!
DANGLE. And the planets.

[3] C 1: Lord.

[4] C 1: DANGLE. Always — it's a rule.
PUFF. Yes — here it is (*looking at the book*). 'Enter Tilburina stark mad in white satin, and her confidant stark mad in white linen.'

[5] C 1 adds: *according to custom.*

[6] C 1 adds: if you please.

[7] C 1 attempts a metrical arrangement of the speech.

[8] C 1: Ha! no, it is my Whiskerandos.

SNEER. Never, while I live.[1]

PUFF. Now then for my magnificence — my Battle[2] — and my procession! — You are all ready?

UND. PROMP. Yes, Sir.

PUFF. Is the Thames dressed?

THAMES. Here I am Sir.

PUFF. Very well, indeed! — See — Gentlemen, there's a River for you![3] —

SNEER. But pray who are these Gentlemen in green with him —

PUFF. Those — those are his Banks.

SNEER. His Banks —

PUFF. Yes[4] — but hey what the Plague you have got both your Banks on one side. — Here here[5] — Ever while you live, Thames, go between your banks. — [*Bell rings.*][6] Now but! — Away! [*Exit* THAMES *between his banks.*

[*Flourish of drums*[7] . . . *trumpets* . . . *cannon, &c. &c*

[1] C I inserts:

PUFF. You observed how she mangled the metre?

DANG. Yes — egad, it was the first thing made me suspect she was out of her senses.

SNEER. And pray what becomes of her?

PUFF. She is gone to throw herself into the sea to be sure — and that brings us at once to the scene of action, and so to my catastrophe — my sea-fight, I mean.

SNEER. What, you bring that in at last?

PUFF. Yes — yes — you know my play is *called* the *Spanish Armada*, otherwise, egad, I have no occasion for the battle at all.

[2] C I adds: my noise!

[3] C I adds: This is blending a little of the masque with my tragedy — a new fancy you know — and very useful in my case; for as there *must be* a *procession*, I suppose Thames and all his tributary rivers to compliment Britannia with a fete in honor of the victory.

[4] C I inserts: one crown'd with alders and the other with a villa! — you take the allusions?

[5] C I: Here, Sir, come round.

[6] C I reads hereafter: There, soh! now for't! — Stand aside my dear friends! — away Thames!

[7] This entire stage-direction and Puff's concluding speech [p. 273] are from C I.

Scene changes to the sea — the fleets engage — the musick plays 'Britons strike home.' . . . Spanish fleet destroyed by fire-ships, &c. . . . English fleet advances . . . musick plays 'Rule Britannia.' . . . The procession of all the English rivers and their tributaries with their emblems, &c. begins with Handels water musick . . . ends with a chorus, to the march in Judas Maccabæus. . . . During this scene, PUFF *directs and applauds every thing —— then*]

PUFF. Well, pretty well—but not quite perfect—so ladies and gentlemen, if you please, we'll rehearse this piece again to-morrow.

CURTAIN DROPS

NOTES

THE RIVALS

PREFACE

3 A circumstance which the Author is informed has not before attended a theatrical trial: The "circumstance," explained in Sheridan's words as "the withdrawing of the Piece, to remove those imperfections in the first Representation which were too obvious to escape reprehension, and too numerous to admit of a hasty correction," had, curiously enough, an immediate parallel in contemporary French drama. *Le Barbier de Séville*, by Beaumarchais, failed at its first performance, February 23, 1775, was withdrawn, cut, and otherwise revised, and finally produced successfully.

4 The uncommon length of the piece: See Appendix, p. 314.

Mr. Harris: Thomas Harris (d. 1820), proprietor and manager of Covent Garden Theatre.

5 On subjects on which the mind, etc.: This passage excited unfavorable comment in an otherwise favorable review of *The Rivals* in *The Monthly Review*, February, 1775: "We are sorry however to see a young writer of so great promise, adopting the vulgar error of dreading imitation, and even asserting in his preface that 'on subjects on which the mind has been much informed, invention is slow of exerting itself.' The contrary is so true, that till the mind is stored with information, invention cannot exist, nor can *imagination body forth the form of things unknown*, till the poet's eye, glancing over the creation, has enabled his pen to copy and combine the images he has contemplated and admired."

As some part of the attack: See Introduction, p. lxv, foot-note 4.

6 The charge of intending any national reflection in the character of Sir Lucius O'Trigger: See Appendix, pp. 316–317.

PROLOGUE

8 11 Sons of Phœbus: "Sons of Phœbus Apollo"—*i.e.* "poets." Cf. Anstey's *Envy, a Poem* (*Works*, 1808, p. 253):

From those industrious sons of PHOEBUS,
Who twine the riddle and the REBUS,
Acrostics weave, and roundelays,
And make new legs for BOUTS-RIMEZ.

8 12 **In the Fleet**: The famous London debtors' prison. Goldsmith, *The Good-Natur'd Man*, iii, 1, plays on the word when Honeywood is trying to pass off as officers the bailiffs who have come to arrest him for debt.

Miss Rich. The gentlemen are in the marine service, I presume, sir?
Honeyw. Why, madam, they do — occasionally serve in the Fleet.

9 29 **Damn'd in Equity, escape by Flaw**: Equivalent to "when really guilty, escape on some technical legal flaw in the suit."

PROLOGUE

SPOKEN ON THE TENTH NIGHT

9 2 **Serjeant**: Of the *first* Prologue.

10 23 **The sentimental Muse**: A hit at the Sentimental Comedy of the day, to which *The Rivals*, except in the characters of Julia and Faulkland, ran counter. Cf. Introduction, pp. xliii–xlv. The "emblems" typify the conscious morality of Sentimental Comedy, whose characters, like Bunyan's, tend often to personify virtue and vice, and to possess such moral virtue as Shakespeare seems to asssociate with "rue" in terming it the "sour herb of grace" (*Richard II*, iii, 4, 105).

10 31 **Harry Woodward,** etc.: These players were all in the original cast of *The Rivals*. Cf. DRAMATIS PERSONÆ, p. 7.

ACT I. SCENE 1

11 3 **Odd's life**: A corruption of "God's life," abbreviated probably to avoid open profanity. Cf. *Odd!* "God" (**11** 17). Note throughout the play the variety of similar mincing corruptions of what Hotspur calls "good mouth-filling oaths."

12 50 **Z—ds**: "Zounds," a corruption of "God's wounds."

12 53 **Thread-papers**: Papers for rolling up skeins of thread. Cf.

Then his waist so long and taper
'Tis an absolute thread-paper.
Isaac Bickerstaffe's *Lionel and Clarissa* (1768), ii, 2.

12 54 **Set of thousands**: "A team of six horses worth thousands of pounds." Cf. "A most rich Coach and Curious Sett of Six Horses to it." T. Lucas, in Ashton's *Social Life in the Reign of Queen Anne*, I, iii.

13 65 **Mort**: Provincial expression for "a great deal."

13 67 **Lounge**: "A resort for idlers." Cf. "She went with Lady Stock to a bookseller's, whose shop served as a fashionable *lounge*." Maria Edgeworth, *Almeria* (*Tales and Novels*, Longford ed., 1893, V, 186).

13 69 **High-roomians and Low-roomians**: The Upper and Lower Rooms of Bath assemblies. In *Rebellion in Bath: or, The Battle of the Upper-Rooms: An Heroico-odico-tragico-comico Poem* (1808), a satirical description is given of fashionable society in the Upper Rooms, where are gathered

> All, save Bath *tradesmen*, and such common stuff,
> Who, banish'd from the fashionable ball,
> Cut vulgar capers in the vile *Town-hall*.

The reverse of the picture is

> that "Serbonian bog,"
> By mortals call'd the *Lower Rooms*,
> Fill'd with frights, and fetid fumes
> Exhaling from the motley crowd,
> Ill-dress'd, vulgar, rude, and loud,
> Who populate the Lower town,
> To fashionable life unknown.

13 74 **Pump-room**: Cf. Introduction, p. lx.

13 86 **Ton**: "Style." Cf. Anstey's *An Election Ball* (*Works*, 1808, pp. 210–11):

> For French is a language so very genteel . . .
> *Savoir vivre — bon ton* . . .

Cf. also Colman, *The Jealous Wife* (1761), ii, 3: "The chief Aim of the *Bon Ton* is to render Persons of Family different from the Vulgar, for whom indeed Nature serves very well."

13 89 **Odd rabbit it**: "God confound it!" but used merely as a mild expletive.

14 96 **Thoff**: "Though." Cf. *tho'ff* (**34** 305).

14 96 **Jack Gauge, the exciseman**: The name, like so many others in Sheridan, is self-explanatory. "Gauger" (gager) is an exciseman (*i.e.* revenue officer) who gages or measures the contents of casks.

14 97 **Ta'en to his carrots**: *i.e.* "Wears his natural head of reddish-yellow hair." Cf. "The lawyers and doctors had took to their own hair" (**13** 88).

14 98 **Bob:** Slang for "wig." Cf. Anstey's *An Election Ball* (*Works*, 1808, p. 212):

> The merry old bob gave his ringlets to flow,
> And dangle like sausages all in a row.

14 102 **Zooks:** A contraction of "Gadzooks." "Gadzooks," according to the doubtful etymology suggested in the *Century Dictionary*, is "apparently a corruption of *God's* (that is, Christ's) *hooks*, with reference to the *nails* with which Christ was fixed to the cross."

14 108 **Gydes' Porch:** "The lower rooms, on the Walks, kept by Mr. Gyde, had, 'from their situation, some advantages of the upper, particularly a good garden, and a retired walk on the margin of the river' (*The New Prose Bath Guide*, 1778)." Note by G. A. Aitken, *Temple* ed. *The Rivals*, p. 168.

ACT I. SCENE 2

14 4 **The Reward of Constancy:** For full discussion of all the books mentioned in this scene, see Introduction, *The Books of Lydia Languish's Circulating Library*, pp. lxviii–lxxvii.

15 9 **Mr. Bull:** J. F. Meehan, *The Famous Houses of Bath and District*, p. 197, tells of a Lewis Bull, a Bath bookseller in 1785.

15 14 **Mr. Frederick's:** Probably the store of William Frederick, a Bath bookseller from 1745 to at least 1772. See *Notes and Queries*, February 24, 1906 (10th S. V, 141).

15 29 **Blonds:** "A silk lace of two threads, twisted and formed in hexagonal meshes." Murray, *English Dictionary on Historical Principles*. Cf.

> Ear-rings, necklaces, aigrets,
> Fringes, blonds, and mignionets.

Anstey's *The New Bath Guide*, Letter iii (*Works*, 1808, p. 17).

15 30 **Sal volatile:** Sufficiently explained by Lydia's next speech. Cf. Mrs. Tryfort in Mrs. Sheridan's *A Journey to Bath* (ii, 2), "I protest I use almost an ounce of salvolatile constantly in my tea."

16 62 **Tall Irish baronet:** The Irish fortune-hunter was a frequent figure at Bath. Cf. "The speculating youth of Irish blood," explained by a foot-note as "a delicate periphrasis for what the vulgar call, in *common language*, an Irish fortune-hunter," in *Rebellion in Bath* (1808), p. 4.

16 63 **Rout:** "Large social gathering or assembly." Cf. Anstey, *The New Bath Guide* (*Works*, 1808, p. 85):

> You've heard of my Lady Bunbutter, no doubt,
> How she loves an *assembly*, *fandango*, or *rout*.

19 157 **Select words so ingeniously misapplied, without being mispronounced**: Cf. the description of Mrs. Tryfort in Mrs. Sheridan's *A Journey to Bath*, i, 5: " 'Tis the vainest poor creature, and the fondest of hard words, which without miscalling, she always takes care to misapply." See also the discussion of Sheridan's indebtedness to Mrs. Tryfort, Introduction, *The Sources of The Rivals*, pp. liii–liv.

19 166 **The Whole Duty of Man**: This "goodly outside" of eminent worthies recalls somewhat Lady Wishfort's chaste library, in Congreve's *The Way of the World* (iii, 1): "There are books over the chimney.—Quarles and Prynne, and 'The Short View of the Stage,' with Bunyan's works, to entertain you." For an account of *The Whole Duty of Man*, see Introduction, p. lxxiii.

20 180 **Thought does not become a young woman**: This, with subsequent phrases of Mrs. Malaprop—*e.g.* "these violent memories don't become a young woman"—recalls Mrs. Tryfort's phrase "so much taciturnity doesn't become a young man." *A Journey to Bath*, ii, 2.

20 182 **Illiterate**: For explanation of this, and of subsequent mistakes of Mrs. Malaprop, consult Appendix, *The Word-Blunders of Mrs. Malaprop*, pp. 320–323.

21 222 **Black art**: "*Necromancy* for a long time was erroneously spelt, under the influence of a faulty derivation; which, perhaps even now, has left traces behind it in our popular phrase, 'the Black Art.' Prophecy, by aid of the dead, as I need not tell you, is the proper meaning of the word." Trench: *English, Past and Present*, lecture viii. The erroneous spelling referred to was caused by false derivation from *niger*, "black," instead of *nekros*, "corpse."

25 335 **Paduasoy**: Rich silk, originally made at Padua. (Padua + *soie*, French, "silk.")

ACT II. SCENE I

26 20 **'Sdeath**: A corruption of "God's death." Cf. *Zounds*.

26 31 **Chairmen**: Sedan-chair bearers. Cf. Introduction, p. lxiii.

26 31 **Minority waiters**: "The explanation of Capt. Dillon is '*Minority* = out of office, out of place; an expression derived from the House of Commons.'" *Notes and Queries*, Jan. 17, 1885 (6th S. XI, 56). Another contributor to *Notes and Queries*, May 16, 1885 (6th S. XI, 391), declares: "Waiters were officers in the employ of the Custom House . . . there were 'extra-ordinary Tide Waiters, allowed no salary but only 3 shill. a Day when Imployed' (Miege, 1691). These last were undoubtedly the 'minority waiters' alluded to, who, having no fixed employment, were at the command of the first bidder."

26 44 **His gentleman**: "A valet de chambre is never called by any other name than a *gentleman* now-a-days; and the gentleman calls for his *gentleman* to come and dress him." *British Theatre* (Leipsic, 1828), *The Rivals*, p. 656, foot-note.

27 76 **Reversion**: "A right or hope of future possession or enjoyment." *Century Dictionary*. The text may be freely paraphrased as follows: "the ultimate prospect of a good inheritance from my father's estate."

30 148 **Odds whips and wheels**: The best explanation of the oaths of Bob Acres is his own (**35** 313–322). Whether Sheridan knew it or not, the "oath referential" of Sir Joseph Wittol, in Congreve's *The Old Bachelor*, is a striking parallel: "Gads-daggers-belts-blades and scabbards," ii, 1.

30 164 **German Spa**: See note on *The School for Scandal* (ii, 2, 141), p. 292.

32 208 **Squallante, rumblante, and quiverante!**: Sufficiently explained by the intonation of Bob Acres's voice.

32 209 **Minims and Crotchets**: "Half-notes" and "quarter-notes" in music. Garrick's *Epilogue* to *The Clandestine Marriage* (1766) introduces Lord Minum, Miss Crotchet, Mrs. Quaver, Colonel Trill, and others.

32 213 **Is not music the food of love**: Recalling the opening line of Shakespeare's *Twelfth Night*, "If music be the food of love, play on."

32 220 **When absent from my soul's delight**: Prolonged but fruitless search through contemporary literature, both musical and dramatic, has resulted in the discovery of no song closer to Sheridan's line than one beginning, "When absent from the nymph I love," *Calliope: or The Vocal Enchantress*, London (1788), p. 176; also in *The Scots Musical Museum*, Edinburgh (1787), p. 54, both containing many songs older than Sheridan's play.

32 222 **Go, gentle Gales!**: The refrain of *The faithful lover: a Choice Song*, given, with the music, in *Clio and Euterpe, or British Harmony* (London, 1762), Vol. III, p. 1. The refrain and opening stanza run as follows:

> Go, gentle gales,
> Go, bear my sighs away,
> And to my love,
> The tender notes convey.

As some lone dove abandoned and forlorn,
With ceaseless plaints my absent love I mourn.

32 224 **My heart's my own, my will is free:** A song sung by Rosetta, in *Love in a Village* (i, 1), a comic opera, by Isaac Bickerstaffe. It may be found in *The British Drama: A Collection of the most esteemed Tragedies, Comedies, Operas, & Farces in the English Language* (London, 1826), II, 1026 (edition of 1837, II, 218). The words, though not ascribed to the author, may be found also in *The Nightingale: A Choice Selection of the Most Admired Popular Songs, Heroic, Plaintive, Sentimental, Humourous and Bacchanalian* (London, n.d. 1830?). There are two stanzas, the first of which runs as follows:

My heart's my own, my will is free,
And so shall be my voice;
No mortal man shall wed with me,
Till first he's made my choice.

32 227 **Catches:** Usually three-part songs, where each of the trio catches up the refrain or words in turn. Cf. *Twelfth Night*, ii, 3, where a catch is sung by Sir Andrew, Sir Toby, and the Clown.

33 265 **Amorous palming puppies:** Cf. *The Winter's Tale*, i, 2, where Leontes suspects Polixines of intriguing with Hermione: "But to be paddling palms and pinching fingers."

33 266 **Managed:** Taught in a riding-school. (French, *manège*).

34 277 **Looby:** Obsolete for "lubber."

34 299 **Frogs and tambours:** *Frogs* were ornamented braided loops to secure the coat or cloak; *tambours* were tambour-frames, or the silk fabrics embroidered on them. Cf. *School for Scandal*, ii, 1 (**129** 36). In the *British Theatre* (1828) is the foot-note (p. 658) on this passage: "The people in England call frenchmen frogs, and at that time our *male* fashions were imported from France; now, we have the advantage, and we have trimmed the Frenchman's jacket these many years. Tambour-work for frills, ruffs, etc."

34 305 **Tho'ff:** "Though." Cf. **14** 96.

35 321 **The oath should be an echo to the sense:** "A parody on Pope's *Essay on Criticism:*

The sound must seem an echo to the sense."

Note by G. A. Aitken, *Temple* ed. *The Rivals*, p. 168.

35 326 **D—ns have had their day:** "There seems to have been a revival of 'strange oaths' about 1775, the year of Sheridan's 'Rivals,' in which we find Bob Acres stating that 'plain damns have had their day':

— old profanities had indeed almost lost their meaning by over use. It was felt that swearing must be modified if it could not be done without; — that is, either softened to suit the aspirations of the time for 'elegance,' or given a turn, quaint, fantastic, or startling." *The Early Diary of Frances Burney*, II, 278, foot-note. (Some interesting contemporary references are given.)

38 432 **Bull in Cox's Museum**: Mr. Cox, an ingenious London jeweler and mechanician, exhibited his collection of fifty-six mechanical curiosities, valued at £197,500, in 1773 and 1774, in Spring Gardens — "Tickets a Quarter-Guinea each." The British Museum contains "A Descriptive Inventory of the several exquisite and magnificent Pieces of Mechanism and Jewellery, comprised in the Schedule annexed to an Act of Parliament, made in the 13th George III., for enabling Mr. James Cox, of the City of London, Jeweller, to dispose of his Museum by way of Lottery." London, 1774. Mention is made of "The Curious Bull." For fuller information see *Notes and Queries*, July 25, 1857 (2d S. IV, 75), and August 11, 1894 (8th S. VI, 118). A scrap of conversational comment on Cox's Museum is in letter 23, Miss Burney's *Evelina* (1778) — in the edition of J. M. Dent & Co. (1901), I, 131.

ACT II. SCENE 2

41 16 **South Parade**: Cf. Anstey's *The New Bath Guide* (*Works*, 1808, p. 52):

> O the charming party's made!
> Some to walk the South Parade.

42 54 **Habeas corpus**: A writ to safeguard personal liberty, "requiring the body of a person restrained of liberty to be brought before the judge or into court, that the lawfulness of the restraint may be investigated and determined." *Century Dictionary*.

ACT III. SCENE 1

48 118 **The Grove**: The "Orange Grove," not far from the North Parade, a fashionable resort named after the Prince of Orange. J. F. Meehan, *Famous Houses of Bath and District* (Bath, 1901), devotes an entire chapter (pp. 145–148) to "The Orange Grove, 1757," and reproduces a picture of the Grove taken from a hand-painted eighteenth-century fan. Cf. Anstey's *The New Bath Guide* (*Works*, 1808, p. 50):

> Whether thou art wont to rove
> By Parade, or Orange Grove.

48 123 **Promethean**; Prometheus, with the aid of Minerva, lighted his torch at the chariot of the sun, and brought down fire to earth, thus enabling man to master nature and wild beasts.

ACT III. SCENE 3

55 89 **Nick**: In present usage, "the nick of time." Cf. iv, 3 (**78** 20).

55 95 **Doubt**: "Suspect," or possibly "fear." Cf. "I doubt some foul play." *Hamlet*, i, 2, 256.

ACT III. SCENE 4

59 3 **An'**: "If."

59 3 **Monkeyrony**: David's corruption of "macaroni," the frequent eighteenth-century word for "dandy." Cf. *School for Scandal*, ii, 2 (**133** 12).

60 12 **Oons!**: Like *Zounds* (**12** 50) a contraction of "God's wounds."

60 19 **Balancing, and chasing, and boring**: Terms of dancing. A foot-note (p. 666) in the *British Theatre* (1828) suggests French explanations: "Balancer, chasser, faire des pas de Bourrée." The *bourrée* was a lively dance, popular especially in Auvergne. In Etheredge's *The Man of Mode; or Sir Fopling Flutter* (1676), Sir Fopling, who has "lately arrived piping hot from Paris," says: "I am fit for nothing but low dancing now, a *corant*, a *bourée*, or a *menuet* (iv, 1).

60 27 **Coupee**: Murray, *English Dictionary on Historical Principles*, defines the noun as, "A dance step formerly much used; the dancer rests on one foot and passes the other forward or backward, making a sort of salutation."

60 33 **Allemandes**: German dances. Cf. Modern "German" in dancing.

60 38 **Antigallican Toes**: "The same thought occurs in the Wasps of Aristophanes, where the old man, on being desired to put on a pair of Lacedemonian boots, endeavours to excuse himself by saying that one of his toes is *πανυ μισολακων* — a sworn enemy to the Lacedemonians." Genest, *Some Account of the English Stage*, etc., V, 461.

62 94 **New room**: The new Assembly rooms were opened in 1771. Sheridan himself wrote some humorous verses on the occasion, which appeared in *The Bath Chronicle*, October, 1771. *The Critical Review*, December, 1774, notices, among new publications, "The Rival Ball Rooms, or, a Collection of all the Pieces published in Favour of the New and Old Assembly-Rooms at Bath, during the Disputes about settling the Public Amusements, in the Autumn Season, 1774." Cf. v, 3 (**102** 274).

62 101 **Pinchbeck:** An alloy of copper and zinc, named after the inventor, Pinchbeck, a London watchmaker of the eighteenth century, who used it in cheap jewelry.

63 102 **The milk of human kindness:** Shakespeare's phrase, *Macbeth*, i, 5, 18.

63 104 **"I could do such deeds":** An inquirer in *Notes and Queries*, March 28, 1896 (8th S. IX, 247), asks if this is "a genuine quotation." To the query is appended this suggestion: "Is not the allusion to Hamlet —

> Now could I drink hot blood,
> And do such bitter business, &c.;

and does not Bob Acres misquote?"

63 129 **King's-Mead-fields:** Towards the southwest of the city. "KING'S MEAD SQUARE is almost South of *Beaufort Buildings*. The Name arises from its being executed on a Piece of Ground called *King's Meadow*." (Quoted from Wood's *History of Bath*, in Earle's *A Guide to the Knowledge of Bath, Ancient, and Modern*, 1864, p. 171.)

ACT IV. SCENE 1

65 9 **Quarter-staff:** Cf. Gurth's quarter-staff contest with the Miller *Ivanhoe*, Chap. 2.

65 10 **Sharps and snaps:** "Sharpers," or, in David's words, "bloodthirsty cormorants." Cf. "Take heed of a *snap*, sir; h' 'as a cozening countenance: I do not like his way." Fletcher, *Spanish Curate*, ii, 1.

65 20 **This honour seems to me to be a marvellous false friend:** With this speech of David, compare Falstaff's "catechism" on honour ending with "Honour is a mere scutcheon." *Henry Fourth*, Part I, v, 1, 143.

ACT IV. SCENE 2

69 14 **Hesperian curls:** The passage which Mrs. Malaprop has so nicely deranged is in *Hamlet*, iii, 4, 56–59:

> Hyperion's curls, the front of Jove himself,
> An eye like Mars, to threaten and command;
> A station like the herald Mercury
> New-lighted on a heaven-kissing hill.

72 105 **Bedlam:** The hospital of St. Mary of Bethlehem (corrupted to "Bedlam") in London, became a hospital for lunatics early in the fifteenth century. Shakespeare uses "Bedlam" for "madman," *King Lear*, iii, 7, 103.

74 163 **"Youth's the season made for joy"**: The opening line of a song in the second act of Gay's *The Beggar's Opera* (in sc. 4, ed. 1728):

Youth's the Season made for Joys,
Love is then our Duty,
She alone who that employs,
Well deserves her Beauty.
Let's be gay,
While we may,
Beauty's a Flower despis'd in decay.

77 250 **Cerberus**: The three-headed dog who guarded the entrance to the infernal regions.

ACT IV. SCENE 3

79 50 **Spring Gardens**: A favorite pleasure resort on the east side of the river, famous for public breakfasts and evening parties. See J. F. Meehan's *Famous Houses of Bath and District*, pp. 24, 85. Cf. also

He said it would greatly our pleasure promote,
If we all for Spring Gardens set out in a boat.

Anstey's *The New Bath Guide*, Letter xiii (*Works*, 1808, p. 86).

80 64 **So that matter's settled**: "This is the general character of the Irish with respect to duelling. Lord Byron says, Don Juan, Cant. IV, when Haidee's father points a pistol at the young hero

But after being fired at once or twice,
The ear becomes more Irish and less nice."

Foot-note, p. 671, *British Theatre*, Leipsic (1828).

81 122 **"Not unsought be won"**: From Milton's *Paradise Lost*, viii, 502–3:

Her virtue, and the conscience of her worth,
That would be wooed, and not unsought be won.

ACT V. SCENE 1

87 156 **Smithfield**: Smithfield was long the cattle-market of London.

87 159 **Scotch parson**: An excellent illustration of the frequent elopements to Scotland is in the under-plot of Goldsmith's *The Good Natur'd Man* (1768), much of which is taken up with the attempt of Leontine and Olivia to elope to Scotland. Especially to the point are the words of the Landlady of the inn where the post-chaise is to meet the lovers. To Olivia she airs her views on "Scotch marriages," and attempts to prove her own dictum, "Scotch marriages seldom turn out well." (v, 1.)

89 228 **Fire-office:** A term used in England for "the office of a fire-insurance company," but here, of course, misused by David in a way worthy of Mrs. Malaprop.

90 246 **Derbyshire Putrifactions:** Probably Mrs. Malaprop means "Petrifactions," for Derbyshire is famous for curious rock formations. Oulton, *The History of the Theatres of London*, 1796, records (I, 75) under date of January 8, 1779, the production at Drury Lane Theatre of a successful pantomime, *The Wonders of Derbyshire: or, Harlequin in the Peak.*

ACT V. SCENE 2

90 1 **A sword seen in the streets of Bath:** Beau Nash passed stringent rules against dueling. Cf. Introduction, *Eighteenth Century Bath*, p. lx. "A duel, fought by torch-light in the Grove between Taylor and Clarke, two notorious gamesters, gave Nash an opportunity of making the law absolute, '*that no swords should on any account be worn in Bath.*'" *Meylers' Original Bath Guide* (Bath, n. d.), p. 14.

ACT V. SCENE 3

94 34 **The Abbey:** The Abbey Church at Bath.
102 274 **New Rooms:** Cf. note on iii, 4, 94 (p. 283).

EPILOGUE

The *Epilogue* to *The Rivals* attracted general commendation. *The Morning Chronicle* (January 18, 1775) calls it "one of the most excellent and poetical epilogues we ever remember to have heard"; a contributor to *The Morning Chronicle* (January 20) declares that the epilogue "after a vein of elegant humour, runs to the conclusion in some as beautiful lines as ever did credit to our language." Many others join in the chorus of praise.
103 9 **Cit:** "Citizen."

THE SCHOOL FOR SCANDAL

DEDICATION

107 A Portrait; addressed to Mrs. Crewe: This was at first circulated in manuscript. In a letter to the Countess of Ossory, Horace Walpole writes, October 8, 1777 [Toynbee edition (1903–5), X, 134]: "My nephew, George Cholmondeley (for I am uncle to all the world), dined here to-day, and repeated part of a very good copy of verses from

Sheridan to Mrs. Crewe. Has your Ladyship seen them? I trust they will not long retain their MS.-hood."

Frances Anne, daughter of Fulke Greville, married, in 1776, John Crewe. She was a famous beauty of Sheridan's day. At Crewe Hall she frequently entertained Sheridan, Burke, and Sir Joshua Reynolds. Frances Burney writes, describing her meeting with the Sheridans, January 27, 1779: "The elegance of Mrs. Sheridan's beauty is unequalled by any I ever saw, except Mrs. Crewe." For proofs of the intimacy between the Crewes and the Sheridans see Fraser Rae, *Sheridan*, II, 125, 128–9, 132, 140–1, 159, 183.

108 25 **Amoret**: Mrs. Crewe is celebrated under the name *Amoret* in Fox's verses printed at Walpole's Strawberry Hill Press, in 1775.

108 36 **Reynolds**: Sir Joshua Reynolds (1723–1792), the famous portrait-painter. "While the comedy of *The Rivals* was applauded and the talk of the Town, Sir Joshua Reynolds was finishing Mrs. Sheridan's portrait as St. Cecilia." Fraser Rae, *Sheridan*, I, 283–4. (See also I, 279.)

108 39 **Granby**: Mary Isabella, Marchioness of Granby. In 1779, four years after their marriage, her husband became Duke of Rutland.

108 40 **Devon's eyes**: Georgina, Duchess of Devonshire. She married the fifth Duke of Devonshire in 1774. The especial beauty of her eyes is illustrated by the story told of a certain dustman who was so far affected as to cry out, "Lord love you, my lady, let me light my pipe at your eyes." In Madame d'Arblay's Diary, June 26, 1781 (Austin Dobson ed. 1904 —, II, 3) is this passage: "Among other folks we discussed the two rival duchesses, Rutland [*i.e. Granby*] and Devonshire. 'The former,' he [a certain Mr. Crutchley] said, 'must, he fancied, be very weak and silly, as he knew that she endured being admired to her face, and complimented perpetually, both upon her beauty and her dress' . . . The Duchess of Devonshire, I fancy, has better parts." An extended discussion is given in *Notes and Queries*, March 28, 1896 (8th S. IX, 256). Cf. Anstey's *Envy, a Poem* (*Works*, 1808, p. 250):

> She breathes her gently-warbling lays
> To beautiful GEORGINA's praise.

110 96 **Greville**: Mrs. Greville, wife of Fulke Greville, envoy extraordinary to the elector of Bavaria, in 1766, and mother of Mrs. Crewe, wrote some verse, notably an *Ode to Indifference*. Sheridan, in dedicating to her *The Critic*, speaks of Mrs. Greville's "dislike to the reputation of critical taste, as well as of poetical talent," and implies that she makes " a fastidious concealment of the most elegant productions of judgment and fancy."

110 99 **Millar:** An eighteenth-century variant for Miller — Lady Miller. Her literary court is fully described in the passages quoted from Horace Walpole and Frances Burney (Introduction, pp. lxi–lxii). A satirical poem, BATH; *its* BEAUTIES *and* AMUSEMENTS (in *The Annual Register*, 1777), speaks of the " mystic vase with laurel crown'd," and the " consecrated ground " where

> Sappho's hands the last sad rites dispense
> To mangled poetry and murder'd sense.

Her followers are

> All Apollo's sons from top to bottom —
> Tho' poor Apollo wonders where he got them.

Anstey has a poem (*Works*, 1808, pp. 259–262) entitled *Winter Amusements*, an Ode, read at Lady Miller's Assembly, December 3, 1778.

DRAMATIS PERSONÆ

111 In addition to the rough indications of Sheridan's manuscript as to *Dramatis Personæ*, the original cast of *The School for Scandal* included *Moses*, Mr. Baddeley; *Snake*, Mr. Packer; *Careless*, Mr. Farren; *Sir Harry Bumper*, Mr. Gawdry; *Lady Teazle*, Mrs. Abington; *Maria*, Miss P. Hopkins; *Lady Sneerwell*, Miss Sherry; *Mrs. Candour*, Miss Pope. *Young Surface*, in Sheridan's list, is, of course, *Joseph Surface*. The part of *Miss Verjuice* was blended with that of *Snake*. *Spunge* became *Trip*, a part taken by Mr. Lamash.

PROLOGUE

111 5 **Vapours:** An exceedingly common ailment of fashionable ladies of the eighteenth century, differing from " an attack of the blues " chiefly in its superior exclusiveness.

111 8 **Quantum sufficit:** " As much as suffices," *i.e.* " plenty."

111 15 **Sal volatile:** See note on *The Rivals*, i, 2, 30 (p. 278).

112 18 **Poz:** A slang abbreviation of " positive," sometimes spelled " pos." Cf. " She shall dress me and flatter me — for I will be flattered, that's *pos.*" Addison: *The Drummer*, iii 2. For interesting comment upon the habit of slang abbreviation see *The Tatler*, No. 230 (written by Swift), and *The Spectator*, No. 135.

112 20 **Dash and star:** A frequent method of reference to the principals in fashionable intrigues. See especially note on the " *Tête-à-Tête in the Town and Country Magazine*," p. 289.

112 22 **Grosvenor Square:** A fashionable residence section of London, not far from Hyde Park.

112 36 **Don Quixote:** The "hydra" which Cervantes took the road to seek was the extravagant romance of chivalry. Sheridan, "our young Don Quixote," first took the road in *The Rivals*. Perhaps Garrick spoke wiser than he was ware of, for in *The Rivals* Sheridan had held up to ridicule the extravagant sentimental novel, as Cervantes in *Don Quixote* held up to ridicule the extravagant romance of chivalry.

ACT I. SCENE I

112 Stage direction: In the current texts, Lappet, the maid, does not appear, and the speeches of Miss Verjuice are transferred to Snake.

113 8 **Demirep.:** A woman of questionable character (*demi+rep* in "reputation"). Cf. "demi-monde."

113 15 **Pallmall:** Pall Mall, the famous London street.

113 27 **A Tête-à-Tête in the Town and Country Magazine:** In Sheridan's day, a striking local allusion. *The Town and Country Magazine, or Universal Repository of Knowledge, Instruction, and Entertainment,* appeared first in January, 1769. The *Tête-à-Têtes* were a series of monthly sketches of fashionable intrigues published uninterruptedly from the first number down to the year of *The School for Scandal*, as well as thereafter. A general explanation of their scope is given at the beginning of the first history, *Dorimant and Maria*, January, 1769: "The gallantry of the present period will, probably, make a greater *eclat* in the annals of the polite world than all the Histories of court intrigues that have engaged the attention of any preceding historian or biographer; and we flatter ourselves the anecdotes which we shall be able to furnish will be a means of handing down to posterity a lively idea of the prevailing beauties, and their most zealous admirers, of this æra." Sometimes assumed names are given, as in the first history. A few random titles will suggest other methods: *Mrs. R—— and the Libertine Macaroni, Memoirs of Lord Le D—— and Miss B——y, Miss P——m and the Hibernian hero.* The purpose of these histories is further explained in the *Advertisements* prefixed to subsequent volumes. In that of January, 1770, for example occurs this passage: "With respect to the History of Têtes-à-têtes, an article received with universal applause, we shall only remark, that it was not undertaken to gratify malignity, or to indulge impertinent curiosity but to hold up a mirror to the *offending* parties by which they might see their own likeness reflected in such a manner, as to force them to renounce the *fashionable vices* of the age; a reformation much more likely to be effected by ridicule than sober reasoning." The *Advertisement*, January, 1771, testifies to " the menaces that have been used on the one hand, and the allurements and bribes which have offered on the other, to suppress the appearance of particular memoirs."

116 130 **Execution**: Here equivalent probably to " a sheriff's sale of property to pay debts."

120 256 **Got rid of her dropsy**: Possibly this may be a reminiscence of Mirabell's words, Congreve's *The Way of the World*, i, 1: " The imputation of an affair with a young fellow, which I carried so far, that I told her the malicious town took notice that she was grown fat of a sudden; and when she lay in of a dropsy, persuaded her she was reported to be in labour."

121 294 **Conversazione**: A meeting for conversation, " primarily on topics connected with literature or art."

122 308 **Petrarch's Laura**: Laura was the heroine of the verses of Petrarch, one of the illustrious classical Italian poets of the fourteenth century.

122 309 **Waller's Sacharissa**: Waller, a seventeenth-century English poet, gave the poetical name of " Sacharissa " to Lady Dorothy Sidney, for whose hand he sued without success.

123 343 **Tunbridge**: Tunbridge Wells, like Bath, a famous English Spa.

124 375 **Old Jewry**: A London street, near the Bank of England. The name, and the remembrance of Charles's dealings with Moses and Mr. Premium, amply explain the context. Cf. Transfer's speech in Foote's *The Minor* (1761), ii: " Then I totter'd away to Nebuchadnezzar Zebulon, in the Old Jewry, but it happen'd to be Saturday; and they never *touch* on the Sabbath, you know."

124 378 **Irish Tontine**: Tonti, an Italian banker, devised a kind of life annuity as a means of obtaining government loans. Essentially the tontine scheme provides for the regular distribution, to surviving members, of the income of a common fund contributed in the first place by the subscribers, the principal going ultimately to the last survivor. *The Wrong Box*, by Robert Louis Stevenson and Lloyd Osbourne, is a laughable story of the struggles of the Finsbury brothers, the last survivors of a valuable tontine. Government tontines usually paid life annuities to surviving contributors, but took possession of the principal of the fund. In the ten years from 1763 to 1773 the Irish National Debt had almost doubled. Failure of the Absentee Bill in the Irish House of Commons cut off expected revenue. " In order to meet immediate wants, £265,000 was raised by the method of Tontine Annuities and Stamp

Duties." Lecky, *A History of England in the Eighteenth Century*, IV, chap. 16 (p. 447, ed. D. Appleton & Co., 1882).

ACT II. SCENE 1

129 21 **Pantheon**: A concert-hall in Oxford Street. Cf. Goldsmith's *She Stoops to Conquer* (ii, 1) where Mrs Hardcastle ignorantly confuses fashionable resorts with vulgar: "But who can have a manner that has never seen the Pantheon, the Grotto Gardens, the Borough, and such places where the nobility chiefly resort?" William B. Boulton, *The Amusements of Old London* (1901), gives (I, 116–118) an interesting account of the opening of the Pantheon in 1772.

129 22 **Fête Champêtre**; "An open-air festival." Cf. review in *The Town and Country Magazine*, August, 1774, of *La Fête Champêtre*: "A *very unpoetical* representation of the rural festival lately given by lord Stanley." Cf. "Beelzebub's Cotillon, or Proserpine's Fête Champêtre," *The Critic*, i, 2 (**240** 246).

129 28 **Oons**: Like "zounds," a contraction of "God's wounds."

129 36 **Tambour**: "Embroidery-frame." Cf. *The Rivals*, ii, 1, (note, p. 281).

130 47 **Pope Joan**: "An old game of cards, resembling its modern derivative newmarket or stop." *Standard Dictionary*.

130 56 **Fly Cap**: A head-dress made, by means of wire, to stand out from the cushion on which the hair was dressed. "Its name seems to come from the resemblance of its sides to wings." *Century Dictionary*.

130 57 **Blew-bottle**: "Bluebottle," an insect with blue abdomen.

132 117 **Rid on hurdles**: The hurdle was a rough cart or sledge on which criminals were taken to the place of execution. See the quotation from Macaulay in the following note.

132 118 **Clippers of Reputation**: The figure of speech is derived from the practice of clipping the edges of coins, a practice that led to milling the edges to prevent loss. "It was to no purpose that the vigorous laws against coining and clipping were vigorously executed.... Hurdles, with four, five, six wretches convicted of counterfeiting or mutilating the money of the realm, were dragged month after month up Holborn Hill." Macaulay: *History of England*, IV, chap. 21 (p. 562, Harper & Bros., 1865).

ACT II. SCENE 2

133 7 **Taking the Dust in High Park**: Hyde Park, the fashionable drive of London. The phrase occurs in some early verses of Sheridan from which he drew Sir Benjamin's quatrain. "And followed by John *take the Dust* in high Park." (See note on **133** 11.)

133 8 **Duodecimo:** The technical term of the book-publisher here means simply "diminutive."

133 11 **'Sure never were seen,** etc.: This quatrain Sheridan reproduced from a set of thirty-six earlier lines. (See Fraser Rae, *Sheridan*, I, 330–331.)

Sure never were seen two such sweet little Ponies
Other horses are clowns, these macaronies.
And to give them this title I'm sure isn't wrong,
Their legs are so slim and their tails are as long.

Moore, *Life of Sheridan*, I, 257–8, calls attention to the similar scene in Congreve's *The Double Dealer*, iii, 10. [There are but three scenes in the act in such modern editions as the *Mermaid*.] His idea that Lady Froth's verses on her coachman may have suggested Sir Benjamin's verses is very probably correct.

133 12 **Macaronies:** The "macaroni" was "a London exquisite of the eighteenth century. Hence arose the use of the word in contemporary doggerel of 'Yankee Doodle' —

(He) stuck a feather in his cap,
And called it *macaroni* —

and its application as a name, in the American revolution, to a body of Maryland troops remarkable for their showy uniforms." Murray, *English Dictionary on Historical Principles*. Cf. Sheridan's line, "In the way I am met by some smart Macaroni," in the verses from which an extract is given in the note on **133** 11.

133 17 **Phœbus:** The reference is to Phœbus Apollo as god of poetry.

135 80 **A character's dead at every word**: More than one critic has instanced the obvious parallel:

At every word a reputation dies.
Pope, *The Rape of the Lock*, iii, 16.

136 98 **The Ring**: Charles II laid out in Hyde Park a drive around an enclosed circle about three hundred yards in diameter. One set of coaches circled the drive in one direction, and another set in the opposite direction, thus affording the fashionable a chance to exchange greetings. The history of "The Ring" is fully described by Boulton, *The Amusements of Old London*, II, 127–137. In Colman's *The Jealous Wife* (1761), a duel is appointed "by the Ring in Hyde-Park" (iv, 1).

137 141 **Spa:** A watering place in Belgium. The name "Spa" was then applied to other places frequented on account of mineral springs. Cf. "The German Spa," *The Rivals*, ii, 1 (**30** 164).

138 181 **Law Merchant:** "Mercantile law."

138 182 **In all cases of slander currency,** etc.: Sir Peter refers to the familiar fact that the endorser of a note is responsible, if the original drawer of it fails to meet its demands.

140 246 **Cicisbeo** : Italian word for "one who plays the gallant to a married woman." The word appears, with various spellings, half a dozen times in Mrs. Sheridan's *A Journey to Bath*. The "little liberties" allowed a *cicisbey* are there discussed by Lady Filmot and Edward, iii, 1.

ACT III. SCENE 1

144 3 **Jet** : "gist." *Century Dictionary* quotes besides the present passage the following: "It often happens that the *jett* or principal point in the debate is lost in these personal contests." Moritz, *Travels in England in* 1782 (trans).

145 37 **A Tear for Pity** : The quotation is from Shakespeare's 2 *Henry IV*, iv, 4, 31–32. Sheridan quotes the lines accurately, except for the insertion of "the" before "day," but the current texts print Rowley's speech,

a heart to pity, etc.

146 77 **Crutched Friars**: A London street, not far from the Tower of London, named from an old Convent of Crossed or Crouched Friars (Fratres Sanctæ Crucis). See Hare's *Walks in London* (5th ed., I, 384).

148 135 **If the borrower is a minor**: The Annuity Bill (see note following) safeguarded minors by providing that contracts with them for annuities should be void. Cf. **148** 144–151.

148 141 **Annuity Bill**: This reference was a decided "local hit." On April 25, 1777, in the House of Commons it was "Ordered, that a Committee be appointed to take into Consideration the Laws now in being against Usury, and the present Practice of purchasing Annuities for the Life of the Grantor; and to report their Opinion thereupon to the House." (*Journals of the House of Commons*, 17 Geo. III, vol. 36, p. 440.) The bill was presented and read April 29 and passed May 12. On May 15 it was reported that "The Lords have agreed to the Bill, intituled, An Act for registering the Grants of Life Annuities, and for the better Protection of Infants against such Grants; without any Amendment." (*Ibid.*, p. 505). (For full report and discussion of Bill, see *Ibid.*, pp. 489–492.)

ACT III. SCENE 2

155 34 **Bags**: "Bags for the hair behind." *British Theatre* (Leipsic, 1828), foot-note, p. 691. Cf. "Bag-wig, and lac'd ruffles." Anstey, *The New Bath Guide* (*Works*, 1808, p. 65).

155 55 **Nobody throws off faster**: "Nobody discards faster from his wardrobe." Cf. Trip's speech, **156** 62–68.

156 65–66 **Reversion** and **post-obit**: Legal terms used by the over-clever servant to signify "future claims on my master's wardrobe."

156 67 **Point**: "Point-lace."

ACT III. SCENE 3

157 15 **Hazard Regimen**: Explained by the previous words of Careless, "Harry diets himself for gaming." Hazard, a dicing game of pure luck, was very popular with eighteenth-century gamblers. Almack's Club (later Brooks's), opened in 1764, was a famous private gaming resort, where Charles James Fox was perhaps the most conspicuous figure. For a full description of hazard, and the gaming at Almack's, see Boulton, *The Amusements of Old London*, I, 134–149.

157 33 **Give a round of her Peers**: "Propose in turn the health of mistresses equal to her."

158 48 **Song and chorus**: In *Notes and Queries*, September 26, 1874 (5th S. II, 245), is made the doubtful contention that Sheridan derived this song from Sir John Suckling's "A health to the nut-brown lass" in his play, *The Goblins*, ii, 1.

159 91 **Wine does but draw forth a man's natural qualities**: The old Latin phrase, "In vino veritas." Thackeray refers to it in the memorable description of Dick Steele, *Henry Esmond*, Book 2, chap. 11: "If there is verity in wine, according to the old adage, what an amiable-natured character Dick's must have been."

161 162 **Bough-pots**: "Pots for holding flowers or boughs."

162 185 **Post-obit**: Here, "a bond for payment of the debt upon Sir Oliver's death." Cf. note on iii, 2, 66 (p. 294, above).

163 229 **Race-cups and corporation-bowls**: "Gold — or silver — cups won at races; bowls received as presents from the city." *British Theatre* (Leipsic, 1828), foot-note, p. 693.

ACT IV. SCENE 1

166 34 **Duke of Marlborough**: John Churchill, Duke of Marlborough (1650–1722), the famous British general of Queen Anne's reign, victor at Blenheim, Ramillies, Oudenarde, and Malplaquet (September 11, 1709). Marlborough and his campaigns figure prominently in Thackeray's *Henry Esmond*, Book II. Hardcastle, in Goldsmith's *She Stoops to Conquer* (1773), is full of "old stories of Prince Eugene [his associate general] and the Duke of Marlborough."

166 49 **Kneller:** Portrait painter (1646–1723), of German birth, but famous for his portraits of many English sovereigns and nobles. "His paintings vary in excellence, the best being of the highest order, while others, even when authenticated, seem unworthy of a great reputation." Lionel Cust in *Dictionary of National Biography.*

167 70 **Woolsack:** "The Chancellor's seat in the House of Lords, is on a woolsack; and it thus applies to all belonging to the law." *British Theatre* (Leipsic, 1828) foot-note, p. 694.

170 177 **Take a hundred pounds of it immediately to old Stanley:** Charles's attitude in money matters is strongly reminiscent of Honeywood's in Goldsmith's *The Good Natur'd Man.* In the opening scene, Honeywood is reproached by Jarvis (who corresponds to Rowley) for sending ten guineas "to the poor gentleman and his children in the Fleet," while he shrugs his shoulders at paying just debts.

171 191 **Hazard:** See note on iii, 3, 15 (p. 294).

ACT IV. SCENE 2

172 38 **With the gloss on:** "This is one of the phrases that seem to have perplexed the taste of Sheridan, — and upon so minute a point, as, whether it should be 'with the gloss on,' or, 'with the gloss on them.' After various trials of it in both ways, he decided, as might be expected from his love of idiom, for the former." Moore, *Life of Sheridan*, I, 247, foot-note.

ACT IV. SCENE 3

181 289 **An absolute Joseph:** The reference to the Biblical Joseph who resisted the temptations of Potiphar's wife (*Genesis*, chap. 39) is, perhaps on the author's part unintentionally, whimsical in the mouth of Sheridan's Joseph.

185 436 **Surface enters just as Charles throws down the Screen:** Cumberland, whom Sheridan later satirized as Sir Fretful Plagiary in *The Critic,* deigned to defend his own use of a screen in *The West Indian* (1771) in these words: "I could name one now living, who has made such happy use of his screen in a comedy of the very first merit, that if Aristotle himself had written a whole chapter professedly against *screens* and Jerry Collier had edited it with notes and illustrations, I would not have placed Lady Teazle out of ear-shot to have saved their ears from the pillory: but if either of these worthies could have pointed out an expedient to have got Joseph Surface off the stage, pending that scene, with any reasonable conformity to nature, they would have done more good to the drama than either of them have done harm; and that is saying a great deal." *Memoirs of Richard Cumberland, Written by Himself* (1807), I, 303.

Moore, *Life of Sheridan*, I, 245, gives a note from Garrick to Sheridan, dated May 11, 1777, containing these remarks: "A gentleman who is as mad as myself about ye School remark'd, that the characters upon the stage at ye falling of the screen stand too long before they speak; — I thought so too ye first night: — he said it was the same on ye 2nd, and was remark'd by others; — tho' they should be astonish'd, and a little petrify'd, yet it may be carry'd to too great a length."

ACT V. SCENE 1

190 79 **Rupees**: Silver coins of India, valued at two shillings.

190 79 **Pagodas**: Gold coins of India, valued at eight shillings, so called since they had on the reverse side the figure of a pagoda.

190 82 **Avadavats**: Small singing-birds of India, having red and black plumage flecked with white, and red beaks. In a letter to her husband (1786), Mrs. Sheridan mentions "my avadavats." Sheridan wrote an "Elegy on the lamented death of an Avadavat," quoted by Fraser Rae, *Sheridan*, II, 121–2.

190 82 **Indian Crackers**: A correspondent in *Notes and Queries* (6th S. II, 199), September 4, 1880, in comment on Sheridan's text, writes: "As well as I can recollect they did not make more or less noise in detonating than those usually supplied by pyrotechnists, but they differed from them in form and were tastefully got up with coloured paper."

ACT V. SCENE 2

195 78 **A thrust in second**: ("Seconde," also "segoon") A term in fencing for "a thrust, parry, or other movement downward toward the left."

195 93 **Salt-Hill where He had been to see the Montem**: It was formerly the custom for Eton school boys to go every third year on Whit-Tuesday to Salt-Hill, a hillock on the Bath road, and there exact contributions, called *salt-money*, from spectators or passers-by, to defray the university expenses of the senior scholar or school captain. (L. *processus ad montem*, going to the hill.)

199 234 **Paragraphs about Mr. S——, Lady T——, and Sir P——**: See note on i, 1, 27 (p. 289).

ACT V. SCENE 3

203 84 **A. B.'s at the Coffee-House**: A reference to appointments made at the coffee-house with intentional concealment of name, much in the present fashion of the use of initials in newspaper advertisements and personals. "It is customary to give one's address in an Advertisement, A. B. at a Coffee-house, or other place." *British Theatre* (Leipsic, 1828), p. 705, foot-note.

EPILOGUE

210 By George Colman: George Colman, the elder, proprietor of the Haymarket Theatre, author, among other plays, of *Polly Honeycombe* (1760), from which Dibdin claimed Sheridan took Lydia Languish.

210 5 **Bayes**: Bayes, a caricature of Dryden, was the principal character in *The Rehearsal* (1671), chiefly written by George Villiers, second Duke of Buckingham. "Bayes" here means "poet" or "dramatist," as in the *Epilogue* to Goldsmith's *She Stoops to Conquer:*

> The Bar-maid now for your protection prays,
> Turns female barrister, and pleads for Bayes.

210 28 **Loo**: A favorite eighteenth-century game of cards.

210 28 **Vole**: Winning of all the tricks.

211 29 **Seven's the main**: A throw of the dice. In hazard, the caster "called his 'main,' by naming any number from five to nine, rattled the dice in the box, and threw them on the table. If the number of his main appeared he won his stake." Boulton, *The Amusements of Old London*, I, 135.

211 30 **Hot cockles**: "*Hot Cockles*, from the French *hautes-coquilles* [a fanciful derivation], is a play in which one kneels, and covering his eyes lays his head in another's lap and guesses who struck him." Strutt, *Sports and Pastimes*, p. 501.

211 32 **Farewell the tranquil mind**: This is a parody on Othello's soliloquy, iii, 3, 347-357:

> O, now for ever
> Farewell the tranquil mind! farewell content!
> Farewell the plumed troop and the big wars
> That make ambition virtue! O, farewell,
> Farewell the neighing steed and the shrill trump,
> The spirit-stirring drum, the ear-piercing fife,
> The royal banner and all quality,
> Pride, pomp and circumstance of glorious war!
> And, O you mortal engines, whose rude throats
> The immortal Jove's dread clamours counterfeit,
> Farewell! Othello's occupation's gone!

211 35 **Drum**: Fashionable card-party (cf. *drum* in "kettledrum").

211 36 **Spadille**: The ace of spades. **Pam**: The knave of clubs.

Basto: The ace of clubs. Pope's classic description of the game of ombre in *The Rape of the Lock*, Canto iii, introduces " Spadillio first, unconquerable lord," " Basto," and " mighty Pam, that kings and queens o'erthrew."

211 50 **Life's great stage**: " All the world's a stage," *As You Like It*, ii, 7, 139.

THE CRITIC

DEDICATION

215 Mrs. Greville: The mother of Mrs. Crewe to whom Sheridan dedicated *The School for Scandal* (see pp. 286–287). Mrs. Greville's interest in literary work is attested by the " poetical talent " of her *Ode to Indifference*, and by the following entry in 1792, in Madame d'Arblay's Diary (1842 ed. *Diary and Letters of Madame d'Arblay*, V, 322): " Mrs. Crewe obligingly promised us the loan, for reading, of a novel begun by her mother, Mrs. Greville, and left in her hands unfinished."

PROLOGUE

217 By the Honourable Richard Fitzpatrick: Richard Fitzpatrick (1747–1813) is remembered chiefly as the intimate friend of Charles James Fox. The two friends lived in the same lodgings in Piccadilly, and had kindred tastes for society, gambling, literature, and the theatre. An earlier product of Fitzpatrick's pen was *The Bath Picture; or a Slight Sketch of its Beauties* (1772). Fitzpatrick had entered the army in 1765, and, though opposed to the war in America, served there in 1777. Subsequent to the appearance of *The Critic* he attained the rank of Lieutenant-General and the post of Secretary of War.

217 1 **Sister Muses**: Melpomene, the Muse of Tragedy — " the tragic queen " (l. 7) — and Thalia, the Muse of Comedy — " her comic sister " (l. 11).

217 6 **When Villiers criticised what Dryden writ**: George Villiers, second Duke of Buckingham, in *The Rehearsal* (1761), burlesqued especially the tragedies of Dryden, then poet-laureate. For full discussion see Introduction, *The Sources of the Critic*, pp. lxxxvi–lxxxviii.

218 33 **A slight remonstrance to the drama's queens**: See Introduction, *Burlesque and Parody of Contemporary Drama in The Critic*, pp. ci–cvii.

218 43 **E'en newspapers themselves defy**: See Appendix, p. 327.

ACT I. SCENE 1

218 1 **Brutus to Lord North**: Frederick North, second Earl of Guilford, better known as Lord North (1732–1792), became First Lord of the Treasury in January, 1770. His attitude toward the American Colonies, especially in favoring the retention of the tea duty, helped to lead to war. The London newspapers contain many communications criticising his various public acts and policies. One of the *Letters of Junius* was addressed to Lord North.

218 2 **To the First L dash D of the A dash Y:** "To the First Lord of the Admiralty." John Montagu, Fourth Earl of Sandwich, First Lord of the Admiralty during the American Revolution, was the target of ceaseless invective aimed at his notorious corruption. See Introduction, *The Element of Actual History in The Critic*, pp. cvii–cviii.

218 3 **Genuine extract of a Letter from St. Kitt's:** Byron, grandfather of the poet, was the English vice-admiral opposing the French fleet in the West Indies. He had been at St. Kitt's in July, 1779. In *The London Chronicle*, September 30 — October 2, 1779, is an "Extract of a Letter from St. Christopher's lately received." In the issue for October 7–9 is an "Extract of a Letter from Basseterre, St. Christopher's, dated July 27."

218 4 **Coxheath Intelligence:** At Coxheath, near Maidstone, had been assembled in July, 1779, a large encampment of militia in view of the threatened hostilities. *The London Chronicle*, October 14–16 and October 16–21, contains news items from the "Camp at Coxheath." *The Camp* (1778), formerly attributed by some to Sheridan, is a "musical entertainment" whose scene is laid at the camp at Coxheath.

218 4 **Sir Charles Hardy:** He had been appointed Admiral of the Channel Fleet to succeed Keppel. (See Introduction, *The Element of Actual History in The Critic*, p. cviii.) Despite the fact that, with a fleet smaller than that of his adversaries, prudence counseled him not to assume the offensive, his conduct met with much hostile criticism. An extract from *The Public Advertiser*, October 25, 1779, runs: "We hear that Sir Charles Hardy, as soon as he returns from the bold Expedition of sailing up and down the English Channel, while the Enemy lie in Harbour, will be created 'Earl of WHOLEBONES.'" One of the verses of a satirical poem in *The Public Advertiser*, October 15, runs:

Where is Sir Charles, and where his Fleet?
Safe anchor'd at Spithead,
Providing Plenty of fresh Meat;
— Enough to strike one dead.

218 7 **The Morning Chronicle:** This newspaper was well known for its theatrical news. William Woodfall, its theatrical critic, probably wrote the review of the first performance of *The Rivals* in the issue for January 18, 1775.

219 11 **The Spanish Armada**: The defeat of the Spanish Armada (1588) had especial significance at the time *The Critic* was produced. A contributor to *Lloyd's Evening Post*, September 29 — October 1, 1779, gives an account of *The* SPANISH ARMOURY, prefaced with this note: "At a time when we are threatened with an Invasion from our inveterate Enemies, the following Account of the Trophies taken from the Spaniards, in 1588, at their grand Invasion, and now preserved in the Tower, I trust will be agreeable to many of your Readers." Viewed in the light of contemporary history, Sheridan's reason for choosing as a title *The Spanish Armada* is clearly expressed in Puff's opening speech in the second act: "Therefore when history, and particularly the history of our own country, furnishes anything like a case in point to the time in which an author writes, if he knows his own interest, he'll take advantage of it — so, Sir, I call my tragedy *The Spanish Armada*." See Introduction, *The Element of Actual History in The Critic*, pp. cviii–cix, and many of the preceding notes to this scene.

219 22 **To make yourself ridiculous by your passion for the theatre**: For an account of the various foibles of Vaughan, supposed to be held up to ridicule in this and other speeches, see Introduction, *Personal Caricature in The Critic*, pp. xcviii–xcix.

219 29 **Letters every day with Roman signatures**: A few of the "Roman signatures" to letters about current politics and history, taken at random from the London newspapers of 1779, are *Coriolanus, Cincinnatus, Pacificus, Rusticus, Patrioticus.*

219 39 **Quidnunc**: "Newsmonger" — literally (*Quid* and *nunc*), one who is continually asking, "What now?"

220 51 **Mr. Fosbrook**: A letter of Mrs. Tickell to her sister, Mrs. Sheridan, November 1785, describing a performance at Drury Lane, says: "I saw Mrs. Siddons after the play in Fosbrook's room." Fraser Rae, *Sheridan*, II, 14.

220 63 **Dorindas**: Dorinda is the daughter of Lady Bountiful in Farquhar's comedy, *The Beaux' Stratagem* (1707).

220 63 **Pollys**: Polly Peachum is the heroine of Gay's famous "ballad opera," *The Beggar's Opera* (1728). Those, however, of Sheridan's commentators who hold that Sheridan's Lydia Languish was the counterfeit presentment of Colman's Polly Honeycombe might consider this allusion proof of their theory.

220 66 **Now that the manager has monopolized the Opera House**: In the year before the production of *The Critic* a coalition between the Drury Lane and Covent Garden theatres had provided for an interchange of actors. An exceedingly caustic satire, directed primarily at Sheridan, the "manager" who had "monopolized the Opera House," was printed in 1779, under this title: *Coalition, a Farce Founded on Facts, and lately performed, with the Approbation, and under the joint Inspection of the managers of theTheatres-Royal.* The preface declares, "That a conspiracy has been formed against the independence of the stage and performers, cannot be denied; no more than the baseness of the intention can be paliated. . . . A total monopoly has taken place." In the farce itself Sheridan appears as Brainsley, Junior, and Harris, manager of Covent Garden, as Harrass. Sheridan's plays, his management of the theatre, even his private life, are savagely attacked. A direct hit at his theatrical "monopoly" is this speech given to Brainsley, Junior: "You must know, I have a notion of applying for two exclusive patents — One to invest in *myself* the sole right of producing theatrical pieces, and the other to exclude all persons composing but by *our* licence."

220 75 **Westminster associations**: The Westminster Associations were bands of volunteer militia. Churchill satirized them in *The Rosciad* (1761), ll. 621–2:

> Like Westminster militia train'd to fight,
> They scarcely knew the left hand from the right.

About 1760, according to the note on this passage in W. Tooke's edition of Churchill's works, the lack of militia in the city of Westminster prompted a Scotch adventurer, Macgregor, to seize the opportunity of raising a regiment. He sold most of the commissions to low tradesmen and sharpers, with financial success that would have done credit to Falstaff. In his day, then, "to be at the head of one of the Westminster associations" was a doubtful compliment. Thomas Vaughan, supposedly represented by Dangle, "about 1782," according to the *Dictionary of National Biography*, "became captain of a company of the Westminster volunteers." In the light of this statement, the question may fairly be raised of the possibility that Vaughan had already (in the latter part of 1779) become interested in "one of the Westminster associations" and had already been, "trailing a pike in the Artillery Ground." The great uncertainty connected with the dates in Vaughan's life — the date of his death, for instance — lends color to the suggestion here offered that Sheridan's passage may be a decided "local hit" at Vaughan, in keeping with other similar hits in the context.

220 76 **The Artillery Ground**: The drill-ground near Bunhill Fields, London, of the Honourable Artillery Company, the oldest military body in England, dating back to Henry VIII's reign.

221 80 **The stage is the mirror of Nature**: The allusion is to Hamlet's speech to the Players (iii, 2, 22ff.): "For anything so overdone is from the purpose of playing, whose end, both at the first and now, was and is, to hold, as 'twere, the mirror up to nature."

221 81 **The actors are the Abstract and brief Chronicles of the Time**: The allusion is to Hamlet's speech to Polonius concerning the Players (ii, 2, 548): "Let them be well used, for they are the abstract and brief chronicles of the time."

222 128 **No, that's a genteel comedy**: A hit at the "true sentimental" comedy of the day, which Sheridan himself had "lately tried to run down." (See Introduction, pp. xliv–xlv.)

222 128 **Not a translation — only taken from the French**: An extract from the exordium to Foote's *The Handsome Housemaid; or Piety in Pattens* (1773), a burlesque of sentimental comedy, is an interesting parallel: "Our modern authors will therefore be spared the mortification of hearing those miserable, melancholy French translations with which our theatres are at present infested."

222 135 **The theatre, in proper hands, might certainly be made the school of morality**: Sheridan's banter is good-naturedly directed at those who praised the "moral excellence" of dramatists like Cumberland, but indulged in such strictures upon the morality of his own plays as are found in "Animadversions on the Moral Tendency of The School for Scandal" (quoted in Appendix, pp. 326–327).

223 143 **Two houses**: Drury Lane and Covent Garden Theatres.

223 147 **Even Vanbrugh and Congreve obliged to undergo a bungling reformation**: A playful allusion probably to Sheridan's own "reformation" of Vanbrugh's *The Relapse* into *A Trip to Scarborough*, produced on February 24, 1777. Though the play grew into considerable favor, it encountered lasting objection in some quarters. The *Critical Review*, November, 1781, in reviewing the first printed edition, says: "In the alteration we find not a spark of that lively wit and easy dialogue that shines forth in the School for Scandal. Some of Vanbrugh's indecencies are taken away, and in that respect the play is mended, but what is added is neither like Vanbrugh nor Sheridan."

223 155 **A comedy, on a very new plan**: This whole speech of Sneer recalls Foote's burlesque of sentimental comedy, *The Handsome Housemaid; or Piety in Pattens* (1773) — the satire which Thomas Davies said (*Life of Garrick*, II, 140) laid Kelly's *False Delicacy*, "and all sentimental comedy, in the dust." Sheridan's *The Reformed House-breaker*, whose "most serious moral" is inculcated "by the mere force of humour," is somewhat akin to Fielding's mock comedy wherein "the maiden of low degree by the mere effects of morality and virtue, raised herself, to riches and honours." At least Sheridan was making sure that the body of sentimental comedy, which Foote had laid in the dust, should not rise again. Dangle might fairly term both *The Reformed House-breaker* and *The Handsome Housemaid; or Piety in Pattens*, "truly moral."

223 168 **Old Bailey**: "The seat of the central criminal court of London, so called from the ancient *bailey* of the city wall between Lud Gate and New Gate, within which it was situated." *Century Dictionary.*

223 171 **Sir Fretful Plagiary**: In this character Sheridan satirized the dramatist, Richard Cumberland. (See Introduction, *Personal Caricature in The Critic*, pp. xciv–xcviii.)

224 192 **Though he is my friend**: This is one of numerous passages in *The Critic* to which Byron refers in his letters: "Though, as Dangle says, 'He is *my* friend,' many of these personages 'were *my friends*,' but much such friends as Dangle and his allies." (*The Works of Lord Byron. Letters and Journals.* Edited by Rowland E. Prothero, VI, 190.) For other allusions in Byron's letters to *The Critic*, see in Prothero's edition of Byron's Letters, II, 149; III, 29, 57.

225 228 **I sent it to the manager of Covent Garden Theatre this morning**: Sheridan may possibly have had in mind Cumberland's *The Battle of Hastings*, produced in 1778, but previously rejected at Covent Garden. See Cumberland's letter to Colman, Introduction, *Personal Caricature in The Critic*, p. xcvi.

226 244 **Steal! — to be sure they may**: Sheridan seems to hit at the foolish story that he had stolen *The School for Scandal*. See Introduction, *Personal Caricature in The Critic*, p. xcviii. For the similarity of the rest of *Sir Fretful's* speech to a passage in Churchill, see Introduction, *The Sources of the Critic*, pp. xcii–xciii.

226 250 **He might take out some of the best things in my tragedy, and put them into his own comedy**: This "palpable hit," whose irony hardly requires Sneer's rejoinder, "That might be done, I dare be sworn," is akin to one of the most familiar anecdotes of Sheridan. The story, whose excellence is less questionable than its veracity, runs that Cumberland's children, at an early performance of *The School for Scandal*, screamed with delight. The unhappy father remonstrated: "What are you laughing at, my dear little folks? You should not laugh, my angels, there is nothing to laugh at!" Then he added in an undertone, "Keep still, you little dunces." The story goes on to say that, when the incident was rehearsed to Sheridan, he replied: "It was ungrateful of Cumberland to have been displeased with his children for laughing at my comedy, for when I went to see his tragedy I laughed from beginning to end." The fretful Cumberland, however, in his

Memoirs (1807, I, 271), offered an elaborate "alibi" whose "proof positive," he asserted, convinced even his "accuser" of the falsity of the charge "that on the first night of *The School for Scandal* I was overheard in the lobby endeavouring to decry and cavil at that excellent comedy."

227 297 **Rises, I believe you mean**: Though so many Sheridan anecdotes turn out to be apocryphal, there is an interesting story in John Taylor's *Records of my Life* (1832), II, 163–4: "Mr. Cumberland came one night to Mr. Sheridan's box in the theatre, somewhat late, and stumbled at the entrance. Mr. Sheridan sprang forward and assisted him. 'Ah! sir,' said Cumberland, 'you are the only man to assist a *falling* author.' Mr. Sheridan, in waggery or forgetfulness, said: 'Rising, you mean,' the very words which Mr. Sheridan has assigned to Sir Fretful Plagiary, in 'The Critic,' a character commonly understood to be drawn for Mr. Cumberland."

228 327 **Newspaper criticisms**: Thomas Davies, whose chapter on Cumberland in *The Life of David Garrick*, 1780 (II, Chap. 48), gives excellent contemporary evidence to the justice of the portraiture in Sir Fretful, says of Cumberland's *The Choleric Man* (1774): "The criticisms thrown out in the news-papers against this play, seem to have affected the author very much. In his Dedication to Detraction, he enters into a long defence of Terence, and his manner of writing comedy, and endeavours to convince his anonymous opponent of malice and ignorance. . . . Mr. Cumberland tuggs too much at the critic's arrow in his side, and yet affects to despise the hand from whence it came." (II, 272–3)

229 361 **Your commonplace-book**: Sheridan quite possibly took the idea from the book of "Drama Common-places" of Bayes, in *The Rehearsal*. See Introduction, p. lxxxviii.

230 378 **Tambour sprigs**: Embroidered ornaments in the form of a spray. The tambour was an embroidery-frame. Cf. *School for Scandal*, ii, 1, 36: "Recollect, Lady Teazle, when I saw you first sitting at your tambour." See Notes, pp. 281, 291.

230 380 **The mimicry of Falstaff's page**: Falstaff's attendant appears in *Henry IV, Part II*, as "his page," in *The Merry Wives of Windsor* as Robin, page to Falstaff, and in *Henry V* as the "Boy." Says Prince Hal (2 *Henry IV*, ii, 2, 75–7): "The boy that I gave Falstaff a' had him from me Christian; and look, if the fat villain have not transformed him ape." Falstaff's page shows "mimicry" even of his master's jests at the expense of Bardolph's nose: "Good Bardolph, put thy face between his sheets, and do the office of a warming-pan" (*Henry*

V, ii, 1, 87–9) — a speech which recalls Falstaff's own remark which the Boy recollects (*Henry V*, ii, 3, 42), after Falstaff's death: "Do you not remember, a' saw a flea stick upon Bardolph's nose, and a' said it was a black soul burning in hell-fire?"

231 421 **These things never fret me in the least:** This and the following speeches of Sir Fretful portray to the life Cumberland's pretended disregard of adverse criticism and his real sensitiveness to it. His own *Memoirs* and letters overflow with unconscious illustrations of this. Sufficient example is in a letter to Garrick (*The Private Correspondence of David Garrick*, II, 285 — Jan. 5, 1778) concerning the reading of one of his own tragedies to the performers. Sheridan, he says, "came in yawning at the fifth act, with no other apology than having sate up two nights running. It gave me not the least offence, as I put it all to habit of dissipation and indolence; but I fear his office will suffer for want of due attention, and the present drop upon the theatre justifies my apprehensions."

232 453 **Where a base and personal malignity usurps the place:** This parting thrust at Sir Fretful reads like a vindication of Sheridan's attitude in holding the mirror up to Cumberland.

235 72 **Winter managers:** The season at Drury Lane and Covent Garden theatres usually extended from the latter part of September to the middle of May; at Haymarket Theatre, from the middle of May to mid-September. Cf. Oulton, *The History of the Theatres of London* (1796, I, 82), where he speaks of the Haymarket season of 1779: "Mr. COLMAN did not open his theatre this season till May 31, the winter houses having continued their performances longer than usual, and most of Mr. COLMAN'S performers being engaged at one or other of them."

236 104 **Hygeia:** The goddess of Health. Cf. Anstey's *The New Bath Guide*, describing "The joys of *Bath*" (*Works*, 1808, p. 50):

> There HYGEIA, goddess, pours
> Blessings from her various stores.

236 110 **Mercury, the God of traffic and Fiction:** Mercury was the patron of travelers, and, as a god of darkness, of thieves and liars. The "Caduceus" was his wand or staff.

237 146 **Marshalsea:** The debtors' prison in London, familiar to all readers of Dickens's *Little Dorrit*.

237 151 **Press'd:** "Impressed into naval service." In Colman's *The Jealous Wife* (1761), Captain O'Cutter recounts (iii, 1) his adventures in roughly pressing men into the service, and is employed to press "into his Majesty's Service" some gentlemen who are obstacles in the way of Lord Trinket's intrigue.

237 156 **Felo de se**: An English law term for "suicide."

238 171 **The Puff direct**: The "various sorts" of puffing are probably suggested by Touchstone's seven stages of the lie (*As You Like It*, v, 4).

239 188 **Mr. Dodd**: He created the part of Dangle. He had been the Sir Benjamin Backbite in the original cast of *The School for Scandal*, and the Lord Foppington in *A Trip to Scarborough*. Boaden says of him (*Memoirs of the Life of John Philip Kemble*, I, 55): "Dodd, with more confined powers [than Palmer], was one of the most perfect actors that I have ever seen. He was the fopling of the *drama* rather than the age. . . He was, to be sure, the prince of pink heels, and the soul of empty eminence." "The character of SIR HARRY" (as the first edition reads) doubtless refers to Sir Harry Bouquet, a part in Tickell's *The Camp* which Dodd created, October 15, 1778.

239 190 **Mr. Palmer**: He created the part of Sneer. He had been the original Joseph Surface. Charles Lamb in the *Elia* essay on *The Artificial Comedy of the Last Century*, which includes the glowing eulogy of "The School for Scandal in its glory," maintained that "its hero, when Palmer played it at least, was Joseph Surface." "Plausible Jack" — so Palmer was nicknamed — was a great favorite, especially with women. The part of "the COLONEL" (to which the first edition adds a reference) may be that of Col. Lambert in *The Hypocrite*, Bickerstaffe's popular revision of Cibber's *The Non-Juror*. Palmer acted the role, November 11, 1779.

239 191 **Mr. King**: He created the role of Puff, and hence was here called upon to pronounce his own eulogy. He had been the original Sir Peter Teazle. Boaden says of him: "Mr. King, though very confined in his powers, was one of the most perfect actors that ever graced the stage." (*Memoirs of Kemble*, I, 59.)

239 195 **Mr. Loutherbourg**: Philippe Jacques De Loutherbourg (1740–1812) came to England in 1771 with considerable Continental reputation as an artist. Garrick secured his services as chief designer of scenery at Drury Lane Theatre. "In this line," declares Lionel Cust (*Dictionary of National Biography*), "De Loutherbourg was without a rival, and the care with which he modelled and studied each detail, and the skill with which he handled the illumination, rendered his scenes real works of art." A newspaper advertisement of the first production of *The Critic* has these significant lines: "The Scenery designed by Mr. De Loutherbourg and executed under his Direction."

239 211 **Lady F four stars F dash E:** The abbreviations of the text for " Lady Fanny Fete " and " Sir Flimsy Gossamer " follow the method in vogue in the *Têtes-à-Têtes* in *The Town and Country Magazine*, alluded to in the opening scene of *The School for Scandal.* (See note, p. 289.)

240 247 **Fête Champêtre:** See note on *The School for Scandal*, ii, 1 (p. 291).

241 259 **Scan. Mag.:** An abbreviation of *scandalum magnatum:* " In law, the offense of speaking slanderously or in defamation of high personages (magnates) of the realm." *Century Dictionary.* In the *Epilogue* to Colman's *The Jealous Wife* (1761), Mrs. Clive, who acted the part of Lady Freelove, an *intriguante* who smacks somewhat of Restoration license in conduct, says: " My Part is *Scandalum Magnatum.*"

241 261 **The Puff oblique, or Puff by Implication:** One of the most amusing charges of imitation brought against Sheridan's text has seemingly attracted no notice. Boaden (*Memoirs of Kemble*, I, 65–68) devotes several pages to pointing the resemblance between Sheridan's account of the " Puff oblique " and " Dr. Barrow's definition of facetiousness," cited in full from the " *Second Sermon on Evil Speaking.* Edition, 1678, p. 44." With Boaden's preliminary statement there must be general agreement: " It was not commonly supposed that Sheridan was a diligent reader of Barrow." The deadly parallel between a page of Sheridan and a page of Dr. Barrow is then supplied, with this comment in a footnote: " Here is an *accidental* parity also — the very PAGES are the same of the two passages."

241 280 **Tablature:** Under the meaning " a tabular representation," the *Century Dictionary* quotes Shaftesbury, *Judgment of Hercules*, Int.: " In painting one may give to any particular work the name of *tablature*, when the work is in reality a single piece, comprehended in one view, and form'd according to one single intelligence, meaning or design."

242 308 **In the style of Junius:** The celebrated *Letters of Junius* appeared in *The Public Advertiser* (1768–1772) attacking the King and his ministers, notably the Duke of Grafton. The mystery of their authorship is still a subject of controversy. In various numbers of *The Athenæum* (1903) Fraser Rae took issue with the prevalent theory ascribing them to Sir Philip Francis. A communication to *The Public Advertiser*, October 12, 1779, laments that " Even JUNIUS has deserted the public cause, and no longer dedicates his life to the Information of his Fellow-Citizens." The " style of Junius " is thus dissected by a modern critic (Saintsbury: *A Short Hist. of Eng. Lit.*, 1898, p. 647): " An affectation of exaggerated moral indignation, clap-trap rhetorical interrogations, the use, clever enough if it were not so constant, of balanced antitheses, a very good ear for some, though by no means many, cadences and rhythms, some ingenuity in trope and metaphor, and a cunning adaptation of that trick of specialising with proper names with which Lord Macaulay has surfeited readers for the last half-century — these, though by no means all, are the chief features of the Junian method."

242 309 **The Thames navigation too is at a stand**: In *The Public Advertiser*, October 26, 1779, but four days before the appearance of *The Critic*, are the following significant passages in an article "On Ramsgate Harbour": "This Harbour, like the Thames and every Harbour and River in the Kingdom, becomes of no Use after Millions of Expence, through Ignorance or Peculation. . . . The Trinity House is supposed to receive 100,000£ a Year for cleansing the Thames from Gravesend to London Bridge; and although by landing Materials raised by improved and more proper Engines, 5,000£ per Annum would carry a First-rate Man of War up to the Tower, yet in several Centuries the Revenue has not been only sunk, but a Gravesend Boat requires the most skilful Pilotage to navigate it safely up to Bilingsgate." The names *Misomud* and *Anti-shoal* (l. 310) seem to continue the satirical reference to "The Thames navigation."

242 312 **To take Paul Jones**: John Paul Jones (1747–1792) was a Scottish-American naval adventurer whose exploits make a brilliant page in the annals of the American Revolution. For some two years before the appearance of *The Critic* he had been a menace to English commerce as he cruised about the British Isles, including the Irish coast where the river "Shannon" (line 312) has its outlet. On September 23, 1779, occurred the famous victory of his *Bonhomme Richard* over the *Serapis*. "Indiamen" were large ships officered and armed by the East India Company for their trade.

242 313 **Reinforce Byron**: John Byron (1723–1786), vice-admiral, had opposed the French fleet in the West Indies, in July, 1779. The indecisive results were due partly to Byron's inexperience and partly to the superior numbers of the French. A satirical poem, *The Alehouse Politicians*, in *The Public Advertiser*, October 15, has this stanza:

A Glass of Peppermint for me;
  What News in the Gazette?
Byron has lost the Victory;
  — Enough to make us sweat.

See also note on "Genuine extract of a Letter from St. Kitts," p. 299.

242 313 **Compel the Dutch — to —**: To "surrender Paul Jones" —

so the phrase should doubtless be completed. This explanation, I believe, is fully warranted by the following extract from *The Public Advertiser*, October 16, 1779: " It is absolutely a Fact (and it is not the only foolish Thing by a Thousand the Ministry have done) that Orders have been sent to our Ambassador at the Hague, directing him to apply to the States for the immediate Surrender of Paul Jones; not however that Government have any Intention, in that Case, of trying him as a Pirate, but as a Murderer, for the Death of a Man some years ago in Scotland. Demanded upon this Ground, Ministry are vain enough to suppose the Dutch will give up Mr. Jones, and that he may be brought to Trial for Murder, and hanged, if convicted, without any Offence to Congress. A gentleman from Holland says, that as soon as it was known that Paul Jones, and his ships were arrived in the Texel, Sir Joseph Yorke, our Ambassador there, applied to the States-General to have him and his ships delivered up, but his request was refused. . . . He says that Jones hath plenty of cash, and it is supposed that as long as his money lasts the Dutch will protect him."

243 316 **To establish the unanimity of the fleet in the Public Advertiser:** *The Public Advertiser* was especially noted for its open letters and communications on all topics of public interest. Though it sought to open its columns impartially to all, it was used chiefly by the opponents of the governmental party. Of numerous criticisms of the fleet an excellent example is in the issue for October 25, five days before the production of *The Critic:* " Our fleet is at last sailed, which seems to confirm the Opinion that the combined Fleets are gone into Harbour. It is a malicious Report, to say that our Fleet has nothing in View in going to Sea — for we are well assured that the Glory of Sailing without Let or Molestation, in our own Channel, after the Enemy is retired into their own Ports, will make a principal Part of the King's Speech, at the Opening of the Session."

243 317 **To shoot Charles Fox in the Morning Post:** *The Morning Post* was as well known for scurrilous personal attacks as was *The Public Advertiser* for communications on matters of public interest, or *The Morning Chronicle* for theatrical intelligence. In politics *The Morning Post* supported the ministry, and hence would be glad " to shoot Charles Fox." Henry Bate, its editor at this time, was a dissolute clergyman, whose abusive career as editor was summarily stopped in 1780 by imprisonment for libelling the Duke of Richmond. (See H. R. Fox Bourne: *English Newspapers*, I, 220–222.)

ACT II. SCENE 1

243 3 **The abstract and brief Chronicle of the Times**: Dangle has already quoted this phrase from *Hamlet*. (See note, p. 302.) Shakespeare's text reads "chronicles of the time."

243 7 **The Spanish Armada**: See Introduction, *The Element of Actual History in The Critic*, and especially the note on i, 1, 11 (p. 300).

243 8 **Tilbury Fort**: This was constructed by Henry VIII to defend the mouth of the river Thames. Here Queen Elizabeth assembled her troops at the time of the Armada (1588).

245 59 **Mr. Hopkins**: Mr. Hopkins, of the Drury Lane Theatre, had already appeared as a stage character as "Prompter" at the Drury Lane Theatre, in Garrick's farce, *A Peep Behind the Curtain; or The New Rehearsal*, 1767. There are frequent references to Mr. Hopkins in *The Private Correspondence of David Garrick* (*e.g.* II, 29, 32, 42).

ACT II. SCENE 2

245 4 **Clock strikes**: For discussion of this and many other burlesque passages in *A Tragedy Rehearsed*, see Introduction, *Burlesque and Parody of Contemporary Drama in The Critic*, pp. ci–cvii.

246 20 **Sir Christopher Hatton**: Hatton (1540–1591) was appointed Lord Chancellor of England in April, 1587. In February of that year he had spoken at length in the House of Commons on the peril of a Spanish invasion. Hence his "cautious conjecture" of danger is highly ridiculous. He was called "the dancing chancellor" because the attention of Queen Elizabeth was attracted to him by his graceful dancing in a mask at court.

246 25 **What! they had been talking before?**: For the possible origin of this and some subsequent passages in Sheridan's text, see Introduction, *The Sources of The Critic*, pp. lxxxvii ff.

247 47 **When virgin Majesty herself I view**: The "Virgin Queen" had reviewed her troops at Tilbury Fort, August, 1588, on a war-horse, armed — "veil'd in steel" — and had exhorted them to arms "with graceful confidence" in these words: "I know that I have but the body of a weak and feeble woman; but I have the heart of a king, and of a king of England too!" *Pictorial History of England*, 1839, II, 674.

247 70 **Philip**: Philip II of Spain. He strove to restore the Roman Catholic religion to the Protestant countries of Europe. (See **248** 74ff.)

250 154 **Nem. con.**: An abbreviation of *nemine contradicente*, "no one contradicting," "unanimously."

251 184 **You couldn't go off kneeling, could ye?:** An *exit* attended with almost equal difficulty is in *The Rehearsal* (iii, 2) where Prince Volscius, torn betwixt Honour and Love, makes his exit " with one Boot on, and the other off."

252 198 **Lord Burleigh:** William Cecil (1520–1598), created Baron of Burghley in 1571, and in the next year Lord High Treasurer of England. " To follow his career from this point to its close would be to write the history of England; for by him, more than by any other single man during the last thirty years of his life, was the history of England shaped." (*Dictionary of National Biography.*)

252 216 **More cannon to fire:** In *Jupiter,* Sheridan had used trouble with stage " ordnance " for comic effect. (See Introduction, p. lxxxv.)

253 222 **The minuet in Ariadne:** *Arianna* (*Ariadne*), an Italian opera, music by Handel, was first represented in London in 1734 (score dated 1733). " The minuet in the first scene was long popular." *Cyclopedia of Music and Musicians,* I, 67. One of Tony Lumpkin's " shabby fellows " at the alehouse says: " May this be my poison if my bear ever dances but to the very genteelest of tunes — *Water Parted,* or the minuet in *Ariadne* " (*She Stoops to Conquer,* i, 2). In Sheridan's *Jupiter* is this line, " This hint I took from Handel." Taken in connection with the previous passage about the " ordnance," it seems evident that Sheridan was here utilizing the material of his earlier farce.

256 340 **Parry Carte:** A " parry in quart " guards against the " thrust in quart," in fencing. The " thrust in tierce " is another regular term in fencing, but the " flankonade " is to be found only in Puff's dictionary. " A palpable hit " is Osric's famous phrase — " A hit, a very palpable hit " (*Hamlet,* v, 2, 292). Sheridan's own " palpable hits " at *Hamlet* must have been especially appreciated by the first-night audience, as *The Critic* was played as an " after-piece " to *Hamlet.*

258 387 **Edge away at the Top:** At the back of the stage.

259 408 **Drake at the Armada:** Sir Francis Drake commanded under Lord Howard in the conflict with the Spanish Armada.

261 466 **Gravesend:** On the south bank of the Thames, some score or more miles below London, and not far from Tilbury Fort.

ACT III. SCENE I

263 32 **Now, pray mark this Scene:** In the burlesque " recognition scene " which follows there may be some instances of specific parody of passages in Home's well-known tragedy, *Douglas* (1756). (See Introduction, p. civ, and especially Appendix, p. 330.)

264 41 **My Name's John Wilkins — Alias have I none**: Sheridan may have intended to parody the most familiar lines in *Douglas* (ii), "My name is Norval," etc. Norval turns out to be the *alias* for young Douglas. It must be remembered, however, that the scene which Dangle pronounces to be "one of the finest Discovery scenes I ever saw" serves as a general burlesque of numerous absurd recognition scenes in contemporary drama.

265 83 **Perdition catch my soul, but I do love thee**: This line which "Shakespeare made use of first" is in *Othello*, iii, 3, 90–91.

266 119 **Lord Burleigh comes forward, shakes his head, and exit**: For a possible hint in Fielding that may have suggested this passage, see Introduction, *The Sources of The Critic*, p. lxxxix.

270 205 **Thrust in tierce**: A fencing term. See note, p. 311.

270 208 **—— nity — he would have added**: Perhaps Sheridan had in mind the conclusion of Hotspur's dying speech: *Hot.* And food for — [*Dies*]. *Prince.* For worms, brave Percy (1 *Henry IV*, v, 4, 86–7).

272 255 **Now then for my magnificence**: For a possible parallel, see Introduction, *The Sources of The Critic*, p. lxxxvii.

272 264 **Those are his Banks**: Sheridan's Thames with his Banks recalls somewhat, as has sometimes been suggested, the dance of Earth, Moon, and Sun in the last act of *The Rehearsal*. Thames fails to remain between his Banks, while, in *The Rehearsal*, "by the very nature of this Dance, the Earth must be sometimes between the Sun and the Moon, and the Moon between the Earth and Sun; and there you have both your Eclipses."

273 (stage direction) **Scene changes to the sea — the fleets engage**: See Introduction, *The Element of Actual History in The Critic*.

273 (stage direction) **Handel's water musick**: A suite of twenty-one movements, "first performed on the Thames, Aug. 22, 1715, when George I. and the Royal family sailed from Limehouse to Whitehall. Handel followed the Royal barge with his orchestra, and performed this suite to the delight of the king, who asked the name of its composer." (*Cyclopedia of Music and Musicians*, III, 566.) The sequel was the restoration of Handel, then in disgrace, to royal favor and an increased pension.

273 (stage direction) **The march in Judas Maccabæus**: Handel's oratorio, *Judas Maccabæus*, was first performed in London in 1747.

APPENDIX

THE RIVALS

I. CONTEMPORARY CRITICISMS OF THE RIVALS

(*a*) On the First Performance, January 17, 1775

The Public Ledger, January 18, 1775.—The *Rivals,* as a Comedy, requires much castigation, and the pruning hand of judgment, before it can ever pass on the Town as even a tolerable Piece. In language it is defective to an extreme, in Plot outré and one of the *Characters* is an absolute exotic in the wilds of nature. The author seems to have considered puns, witticisms, similes and metaphors, as admirable substitutes for polished diction; hence they abound in every sentence; and hence it is that instead of the '*Metmorphosis*' of Ovid, one of the characters is made to talk of Ovid's 'Meat-for-Hopes,'[1] a Lady is called the 'Pine Apple of beauty,' the Gentleman in return 'an Orange of perfection.' A Lover describes the sudden change of disposition in his Mistress by saying, that 'she flies off in a tangent born down by the current of disdain'; and a second Tony Lumkin, to describe how fast he rode, compares himself to a 'Comet with a tail of dust at his heels.'

These are shameful absurdities in language, which can suit no character, how widely soever it may depart from common life and common manners.

Whilst thus censure is freely passed, not to say that there are various sentiments in the Piece which demonstrate the Author's no stranger to the finer feelings, would be shameful partiality. . . .

[1] This passage shows how Sheridan did apply "the pruning hand of judgment" in the revision of the play for January 28. A contributor to *The Morning Chronicle* (January 20, 1775) writes, "The miserable pun used by a footman to a coachman of *meat for horses*, instead of *metamorphosis*, is much too contemptible even for a postilion."

Many of the parts were improperly cast. Mr. Lee [Sir Lucius O'Trigger] is a most execrable Irishman. Miss Barsanti [Lydia Languish] is calculated only for a mimic; she has the archness of look and manner, that shrug of the shoulders, which must for ever unqualify her for genteel Comedy; and when she is represented as a girl of thirty thousand pounds fortune, we curse the blind Goddess for bestowing her favours so absurdly; then she has the agreeable lisp of Thomas Hull, and cannot be expected to articulate her words so as to be understood, unless her tongue first undergoes a cutting.

The Morning Chronicle, January 20, 1775. — To the Printer, Sir, There is certainly some evil genius attends the proceedings of Covent Garden Theatre. Our expectations have been some time raised with the hope that they were at last to produce us a truly good comedy; the hour of proof arrives, and we are presented with a piece got up with such flagrant inattention, that half the performers appear to know nothing of their parts, and the play itself is a *full hour* longer in the representation than any piece on the stage. — This last circumstance is an error of such a nature as shows either great obstinacy in the Author, or excessive ignorance in the managers; but the casting Mr. Lee for the part of *Sir Lucius O'Trigger*, is a blunder of the first brogue, which Mr. Lee plainly shewed as he was not *Irishman* enough to have committed for himself. If there had been no one in the theatre fit for the part, it should have been taken out of the piece which is full exuberant enough to spare it. As I find the further representation of it is put off for the present, I suppose this will be the case; for to attempt to continue him in the character will inevitably damn the play. . . . The character of Faulkland is touched with a delicate and masterly hand. . . . There is as much true humour in *Acres* and *David* as in any character on the stage whatever. What the characters of *Sir Anthony* and *Sir Lucius ought* to have appeared I cannot take upon me to say, but Shuter, from being imperfect appeared to ruin some scenes, which, from the situations, seemed to promise noble effects from his *vis Comica*. . . . Yours &c. *A Friend to Comedy.*

The Morning Chronicle, January 20, 1775. — Sir, — I cannot avoid taking the earliest opportunity of reprehending, in the severest manner, one of the performers of Covent Garden Theatre, for his shameful negligence, in not being perfect in a single sentence, at the representation of The *Rivals* on Tuesday last. Before I name the man, every lover of the drama, will, I am persuaded, point him out: for fear, however, the town should be wrong in their conjecture, and any other person should suffer by it, I will give you, Mr. Printer, his name in capitals. The person I allude to is MR. SHUTER. I will treat him like a gentleman in my appellation, though he probably may not deserve it. If his incorrectness arises from his strong feelings, I really pity his condition, and a public declaration of this kind would do him service, but if it is the effect of *inattention*, I will be bold to tell him, that, in an equitable consideration, he is more immoral and unjust than a highwayman; for by this shameful usage, he, in all probability may rob an author of four or five hundred pounds, besides what is as dear to man as his existence — his reputation. . . . *One of the Pitt.*

The Morning Post, January 20, 1775. — Sir, Next to the torment of sitting out a very dull Comedy, I know not a more uneasy situation than that of hearing an apparently good one mangled in the representation. I think I never saw a performance more disgraceful to a Theatre-Royal than the manner in which the *Rivals* was performed at Covent Garden; none of the performers seemed to be tolerably perfect except Mrs. Bulkley and Miss Barsanti; Shuter did not know any two lines together, and whenever he was out, he tried to fill the interval with oaths and buffoonery; in all his scenes with Woodward he put him out; and for the Irishman, of all disgusting attempts that ever was damn'd in a strolling company, nothing ever came up to this. The audience shewed great partiality and lenity for the author, in making a distinction between the merit of the piece, and the excessive demerit of the representation of this character; which one would have thought must have damned the best play that ever was written: as it stands, it is absolutely impossible that the piece can go on; the others may get perfect, and do justice to their parts, but *Lee* never can be suffered in this character, and his deportment in it, is literally such, as will bully even the Author's friends into hissing. Yours, &c. Hibernicus.

The Morning Post, January 21, 1775. — MR. EDITOR, I am the last man in the world who would step forth to upbraid a degraded poet, but when I find a performer is execrated by the wretched puffs of the author's friends, in order to throw the principal part of the odium from his own shoulders on those of the player, I own I cannot help taking fire. I shall be acknowledged no partisan, either of Mr. *Lee* or Mr. *Shuter*, when I confess their performance was in every way reprehensible, nay shocking — but at the same time I will aver, that neither of them were invested with anything like a *character: Sir Lucius O'Trigger* was so ungenerous an attack upon a nation, that must justify any severity with which the piece will hereafter be treated: it is the first time I ever remember to have seen so villainous a portrait of an Irish Gentleman, permitted so openly to insult that country upon the boards of an English theatre. For the rest of the piece, the author has my pity; but for this unjustifiable attack, my warmest resentment.

Yours, &c. A BRITON.

The Town and Country Magazine, January, 1775. — If we examine this comedy by the rules of criticism, many objections may be made to it. Few of the characters are new, and scarce any well supported: those of Falkland and Miss Melville (*sic*) are the most *outré* sentimental ones that ever appeared upon the stage: the acts are long, in many parts uninteresting, and of course tedious. But the most reprehensible part is in the many low quibbles and barbarous puns that disgrace the very name of comedy. Nevertheless, there are some scenes lively, spirited, and entertaining; and if it were properly pruned by a competent judge of what is called the *Jeu de théatre*, it might probably go down with less opposition.

(*b*) ON THE REVISED PERFORMANCE, JANUARY 28, 1775

The British Chronicle, January 27–30, 1775. — At the second representation of the new Comedy of the Rivals, it was received with the warmest bursts of approbation by a crowded, and apparently impartial audience. The Author has very judiciously removed everything that could give offence in the character of Sir Lucius

O'Trigger; and Mr. Shuter exerted himself in a manner which entirely recovered his credit.

The Morning Chronicle, January 30, 1775. — We heartily wish it was a general custom for authors to withdraw their pieces after a first performance, in order to remove the objectionable passages, heighten the favourite characters, and generally amend the play. The author of the RIVALS has made good use of his time; his comedy is altered much for the better since it was first acted. The cast of it is improved, and all the performers are now perfect, and better acquainted with their several parts. It comes within a reasonable compass as to the time taken up in the representation, and the sentiments thrown into the mouth of Sir Lucius O'Trigger produce a good effect, at the same time that they take away every possible idea of the character's being designed as an insult on our neighbours on the other side of St. George's Channel. In the room of the objectionable and heavy scenes which are cut out, two new ones of a very different turn are introduced, and we remarked more than one judicious alteration in the Prologue. — The RIVALS will now stand its ground; and although we cannot pronounce it, with all its amendments, a comic chef-d'ouvre it certainly encourages us to hope for a very capital play from the same writer at a future season; he therefore, from motives of candour and encouragement, is entitled to the patronage and favour of a generous public.

The London Chronicle, January 28–31, 1775. — On Saturday evening last, Mr. Sheridan's comedy of 'The Rivals,' was performed for the second time with additions and alterations, at the Theatre Royal, Covent-garden. Its present state is widely different from that in which we found it on the first night's representation. Sir Lucius O'Trigger being retouched, has now the appearance of a character; and his assigning Beverley's reflection on his country as the grounds for his desire to quarrel with him is a reasonable pretence, and wipes off the former stigma undeservedly thrown on the sister kingdom: It is due to the merit of Mr. Clinch to say he did the strictest justice to the part, and from his ease in this character we soon expect to see him fill more capital walks in genteel comedy with credit to himself and pleasure to his audience.

An alteration of a principal incident gave a very favourable turn to the fable and the whole piece, viz. that where young Acres now delivers his challenge to his friend Absolute, begging him to carry it to his rival Beverly, not knowing the two characters composed but one man; its being at first given to Sir Lucius, the person who indited it, was highly inconsistent. — The cuttings have been every where judicious, except where they have deprived Lydia of that comic and picturesque description of her lover, standing like a *dripping-statute*[1] (*sic*) in the garden, &c. — The hiss that occasioned this cut was that of party or ignorance, not of judgment.

The performers were very attentive to the discharge of their duty; and though honest Ned Shuter was unfortunately reprehensible the first night, he has now wiped off the odium, and charmed as much as he had before displeased.

(*c*) The Judgment of the Literary Reviews

The Monthly Review, February, 1775. — The Author of this Comedy speaks so modestly of his performance, presumes so little on supposed abilities, and so candidly acknowledges his youth and inexperience, that even remorseless critics are inclined rather to promise themselves much future entertainment from the rays of genius that shine through particular passages of his Comedy, than to censure with acrimony its irregularities and defects. The fable indeed is neither new nor probable, nor the characters original or well sustained; but there are many just observations on human life and manners, many beauties of sentiment, and much excellent dialogue.

The Critical Review, February, 1775. — This comedy affords a singular proof of the ingenuity of the writer, and the candour of an English audience. Some parts of it were much disliked on the first representation: the author therefore instantly withdrew his performance, altered a great part of it, and *in a few days* produced, as it were, a new play; which was immediately brought on the stage, and received with applause.

There is variety, and some degree of novelty, in the following characters: [Then follows some account of the chief characters,

[1] This passage is now restored, v, 1.

largely made up of quotation of characteristic passages — *e.g.*, some of Mrs. Malaprop's word-blunders, and some of Bob Acres's referential oaths.]

The principal persons abovementioned are thrown, by their caprice, folly, or mistake, into several perplexities and ludicrous situations, which produce some entertaining scenes of comic humour.

The Gentleman's Magazine, March, 1775. — The dialogue of this comedy is, in general, natural and pleasing: as to the plot, though we have often heard of younger brothers, and fortune-hunters assuming fictitious titles and estates, as credentials to rich heiresses, it seems very unlikely that real rank and fortune should be deemed an objection, and therefore disclaimed, as in the piece before us. Here the marvellous and romantic seem to lose sight of the natural and probable; as they also do in Lydia's indifference to the man of her choice, as soon as she discovers his real character, and that there are no impediments to their union.

(*d*) On the First Performance at Bath, March 8, 1775

The Bath Chronicle, March 9, 1775. — Mr. Sheridan's comedy of 'The Rivals' was performed for the first time at our theatre last night; and we have the pleasure to say that it was received with every mark of approbation and applause from a numerous and polite audience.

Letter of Mary Linley to Mrs. Sheridan, March 9, 1775. — March 9, 1775. You will know, by what you see inclosed in this frank, my reason for not answering your letter sooner was that I waited the success of Sheridan's play at Bath; for, let me tell you, I look upon our theatrical tribunal though not in quantity, in quality as good as yours, [*i.e. London*] and I do not believe there was a critic in the whole city that was not there. But, in my life, I never saw anything go off with such uncommon applause. I must first of all inform you that there was a very full house; the play was performed inimitably well; nor did I hear, for the honour of our Bath actors, one single prompt the whole night; but I suppose the poor creatures never acted with such shouts of applause in their lives, so that they were incited by that to do their best. They lost many of Malaprop's good sayings by the applause; in short, I never saw or heard anything like it; before the actors spoke they began their clapping.

(*e*) On Other Early Performances

Letter of Mary Linley to Mrs. Sheridan, August 22, 1775. — Bath. 22. August. 1775. — Tell Sheridan his play has been acted at Southampton: — above a hundred people were turned away the first night. They say there never was anything so universally liked. They have very good success at Bristol, and have played *The Rivals* several times. — Miss Barsanti, Lydia, and Mrs. Canning, Julia.

II. THE WORD-BLUNDERS OF MRS. MALAPROP[1]

The actual introduction of Mrs. Malaprop to the stage is anticipated by Julia's reference to "her select words so ingeniously *misapplied*, without being *mispronounced*." "Improprieties" of speech, the rhetorics would style these words, correct in themselves, but wrong in usage. Though most of these blunders are at once self-explanatory, in many instances the mistakes are far more obvious than the explanations.

The simplest and by far the most frequent form of blunder perpetrated by Mrs. Malaprop consists of the misuse of one word for another similar to it in sound. A random illustration is sufficient — "Sure, if I reprehend (*apprehend*) any thing in this world it is the use of my oracular (*vernacular*) tongue, and a nice derangement (*arrangement*) of epitaphs! (*epithets!*) (iii, 3). Since, unfortunately, not every "derangement of epitaphs" is "nice" for explanation, the subjoined Glossary is compiled so that the reader who has but a "supercilious knowledge" of "orthodoxy" may "reprehend the true meaning of what she is saying." Furthermore, it will not merely prove the statement that most of the blunders consist simply of the misuse of one word for another similar to it in sound, but will emphasize the variety and frequency of the blunders.

Since this Glossary includes only those more readily catalogued

[1] For discussion of the literary antecedents of Mrs. Malaprop, see Introduction, pp. lii–liv, and various parallel passages from Mrs. Sheridan's *A Journey to Bath*, quoted in Notes, pp. 278, 279.

mistakes of one word for another similar in sound, it will be well first to discuss briefly word-blunders of other sorts. When Mrs. Malaprop exclaims (iv, 2), "We will not anticipate the past; — so mind, young people — our retrospection will be all to the future," the mistake consists, obviously, in confusing not words similar in sound, but words opposite in meaning. If "retrospection" were here used, for example, for "introspection," the blunder would be of the most characteristic and frequent class. Here, evidently, the blunder lies in using "anticipate" and "retrospection" in exactly inverted senses. Another blunder of this sort is "Lead the way, and we'll precede" (v, 1).

There remain a number of individual words and passages whose derangement almost defies classification. They may be best grouped, perhaps, simply as words whose sound, but not whose sense, has caught the ear of Mrs. Malaprop — words deranged neither by mistake for words similar in sound, nor by mistake for words opposite in meaning, but used simply as mouth-filling epithets. In commenting upon Mrs. Malaprop's letter read by Sir Lucius (ii, 2) a critic of 1828 (in the *British Theatre*, Leipsic), one of the earliest of the few commentators who have wrestled with the real puzzles of Mrs. Malaprop's speech, has shown the difficulty of comment, and perhaps the best answer to the problem, in this note (p. 660) on "the last criterion of my affections": "This word has no business here; but it is not easy to hit upon any one sounding something like it with a meaning any way suitable. Our readers will observe that Mrs. Malaprop knows a great many hard words; but has not a very correct ear in applying them." A typical passage to show her use of mouth-filling epithets is this (i, 2): "I would never let her meddle with Greek, or Hebrew, or Algebra, or Simony, or Fluxions, or Paradoxes, or such inflammatory branches of learning — neither would it be necessary for her to handle any of your mathematical, astronomical, diabolical instruments."

In the following Glossary, however, are grouped the vast majority of Mrs. Malaprop's word-blunders — mistakes of words for others similar in sound. Obviously such a list must necessarily be suggestive, rather than mathematically exact.

Partial Glossary of the Word-Blunders of Mrs. Malaprop

Accommodation — recommendation. **52** 2.
Affluence — influence. **70** 47.
Allegory — alligator. **58** 199.
Analyzed — paralyzed. **76** 243.
Antistrophe — catastrophe. **88** 189.
Caparisons — comparisons. **69** 6.
Compilation — appellation. **73** 147.
Commotion — emotion. **42** 36.
Conjunction — injunction. **53** 30.
Contagious — contiguous. **22** 261.
Controvertible — incontrovertible. **20** 197.
Delusions — allusions. **99** 194.
Derangement — arrangement. **54** 71.
Dissolve — disclose (?), solve (?). **100** 222.
Enveloped — developed. **88** 191.
Envoy — convoy. **90** 253.
Epitaphs — epithets. **54** 72.
Exhort — escort. **90** 252.
Exploded — exposed (?). **53** 30.
Extirpate — exculpate (extricate?). **20** 196.
Felicity — velocity (?), celerity (?). **90** 248.
Geometry — geography. **22** 260.
Harry Mercury — the herald Mercury. **69** 16.
Hesperian — Hyperion's. **69** 14.
Hydrostatics — hysterics. **53** 36.
Illegible — ineligible. **23** 294.
Illiterate — obliterate. **20** 182.
Illuminate — elucidate. **100** 223.
Incentive — instinctive. **42** 34.
Induction — seduction. **42** 35.
Ineffectual — intellectual. **53** 12.
Infallible — ineffable. **42** 41.
Ingenuity — ingenuousness. **52** 3.
Interceded — intercepted. **53** 38.
Interested — disinterested. **42** 38.
Intricate — obstinate (?). **21** 218.
Intuition — tuition. **24** 303.

Job — Jove. **69** 15.
Laconically — ironically. **22** 245.
Locality — loquacity (venality ?). **24** 321.
Malevolence — benevolence. **24** 320.
March — Mars. **69** 15.
Meretricioxs — meritorious (?). **42** 42.
Misanthropy — misanthropist. **21** 224.
Oracular — vernacular. **54** 71.
Orthodoxy — orthography. **22** 262.
Particle — article (?). **53** 33.
Participate — precipitate. **89** 239.
Perpendiculars — particulars. **88** 206.
Persisted — desisted. **53** 37.
Physiognomy — phraseology. **69** 12.
Pine-apple — pinnacle (?). **53** 22.
Preposition — proposition. **53** 32.
Profane — profuse (?). **54** 49.
Progeny — prodigy. **22** 250.
Punctuation — punctilio (?). **42** 40.
Putrifactions — petrifactions. **90** 246
Reprehend — apprehend (comprehend ?). **22** 264; **54** 70.
Similitude — simile. **69** 17.
Simulation — dissimulation. **88** 188 (R 3).
Supercilious — superficial. **22** 259.
Superfluous — superficial. **42** 37.
Superstitious — superfluous. **23** 267
Vandyk — vandal (?). **100** 230.

III. MR. JOSEPH JEFFERSON'S ACTING VERSION OF THE RIVALS

While the primary interest of the reader and student of Sheridan's plays lies emphatically in the text of his plays as he wrote them, secondary interest attaches to alterations of the text for dramatic representation. To compare lesser things with greater, modern stage versions of *The Rivals* bear somewhat the same relation to Sheridan's own text as the various acting versions of *The Merchant of Venice* bear to the text of the First Folio. Not to dwarf interest or obscure the comparison by an inextricable mass of detail, the present purpose is best served by a brief account of the alterations made in a single representative stage version — that of Mr. Joseph Jefferson,[1] to American audiences the most familiar Bob Acres of the modern stage.

Most noteworthy is the almost complete excision of the Julia–Faulkland under-plot. Julia's part is entirely omitted, while Faulkland is retained simply in the scene with Bob Acres. To the sentimental taste of Sheridan's own day Julia and Faulkland appealed strongly. To-day, however, that excess of sentiment, at times degenerating into the sentimentality which Sheridan himself held up to ridicule, wearies the reader, and irritates the playgoer. This radical excision is accomplished so simply as to fortify the common criticism that Sheridan failed to weld together firmly plot and and under-plot in *The Rivals*. In Mr. Jefferson's version, in i, 2, after Lydia's speech (**15** 39-40) Lucy remains on the stage, and replies immediately with her later speech (**19** 150). iii, 2, is omitted entirely, while v, 1, begins with the entrance of Mrs. Malaprop and David (**88** 187), to whom Lydia is added to take the few short speeches remaining in Julia's part. The play is ended, save for the epilogue, at Mrs. Malaprop's "Men are all barbarians!" (**101** 247). No other changes are necessary.

Other changes made by Mr. Jefferson are the omission of Sheridan's opening scene; a dramatic "curtain" at the exit of the irate Sir Anthony after the stormy interview with his son (which forms the end of Act I, in Mr. Jefferson's version); the running together of the two scenes on "the North Parade" (Sheridan's, ii, 2, and iii, 1) into the first scene of his second act; the similar running together of two successive scenes at "Acres' Lodgings" (Sheridan's iii, 4, and iv, 1); at the conclusion of this scene, another dramatic "curtain" by making Acres reiterate to the departing Captain Absolute, "Tell him I generally kill a man a week." — *Acres faints on sofa ;* and, finally, the omission of iv, 3.

Such, essentially, are the changes by which Mr. Jefferson removed from his acting version of *The Rivals* the scenes least effective dramatically, notably those in the Julia–Faulkland under-plot, and

[1] Mr. Jefferson courteously supplied me with a copy of the play "cut as we do it."

heightened the stage effectiveness of some scene-ends by dramatic, but not melodramatic, "curtains."[1]

THE SCHOOL FOR SCANDAL

CONTEMPORARY CRITICISMS OF THE SCHOOL FOR SCANDAL

The Public Advertiser, May 9, 1777. — [After three-quarters of a column devoted to an outline of the plot and characters.] This is a short Sketch of the Fable; to the Conduct and Originality of which it is impossible to do Justice in so brief a Detail.

The Persons of the Drama have all of them something particular marked in their Characters, and the Humour of each belongs to that Character, and is admirably well sustained throughout. The Satire is forcible, and in many Places as severe as Comedy can admit of. The Situations are so powerfully conceived, that little is left for the Performers to do, in Order to produce what is called Stage Effect; and the Circumstance of the Screen and Closet in the fourth Effect, produced a Burst of Applause beyond any Thing ever heard perhaps in a Theatre. With such Support it is needless to add that the whole was received with an extravagant Warmth of Approbation, which seemed to shew that a generous British Audience will still overpay the strongest efforts of Genius.

The London Chronicle, May 8–10, 1777. — The School for Scandal is the production of Mr. Sheridan, and is an additional proof of that gentleman's great abilities as a dramatic writer. The object of the satire is two-fold — detraction and hypocrisy, which are the prevailing vices of the times; by the first the good are reduced to a level with the worthless, and by means of the second, the latter assume the appearance of men of virtue and sentiment. Nothing, therefore, could have been more seasonable than this comedy, which, in point of execution, is equal, if not superior, to most of

[1] An interesting account of many minor changes in the text made by Mr. Jefferson, and the reasons therefor, is in *The Technique of the Drama*, by W. T. Price, pp. 183–188. I am indebted to Mr. Jefferson for a copy of the book, with the comment, "I do not know Mr. Price, but he seems to have not only found out what I did, but why I did it."

the plays produced for the last twenty years. The characters are drawn with a bold pencil, and coloured with warmth and spirit. The two principal, Joseph and Charles Surface, are the Blifil and Tom Jones of the piece. . . .

The dialogue of this comedy is easy and witty. It abounds with strokes of pointed satire, and a rich vein of humour pervades the whole, rendering it equally interesting and entertaining. The fable is well conducted, and the incidents are managed with great judgment. There hardly ever was a better dramatic situation than that which occurs in the fourth act, where Sir Peter discovers Lady Teazle in Joseph Surface's study. The two characters of the brothers are finely contrasted, and those of the Scandal Club well imagined. . . . Upon the whole, the School for Scandal justifies the very great and cordial reception it met with; it certainly is a good comedy, and we should not at all wonder if it becomes as great a favorite as the Duenna, to which it is infinitely superior in point of sense, satire, and moral.

Horace Walpole, to Robert Jephson, July 13, 1777. — To my great astonishment there were more parts performed admirably in *The School for Scandal*, than I almost ever saw in any play. Mrs. Abington was equal to the first of her profession, Yates (the husband), Parsons, Miss Pope, and Palmer, all shone. It seemed a marvellous resurrection of the stage. Indeed, the play had as much merit as the actors. I have seen no comedy that comes near it since *The Provoked Husband.* [*The Letters of Horace Walpole*, Toynbee ed. (1903-5), X, 82.]

The Gentleman's Magazine [*Communication*], *February*, 1778

Animadversions on The Moral Tendency of The School for Scandal

[*The School for Scandal* is] a play which is at least as defective in morality, as abundant in wit; and more dangerous to the manners of society, than it can possibly tend to promote its pleasure.

Affection of Sentiment, and love for scandal, are the foibles satirized by this comedy: the former is not a reigning vice of the times; on the contrary, a shameless depravity of disposition, which glories in the faults it commits, gains ground every day, and that unblushing impudence which formerly characterized the veteran in iniquity, may now be found in a school-boy. . . .

Lady Teazle is certainly more likely to excite imitation than disgust. . . . In comparing these two characters [*i.e.* Joseph and Charles] I do not contend for the merit of Joseph, but I wish to shew that there is not that balance in favour of Charles which there ought to be for the *exemplary* character in a piece when weighed against him who is exhibited as an object of unlimited aversion. . . .

It has been said that this is a second attempt to destroy the taste for sentimental comedy revived by Mr. Cumberland. It will be readily acknowledged, that the plays of that gentleman may tend to produce an affectation of sentiment; but it is better to affect sentiment than vice: and Mr. Cumberland has judiciously executed the whole duty of an author, which is, not *only* to paint nature, but to paint *such* parts of it, as every good man would wish to see imitated.

THE CRITIC

CONTEMPORARY CRITICISMS OF THE CRITIC

(*a*) On the First Performance, October 30, 1779

The Public Advertiser, November 1, 1779. — After so long a Dearth of dramatic Novelty, the Expectation of the Public, which had presaged every Excellence from the Pen of their favourite Author, was at length fully gratified by the Representation on Saturday of *The Critic*, a Dramatic After-piece,[1] in Three Acts.

The two leading Objects of this witty *Stage Satire* appear to be these — First, to expose the mock Comments of News-paper and other minor Critics; and next, to ridicule the false Taste and brilliant Follies of modern dramatic Composition. — The Abuse of Criticism has always led to a Degeneracy of Stile. To mark therefore its present Perversion was the best Preliminary to a Satire on modern Tragedy — And nothing can be more lively and well pointed

[1] Explained by the following announcement in *The Public Advertiser*, Thursday, October 28, 1779: *Drury Lane Theatre. On Saturday next the tragedy of Hamlet, after which will be presented for the* 1st *Time, a Dramatic After-Piece, in two Acts, called The Critic, or a Tragedy Rehearsed.*

than the Execution of this Plan. The first Act ridicules the several Species of petty Patronage, and mock Consequence of a self-elected Critic, in the Character of *Dangle ;* and of bitter Pleasantry and merry Malice in the cold sarcastic Severity of *Sneer.* — These Characters are introduced at *Dangle's* Theatrical Levee, and are succeeded by Sir *Fretful Plagiary,* whose Name is a Definition of himself. Upon him the Author seems to have employed the whole Force and finest Powers of his Wit. — He is at once original and striking. With an affected Candour he importunes his Friends for Comments which his Vanity has predetermined him to reject. His false Humanity is at perpetual Variance with his real Arrogance; and while this wou'd-be Stoic of Parnassus affects to be above all petty Censure, and even to be diverted by it, he becomes doubly ridiculous by betraying the meanest Subservience to those very Passions which he most affects not to feel. — Whether Sir *Fretful Plagiary* is drawn from Nature, or is only the Coinage of Fancy, we will not determine; but if the former is the Case, this Original certainly bids as fair for an enduring Ridicule as *Dryden* in *Bayes.* —

After a Scene of such Novelty and Wit, however judicious it might at first appear to lighten the Dialogue by the Intervention of some Incident, we cannot however think that the Introduction of the Operatical Candidates was in the least Degree necessary; or that any Relief was wanting to the bold Humour of the succeeding character. — Mr. *Puff* is the finished Portrait of the Art he professes. He is announced as a *Practitioner in Panegyric ;* and to use the Author's words, "*advertises* himself vivâ voce." — This Character is undoubtedly taken from Nature, and is peculiar to the present Times. It is not however the Portrait of any single *Individual,* but the Display of a whole *Species;* whose ridiculous Abuse of the Liberty of the Press, though too low an Office for serious Severity, was of all others the properest Theme for the Author of The School for Scandal; the News-papers having of late superseded the more contracted Practices of private Defamation, by giving a wider Circulation to secret Malice, and becoming the open Registers of anonimous Detraction. With the liveliest Display of this Science, the first Act of *The Critic* closes.

The second and third contain *The Rehearsal of the Tragedy,* — and in these, considering how much of the *general* Subject had originally being [been] pre-occupied by the Duke of Buckingham, and how frequently also several Authors of a later Date have ridiculed the *particular* Affectations of Tragic Writers, it is astonishing with what Novelty and Ingenuity the striking Faults of our present Compositions in this Line are here satirized: The tedious and unartificial Commencements of modern Tragedies, the inflated Diction, the figurative Tautology, the *Feu de Theatre* of Embraces and Groans, Vows and Prayers, florid Pathos, whining Heroism, and, above all, the Trick of Stage Situation, are ridiculed with a Burlesque which perhaps may be thought rather too refined for the Multitude, but certainly is perfect in its Stile; and which, when its due Force is more fully given by the Actors, will as certainly amuse and divert an Audience, as delight the true Critic.

Such is the Outline of this most witty and fanciful Composition, wherein the Author has lighted a friendly Beacon for future Adventurers on the Dramatic Ocean — it is a luminous and bright Guide for them to steer by, — and while it blazes with the Fragments of their shipwrecked Predecessors, it may turn them from Rocks or *Flats*, on which the former have perished.

Of the Actors, Dresses, miraculous Scenery, &c. &c. Mr. *Puff* himself has for once said so entirely the Truth, that it would be the most unnecessary Presumption for any Minor Critic to add a Word to so perfect a Panegyric.

The London Chronicle, October 30 — *November* 2, 1779. — This dramatic satire is the avowed production of Mr. Sheridan, the two leading objects of which appear to be, to expose the mock comments of News-papers and other minor critics, and to ridicule the false taste and brilliant follies of modern dramatic composition. . . .

[Then follows a long account of the plot.]

The scene of Tilbury Fort, with a view of the river Thames and the town of Gravesend — the scene of the camp, and the scene of the battle with the Armada, were executed in the most masterly manner. The motion of the sea, the engaging of the ships, and the destruction occasioned by the fire-ships, were happily contrived and accurately represented. The dresses in the tragedy were characteristic, rich, and magnificent. The performers were highly worthy of praise for the justness of their performance, and the attention they paid to their several parts; and the chorus and dance, which finished the piece, had a pleasing effect.

[Then follows an account of Fitzpatrick's Prologue.]

The *Critic* was by far too long for an after-piece, but on the whole gave general satisfaction.

(*b*) On the First Printed Edition of The Critic, 1781.

The Monthly Review, October, 1781.—*The Critic: or, A Tragedy Rehearsed.* A Dramatic Piece, in Three Acts. As it is performed at the Theatre-Royal in Drury Lane. By Richard Brinsley Sherihan, Esq. 8vo. 1s. 6d. Becket. 1781.

This *Tragedy Rehearsed* proceeds too closely in the beaten track of the Duke of Buckingham's *Rehearsal*. The mode and objects of ridicule are generally the same; except that the Author of the Critic has too indiscriminately attacked Tragedy in general, and levelled some of his severest traits against the very best modern tragedy in our language, we mean the tragedy of Douglas! The theatrical rage, however, for *situation*, *attitude*, *discoveries*, *processions*, &c. is properly and humorously exposed.

Leaving, however, *the Tragedy Rehearsed*, which occupies the two last Acts of this *dramatic piece*, we revert with pleasure to the first of the three, which abounds with wit, humour, and a masterly display of character. *Mr. and Mrs. Dangle*, though not very original, are natural and spirited; *Sneer* is drawn with a finer pencil; the *Unintelligible Interpreter* is truly pleasant; and the treatise on panegyric, delivered by *Puff*, is lively, shrewd, and satirical though rather narrative, than dramatic. From his own delineation of his character in the first Act, we should not expect to see him dwindle into the Bayes of the two last. That part might perhaps have been more properly sustained by *Sir Fretful Plagiary*, for whose sake, we are inclined to believe that the whole piece was written.

In order to do justice to a picture, so highly finished, we must give it at full length.

[Then follows extensive quotation from the latter part of the opening scene of *The Critic*.]

This dramatic piece is ushered in by a well-turned Dedication to Mrs. Greville, and a well-turned Prologue, by the Honourable Richard Fitzpatrick. We do not quite comprehend, why this drama is entitled *The Critic.*[1]

The Critical Review, November, 1781. — This piece has been seen and admired by every body; and the oftener it is seen, and the oftener it is read, the more it will be applauded. Hypercritical remarks on it would therefore be totally unnecessary. There is, indeed, more true wit and humour crouded (*sic*) into this little performance, than has, perhaps, appeared since the days of Wycherley and Congreve. The impartiality of cool reflection obliges us, at the same time, to condemn that which we cannot but admire. Ridicule is a dangerous and destructive weapon, which, Drawcansir-like,[2] destroys every thing before it, without mercy and without distinction. Wantonness of wit, and exuberance of fancy, have carried the ingenious author of the Critic beyond the limits of reason, justice, and impartiality. Not content with lashing the false sublime, bombast, and all the stage-trick of modern tragedy, he has attacked tragedy itself, and endeavoured, but too successfully, to render it an object of ridicule and sarcasm. How far it may be consistent with the character of a manager of a theatre to weaken one of its best supports, we leave Mr. Sheridan to determine. Certain however it is, that since the exhibition of the Critic, tragedy, which a celebrated writer has declared to be one of the greatest exertions of the human mind, is fallen into contempt; it will be some time at least before she can recover the blow. We hope, notwithstanding, for the credit of a British audience, that they will not be laughed out of their feelings, or suffer themselves to be deprived of that pleasure, not to mention the profit and instruction, which may arise from the exhibition of a good tragedy well performed, for any thing that such a wicked wit as our author can say against it.

[1] A conjectural explanation is that the title is derived from Molière's *Critique de l'École des Femmes.*

[2] A character in *The Rehearsal* which burlesqued especially Dryden's Almanzor in *The Conquest of Granada.*

www.ingramcontent.com/pod-product-compliance
Lightning Source LLC
LaVergne TN
LVHW010529100826
845148LV00001B/136
* 9 7 8 1 4 2 5 5 7 3 4 8 5 *